W9-AEJ-056

Investing in REITs

Since 1996, Bloomberg Press has published books for financial professionals, as well as books of general interest in investing, economics, current affairs, and policy affecting investors and business people. Titles are written by well-known practitioners, BLOOMBERG NEWS® reporters and columnists, and other leading authorities and journalists. Bloomberg Press books have been translated into more than 20 languages.

For a list of available titles, please visit our web site at www.wiley.com/go/bloombergpress.

Investing in REITs

REAL ESTATE INVESTMENT TRUSTS

FOURTH EDITION

Ralph L. Block

HALF HOLLOW HILLS
COMMUNITY LIBRARY
55 Vanderbilt Parkway
Dix Hills, NY 11746

BLOOMBERG PRESS
An Imprint of
WILEY

Copyright © 2012 by Ralph L. Block. All rights reserved.

Published by John Wiley & Sons, Inc., Hoboken, New Jersey.

Published simultaneously in Canada.

NAREIT makes no warranties, express or implied, as to the accuracy, timeliness, completeness or noninfringment of the Material and will prominently note such disclaimer in any work containing the Material.

No part of this publication may be reproduced, stored in a retrieval system, or transmitted in any form or by any means, electronic, mechanical, photocopying, recording, scanning, or otherwise, except as permitted under Section 107 or 108 of the 1976 United States Copyright Act, without either the prior written permission of the Publisher, or authorization through payment of the appropriate per-copy fee to the Copyright Clearance Center, Inc., 222 Rosewood Drive, Danvers, MA 01923, (978) 750-8400, fax (978) 646-8600, or on the Web at www.copyright.com. Requests to the Publisher for permission should be addressed to the Permissions Department, John Wiley & Sons, Inc., 111 River Street, Hoboken, NJ 07030, (201) 748-6011, fax (201) 748-6008, or online at http://www.wiley.com/go/permissions.

Limit of Liability/Disclaimer of Warranty: While the publisher and author have used their best efforts in preparing this book, they make no representations or warranties with respect to the accuracy or completeness of the contents of this book and specifically disclaim any implied warranties of merchantability or fitness for a particular purpose. No warranty may be created or extended by sales representatives or written sales materials. The advice and strategies contained herein may not be suitable for your situation. You should consult with a professional where appropriate. Neither the publisher nor author shall be liable for any loss of profit or any other commercial damages, including but not limited to special, incidental, consequential, or other damages.

For general information on our other products and services or for technical support, please contact our Customer Care Department within the United States at (800) 762-2974, outside the United States at (317) 572-3993 or fax (317) 572-4002.

Wiley also publishes its books in a variety of electronic formats. Some content that appears in print may not be available in electronic books. For more information about Wiley products, visit our web site at www.wiley.com.

Library of Congress Cataloging-in-Publication Data:

Block, Ralph L.
  Investing in REITs : real estate investment trusts / Ralph L. Block. – 4th ed.
    p. cm. — (Bloomberg ; 141)
  Includes index.
    ISBN 978–1–118–00445–6 (cloth); ISBN 978–1–118–11258–8 (ebk);
    ISBN 978-1-118-11259-5 (ebk); ISBN 978-1-118-11260-1 (ebk)
  1. Real estate investment trusts. I. Title.
HG5095.B553 2012
332.63'247— dc22

                                        2011012859

Printed in the United States of America

10 9 8 7 6 5 4 3 2 1

To my father, Jack,
who led me into REITville,
and without whom this book,
in more ways than one,
would never have been possible.
My only regret is that he was not
able to witness its birth and popularity.

Contents

Part IV   Risks and Future Prospects

Introduction

*"Men, it has been well said, think in herds; it will be seen that they
go mad in herds, while they only recover their senses slowly and one
by one."*

—Charles MacKay, *Extraordinary Popular
Delusions and the Madness of Crowds*, 1852

All of us think we know real estate, and we have all been involved
with it in one way or another since our arrival in the hospital delivery room. That building, our earliest impression of the world,
is real estate; the residence we were taken home to, whether a
single-family house or an apartment, is real estate; the malls and
neighborhood centers where we shop, the factories and office
buildings where we work, the hotels and resorts where we vacation,
even the acres of undeveloped land we have walked across or played
baseball on—all are real estate. Real estate surrounds us. But do we
really understand it?

For many years we've had a strange relationship with real estate.
Despite the housing market problems of recent years, we still love
our homes and fully expect that they will, over time, appreciate
in value. We admire real estate tycoons, past and present, such as
Joseph Kennedy, Conrad Hilton, and the Rockefellers; we even find
Donald Trump fascinating. Yet we believe real estate to be a risky
investment and marvel at how supposedly sophisticated institutional
investors have spent hundreds of millions of dollars on hotels,
major office buildings, and other "trophy" properties, only to see
their values plummet in real estate recessions, most recently from

2007 through 2009. During the past 10 years, as in prior cycles, we've experienced gut-wrenching changes in property valuations.

Is real estate a good investment? Real estate investment trusts, or "REITs," own, and sometimes develop, commercial real estate and have delivered excellent returns to their investors—but will this continue? Can we still make money in REITs, regardless of the inevitable ups and downs of real estate cycles?

This book seeks to answer those questions and many others. I believe it makes a convincing case for investing in REITs, but also provides the details, background, and guidance investors should have before delving into these often misunderstood but highly rewarding investments. Here's what's in store:

Part I: Meet the REIT serves as an introduction to REITs. The first order of business is to explain why REITs have been, and will continue to be, excellent long-term investments that belong in every well-diversified portfolio. From there, we'll explore the "nature of the beast," and obtain a good working familiarity with REITs and their characteristics. We will follow with a description of the types of properties REITs own and the investment characteristics of each. And, finally, this section compares REITs with some other traditional investments and also describes the structure and evolution of REITs.

Upon reaching **Part II: History and Mythology**, readers should find REITs such an intriguing investment that they'll wonder why these solid and profitable companies have been neglected for much of their history. This section answers this question and dispels some common myths and misperceptions about REITs. We'll take a step back and study the 50-year history of the REIT world since its inception in 1960, and trace REITs' progress up to today.

Part III: Investing in REITs Intelligently provides the basic tools investors need to understand the dynamics of REITs' revenue and earnings growth, identify those REITs that have the capacity to create the most value for their shareholders, and consider ways of valuing the shares of a particular REIT. It will also get into the nitty-gritty of building REIT portfolios with adequate diversification. A new chapter for this edition of *Investing in REITs*, written by well-respected REIT industry veterans Kenneth Campbell and Steve Burton, discusses investing in non-U.S. REITs and real estate companies.

Near the end of the book, **Part Four: Risks and Future Prospects** contains a discussion of the risks that investors should be aware of as they wend their way through the streets of REITville. In addition, we'll speculate a bit and consider how current and future trends may change the landscape of the REIT world and how new opportunities may evolve.

By the time you finish this book, you will have a firm understanding and appreciation of one of the most rewarding investments on Wall Street. Even more important, you will be able to build your own portfolio of outstanding real estate companies that should provide you with attractive current dividend yields and the prospects of significant capital appreciation in the years ahead. REIT investors, of all shapes and sizes, have been able to earn total returns averaging close to 12 percent annually over the past 30 years, along with, during most market periods, steady income, low market price volatility, and investment safety.

REIT investors today have a much wider choice of investment properties than ever before and can choose from some of the most experienced and capable management teams that have ever invested in and operated real estate in the United States. As you read on, you'll see why REITs should be an essential part of every investor's portfolio.

Finally, I hope you will permit me a few personal thoughts. Just like the REIT industry itself, *Investing in REITs* has evolved significantly since the first edition was published approximately 15 years ago. That first edition was written primarily for "mom and pop" investors, who might be looking to diversify their investments and to obtain stable performance and above-average dividend yields. But as one edition followed another, I realized that an increasing portion of the book's readers consisted of real estate people, including many in REITland, as well as professional investors. Thus, the tone of the book has generally become less folksy and has assumed more investment knowledge on the part of the reader. And, there has been another change from prior editions: recent events have taught us how increasingly complex today's world has become— now almost everything comes in shades of gray. The REIT world is no different, and I have tried to remind readers of that in this edition.

Some readers will note that I have not included in this book a large number of graphs and charts. They tend to absorb lots of page space and, although they can illustrate where we've been and where we are now, they don't necessarily tell us much about where we're headed. I have thus concluded that a full textual discussion of the most important aspects of REITs and REIT investing, rather than a plethora of graphs and charts, will be most helpful to most readers, and hope that you will agree.

An old Chinese proverb claims, "Give a man a fish and he will eat for a day. Teach him how to fish and he will eat for a lifetime." My objective in writing this book was not to provide the names of particular REITs in which investors should put their hard-earned investment dollars—indeed, there are no specific REITs that are recommended for investment anywhere within its covers. Rather, *Investing in REITs* is intended to provide investors and others with a basic understanding of these interesting critters, who have treated me and my fellow REIT shareholders very well over many decades. It offers some historical perspective, some characteristics—both good and bad—to watch for, and some basic tools for investing intelligently in this quite remarkable asset class. I have done the best I could, but only you, dear reader, can judge whether I've succeeded.

Acknowledgments

"Writing is easy. All you have to do is sit down at a typewriter and open a vein."

—Red Smith

Much to my surprise and delight, *Investing in REITs* has been popular enough to justify a fourth edition, this one under the aegis of John Wiley & Sons, Inc. I cannot, of course, claim more than a modicum of credit for the book's prior success. REITs' transition from the sleepy backwaters of the world of equities to a mainstream investment choice has been the principal contributor to the interest in *Investing in REITs*. Even more important, many kind, perceptive, and dedicated professionals have midwifed the birth of the original edition of the book and its subsequent revisions. I would be remiss if I didn't mention a few of these outstanding individuals.

Bill Schaff and Gary Pollock provided the essential encouragement and support for the book's predecessor, *The Essential REIT*, and Alan Fass, Jared Kieling, John Crutcher, and many other outstanding professionals at Bloomberg Press helped to transform that first book into *Investing in REITs*, and exposed it to the marketplace—to sink or swim. More recently, it has been my great pleasure to have worked with Laura Walsh, Judy Horwarth, Donna Martone, and Adrianna Johnson at John Wiley & Sons; they have given me the opportunity to bring the book up to date through a fourth edition, for which I am very appreciative.

I'd also like to express my thanks, again, to Mike Kirby and the all-star analysts at that quintessential research firm, Green Street

Advisors, for their outstanding research and analysis on REITs over the years. Thanks, also, to Kenneth D. Campbell, who introduced me to the world of institutional REIT investors many years ago and who, along with his colleague, Steve Burton, wrote Chapter 11 on investing in real estate overseas. Malcolm Bayless, who—like me—continues to search for the Holy Grail of investing, was very helpful as I labored through the creation of this fourth edition. I have learned much from many REIT experts and fellow investors over the years, and wish I could name all of them here.

I'll never be able to repay my debt to Milton Cooper. He is truly a giant of the REIT world and a gentleman in every respect. Milton provided me with the necessary moral support and encouragement to undertake my first book on REIT investing, which led ultimately to *Investing in REITs*. I owe much to the folks at the National Association of Real Estate Investment Trusts (NAREIT), including Mark Decker (now managing director at Robert W. Baird), Steve Wechsler, Michael Grupe, Kurt Walten, and many of their associates who have been supportive in every way and generous in providing me with useful REIT statistics and information. Limited space prevents me from noting specifically the many other individuals whose support and assistance has made this book possible.

Finally, allow me to express my gratitude to my lovely wife, Paula, who has put up with a great deal of "benign neglect" during the time it's taken me to complete this book and its revised editions.

R. L. B.

MEET THE REIT

REITs: What They Are and How They Work

"Buy land. They ain't makin' any more of the stuff."
—Will Rogers

What's your idea of a perfect investment? That's a trick question—there is no perfect investment! Greater returns come with greater risk. But those looking for above-average current returns, along with reasonably good price appreciation prospects over time—and with only modest risk—will certainly want to consider apartment communities, office and industrial buildings, shopping centers, and similar investments. In other words, commercial real estate that can be leased to tenants to generate reliable streams of rental income.

Sure, you might say, but only if there were an easy way to buy and own real estate, where an experienced professional could handle the business of owning and managing it well and efficiently, and give you the profits. And only if you could sell your real estate—if you wanted to—as easily as you can sell a common stock like General Electric or Intel. Well, read on. This is all possible with real estate investment trusts, or REITs (pronounced "reets").

REITs have provided investors everywhere with an easy way to buy major office buildings, shopping malls, hotels, and apartment buildings—in fact, just about any kind of commercial real property you can think of. REITs give you the steady and predictable cash flow that comes from owning and leasing real estate, but with the benefit of a common stock's liquidity. Equally important, REITs usually have ready access to capital and can therefore acquire and build additional properties as part of their ongoing real estate business.

Besides that, REITs can add stability to your investment portfolio. Real estate as an asset class has long been perceived as an inflation hedge and has, during most market periods, enjoyed fairly low correlation with the performance of other asset classes.

REITs have been around for nearly 50 years, but it's only been in the past 20 that these appealing investments have become widely known. From the end of 1992 through the end of 2010, the size of the REIT industry has increased by more than 20 times, from just under $16 billion to $389 billion. But the REIT industry, having so far captured only about 10 to 15 percent of all institutionally owned commercial real estate, still has plenty of room left for growth.

Stan Ross, former managing partner of Ernst & Young's Real Estate Group, defined REITs by saying, "They are real operating companies that lease, renovate, manage, tear down, rebuild, and develop from scratch." That helps define a REIT, but investors need to know what they can expect from it in terms of investment behavior. That's really what this book is about.

REITs provide substantial dividend yields, which have historically exceeded the yields of most publicly traded stocks, making them an

REITs Are a Liquid Asset

A *liquid asset* or investment is one that has a generally accepted value and a market where it can be sold easily and quickly at little or no discount to that value. Direct investment in real estate, whether it be a shopping mall in California or a major office building in Manhattan, is not liquid. A qualified buyer must be found, and even then, the value is not clearly established. Most publicly traded stocks *are* liquid. REITs are real estate–related investments that enjoy the benefit of a common stock's liquidity.

ideal investment for an individual retirement account (IRA) or other tax-deferred portfolio. Their actual dividend yields tend to be somewhat correlated with—and generally higher than—yields on 10-year U.S. Treasury bonds. But, unlike most high-yielding investments, REIT shares have a strong likelihood of increasing in value over time as the REIT's properties generate higher cash flows, the values of their properties increase, and additional properties are added to the portfolio.

TIP

REITs own real estate, but when you buy a REIT, you're not just buying real estate, you're also buying a business.

When you buy stock in Exxon, for example, you're buying more than oil reserves. And with REITs, you own more than its real estate. The vast majority of REITs are public real estate companies overseen by financially sophisticated, skilled management teams who have the ability to grow the REIT's cash flows (and dividends) at rates in excess of inflation. Adding a 4 percent dividend yield to capital appreciation of 4 percent, resulting from 4 percent annual increases in operating cash flow and property values, provides for total return prospects of 8 percent annually.

A successful REIT's management team will accept risk only where the odds of success are high. REITs must pay out most of their earnings in dividends to shareholders, and thus must be very careful when they invest retained earnings. REITs operate their properties in such a way that they generate steady income; but they also have an eye to the future and are interested in growth of the property portfolio, its values and its cash flows, and in taking advantage of new opportunities.

Types of REITs

There are two basic categories of REITs: equity REITs and mortgage REITs.

An equity REIT is a publicly traded company that, as its principal business, buys, manages, renovates, maintains, and occasionally sells real estate properties. Many are also able to develop new properties when the economics are favorable. It is tax advantaged in that it is not taxed on its income and, by law, must pay out at least 90 percent of its net income as dividends to its investors.

A mortgage REIT is a REIT that makes and holds loans and other debt instruments that are secured by real estate collateral.

The focus of this book is equity REITs rather than mortgage REITs. Although mortgage REITs have higher dividend yields and can, at times, deliver spectacular investment returns, equity REITs are less vulnerable to changes in interest rates and have historically provided better long-term total returns, more stable market price performance, lower risk, and greater liquidity. In addition to that, equity REITs allow the investor to determine not only the type of property he or she invests in, but also, quite often, the geographic location of the properties.

General Investment Characteristics

Performance and Returns

Although the long-term performance of equity REITs varies with the measurement period used, they have, during most time horizons, compared quite well with that of broader stock indices such as the S&P 500 index. For example, according to data provided by the National Association of Real Estate Investment Trusts (NAREIT), shown in Figure 1.1, during the 35-year period ending December 31, 2010,

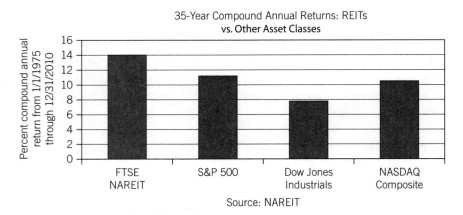

Figure 1.1   35-year Total Returns for REITs vs. Other Asset Classes
Source: NAREIT REITWatch January 2011.

equity REITs delivered an average annual total return of 14.0 percent. This compares quite well with the returns from various other indices during the same time period.

However, if REITs' performance was merely comparable to the Standard & Poor's (S&P) 500, you wouldn't be reading a book about them. And the performance of many high-risk stocks has substantially exceeded the returns provided by the broad market. Here's the difference: REITs have provided total returns comparable to the S&P 500 index despite having benefits not usually enjoyed by stocks that keep pace with the market, including only modest correlation with other asset classes, less market price volatility, more limited investment risk, and higher current returns. Let's look at each of these.

Lower Correlations

Correlations measure how much predictive power the price behavior of one asset class has on another to which it's compared. In other words, if we want to predict what effect a 1 percent rise (or fall) in the S&P 500 will have on REIT stocks, small caps, or bonds for any particular time period, we look at their relative correlations. For example, if the correlation of an S&P 500 index mutual fund with the S&P 500 index is perfect, that is, 1.0, then a 2 percent move in the S&P 500 would predict that the move in the index fund for the same period would also be 2 percent. Correlations range from a perfect +1.0, in which case the movements of two investments will be perfectly matched, to a −1.0, in which case their movements will be completely opposite. A correlation of 0.0 suggests no correlation at all. Correlations in the investment world are important, as they allow financial planners, investment advisers, and individual or institutional investors to structure broadly diversified investment portfolios with the objective of having the ups and downs of each asset class offset one another as much as possible. This, ideally, results in a smooth increase in portfolio values over time, with much less volatility from year to year or even quarter to quarter.

According to NAREIT, as summarized in the graph in Figure 1.2, REIT stocks' correlation with the S&P 500 during the period from December 1980 through December 2010 was just 0.55. Thus, price movements in REIT stocks have had only a 55 percent correlation

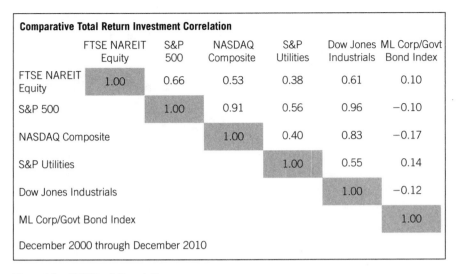

Comparative Total Return Investment Correlation

	FTSE NAREIT Equity	S&P 500	NASDAQ Composite	S&P Utilities	Dow Jones Industrials	ML Corp/Govt Bond Index
FTSE NAREIT Equity	1.00	0.66	0.53	0.38	0.61	0.10
S&P 500		1.00	0.91	0.56	0.96	−0.10
NASDAQ Composite			1.00	0.40	0.83	−0.17
S&P Utilities				1.00	0.55	0.14
Dow Jones Industrials					1.00	−0.12
ML Corp/Govt Bond Index						1.00

December 2000 through December 2010

Figure 1.2   REIT Stock Correlations
Source: NAREIT REITWatch, January 2011.

with the broad market, as represented by the S&P 500, during that period. Accordingly, in markets where stocks are rising sharply, REITs' relatively low correlation suggests that they may lag relative to the broad stock market indices. This happened in 1995, when REIT stocks underperformed the popular indices—but still provided investors with total returns of 15.3 percent—and in 1998 and 1999, when REITs' returns were actually *negative* despite strength in the technology-led S&P 500. Conversely, during many bear markets in equities, such as in 2000 and most of 2001, lower correlating stocks such as REITs tend to be more stable and may suffer less. And yet there are some markets, as in 2008 and 2009, when virtually *every* investment, including REITs, will drop by similar amounts. When investors decide to unload everything, there is no place to hide!

A study of correlations by Ibbotson Associates completed in 2001 and updated in 2003 concluded that the correlation of REITs' stock returns with those of other equity investments has declined significantly when measured over various time periods since 1972, when NAREIT first began to compile REIT industry performance data. Nevertheless, correlations will vary over time—particularly during short time frames—and REIT stocks have been more closely correlated with other stocks during the market turmoil of the past few years. However, because commercial real estate is a distinct asset class, and due to the unique attributes of REIT investing as discussed in this chapter and elsewhere in this book, it is reasonable to expect that REIT stocks will maintain fairly low correlations with other asset classes over reasonably long time periods.

Lower Volatility

A stock's "volatility" refers to the extent to which its price tends to bounce around from day to day, or even hour to hour. My observations of the REIT market over the past 35 years have led me to the conclusion that REIT stocks are, most of the time, simply less volatile, on a daily basis, than other equities. Although REITs' increased size and popularity, particularly over the past 5 years, has brought in new investors with different agendas and shorter time horizons, and thus created more volatility, REIT stocks should remain less volatile than their non-REIT brethren.

TIP

REITs' higher current yields often act as a shock absorber against daily market fluctuations.

There is a predictability and steadiness to most REITs' operating and financial performance from quarter to quarter and from year to year, and there is simply less risk of major negative surprises that can stoke volatility.

Another factor that should help to dampen the volatility of REIT stocks is their higher dividend yields. When a stock yields next to nothing, its entire value is comprised of all future earnings, discounted to the present date. If the perceived prospects for those earnings decline just slightly, the stock can plummet quickly. Much of the value of a REIT stock, however, is in the REIT's current dividend yield, so a modest decline in future growth expectations will have a more muted effect on its trading price. The volatility of REIT stocks spiked from 2007 through 2009, due to concerns about REITs' balance sheets and our nation's space markets, but those issues were pretty much resolved by 2010, and a reasonable assumption for REIT investors is that REIT stock volatility will, in the future, as in most of the past, be lower than that of other equities.

This is important because our biggest investment mistakes tend to be the result of fear. When our stocks are going up, it's human nature to ignore risk in our pursuit of ever greater profits. But, when our stocks are dropping, we often tend to panic and dump otherwise sound investments because we're afraid of ever greater losses. When is the "right" time to sell or buy? There is no easy answer to this question, but prudent investors have learned through experience to control their emotions; low volatility in a stock can make patient and disciplined investors of us all.

Sometimes our financial decisions are not based on long-term investment strategy but on some unexpected personal event that requires that we liquidate some of our holdings. That can be very unpleasant if it occurs during a sizeable market downturn. But if we own ample amounts of REIT shares, chances are we can sell some of them at prices that are reasonably close to where they were trading a week or a month ago, even in soft markets.

Less Risk

There's just no way to avoid risk completely. Even simple preservation of capital carries its own risk—inflation can impact the real value of even seemingly low-risk investments such as investment grade bonds. Real estate ownership and management, like any other business or commercial endeavor, is subject to all sorts of risks. Mall REITs are subject to the changing spending habits of consumers; apartment REITs are subject to changes in the popularity of single-family dwellings and declining job growth in the areas where their properties are located; and health care REITs are subject to the politics of government cuts in health care reimbursement, to cite just a few examples. In general, all REITs are subject to an increased supply of rental properties and demand-weakening recessions.

Yet, despite this, owners of commercial real estate can limit risk, including the risk of tenant bankruptcies—if they are diversified by sector, geographic location, and tenant roster. For example, if some tenants are doing badly, there are usually other tenants who are doing fine. This has happened repeatedly in the history of the retail industry, and the retail REITs have remained resilient; they continually find new tenants to replace those that must close their doors.

Holders of most common stocks must contend with yet another type of risk, related not to the fundamentals of a company's business but to the fickle nature of the financial markets. Let's say you own shares in a company whose business is doing well. The earnings report comes out and the news is that earnings are up 15 percent over last year. But because analysts expected a 20 percent increase, the price of the stock drops precipitously. This has been a common phenomenon in the stock market in recent years, but REIT investors have rarely suffered from this syndrome.

 TIP

Analysts who follow REITs are normally able to accurately forecast quarterly results, within one or two cents, quarter after quarter.

This is because of the stability and predictability of REITs' rental revenues, occupancy rates, and real estate operating costs. Long-term leases enjoyed by most commercial real estate owners provide earnings stability and make this asset class more "bondlike." The risks, therefore, are reduced.

Few REITs have gotten themselves into serious financial difficulties over the years. Those few instances of severe financial stress have generally been caused by risky balance sheets, for example, General Growth Properties, or poor allocation of their investment capital. Remember, there is no such thing as zero risk. If you're investing primarily in the higher-quality REITs (we'll review the nature of "blue-chip" REITs in a later chapter), the long-term risk of REIT investments is far lower than that of most other common stocks.

Higher Current Returns

As we'll see in Chapter 3, REITs must, by law, pay out at least 90 percent of their pretax income to shareholders in the form of dividends. As a result, REITs' dividends tend to be higher than those of other companies as a percentage of their free cash flows, and REIT shares normally trade at higher dividend yields (see Figure 1.3).

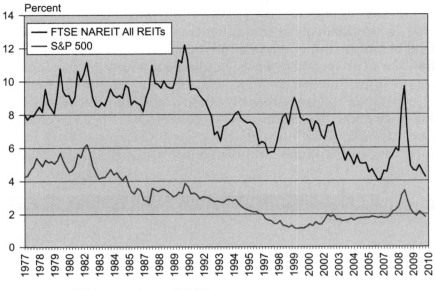

Dividend Yields: FTSE NAREIT All REITs vs. S&P 500
(Quarterly dividend yields, 1977 to 2010)

Figure 1.3   REIT Yield Comparison vs. S&P 500
Source: NAREIT REITwatch, January 2011.

Although many academics claim that it shouldn't matter to shareholders how much of its net income a corporation pays out in dividends, many argue that dividends really do matter with respect to shareholders' total returns. According to Ed Clissold, an equity strategist at Ned Davis Research (as referred to in a *Barron's* article of September 20, 2010), the S&P 500 index has delivered average annual price appreciation since the end of 1929 of 4.92 percent, but its average annual total return has been 9.16 percent. Thus, dividends have provided approximately 46 percent of those total returns. Dividends *do* count.

Perhaps another benefit of owning REIT stocks, relating to REITs' dividend payment requirement, is that its shareholders are legally entitled to 90 percent of the REIT's income each year. This allows the shareholder to participate in income reinvestment decisions. He or she can plow the dividend income back into the REIT by buying additional shares (albeit on an after-tax basis if owned in taxable accounts), investing elsewhere, or spending it on a vacation in Hawaii. Shareholders in non-REIT companies don't have this advantage, and must accept the decisions of the company's board of directors with respect to dividend policy.

Another key advantage to owning higher-yielding investments is that they provide a steady income even during the occasional bear market. This can often prevent the investor from becoming discouraged enough to sell out at bear market lows. With REITs, we get "paid to wait."

REIT stocks' current dividend yields are often below those of many corporate bonds. However, bond interest payments do not increase, while the REIT industry has a long-term track record of increasing dividends on a regular basis. Although this track record was marred during the recent traumatic period commonly referred to as the "Great Recession," as many REITs reduced their dividends in response to weak and uncertain space and capital markets, REITs have been able, over time, to increase their dividends at a rate above the rate of inflation (Figure 1.4).

Finally, there's an intangible psychological benefit in seeing significant dividends roll in each month or each quarter. If, like most of us, you have to work to earn a salary, seeing a check come in for several hundred dollars—without your having to show up at the office—provides substantial comfort regardless of whether you intend to spend it or reinvest it.

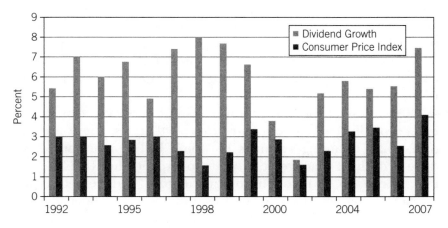

Figure 1.4   Equity REIT Dividend Growth vs. CPI
Source: www.reit.com.
Note: Data as of December 31, 2007.

Do High Current Returns Mean Slow Growth?

It doesn't take a PhD to figure out why many investors like REITs' substantial dividend yields. But what effect does the high payout ratio have on a REIT's growth prospects? With investors receiving at least 90 percent of pretax income, a REIT can retain only modest amounts of capital with which to expand the business and, therefore, to grow its future operating income. Thus, to the extent that stock price appreciation results from rapidly rising earnings growth, a REIT's share price should normally rise at a slower pace than that of a non-REIT stock. However, the REIT investor doesn't mind that; he or she expects to make up much, or even all, of the difference through higher dividend payments over time, and thus maintain a high *total* return.

And it isn't even clear that paying out most of a REIT's income in dividends condemns it to slower growth. A study appearing in the January/February 2003 issue of *Financial Analysts Journal*, entitled "Surprise! Higher Dividends = Higher Earnings Growth," by hedge fund manager Cliff Asness (AQR Capital Management) and academic Robert Arnott (Research Affiliates) concluded that earnings growth rates of companies with above-average dividend payments are actually higher than those of companies with lower dividend payments. These results tend to defy logic, but the implication is that many companies with low payout ratios may not be doing a very good job of reinvesting their retained capital, perhaps investing it in poorly conceived acquisitions. One may therefore speculate whether the higher dividend payments required by the tax laws applicable to REITs, by creating a situation of "opportunity triage," has been a key element in REIT stocks' excellent relative performance over the years.

Regardless of the conclusion of Asness and Arnott or the relevance of dividend payout rates to growth rates, there are ways other than retaining earnings by which REIT organizations can drive growth. If management wants to expand the REIT's growth rate, it can do so through additional stock and debt offerings, by exchanging new shares or partnership units for properties, or by selling mature properties and reinvesting in higher-growth properties. There are some times when such capital is freely available to a REIT, sometimes when it dries up altogether, and still other times when it is available but at a price that is dilutive to the existing shareholders. Generally, however, high-quality REITs can expect to have reasonably good access to expansion capital during most market environments.

> **TIP**
>
> When selecting REITs for investment, remember that it is the strong ones that can attract additional capital—and this provides the greatest long-term growth potential.

Because being able to attract reasonably priced capital is an important advantage for a REIT, those companies with excellent reputations in the investment community and strong balance sheets have a potent tool at their disposal.

Nevertheless, let's be conservative. The need to raise additional capital to fund significant external growth opportunities, such as acquisitions or developments, normally means that REITs will be slower-growing investment vehicles. In the mid-1990s, however, some REITs were acting in a very un-REITly way, growing by 10 to 20 percent annually. It was as if tortoises were actually sprinting faster than hares. What happened? The phenomenon can probably be explained by the fact that many REITs during that period combined their capital-raising capabilities with many institutions' need to liquidate their real estate investments, and thus many REITs created rapidly growing cash flows through numerous property acquisitions. This trend ended in 1998, and REITs' growth rates returned to the more normal single-digit range thereafter.

Some have speculated that the gut-wrenching recession that began late in 2007 and ended in the middle of 2009—the Great Recession—and related problems in the U.S. real estate markets, along with the vast amounts of mortgage loans whose principal amounts were greater than the values of the underlying properties, might create similar acquisition and growth opportunities for REITs over the next few years. While this could happen, there has been much competition among buyers for "distressed real estate," and it is unlikely that REITs will be able to generate double-digit earnings growth by buying huge volumes of cheap properties.

Of course, investors in REITs shouldn't assume that these organizations will be able to grow earnings each and every year. Cash flow growth went negative for many REITs in the early years of the twenty-first century, due to weak office, industrial, and apartment rental markets, but these markets later stabilized, and modest cash flow growth resumed in late 2005. Then, beginning in 2008, when many of our leading investment banks either failed or had to be rescued by the federal government and a deep recession ensued, REITs' cash flows declined due to lower occupancy and rental rates. Property markets began to stabilize, yet again, in 2010. Real estate is a cyclical industry, and there will be down years. However, rental rates *do* grow over time, and REITs' cash flows will grow also. But REIT investors would be wise not to expect more than mid-single-digit growth over relatively long time frames.

This chapter has suggested some long-term advantages of owning REIT shares as part of a broadly diversified investment portfolio. By the time you finish this book, you will understand what REIT stocks are capable of and why. There is, indeed, a great deal to like; however, I am not promising instant riches or even perpetual investment tranquility. As noted earlier, commercial real estate, like virtually all global markets, is cyclical, and so are the markets for real estate space and property valuations. Furthermore, investment trends, like fashion trends, change quickly and are not easily predictable. In some years, REIT stocks will simply become unpopular due to the oft-fickle nature of investors. Also, the rise of hedge funds, sometimes with very short time horizons, has added another wild card to the deck; REIT stocks have, at times, become the sandbox in which these funds like to play. As a result, REIT stocks will often be more volatile than warranted by the stability and predictability of their property cash flows. We must remember that REITs are a unique blend of equity and real estate.

The bottom line here is that REIT stocks are not without risk, particularly for those with short time horizons; unexpected economic events and changes in investor preferences can, and do, affect REIT prices from time to time. But that does not detract from REITs' value as excellent long-term investments, as we'll see throughout the rest of this book.

Summary

- REITs own real estate, but when you buy a REIT, you're not just buying real estate—you're also buying a business run by an experienced management team.
- REITs' total returns, over reasonably long time periods, have been very competitive with those provided by the broader market.
- The vast majority of REITs offer the liquidity provided by public equities markets.
- REITs provide diversification to your portfolio because their price movements, during most periods, are not highly correlated with the rest of the market.
- REITs' higher current yields frequently act as a shock absorber against daily market fluctuations.
- Analysts who follow REITs are normally able to forecast quarterly results within one or two cents, quarter after quarter, year after year, thus minimizing the chances for "negative surprises."
- REITs' higher yields raise the overall yield of the portfolio, thus reducing volatility and providing stable cash flows regardless of market gyrations.
- REIT stocks are equities, as well as real estate, and thus are subject to the prevailing winds that blow across the investment world.

CHAPTER

REITs versus Competitive Investments

"The question is not do you take money out of stocks and put it into real estate, or the reverse. There's so much money out there looking for a home. I don't think it's either/or."

—Sam Zell

Before you decide if REITs are an appropriate investment for you, it might be helpful to compare their merits with those of other investments. This exercise becomes more meaningful, of course, if the comparison is made with investments that are truly similar.

But this is not as easy as it may seem. Most investors acknowledge that commercial real estate is a unique "asset class," and some believe that REITs—being a hybrid of both equity and real estate—comprise yet another asset class. But compare we shall, and so in this chapter we'll compare REITs to other investments that often compete with them for investors' capital.

Even though REITs trade as stocks, is it appropriate to compare REITs with *all* common stocks, or does it make more sense to compare them with the narrower segment of high-yield stocks and other similar investments? Up to this point we've been comparing them to the broad spectrum of common stocks, which, technically, they are. Many investors, however, see them as somehow different from stocks of such companies as General Electric, Microsoft, or Disney because of their higher dividend yields and more modest capital appreciation prospects.

Thus, while it is always informative to compare REITs to the broad equities markets, REITs might be more meaningfully compared to securities investments with higher yields: bonds, convertible bonds, preferred stocks and higher-yielding common stocks, and even master limited partnerships (MLPs). These are the investments of choice for those who normally invest primarily for income, and that offer lower volatility, zero to modest capital appreciation prospects, and reduced investment risk. Another appropriate comparison, discussed below, is to other real estate investment vehicles.

Bonds

Bonds, particularly high-yield, or "junk," bonds, usually provide higher yields than the average REIT stock, but the investor gets only the interest coupon and no growth potential. Bonds do offer something that REITs cannot provide: a promise of repayment of principal at maturity so that, in the absence of bankruptcy or other default, investors will always get back their investments. It is this feature that makes the comparison between REITs and bonds less meaningful. For that reason, if absolute safety of capital is paramount regardless of the cost in total return or protection against inflation, REITs may not be the ideal investment for you. But let's look at the returns each can provide.

With bonds, what you see is what you get: pure yield and very little else. Let's assume that you invest $10,000 in a bond that yields 5 percent and matures in 10 years. At the end of 10 years, you will have your $10,000 in cash, plus the cumulative amount of the interest you received (10 × $500), or a total of $15,000, less taxes on the interest received.

If, however, you invest the same amount of money in a typical REIT, the total return would probably calculate something like this: Assume the purchase of 1,000 shares of a REIT trading at $10 per share, providing a 4 percent yield (or $0.40 per share). Let's also assume that the REIT increases its adjusted funds from operations (AFFO)—which, as we'll discuss in more detail in a later chapter, is a rough approximation of free cash flow—by 4 percent annually and increases the dividend by 4 percent annually. Finally, let's assume that the shares will rise in price proportionately with increased AFFO and dividend payments. Ten years later, the REIT will be paying $0.593 in dividends, and the total investment will be worth $19,812 ($4,992 in cumulative dividends received plus $14,820 in share value at that time). That's $19,812 from the REIT investment, versus only $15,000 from the 10-year bond, or a difference of $4,812 (see the chart in Table 2.1). Taxes, of course, will have to be paid on both the bond interest and the dividend payments. Conventional wisdom says that REITs *should* provide a higher total return, because they are riskier than bonds. However, that's not necessarily true if we consider the bond owner's exposure to inflation.

Unlike bonds, REIT shares offer no specific maturity date, and there is no guarantee of the price you'll get when you sell them. However, with bonds you get no inflation protection, and so you are at a substantial risk of the declining purchasing power of the dollar. It's all a question of how one measures risk.

Table 2.1 REITs Should Produce Better Total Returns than Bonds

REITs: 4% annual dividend, compounded at a 4% annual growth rate

End Year	Stock Price	Per Share Div.
1	$10.40	$0.400
2	$10.82	$0.443
3	$11.25	$0.450
4	$11.70	$0.468
5	$12.17	$0.487
6	$12.66	$0.506
7	$13.17	$0.527
8	$13.70	$0.548
9	$14.25	$0.570
10	$14.82	$0.593
		$4.992
× 1,000 shares	$14,820	$4,992
Total Investment value		$19,812

TIP

If history is any guide, REITs, unlike bonds, will appreciate in value as the value of their underlying real estate appreciates and the rental income from their tenants increases over time.

If inflation rises, so generally will interest rates, which reduces the market value of the bond while it's being held and results in a real loss of capital if the bond is sold prior to maturity. However, if interest rates decline, perhaps due to lower inflation, many bonds may be called for redemption before their maturity dates. This deprives investors of what, with hindsight, was a very attractive yield and forces them to find other investment vehicles, but ones that will pay a lower rate of interest. (Of course, a REIT's stock price may decline in response to higher interest rates, but higher interest rates are often due to a fast-growing economy, which helps to grow REIT cash flows over time.)

U.S. Treasury bonds are not callable prior to maturity and entail no repayment risk, but their yields are lower than those of corporate bonds and also fluctuate with interest rates. Bonds are certainly suitable investments for most investors; however, for the reasons stated above, they should not be regarded as good substitutes for REIT stocks in a broadly diversified portfolio.

Convertible Bonds

Convertible bonds may provide more competition for REITs. These securities offer yields comparable to those of many REITs *as well as* appreciation potential—if the common stock into which these bonds may be converted rises substantially. Convertible bonds provide the security of a fixed maturity date in case the underlying common stock fails to appreciate in value. They can be relatively attractive investments.

The problem with convertibles is that most companies just don't issue them. If they can be found, and if the underlying common stock appears to be a good investment, the convertible may also be a good investment. Some REITs have occasionally issued convertible securities, including convertible preferred stock. The investor should consider whether the extra safety of these convertibles outweighs the often substantial conversion premium and their relative lack of liquidity.

Preferred Stocks

Many investors seeking higher yields have become interested in preferred stocks, some of which have been issued by REITs. Unlike bonds, however, preferred stocks do not represent a promise by the issuing company to repay a specific amount at a specified date in the future; furthermore, in the event of liquidation or bankruptcy, preferred shareholders' rights are subordinated to those of the corporation's creditors. However, holders of preferred stock do have seniority relative to common shareholders, and most preferred stocks specify that common dividends cannot be paid unless preferred dividends are current.

Accordingly, preferred stocks are treated as "equity" by the credit rating agencies, and many companies like to issue them; they regard them as "permanent capital" that doesn't dilute the interests of holders of the common shares.

The dividend rate for a preferred stock is set at the time of original issuance, and remains the same for as long as the shares are outstanding. Accordingly, unlike common stockholders, preferred holders don't participate in the growth in earnings of the issuing company. And there are other disadvantages. They can usually be redeemed by the issuing company after a period of time, usually five years after issuance, at the price at which they were originally issued—so, if interest rates fall, the preferred shareholder may be deprived of what had been a good, high-yielding investment. Also, the liquidity of preferred shares is usually a significant issue; it can be difficult to buy or sell them in substantial size, and often there is a significant spread between bid and ask prices. Should the issuer be acquired or go private, the preferred shareholder will sometimes be negatively affected by the lack of disclosure of company information or by higher debt leverage at the newly private company.

So why would anyone want to own these odd investments? Dividend yields are higher than on most common stocks, and they are higher than the yields on corporate bonds (assuming comparable credit quality). The dividends on preferred stocks also have priority over those of the related common stocks. This will be particularly important to investors when the direction and strength of the U.S. economy is uncertain, as it was in 2008 to 2010.

Because they lack meaningful, if any, appreciation potential or the prospects of rising dividends over time, REIT preferred stocks are not substitutes for REIT common stocks. However, some may regard them as "bond proxies," and due to their higher dividend yields and safety relative to common shares, REIT preferreds will be attractive to some conservative investors as a supplement to their REIT common share holdings.

Other High-Yielding Equities

REIT stocks are regarded, quite properly, as higher-yielding equities, and thus compete for investment capital, to some extent, with other equities that have historically provided higher than average dividend yields to shareholders. Let's take a brief look at just two of these higher-yielding publicly traded securities: utility shares and master limited partnership interests.

Utility stocks have been a staple of the investment world almost forever, and have often been a favorite of those looking for higher dividend yields as well as lower investment risk. The industry's total market cap is large, at $487 billion as of September 2010. Utility shares represent equity interests in companies that provide basic services, such as electricity, natural gas, water, and wire line telephony, to individuals and businesses. As competition is not practical in most of these industries, many utility companies have been given a legal monopoly on the provision of services in their trade areas.

This is both good and bad for their shareholders. On the one hand, the utility doesn't have to compete with other providers, so its earnings and dividends are often quite stable. On the other hand, it can charge customers only what the regulatory authority will permit, so it runs the risk of fickle, and sometimes politically motivated, regulators. Holders of utility stocks also understand that, because the need for utility services grows slowly, earnings and dividends will also grow slowly—perhaps 2 to 4 percent annually.

In recent years, there has been an "unbundling" of services that some utilities provide. Companies that generate or purchase power and sell it to other service providers have become much less regulated, so their growth prospects are better than regulated utilities. But their earnings are much less certain, and their dividend yields tend to be much lower. Companies that remain heavily regulated may see their earnings grow even more slowly without the ability to wholesale power in open markets.

Accordingly, utility stocks, such as Duke Energy and Southern Company, may compete, to some extent, with REITs for the investment dollars of those investors who favor higher dividend yields, and they have been less volatile than REIT shares in recent years. Therefore, they can be a good choice for those investors with very modest capital appreciation expectations and total return requirements.

Another type of publicly traded higher yielding investment is the master limited partnership (MLP). An MLP can conduct almost any business, but the vast majority of public MLPs are engaged in energy infrastructure, such as gas pipelines, storage facilities, and similar businesses. They vary in the extent to which they have exposure to the prices of natural resources. According to a Legg Mason report, the total market capitalization of the energy MLPs has grown rapidly, to $174 billion in June 30, 2010.

Their dividend yields, which were close to 6 percent in early 2011, are generally higher than those of REIT stocks, and thus provide the investor with high current income, along with diversification. And, thanks to depreciation and other tax advantages applicable to the oil and gas industry, much of those cash distributions are not currently taxable as ordinary income.

But, while MLPs may trade like stocks, they are *not* stocks. Rather, investors receive a partnership K-1 form at the end of each year, which can make tax return preparation quite challenging indeed. And, if held in an individual retirement account (IRA) or other tax-deferred account, they may, in some cases, give rise to "unrelated business taxable income," and thus their dividends may be subject to tax under certain circumstances. As they distribute most or all of their free cash flow to their partners, they will need to raise outside capital from time to time if they want to grow. Such capital won't always be available.

MLPs will thus compete with REITs for investment capital; however, as most of their investment characteristics are different from REITs, it should not be an "either/or" proposition for investors.

Other Real Estate Investment Vehicles

As an asset class, and particularly if not financed with large amounts of debt, real estate has normally been a very good and stable investment. A well-situated, well-maintained investment property should grow in value over the years, and its rental revenues are likely to grow with it. While buildings may depreciate over time and neighborhoods change, only a finite amount of land exists upon which an apartment community, retail center, or office building can be built. If you own such a property in the right area, it can be, if not a gold mine, a cash cow whose value is likely to increase over the years. New, competitive buildings will not be built unless either rents or property values are high enough to justify the development costs. In either such event, owners of existing properties will be wealthier.

It's interesting to note that, contrary to popular wisdom, the extent to which commercial real estate owners directly benefit from inflation isn't all that clear. There have been studies done on this issue; for example, David J. Hartzell, professor of real estate at the University of North Carolina, along with R. Brian Webb, concluded that property "returns tend to exhibit stronger relationships with inflation and its components" during periods of low vacancy rates. Inflation may therefore not benefit real estate owners when property markets are weak. That said, well-maintained properties in economically healthy areas, particularly if they are protected against competing properties because of land scarcity or entitlement restrictions, are likely to rise in value over time. We'll explore the inflation conundrum in more detail in Chapter 5.

 TIP

REIT ownership resolves the issues raised by every other real estate investment vehicle: REITs offer diversification, liquidity, expert management, and, in most cases, zero or very limited conflicts of interest between management and investors.

Accepting that well-located and well-maintained commercial property is likely to remain a good long-term investment, how does real estate as an asset class fit within a well-diversified portfolio? Since it has historically behaved differently from other assets—stocks (both foreign and domestic), bonds, cash, or possibly gold or art—it adds another dimension and therefore helps to diversify one's asset base. There are a number of ways, however, in which we can choose to hold real estate.

Direct Ownership

Direct ownership means being in the real estate business. Do you have the time to manage property, or do you already have a full-time career? Do you know the best time to buy or sell? Buying real estate at cheap prices and then selling it is often more profitable than holding and managing it, depending on the market climate. But would you recognize when it's smarter to sell the property than to hold on to it? For most individual investors, having a real estate professional make this decision is far wiser than being in real estate directly. Effective and efficient property management is also crucial; the importance of competent, experienced management cannot be overstated, and individuals often lack the resources—time, money, or expertise—to accomplish this.

TIP

Direct ownership may sometimes offer higher profits than investing in REITs, but most individuals don't have the time or experience to be in the real estate business.

Although it is sometimes more profitable not to have to share returns from a great real estate investment with other investors, it is also clearly riskier. The investment value of real estate quite often is determined by the local economy; at any given time, apartment buildings may be doing well, say, in Manhattan, but poorly in Los Angeles. Most individuals simply do not have the financial resources to buy enough properties to be safely diversified, either by property type or by geography.

Then there is the problem of liquidity: Selling a single piece of real property may be very time-consuming and costly. Furthermore, it may not happen when you want it to, although selling may sometimes be your only way to cash out.

Finally, even if you are willing to accept all the inconveniences and disadvantages of inexperience, limited diversification, and illiquidity, would you want to be the one who gets the call that there's been a break-in, or the air conditioning isn't working, or the elevator is stuck? And if you use an outside management company, your profits may be significantly reduced.

Some investors claim that they don't need REIT investments, as they own their own home—which, of course, is real estate. However, the dynamics of home values and their price fluctuations are often very different from those of commercial real estate, as will be discussed briefly in Chapter 4. Further, there is no diversification if the only real estate an investor owns is one's home. Another key point is that capturing the appreciated value in a single-family residence requires its sale, and most individuals would be reluctant to sell their beloved home and move into an apartment building or find another home in a different location. Of course, equity can be pulled out of one's home through a refinancing, but this will usually require substantially higher monthly mortgage payments. Simply stated, owning a home is no substitute for owning commercial real estate.

Private Partnerships

Ownership through a private partnership—whether with 2, 10, or 20 partners—is yet another option for real estate ownership. Here, the investor gets to delegate, either to a general partner or to an outside company, the tasks of property leasing and management—at a price, of course. Usually, however, most private partnerships of this type own only one or very few properties, and those properties are rarely sufficiently diversified in terms of property type or location.

In a private partnership, liquidity may depend on the financial strength or solvency of the investor's partners. Although it might be theoretically possible for one partner to sell his or her interest to another partner without the underlying property being sold, that alternative is often problematic. Also, in private partnerships, conflicts of interest often abound between the general partner and the limited partners, perhaps with regard either to compensation or to the decision to sell or refinance the partnership property. Finally, there is the question of the personal liability of the individual partners if the partnership experiences financial difficulties, a situation not uncommon a number of years ago.

These private partnerships can sometimes be good investments, but they do have issues—particularly a lack of liquidity and property diversification—that will make public REITs a better choice for most investors.

Publicly Traded Limited Partnerships

Publicly traded real estate limited partnerships were very popular with investors for a period of time up until 1990. There is a world of difference between REITs and real estate limited partnerships, and these differences have cost many investors in the latter dearly. The limited partnership sponsors of the 1980s plucked billions of dollars from investors who were seeking the benefits of real estate ownership combined with tax breaks. Unsuspecting investors during that time did so poorly that they were lucky to recover 10 or 20 cents on the dollar.

There were several reasons for their failure: Sometimes it was that fees were so high that there were no profits for the ultimate owner, the investor. Sometimes it was that the partnerships bought too late in the real estate cycle. After they grossly overpaid for the properties, they hired mediocre managers, failing to recognize that, particularly in the 1990s, real estate was—and still is—a very management-intensive business. At other times, these limited partnerships had conflicts of interest with the general partners, to the detriment of the investors.

Publicly traded limited partnerships are not popular today—for good reason!

The Private REIT Phenomenon

Beginning in 2000, another real estate alternative to public REITs burst on the scene—non–publicly traded, or "private," REITs. These entities are organizations that comply with the U.S. REIT laws, but their shares do not trade in public markets. Sponsored by various real estate organizations, for example, Inland American or Wells Real Estate, they are usually sold to small investors by financial planners and investment advisers. Like public REITs, a nonpublic REIT will own a number of commercial properties, usually in different locations, and the income from the properties is distributed to the REIT's shareholders as dividends. The yields to investors are normally higher than available from an investment in public REITs.

However, there are a number of drawbacks to nonpublic REITs that investors should be aware of. Perhaps most important, they are not liquid investments. Although some nonpublic REITs promise to offer to repurchase a number of shares at certain times and under certain conditions, shares cannot be quickly sold by calling one's broker. Furthermore, nonpublic REIT shares are normally sold with large commissions going to the selling agent (often exceeding 10 percent), so fewer investment dollars are available for real estate investment; and, quite often, the sponsor earns significant additional revenues via property acquisitions and management fees. Accordingly, prospective investors in nonpublic REITs should be aware of potential conflicts of interest that may result from a desire of some sponsors to grow the size of the REIT merely in order to generate increasing revenues for itself.

Investors therefore should carefully balance the promised benefits of these REITs against their inherent disadvantages (including very limited liquidity, large offering commissions, and potential conflicts of interest), and should carefully analyze their organizational structure, balance sheet, acquisition criteria, operating costs and fee payments, prospective cash flows, and dividend coverage from recurring free cash flows.

To summarize, bonds, preferred stocks, utility stocks, MLP interests, and other high-yielding non-REIT stocks, as well as other forms of commercial real estate ownership, can, and do, provide alternatives to REIT investing. But REITs are different from each of them. They are all about commercial real estate, and their stocks have both liquidity and reasonable prospects for capital appreciation over time. REIT management teams are experienced and dedicated professionals, and their interests are closely aligned with the REIT's shareholders. And REITs' financial condition and operating results are quite transparent via Securities and Exchange Commission disclosure requirements and industry practice.

Accordingly, REIT shares are unique and distinguishable from other higher-yielding investments, including other forms of commercial real estate ownership. The key point is this: It need not be "either/or," and a wise investment strategy is to own both REITs *and* other higher-yielding stocks, as well as other investments. The *real* issue is the "right" investment mix, which will depend on the investor's financial circumstances, return requirements, and tolerance for risk. We'll discuss this issue later in the book.

Summary

- REITs benefit from U.S. economic growth and thus are not as interest rate sensitive as most bonds and preferred stocks.
- Bonds and preferred stocks, unlike REITs, have no potential for dividend income growth, but preferreds, in particular, offer higher current dividend yields, and bonds promise the repayment of the principal amount at maturity.
- Higher-yielding equities, such as utility stocks and MLPs, compete with REITs for the investment dollars of yield-oriented investors, but only REITs provide for the indirect ownership of commercial real estate.
- Direct real estate ownership may sometimes deliver higher profits than investing in a REIT, but most individuals don't have the time or experience to be in the real estate business full time.
- Owning REIT shares eliminates the vexing issues raised by every other real estate investment vehicle: REITs offer diversification and liquidity, provide expert and experienced management and investor transparency, and, in the vast majority of cases, avoid conflicts of interest between management teams and their investors.

CHAPTER

Today's REITs

*"Ninety percent of all millionaires become so through
owning real estate."*

—Andrew Carnegie

Now that you have a general sense of what REITs are and how they compare to other investments, let's take a closer look at the nature and structure of REITs, how they've changed, and how they've adapted to changing market conditions over the years.

The First REIT

The REIT was defined and authorized by the U.S. Congress, in the Real Estate Investment Trust Act of 1960, and the first REITs were organized in that year. This legislation was intended to provide individual investors with the opportunity to participate in the benefits, already available to large institutional investors, of owning and/or financing a diversified portfolio of commercial real estate.

TIP

The avoidance of "double taxation" is one of the key advantages to the REIT structure.

A key hallmark of the REIT structure is that the REIT can deduct from its pretax net income all dividends paid to its shareholders—thus, the REIT pays no corporate taxes if it distributes to shareholders all otherwise taxable income. By law, however, it must pay out at least 90 percent of its net income to its shareholders. The shareholders, of course, must pay income taxes on the dividends, unless the REIT shares are held in an individual retirement account (IRA), 401(k), or other tax-deferred account. Often, however, a portion of a REIT's dividend is not immediately taxable, and another portion may be taxable at lower capital gain rates, as we'll see later.

There are other basic legal requirements applicable to REITs, as described in the following box:

Unique Legal Characteristics of a REIT

1. A REIT must distribute at least 90 percent of its annual taxable income, except for capital gains, as dividends to its shareholders.
2. A REIT must have at least 75 percent of its assets invested in real estate, mortgage loans, shares in other REITs, cash, or government securities.
3. A REIT must derive at least 75 percent of its gross income from rents, mortgage interest, or gains from the sale of real property. And at least 95 percent must come from these sources, together with dividends, interest, and gains from securities sales.
4. A REIT must have at least 100 shareholders and must have less than 50 percent of the outstanding shares concentrated in the hands of five or fewer shareholders.

The Tax Reform Act of 1986

The Tax Reform Act of 1986 was a significant milestone in the REIT industry, as it relaxed some of the restrictions historically limiting REIT activities. Originally, management was legally obliged to hire outside companies to provide property leasing and management services, but this new legislation allowed REITs to perform these essential services within their own organizations. This change was highly significant because imaginative and efficient leasing and property management are key elements of successful and profitable property ownership.

The vast majority of today's REITs are fully integrated operating companies that can handle all aspects of real estate operations internally:

- Acquisitions and sales of properties
- Property management and leasing
- Property rehabilitation, retenanting, and repositioning
- New property development

UPREITs and DownREITs

In studying different REITs, you might come across the terms *UPREIT* and *DownREIT*. These are terms used to describe differences in the corporate structure of REITs. The UPREIT concept was first implemented in 1992 by creative investment bankers. Its purpose is to enable long-established real estate operating companies to bring properties they already own into a new REIT structure, without having to sell the properties to the new REIT. Such a sale would likely cause the existing owners to incur significant capital gains taxes.

UPREIT just means "umbrella partnership REIT." Generally, it works like this: The REIT itself might not own any properties directly; what it *does* own is a controlling interest in a limited partnership that, in turn, owns the real estate. The other limited partners often include management and private investors who had indirectly owned the organization's properties prior to its becoming a REIT. The owners of the limited partnership units have the right to convert them into shares of the REIT, to vote as if they were REIT shareholders, and to receive the same dividends as if they held publicly traded REIT shares. In short, they enjoy virtually the same attributes of ownership as the REIT's public shareholders.

DownREITs are structured similarly but are usually formed *after* the REIT becomes a public company, and generally do not include members of management among the limited partners in the controlled partnership.

REITs structured as UPREITs or DownREITs can exchange operating partnership units (OPUs) for interests in other real estate partnerships that own properties the REIT wants to acquire. Such an exchange enables the sellers to defer capital gains taxes. By receiving

OPUs in a "like-kind" exchange, the sellers can then not only defer the payment of taxes but also gain the advantage of having a more diversified form of investment, that is, an indirect interest in many properties. These structures can give the UPREIT or DownREIT a competitive edge over a regular REIT when it comes to making a deal with tax-sensitive property sellers (see Figure 3.1).

TIP

Originally conceived as a tax-deferral device, the UPREIT structure has also, at times, been an attractive acquisition tool for the REIT.

One negative aspect of the UPREIT structure, however, is that it creates the possibility of conflicts of interest. Management may own units in the UPREIT's partnership rather than, or in addition to, shares in the REIT, and their OPUs will usually have a low cost basis.

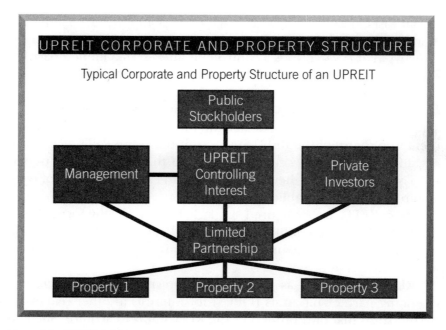

Figure 3.1   UPREIT EPS Diagram

Since the sale of a property could trigger taxable income to the holders of the UPREIT's units but not to the shareholders of the REIT, management might be reluctant to sell a property, or even the REIT itself—even if the property may not be performing well or the third-party offer is a generous one. Investors should watch how management handles the conflict issues. There is less concern, of course, in a Down-REIT structure, where management usually owns no OPUs.

REIT Modernization Act and RIDEA

In December 1999, President Clinton signed into law the REIT Modernization Act (RMA). The most important feature of this new legislation enables every REIT organization to form and own a "taxable REIT subsidiary" (TRS). Thus, a REIT, through ownership of up to 100 percent of a TRS, can develop and quickly sell properties and provide substantial services to its property tenants, as well as others, without jeopardizing the REIT's legal standing; this had been a major issue in the past. This law also greatly expanded the nature and extent of activities that a REIT may engage in, which may now include concierge services to apartment tenants, "merchant" property development, and engaging in a variety of real estate–related businesses; the TRS may also participate in joint ventures with other parties to provide additional services.

However, certain limitations do apply. For example, the TRS cannot exceed certain size limitations (originally no more than 20 percent, but changed by the REIT Investment Diversification and Empowerment Act of 2007 [RIDEA] to 25 percent, of a REIT's gross assets may consist of securities of a TRS). Loan and rental transactions between a REIT and its TRS are limited, and a substantial excise tax is imposed on transactions not conducted on an arm's-length basis. Income from the TRS is subject to taxes at regular corporate income tax rates.

Prior restrictions on hotel and lodging REITs, which prevented them from leasing properties to a "captive" or controlled subsidiary, were relaxed by the RMA. Thus, these REITs became empowered to enter into such leases, provided that each property is operated on behalf of the TRS by an outside manager or independent contractor. This enables a lodging REIT to potentially capture more of the economic benefits of ownership for its shareholders.

The provisions of RIDEA, almost all of which were incorporated into the Housing and Economic Recovery Act of 2008, signed by President Bush in July 2008, provide REITs with more certainty and flexibility relating to the purchase and sale of assets, the size of the TRS relative to a REIT's total assets, and more clarity regarding overseas investments and foreign currencies. This legislation also provides to REITs that own health care properties the same flexibility regarding the leasing of properties to a TRS that was given to hotel and lodging REITs in the RMA.

The National Association of Real Estate Investment Trusts (NAREIT) has suggested several potential benefits to REIT organizations arising from the RMA. These include the ability to provide new services to tenants (thus allowing them to be competitive with non-REIT property owners), better quality control over the services offered (which may now be delivered directly by the REIT's controlled subsidiary), and the prospects of earning substantial nonrental revenues for the REIT and its shareholders.

The RMA and subsequent legislation, by expanding the scope of business activities allowed to REIT organizations, can be regarded as an important tool that may be used to create value for a REIT's shareholders. However, any tool can be used wisely or carelessly and, despite the enthusiasm with which many REITs greeted the passage of the RMA and the ability to create a TRS, its value is still subject to debate. Many early TRS ventures, particularly with respect to technology and Internet investments in the late 1990s, have been failures. More recent TRS activities, such as merchant developments (development of new properties, leasing them up and selling them) performed well until the Great Recession. Kimco Realty, long a widely respected retail REIT that took advantage of the RMA to engage in a number of nonrental businesses, is refocusing on its basic property ownership business—although its business of forming joint ventures with institutional investors to buy and manage retail properties for them, in the United States and elsewhere, remains a valuable profit generator.

The RMA and RIDEA are clearly positive developments for the REIT industry, but investors should pay close attention to a REIT's non–property ownership businesses and try to assess whether it is using these tools wisely. Will the potential rewards of more rapid earnings growth and value creation be worth the added risks? The answer will be specific to each REIT.

Lending REITs versus Ownership REITs

Earlier, we discussed the statutory requirements for a REIT. The laws applicable to REIT organizations do not require that a REIT *own* real properties. It is legally permissible for the REIT to merely lend funds on the strength of the collateral value of real estate by originating, acquiring, and holding—and even securitizing—real estate mortgages and related loans. These mortgages might be secured by residential or commercial properties. As of the end of 2010, there were 26 mortgage REITs, split almost evenly between residential and commercial. Hybrid REITs, which both own properties and hold mortgages on others, were popular some years ago, but are not widely prevalent in today's REIT industry.

In the late 1960s and early 1970s, lending REITs were the most popular type of REIT, as many large regional and "money-center" banks and mortgage brokers formed their own captive REITs. Almost 60 new REITs were formed back then, most of them lending funds to property developers. However, interest rates rose substantially in 1973, new developments couldn't be sold or leased, nonperforming loans spiked to fearsome levels, and most of these REITs crashed and burned, leaving investors holding the bag. A decade later, a number of REITs sprang up to invest in collateralized mortgage obligations (CMOs), and they didn't do much better. In recent years, however, the quality of mortgage REITs has improved substantially, and their shares have performed better than they had in the past. However, a number of them, particularly residential mortgage REITs, performed very poorly as a direct result of the Great Recession and related credit squeeze; many of them lost most of their value.

Mortgage REITs present several challenges for the REIT investor. They tend to be more highly levered with debt than the "equity" REITs that own real estate, and this increased leverage can make earning streams and dividend payments much more volatile. Also, mortgage REITs tend to be more sensitive to interest rates and interest rate changes than equity REITs, and a general increase in interest rates (or even a significant change in the spread between short-term and long-term interest rates) can impact earnings substantially. Finally, as they do not own real estate whose values can be estimated, the shares of mortgage REITs can be very difficult to value properly.

Thus, mortgage REITs are perhaps best viewed as trading vehicles, and their business strategies, balance sheets, and sensitivity to interest rates must be constantly and carefully monitored. They can be good investments, particularly if well managed, but they do occupy a specialty niche in the REIT world. Accordingly, most conservative long-term investors will prefer to put most of their REIT investment funds into equity REITs.

TIP

The vast majority of today's REITs own real property rather than make real estate loans.

Throughout the rest of this book, then, the term *REIT* will refer to REITs that *own* real estate of one property type or another.

Expansion of REIT Property Sector Offerings

In Chapter 1, we briefly considered some of the various commercial real estate sectors in which today's REITs own properties. This, too, is a story that has evolved over time. In the beginning and until 1993, only a limited number of property types were owned by REITs: neighborhood (or "strip") shopping centers, apartments, health care facilities (primarily nursing homes), and, to a very limited extent, office buildings. If you wanted to invest in another sector, such as major shopping malls or self-storage properties, you were out of luck.

By the end of 1994, however, as a result of a huge increase in the quantity and dollar amounts of many new and secondary public offerings, the REIT industry had grown substantially. According to NAREIT statistics, the amounts of stock sold in those two years were $18.3 billion and $14.7 billion, respectively—about 117 percent and 46 percent of the total REIT market capitalization in each prior year.

The size of the REIT industry has continued to grow since then, although it has also contracted at times. These occasional contractions can be due to a REIT bear market, which reduces the market capitalizations of virtually all REITs, or a "going private" environment in which commercial real estate becomes more valuable in private hands than in securitized form. This occurred most recently from 2005 through early 2007, as we'll see in a later chapter. REITs' total equity market capitalization fell from $330.7 billion at the end of 2005 to $191.7 billion at the end of 2008, according to NAREIT; this substantial decline was due to the large number of REIT privatizations in 2006 and 2007, as well as REITs' bear market in 2007 and 2008. However, by the end of 2010, REITs' total equity market capitalization had rebounded to $389 billion, including 153 publicly traded equity REITs. The importance of the increased size of the REIT industry and the greatly expanded array of investment choices cannot be overemphasized; it has contributed substantially to both the credibility of the REIT industry and its attractiveness to investors of all types.

TIP

The 1993 to 1994 REIT initial public offering (IPO) boom changed the REIT industry forever. Today's investor has a choice of many well-managed REITs owning various distinct property types.

Each property type, which we'll discuss in the next chapter, has its own set of investment characteristics, including its individual economic cycles and particular risk factors, competition threats, and growth potential. Each sector might, at any particular time, be in a different phase of the broad real estate cycle. Conservative REIT investors will be well diversified among the different property sectors, while those seeking the best relative performance may seek to avoid those whose market cycles appear to create an unfavorable risk-reward ratio. For the long-term investor, investing in REITs led by management teams that are knowledgeable, creative, and experienced, and that finance their properties and businesses conservatively, should continue to provide favorable total returns over many years.

Summary

- Most REITs are operating companies that own and manage real property as a business and must comply with certain technical rules that generally do not affect them as investments.

- The avoidance of double taxation is one of the key advantages to the REIT structure.
- Originally conceived as a tax-deferral device, UPREIT and DownREIT structures have also, at times, been attractive acquisition tools for REITs.
- The REIT Modernization Act and subsequent legislation allow today's REITs to form taxable subsidiaries, enabling them to engage in various real estate–related businesses.
- The vast majority of today's REITs are in the business of owning, managing, and even developing real property rather than making real estate loans.
- Mortgage REITs can, at times, provide good returns to the discerning investor, but must be closely monitored, particularly with respect to interest rate movements.
- The 1993 and 1994 REIT IPO boom changed the REIT industry forever. Today's investor has a choice of many well-managed REITs, most of which specialize in one particular property type.

CHAPTER

Property Sectors and Their Cycles

"There must certainly be a vast Fund of Stupidity in Human Nature, else Men would not be caught as they are, a thousand times over, by the same Snare; and while they yet remember their past Misfortunes, go on to court and encourage the Causes to which they were owing, and which will again produce them."
—Cato's Letters, January 1721

Certain things are true of *all* commercial properties: their value and profitability depend on property-specific issues, such as location, lease revenues, property expenses, occupancy rates, prevailing market rental rates, tenant quality, and replacement cost; real estate issues such as market "cap rates" and supply/demand conditions; competition from nearby properties; and such "macro" forces as the economy, employment growth, consumer and business spending, interest rates, and inflation.

But despite generalizations and expectations that can be applied to commercial real estate generally, properties themselves can be quite dissimilar. The owner of a large, luxury apartment complex, for example, has financial concerns very different from the owner of a neighborhood strip mall or a large office building. And those are just three of the more common property types.

TIP

The four principal commercial property types are residential (primarily apartment communities), industrial properties, office buildings, and retail shopping centers. Some of these property types have subtypes with their own unique characteristics, including manufactured home communities, student housing, medical office buildings, lab and research space, and data centers. And there are still other important property types, including hotels and lodging, self-storage, and several kinds of health- and senior-related properties. There are even timberland REITs, and a movie theater REIT.

Figure 4.1, based on data compiled by the National Association of Real Estate Investment Trusts (NAREIT), provides a glimpse of the diversity within the world of REITs.

The point is that investors may choose to invest only in certain property types—or they can invest in all of them. The choices are wide indeed. But, to make intelligent choices, we must have some familiarity with the specific investment characteristics that set each

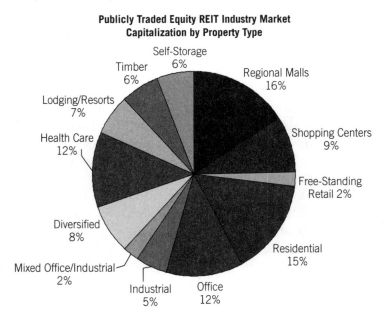

Figure 4.1   Sector Pie Chart
Source: FTSE NAREIT All Equity REITs Index, as of December 31, 2010.

type of property apart. While REIT investors need not be experts on apartments, malls, or any other specific sector, they should know some of the basics.

Ups and Downs

Before we examine the characteristics of the property types owned by REITs, let's first look at the general nature of real estate. Real estate prices and profits move in cycles, often predictable in type but not in length or severity. And there are two kinds of cycles: one is the "space market" cycle, which describes the supply of, and demand for, real estate *space,* and the other is the "capital markets" cycle, which relates to levels of investor demand for commercial real estate assets and the prices and valuations at which they trade.

If you're a long-term, conservative REIT investor, you might choose to buy and hold your REIT stocks even as their properties move through their inevitable up and down cycles. Nevertheless, you should understand and be aware of these cycles, as they can significantly affect a REIT's cash flow and dividend growth, as well as its stock price, from time to time. If you consider yourself more of a short-term market timer, you may try to structure your REIT portfolio in accordance with either real estate space or capital market cycles, even the cycle of an individual property sector. Like many investment strategies, however, this is easier said than done well.

TIP

The phases of the real estate cycle are depression, recovery, boom, and overbuilding and downturn.

The Real Estate Cycles

The following phases refer to the space market cycle, as opposed to the capital market cycle. No two cycles are exactly alike, but they all share similar characteristics.

- **Phase 1: The Depression**. Vacancies are high, rents are low. Concessions to tenants in the form of free rent and tenant improvement allowances are prevalent and substantial. Many properties, particularly those financed with excessive debt, may be in foreclosure. There is little or no new construction.

- **Phase 2: The Gradual Recovery.** Leasing activity accelerates, and occupancy rates stabilize; rents firm and begin to increase gradually, and bargaining power between owners and tenants approaches equilibrium. There is still little or no new building, but developers begin to seek new entitlements from planning commissions and try to line up financing for new projects.

- **Phase 3: The Boom**. After a while, the most desirable vacant space has been absorbed, allowing property owners to boost rents more aggressively. With higher occupancy and rising rents, landlords are getting good returns. Properties may begin to trade at prices above replacement cost. New construction is expected to provide strong investment yields, and developers are flexing their muscles. Investors and lenders are confident and provide ample financing. During this phase, some will argue that "it's different this time."

- **Phase 4: Overbuilding and Downturn**. After rents have been rising rapidly, overbuilding frequently follows as too many players try to capitalize on the high profits being earned by real estate owners. Vacancy rates therefore increase, and rental rates flatten or decline in response to the new supply. Conditions will deteriorate further in the event of an economic recession, perhaps brought about by high interest rates or an unexpected shock to the U.S. economy. As the return on real estate fails to meet excessively rosy expectations, new developments are canceled. Eventually, this downturn phase may turn into a depression phase, depending on the severity of overbuilding or the economic recession. Now the cycle is complete and begins anew with Phase 1.

Sometimes the capital and space markets are in sync, and property prices and owners' cash flows rise and fall together or with a modest lag. However, there are other times, as in 2000 to 2004, when prices seem to be "disconnected" from real estate profitability and market fundamentals. Ultimately, however, real estate market conditions and asset pricing tend to converge. Existing and prospective "conditions on the ground" will always be an important—but not the *exclusive*—component of commercial real estate pricing.

Why do these cycles occur? Commercial real estate is tied closely not only to the national economy, but also to local economies. Years ago, for example, when the steel mills in Pittsburgh or the rubber companies in Akron laid off workers, the local economy, from retail to real estate, became depressed. The part of the country known as "Smokestack America" very quickly became "Rust Belt America." Families doubled up, with young adults moving in with parents or leaving for greener pastures elsewhere. As the number of households declined, apartment vacancy rates rose and office and industrial space went begging.

Conversely, when the Olympic Committee decided to hold the summer games in Atlanta, or when Michelin Tires decided to build a plant in Greenville, South Carolina, the entire local economy picked up. Business improved for all the local residents, from dentists to dry cleaners, and job growth expanded. Recessions and booms can be local or national in scope, but commercial real estate markets will always be sensitive to economic conditions. As economies are cyclical, so is real estate.

Sometimes capital market cycles become even more extreme than is justified by real estate space market conditions, however, and prices can become truly manic—or depressive. In 2006 and into 2007, our nation's space markets were healthy, but the prices of commercial real estate rose to levels consistent only with spectacularly good space markets. Many buyers were willing to accept historically low initial investment returns of 4 percent or less, hoping to garner acceptable total returns by making some very aggressive assumptions about future rent and operating income growth.

Of course, it's not just commercial real estate that's cyclical, and bubbles can form when cycles go to extreme levels. We've seen manic cycles in the stock and single-family home markets. During bull market conditions, investors often throw caution to the wind and expect prices to rise forever. New York City's shoeshine operators and taxi drivers handed out stock tips in the late 1920s. Seventy years later, cocktail party chatter and Internet discussion groups were replete with details of the latest killing on Wall Street. And I need not remind anyone of the more recent home buying mania.

When real estate is booming, there may be—shall we say—"irrational exuberance," but the exuberance isn't limited to investors. When commercial real estate prices, rents, and operating income are rising rapidly, developers, syndicators, private equity managers, and even lenders want a piece of the action. The traditional use of debt to leverage real estate investments can exacerbate the situation. This was the scenario that commenced in the mid-1980s. Investors were buying up apartments at furious rates—individually, through syndications, and through limited partnerships. Developers were building everywhere. The banks and savings and loans (S&Ls) were only too eager to provide the necessary liquidity to drive the boom ever higher. Even Congress got into the act, passing legislation to encourage real estate investment by allowing property owners to shelter other income with depreciation expenses and allow faster depreciation write-offs.

Eventually, and not surprisingly, apartments, office buildings, shopping centers, and other property types all over the nation became overbuilt, and property owners had to contend with depression-like conditions for several years thereafter.

A little over 20 years later, history repeated itself, as it often seems to do. Commercial real estate prices were bid up to levels that would be sustainable only if everything went right for at least several more years, and property acquisitions were financed by lenders who loosened their underwriting standards at exactly the wrong time. This process was exacerbated by a mushrooming market for commercial mortgage-backed securities (CMBS), which allowed lenders and investment bankers to package real estate mortgage loans and sell them to investors who were willing to sacrifice acceptable returns on the altar of "diversification." As is often the case when investors and lenders become complacent, there wasn't a happy ending. The bottom line is that REIT investors should expect that their investment returns will, as is the case with every asset class, be cyclical. As we endure the painful portions of these cycles, investors must repeat to themselves, "This, too, shall pass." The value of a blue-chip REIT stock, as is true of a quality building in a good location, will fluctuate but never disappear.

Before we move on to a discussion of the various property types, I'd like to just note here that the cyclical nature of real estate demonstrates an important irony of REIT investing:

TIP

The cyclical nature of commercial real estate markets has meant that, quite often throughout REITs' history, very strong property markets have deprived REITs of investment opportunities and have spawned other problems, while poor markets have proven a boon.

Strong markets often eventually lead to overbuilding—which heightens competitive conditions and can depress operating income for up to several years into the future. Weak and troubled markets, conversely, can offer unusually good growth opportunities. Because financially solid REITs frequently have far better access to reasonably priced capital during weak markets than do other prospective buyers, they may have the ability to buy properties with good long-term prospects at bargain-basement prices. And they may be able to earn even higher returns on these new investments by upgrading them and bringing in new and more attractive tenants. Of course, the extent of the opportunities presented during major market downturns must be weighed against prospective declines in a REIT's cash flows from its *existing* properties. The quality of a REIT's management team and its access to capital, while always important, are particularly critical during times of overbuilt markets or depressed economic conditions. Difficult times create the most opportunities for those who can take advantage of them.

Property Sectors

REIT investors are now able to invest in businesses that own and operate many different property types. There are apartment communities, shopping centers, office buildings, industrial parks, factory outlet centers, health care facilities, and many others. REIT organizations participate in each of these property types, and each type has specific advantages, risks, idiosyncrasies, and cycles that

Commercial Real Estate versus Homes

Before we look at the property sectors available to REIT investors, let's take a very quick detour and consider how commercial real estate differs from residential real estate. Yes, they are both "real property," but there are major differences between them. Despite the excessive home speculation that crested a few years ago, residential real estate is primarily bought for shelter and, perhaps, a lifestyle, not income. And, when bought for rental income, its cash flow will usually be very modest due to mortgage payments, real estate taxes, insurance, and maintenance expenses. Also, residential real estate quite often experiences pricing cycles different from commercial real estate, and is frequently influenced by families who are primarily concerned with affordability, neighborhood, and schools.

Unlike commercial real estate, which is difficult to finance at more than 50 to 60 percent debt leverage, residential real estate can, at times, be bought using 90 percent debt leverage—and at times even more; this can make prices much more volatile, particularly during economic downturns. In certain types of economies, the prices of residential and commercial real estate have moved in similar directions, as in 2008 and 2009, but investors would do well to differentiate between them. Owning a home may be a good investment if bought cheaply enough, but it's not at all equivalent to owning commercial property.

set them apart from the others. The difficulty for the investor is deciding how much weight to give to each factor when trying to evaluate them. The pie chart near the beginning of this chapter shows the percentages of the REITs' aggregate market value represented by the various sectors of REIT properties near the end of 2010. There's a veritable feast of offerings.

Apartments

Before the 1993 and 1994 tsunami of new REIT public offerings, there were only four major apartment REITs: United Dominion, Merry Land, Property Trust of America, and South West Property Trust. By late 1996, that number had grown to at least 30 residential equity REITs, each with an equity market cap of more than $100 million; many of these have continued to grow in size, while others have gone private or merged with other REITs. At the end of 2010, there were a dozen apartment REITs (not including three student housing REITs), of which Equity Residential, with an equity market cap of $14.6 billion, was the largest. These REITs own and manage apartment communities in various geographic areas throughout the United States. Some have properties located only in very specific areas, while others own units in markets across the country. Some management teams have specialized development skills that enable them to build new properties in healthy markets where rents and occupancy rates are expected to rise quickly or where profitable niche markets exist.

Based on data from the National Council of Real Estate Investment Fiduciaries (NCREIF), apartment owners have, since 1986, enjoyed average annual total returns of 7.8 percent (see Figure 4.2). Today, most apartment cap rates range from 5 to 7.5 percent, depending on location, property quality, age, condition, and supply/demand factors.

Apartment owners do well when the economy is expanding because of the new jobs thereby created and the rise in the formation of new households. Because apartments compete for residents, conditions in the single-family home market are also important. These conditions include home prices, affordability (mortgage payments relative to household income), the cost and availability of home financing, and even the perceived attraction of houses and condominiums as an investment. In 2010, despite low home mortgage rates and improved affordability due to the large decline in single-family home prices, apartment owners captured a larger percentage of prospective residents—home ownership rates declined, and owning a single-family dwelling was no longer viewed with the enthusiasm of several years earlier.

What Is a "Cap Rate"?

The term *cap rate* (capitalization rate) will be used frequently in this book; it refers to the unleveraged return expected by a buyer of a commercial real estate property, expressed as the anticipated cash flow return (before depreciation expense) as a percentage of the purchase price. For example, paying $1 million for a property expected to return to the investor $70,000 in the first full year of ownership (excluding both depreciation expenses and the capital expenditures needed to keep the property competitive) will result in a cap rate of 7 percent.

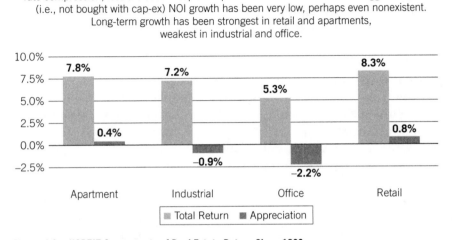

Components of Real Estate Return since 1986
The vast majority of the return generated by real estate comes from the income return (i.e., the initial yield). The appreciation return is driven by NOI growth and cap rate compression, less the cost of capital improvements. The NCREIF data suggests that true (i.e., not bought with cap-ex) NOI growth has been very low, perhaps even nonexistent. Long-term growth has been strongest in retail and apartments, weakest in industrial and office.

Figure 4.2   NCREIF Components of Real Estate Return Since 1986
Source: Green Street Advisors.

Another very important factor for apartment owners is the rate of construction of new units in the local area. Such competing properties, if built when demand for apartment space is slowing, can force the owners of existing units to reduce rents or to offer concessions, and often results in lower occupancy rates and reduced income.

Inflation also determines an apartment owner's economic fortunes, as inflation can cause higher operating expenses for everything from maintenance to insurance to interest on debt, which cannot normally be passed along to the tenant. But inflation can be a boon as well as a curse. Should owners of newly constructed apartment communities need to charge higher rents because of inflated construction costs, owners of existing units may then, as the new buildings become fully occupied, raise their own rents. Eventually, as land prices and inflation increase further, new construction may no longer even be profitable. The pressure on apartment owners' cash flows resulting from the Great Recession would have been a lot worse if development had not been held in check by high land prices and construction costs in 2005 to 2007.

Like all REIT and commercial real estate investors, apartment REIT investors need to be mindful of certain risks. Even if the national economy is doing fine, the regional or local economy can drop into a recession or worse, causing occupancy rates to decline and rents to flatten or even fall. This will be more of an issue for apartment REITs that focus on narrow geographic areas. Overbuilding can occur, especially where land is cheap and available to developers and the entitlement process is easy. Poor property management, including a failure to respond quickly to changing market forces, can also result in a general deterioration of the value or profitability of apartment assets.

Fortunately, these adverse developments rarely occur overnight, and vigilant apartment REIT owners will often be able to spot negative trends early enough to react to them. The trick, of course, is to be able to distinguish a temporary blip from a long secular decline.

 TIP

As an additional safety measure, the well-diversified REIT investor will normally own several apartment REITs in order to spread the investment risk over many geographic areas and management teams.

Like other property types, the profits from apartment ownership are cyclical. During the late 1980s and early 1990s, earning reasonable returns from apartment ownership was difficult. The loan largesse of the banks and S&Ls, along with real estate limited partnerships and other syndicators, had sharply accentuated the boom phase. Hapless investors put large amounts of capital into new construction, only to have many buildings fall into the hands of the Resolution Trust Corporation (RTC). Rents fell, and free rent was offered to attract tenants. Occupancies declined, and market values diminished.

Eventually, beginning in 1993 to 1994, the supply-demand imbalance began to right itself as the economy strengthened, and very few new units were built. By 1995, rents were rising once more and, by the end of the following year, occupancy levels rose to over 90 percent. Occupancy rates remained firm and market rents rose steadily throughout the rest of the decade, but softened beginning in 2001 due to the national recession. Weak job growth and competition from single-family housing, spurred by low mortgage rates, negatively impacted the profitability of apartment REITs until the cycle bottomed in 2004.

Conditions were favorable for apartment owners for several years thereafter, and—spurred in part by condo converters who tried to feed the insatiable appetite for home ownership—prices for apartment communities rose rapidly into 2007, while the apartment space markets were in good shape. But the Great Recession that began in late 2007 caused the cycle to reverse itself once again, and owners experienced a decline in rental revenues and operating income similar to that of the recession of 2001 to 2003. By mid-2010, however, apartment markets again began to stabilize, driven, in large part, by a significant decline in the rate of home ownership in the United States.

As commercial real estate is often financed with debt, the availability and cost of mortgage financing have been important factors in real estate prices. Fortunately for apartment owners, even during the credit crunch lasting from 2008 to well into 2009, financing has been available for apartment property acquisitions and related transactions from government-sponsored entities such as Fannie Mae and Freddie Mac. This helped to support apartment community prices during the major commercial real estate price decline beginning in late 2007 and, as long as such financing continues to be available, will continue to mute the cyclicality of prices in this sector.

New construction has not, in recent years, exceeded demand, and remains below the peak levels of the 1980s; as this book went to press, the supply-demand equation was again favoring apartment owners. However, beginning in a year or two, there will be more development completions. And, it's certainly possible that we'll see a renewal of demand for single-family homes and condos, driven by increasing home ownership affordability and low financing costs; these factors may siphon off some tenants and thus could impact the rate of owners' cash flow growth. However, unlike owners of some other property types, apartment owners may be relatively unaffected by moderately rising interest rates, which could retard demand for single-family housing.

The demographics for apartment owners are quite favorable. A 2010 report on the apartment industry, prepared by Marcus & Millichap, the United States' third-largest apartment broker, notes that there are over 70 million "Echo Boomers" (a term used to describe the large baby cohort born between 1982 and 1995), many of whom are just now graduating from college. The size of this cohort is huge, "only moderately smaller than the 80 million Baby Boomers." As Bryce Blair, CEO of AvalonBay Communities told REIT.com recently, "these 20-somethings are renters, not homeowners." The Marcus & Millichap report's authors, Harvey E. Green and Hessam Nadji, conclude, "It is simply a matter of time before an expanding economy releases this powerfully favorable demographic into the renter pool."

Assuming a reasonably stable economy and moderate job growth—and if the assets are properly managed—apartment ownership looks as though it will continue to be a rewarding investment for REIT investors despite occasional blips in local markets and recurring real estate cycles. My expectation is that apartment owners in most areas should be able to get, over time, average annual rent increases of close to 3 percent, while expenses should rise with inflation. This would add up to some pretty good total returns, and with less risk than in most other property sectors.

Other Residential: Manufactured Home Communities and Student Housing

Although apartment communities comprise the largest space within the "residential" property category, there are two other worthy residential types in which REIT investors can participate.

Over 50 years ago, an enterprising landowner brought a number of trailers, together with their owners, to a remote parcel of land, semi-affixed them to foundations, and called the project a "mobile home park." Many of today's modern "manufactured home" communities, however, bear little resemblance to yesterday's mobile home parks. The homes, manufactured off-site, are rarely removed from the communities, and generally have the quality and appearance of site-built homes. The homeowners enjoy amenities such as an attractive main entrance, clubhouse, pool, tennis courts, putting greens, exercise rooms, and laundry facilities. According to Equity Lifestyle Communities, a manufactured home community REIT, there are approximately 50,000 manufactured home communities in North America. Approximately 19 million people (6 percent of our nation) live in them (based on data from the Manufactured Housing Institute [MHI]).

Manufactured homes are less expensive and help to satisfy America's need for affordable housing; the average construction cost per square foot of a manufactured home is, according to MHI estimates, 10 to 35 percent less than a site-built home, excluding land costs. The average unit selling price for a double-wide home in 2009 was just $74,400, less than half the median price for site-built houses and condos. The residents own their own homes but lease the underlying land at varying rates, generally ranging from $200 to more than $500 per month, from the community's owner. Some of the communities cater only to seniors, while others are "all-age."

Despite declining occupancy rates at the all-age communities and a substantial multiyear decline in new home shipments (a key indicator of industry health), turnover rates have been low and the business of owning manufactured home communities has been stable and somewhat recession resistant. And the community owner's capital expenditures are limited to upkeep of the grounds and common facilities; the maintenance of each home is the park tenant's responsibility. Overbuilding has rarely been an issue, due to the difficulty of getting property zoned and entitled, and the long lead times necessary to fill these communities. Providing space to users of recreational vehicles and campers may become an increasingly important source of revenue for the manufactured home community REITs.

As with every sector, of course, there are challenges, including occasional flare-ups of calls for rent control. Perhaps the largest issue for park owners has been the inability of manufactured home buyers to obtain financing on terms even close to those available to buyers of site-built homes; according to a September 30, 2010, *Wall Street Journal* article, interest rates on these loans "are 7 percent to 11 percent, compared with less than 5 percent for conventional home loans." Also, development of new and expansion communities is time- and capital-intensive. And competition from site-built homes will always be an issue. Nevertheless, this property type will appeal to investors who appreciate stable cash flows, predictable rent increases, and very modest capital expense requirements; three REITs—Equity Lifestyle Properties, Sun Communities, and UMH Properties—serve this niche.

Another property type that has recently become available to REIT investors is student housing. American Campus Communities, Education Realty Trust, and Campus Crest Communities, which specialize in these types of properties, went public in August 2004, January 2005, and October 2010, respectively. This type of property is uniquely designed for temporary residence for college students, who lease the space on an annual basis over a college year. A typical student housing community can accommodate from several hundred to over 1,000 students, at monthly lease rates from about $300 to $700 per bed. American Campus's average monthly rate, for example, was $490 per bed at the end of 2009.

There are several unique characteristics of student housing properties. Demand is, of course, driven by college enrollment. And the demographics appear to be favorable. According to Michael H. Zaransky, author of *Profit by Investing in Student Housing: Cash in on the Campus Housing Shortage* (Kaplan Publishing, 2006), "more than 80 million people will turn 18 over the next decade," and the "Echo Boom" cohort is likely to drive demand. Students can read the unemployment statistics as well as anyone, and they are learning that employment prospects are much better for those with college educations. College enrollment should continue to grow at a healthy pace, although rising tuition costs and cutbacks in student aid may become more of an issue.

Many public universities, in particular, may not have the resources to develop their own student housing, and are likely to increasingly turn to private developers and owners to build and manage them. Although operating expenses are higher than for apartment communities, and there is substantial turnover from year to year, a large room that houses three students generates substantially higher revenue than that of an average apartment unit.

There are also particular risks that need to be considered. According to an April 13, 2006, Green Street Advisors report on the industry, tenant retention is low (about 33 percent) and turnover costs are substantial. Furthermore, leasing occurs each year during a very narrow window—usually the first two weeks of August. As a result, a poor leasing season can negatively affect operating results for the ensuing year. Property management can be intensive and requires unique skills. There is also likely to be increasing competition from private builders, institutional investors, and possibly even apartment REITs. Location is important, as is the case in other property sectors, and the best properties are located on campus, rather than a few miles away.

Due to the expected substantial increase in demand for college rooms, and what could be a dearth in new supply, as well as only modest sensitivity to recessions, the supply-demand equation for college housing appears favorable, and an investment in this sector is worth considering. REIT organizations, due to their experience and relationships with college administrators, will be strong competitors in this property type. These REITs may also benefit from external growth opportunities, such as new developments, forming new joint ventures with colleges and universities, and property acquisitions.

Retail Properties

TIP

Retail REITs are available to investors in two primary colors: neighborhood shopping centers and large shopping malls.

For most of the twentieth century, shoppers bought everything locally at the small stores on Main Street or in downtown shopping areas. But the world of retail real estate changed in 1956, when the first enclosed shopping mall (Southdale Center) was built in Edina, Minnesota. Since then, the number of shopping alternatives and retail venues has exploded, and today's shoppers can spend money in ways never imagined by their grandparents.

They can shop at large, enclosed malls, where friends and family often shop together in attractively designed environments with fountains and waterfalls, attend movies, and eat at food courts; at neighborhood shopping centers, where goods and services of convenience are readily available close to home; at "big box" megastores, for example, Wal-Mart, Costco, Target, and Ross, where a wide selection of items can be bought at discount prices; at outlet centers located along the highway or in major tourist destinations, featuring a wide variety of stores offering discontinued and other brand-name items at tantalizing prices; and at new "lifestyle" centers, which offer restaurants, entertainment options, and new store concepts in attractive outdoor settings.

Neighborhood Shopping Centers   Although the traditional neighborhood shopping center has had to contend with these other, newer competitors, Americans still love their conveniences, and proximity is a great time saver. For certain run-in-and-run-out errands, such as grocery shopping, buying take-out sandwiches for lunch, picking up drug prescriptions, dry cleaning, and shoe repair, most people don't want to be bothered with a mall or a mega-store, or to take the time to drive to one.

A desirable neighborhood shopping center is usually anchored by one or two major stores—most often a supermarket or a drugstore—and contains a number of additional stores that offer other basic services and necessities. As a result, these centers tend to be relatively resilient even in the face of recessions. The property owner charges a minimum rent to the tenants, and the lease is often structured to contain fixed "rent bumps" that increase the rental obligation each year. In addition, or in lieu of fixed rent bumps, the lease may contain "overage" rental provisions, which obligate the tenant to pay increased rent if its annual sales exceed certain minimum levels. Often, "triple-net" leases are signed, which make expenses like real estate taxes and assessments, repairs, maintenance, and insurance the responsibility of the tenant.

Industry observers often question whether retail properties have been overbuilt in the United States. According to the International Council of Shopping Centers (ICSC), there were more than 1.1 million retail establishments and 7 billion square feet of shopping center space in the United States at the end of 2009; with a population of over 304 million, that's 23.1 square feet per capita of shopping center space. In view of earlier Bear Stearns estimates of 18.1 and 13.1 square feet per capita, in 1990 and 1980, respectively, one may easily conclude that we have "grossed out" on retail space (see Figure 4.3).

And yet, despite an always competitive retail landscape and the continual "creative destruction" occurring in the industry, occupancy and rental rates have held up pretty well, even recently. Some retailers go out of business or file bankruptcy, but they are replaced with others. The retail business remained healthy during the 2000 to 2002 recession and, although occupancy and rental rates were negatively impacted by the recent Great Recession, most large national and regional retailers remain financially healthy, and occupancy rates were firming in 2010. There were surprisingly few closings and bankruptcies despite the substantial cutbacks in consumer spending.

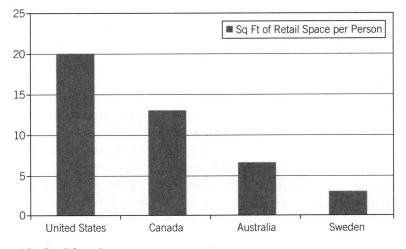

Figure 4.3   Retail Capacity

Source: Used with permission. John Wiley & Sons, Inc. Ellen Dunham-Jones and June Williamson, "Retrofitting Suburbia" (December 2008).

Neighborhood shopping center owners, not surprisingly, face perpetual challenges. The retail environment remains very competitive, and the prospect of retailer failures, store closings, and consolidations is always a concern. And the continual inroads being made by Wal-Mart and other powerful discounters upon supermarkets and other neighborhood shopping center anchors and smaller shops, as well as competition from Internet retailers, remain a long-term issue.

But concerns such as reductions in consumer spending growth and excess capacity shouldn't discourage investors from this sector of REITdom. We have learned that the American consumer is resilient and very diverse in his or her shopping tastes, and likes to patronize a number of different stores and partake of many divergent product offerings. A key element for the investor, however, is location. A neighborhood shopping center located near one or more major residential areas, leased to tenants offering an assortment of necessity-based products and services, will continue to thrive—particularly if the center is attractive and well maintained. If one or a few stores underperform or must close for lack of business, the owner of an attractive and well-located center will be able to find new replacement tenants that can attract shoppers. Location is very important for all commercial real estate owners, but in the retail sector it is crucial.

Many neighborhood shopping center REITs have been prolific developers. We'll talk a bit more about development later in the book, but here I'd like to just note that development can, at certain times, be a very good business for retail REITs. Many of them created substantial value for their shareholders during the great housing boom in the middle years of the past decade by building and filling new neighborhood shopping centers where new houses were appearing virtually every week; value was created by the spread between the cost of the new development and its value after the property was substantially leased. But the popping of the housing bubble resulted in high vacancy rates in many of these newly built shopping centers and, at times, shareholder value was actually destroyed. Building to "follow the rooftops" can, at times, be an effective business strategy, but good timing is essential.

Regional Malls If neighborhood shopping centers provide the basics, large regional malls provide greater consumer choice and more luxury items. From alarm clocks to stuffed zebras, the mall offers almost anything desired by today's shoppers. The concept of an enclosed, large shopping mall is that shopping is not necessarily related to need; it is a *recreational* activity.

The economics of malls are very different from those of neighborhood shopping centers. Rent payable by the tenant is higher, but so are the sales per square foot. Despite higher rent, a retailer can do very well in a mall because of the high traffic and larger sales potential per store. Due to higher overhead costs, however, stores that don't generate strong sales can quickly flounder; accordingly, it is crucial that mall owners find and sign leases with the most successful retailers. Some mall REITs own prestigious supermalls, containing more than 1 million square feet, where rental rates are high (in many of them, rents easily exceed $40 per square foot) and sales per square foot can reach well in excess of $500. Other owners specialize in smaller malls, usually located in less densely populated cities where rental rates are in the mid-$20 range per square foot and sales per square foot don't get much above $300.

Mall owners are, in fact, in the retail business. Their long-term success depends on keeping their malls attractive and exciting for shoppers, and leasing to successful retailers who can attract the fickle and demanding customer. Over the shorter term, mall owners are subject to the strength of the national, regional, and local retail economies, and trends in consumer spending, household net worth and income growth.

TIP

Mall REITs were unavailable to REIT investors until 1992, when several large mall owners went public.

Before 1992, most malls were owned only by large, private real estate organizations and by institutional investors; there was no way a REIT investor could own a piece of the great "trophy" shopping properties of America. However, between 1992 and 1994, large shopping mall developers and owners such as Martin and Matthew Bucksbaum, Herbert and Melvin Simon, and the Taubman family "REITized" their empires by going public as REITs. There are now six REITs that own and operate regional and super-regional shopping malls, along with Tanger Factory Outlet Centers, which owns only outlet center properties.

Are malls, and the REITs that own them, good investments? Before we tackle this question, let's first take a quick look at some mall history. The 1980s launched a golden era for the regional mall. Women were starting careers in record numbers, and they had to buy clothes for the workplace. Baby Boomers were spending their double incomes on all types of consumer goods. Tenant sales rose briskly, major national and regional retailers felt compelled to have space in all the malls, and mall owners could increase rental rates easily. Malls were truly attractive investments, and most large property-investing institutions wanted to own them.

By the early 1990s, however, this great era of consumerism stalled, due to the same recession that knocked President George Bush (the elder) out of office and created waves of corporate restructuring. Wage gains were hard to come by, fears of layoffs were rampant, and consumer confidence declined. "Deep discount" became the American consumer's rallying cry. Further, on a longer-term basis, many Baby Boomers began to consider the prospect of their own retirements, deciding that investing in mutual funds was at least as important as buying Armani suits.

These developments took their toll on mall owners and their tenants until the mid-1990s, when sales rebounded briskly and continued until the latter part of that decade, driven by full employment, strong wage gains, and a buoyant stock market. Sales slowed again in 2001 with the onslaught of another recession. However, low interest rates and some well-timed tax cuts soon restored consumer confidence, and mall sales and occupancy rates again began to trend higher. The cycle repeated itself during the Great Recession. Household net worth declined due to falling stock markets, home prices cratered, unemployment spiked, and consumers decided that it might not be wise to spend over 100 percent of their disposable income. Retailers and mall owners suffered the consequences. According to a September 15, 2010, Green Street Advisors report, average mall "in-line" tenant sales fell 4.5 percent and 6.9 percent in 2008 and 2009, respectively, while average mall occupancy fell from 92.8 percent at the end of 2007 to 90.8 percent at the end of 2009. However, thanks, in part, to good balance sheet management and inventory control by the large retailers, tenant bankruptcies were modest, and occupancy rates began to stabilize—and even move modestly higher—in 2010.

Malls have thus proven to be quite resilient, notwithstanding their sensitivity to the changing financial health and spending habits of the American consumer. Nevertheless, it is fair to question whether mall owners' high rates of growth in net operating income enjoyed in the years leading up to the Great Recession will be reestablished within the next few years.

Another concern for mall REIT investors has been their modest external growth opportunities. REITs can generate "external" profit growth, that is, growth beyond increased revenues from owned properties, by developing or acquiring additional real estate. However, new development opportunities are scarce, as most of the best locations for malls have already been exploited. According to CoStar, which provides real estate information to the real estate industry, there are approximately 1,400 malls in the United States, but only a few new ones are under development. Of course, mall

REITs have bought independently owned malls (and even other mall REITs) from time to time, but these opportunities appear to be waning as REITs become the dominant owners of this property type. So mall REITs may have to rely primarily on internal growth, that is, higher revenues within each mall through increases in tenants' rents, better occupancy rates, and "specialty retailing" via kiosks at the malls, if they want to produce above-average increases in cash flows.

But does this make mall REITs the slowest growers in the REIT industry? Should REIT investors forget mall REITs altogether and look for better prospects elsewhere? No. Most mall REITs should continue to enjoy reasonably good profit growth. As the cost of building a new mall can easily reach $100 million or more, overbuilding within a given geographic area rarely has been a major concern. This, along with excellent locations and moderate but steady growth in mall shop retail sales, reduces risk and provides for predictable and growing cash flows.

Another advantage of mall ownership is that many major retailers continue to rely on malls for most of their total sales. It's significant that, despite the widely heralded problems of many retailers resulting from the Great Recession, malls' occupancy rates have rebounded from their 2009 lows. Although the large department stores' performance has been disappointing in recent years, which has created a wave of industry mergers and consolidations, most profits of mall owners come from smaller "in-line" specialty stores that have generally performed better. And while there are always retailers who disappoint, capable mall owners historically have been able to reconfigure retail space and bring in new tenants to meet changing consumer demands. Many of them have been adding entertainment venues to their malls, attracting such new tenants as theaters, restaurants, family entertainment, and other special attractions; "specialty leasing" at mall kiosks is another good revenue source.

Malls have had to deal with numerous challenges, including the increased numbers of working spouses who no longer spend their days shopping, periodic retailer bankruptcies, the ups and downs of the apparel industry, problems of the major department store chains, inroads being made by the big-box discounters, and the advent of e-commerce. A more recent competitor is the "lifestyle" center, which is usually smaller, open-air, more easily accessible, and entertainment oriented (some mall owners have even developed these properties themselves). But the best mall owners are nothing if not imaginative, and they have been able to keep their malls attractive to both important retailers and the shopping public.

A fairly recent trend in retail real estate is that a significant number of retailers are diversifying away from the traditional retail formats they have long used, and are experimenting with others. Thus, Saks and a few other traditional mall tenants are experimenting with lifestyle centers, and well-known discounters such as Wal-Mart and Target are considering (and accepting) invitations to become mall tenants. Even a few auto dealers, according to Simon Property Group's president and chief operating officer, Richard Sokolov, are beginning to lease space in malls. Simon has had success getting mall tenants to lease space in the Chelsea outlet centers that Simon acquired in 2004. This new trend is due to changing consumer shopping patterns and the needs and preferences of both retailers and retail real estate owners, all of which have been influenced by the waning popularity of the traditional department store.

A related trend is that the lines between different types of retail formats are becoming less clear and defined. "No longer can you look at a tenant and say, 'That's someone that goes into a mall,'" says Gwen MacKenzie, vice president of retail investment for Sperry Van Ness, commercial real estate advisers. "All retailers and landlords are playing. There's a lot of blurring going on." Mall REIT management teams are very much aware of this trend, and are seeking to turn it to their advantage.

Before we leave the topic of shopping malls, investors might want to ponder one other issue. The Great Recession seems to have taken its greatest toll on consumers in lower income brackets. In November 2010, the unemployment rate among college graduates, according to the Bureau of Labor Statistics, was 5.1 percent, but the overall rate of unemployment was 9.8 percent. This suggests that "high-end" malls—those serving the relatively affluent shopper—may, at least over the next few years, perform substantially better than their peers. The Green Street Advisors report, mentioned earlier in this chapter, reports that tenant sales in its group of "higher-productivity" malls (generally, those with higher sales per square foot) rebounded 7 percent in the first half of 2010, compared with just 3 percent for its group of "lower-productivity" malls. One may draw the conclusion that, if this disparity continues, the most productive malls will enjoy better growth rates in net operating income over the next few years. After all, tenant sales is a key driver of mall lease rates, and, over time, mall owners can increase rents only to the extent that tenants are able to increase their sales.

Factory Outlet Centers   Factory outlet centers have enjoyed increasing popularity with consumers since the early 1990s. These centers' primary tenants are major manufacturers, such as Gap, Old Navy, Bass Shoes, Liz Claiborne, and Polo Ralph Lauren. The centers are normally located some distance from densely populated areas, primarily because retail product manufacturers don't want to compete with their own customers, such as the mall retailers. However, many very profitable outlet centers are located at tourist destinations, such as Myrtle Beach and Hilton Head, South Carolina, and Branson, Missouri.

While most outlet center tenants are manufacturers who normally sell to major retailers, for example, Polo Ralph Lauren, the outlet center allows them to also sell directly to the public at cut-rate prices. Their strategy is to sell overstocked goods, odd sizes, irregulars, or fashion ideas that just didn't click. The goods, priced at 25 to 35 percent below retail, often move quickly.

Although almost all of the early outlet center REITs disappeared (some were acquired, while others were victims of poor management), this type of property has performed quite well over the years. During the Great Recession, in particular, outlet centers have significantly outperformed their mall peers in tenant sales growth. Americans love a bargain, but are particularly attracted to them when times are tough. Tanger Factory Outlets, the only remaining pure outlet center REIT, was the only company among mall REITs to report positive same-store sales in 2009, and did better than its peers in 2010.

Perhaps the biggest risk in this property subtype is that it has performed so well that new developers are being attracted to it, including private developers and even retail REITs. CBL & Associates, a mall REIT, has partnered with Horizon Group Properties to build a new outlet center in Oklahoma City, and Taubman Centers, another mall REIT, is entering this business (after converting two of its existing malls to outlet center formats in 2010). According to the ICSC, approximately 40 new outlet centers were being planned near the end of 2010, compared with about 214 that now exist.

This interesting retail real estate niche is likely to continue to perform well, and tenants will remain attracted to them due to their low occupancy costs (which are generally 8 to 9 percent of tenant sales compared with close to 13 percent for the typical mall), the prospects of selling excess inventory to price-sensitive consumers in an efficient manner, and as a way of expanding brand-name recognition.

One other retail format should be mentioned. In recent years, the American shopper has seen the rise of the powerful discounter, perhaps typified by Wal-Mart, Target, and Home Depot, which utilize "big-box" formats of very large size, typically 100,000 to 200,000 square feet of space per store. These tend to be stand-alone properties, although they are sometimes clustered in a group as "power centers," and often specialize in one type of product, such as consumer electronics, for example, Best Buy or Fry's Home Electronics, or home furnishings, such as Bed Bath & Beyond. Each property is occupied by a single tenant.

Few REITs have specialized in this property type, perhaps because many of these large discounters have traditionally owned their own stores; for example, in January 2010, only 8 percent of Target's 1,740 stores were leased. However, a few retail REITs are participating in this niche, such as Developers Diversified Realty, whose four largest tenants at the end of 2010 were Wal-Mart, T.J. Maxx, PetSmart, and Bed Bath & Beyond. In addition, "free-standing property" REITs own properties that are leased to a single user on a "triple-net" basis. Many of these properties are retail oriented. For example, at the end of 2010, the largest of these REITs, Realty Income Corporation, owned 2,496 properties leased to a wide array of tenants, including drugstores, automobile parts retailers, and sellers of home furnishings and general merchandise.

These properties are characterized by long-term leases, which generate stable and predictable cash flows for the property owners, often at initial returns higher than those available on multitenant properties, but often lack significant opportunities for increased rents.

Offices and Industrial Properties

Office buildings and industrial properties are often grouped together by many REIT investors. They are the primary types of properties leased directly to businesses that don't rely on consumer traffic. In that respect they are quite different from apartments, retail stores, self-storage facilities, manufactured home communities, college dorms, or even health care properties. In addition, some REITs own both office buildings and industrial properties. And yet, due to the many significant differences between office and industrial properties, we'll discuss them separately.

Office Buildings   Office buildings historically have been a fairly stable property type; after all, millions of employees who provide service to customers and clients must have an office somewhere from which to serve them. And due to the longer-term leases of these properties, owners' cash flows tend to be more stable than the office markets themselves. But due to the long lag time between beginning construction of a major office building and its completion, overbuilding in this sector has, at times, been a problem for investors. As much as overbuilding was an issue for apartment owners in the late 1980s and early 1990s, it was far worse for office property owners; vacancy rates, which normally average about 10 percent, rose to more than 20 percent in some major markets. Vacancy rates spiked again in 2001 to 2003 and in 2009 to 2010, to 17 percent—although these more recent vacancy increases were due to recession-induced declines in tenant space demand rather than excessive development.

Office leases are normally long term in nature, frequently 5 to 10 years in duration. Rental rates are fixed during the term of the lease, with perhaps small annual rent increases tied to an inflation index such as the Consumer Price Index (CPI). Many leases, even "gross leases" that require the owner to pay utility costs, repairs, and other expenses, contain provisions requiring tenants to pay a pro rata portion of increased building operating expenses and property taxes incurred by the owner beyond a base year.

The long-term nature of office leases can, to some extent, protect owners' cash flows during cyclical downturns in office space markets caused by overbuilding or weak space demand. However, the need to provide more free rent and to expand tenant improvement allowances, as well as the effects of rising vacancy rates, during such periods means that net operating income can decline during recessions. And yet, it's interesting to note that despite very weak office market conditions during the Great Recession, which began in December 2007, few office REITs reported more than 1 to 2 percent declines in net operating income in 2009. Conversely, office markets are generally slower to recover when coming out of recessions. Even after market conditions begin to improve, rental rates in new leases for office space are "rolled down" to market rents, which may be below expiring rents.

For example, many office property owners saw their cash flows diminish from 2001 through 2005, as many leases signed in 1999 and 2000 at very high rental rates were reset to new and lower prevailing market rental rates. History repeated itself in 2008 through 2010. Thus, periodic episodes of overbuilding and sudden but unforeseeable reductions in demand for office space almost ensure that the office property sector will remain cyclical. Investors in office REITs should look not only at current cash flows earned by the REIT but also at existing conditions such as market rents, net effective rents (which factors in free rent and other tenant concessions) and occupancy rates, which will affect future cash flows. And, as investors do look ahead, the shares of office REITs will be priced to reflect future prospects as well as current operating results.

As noted earlier, a problem unique to the office sector is the long lag time between obtaining building permits and final completion. Once the development process has begun, even if the builder or lender realizes that there is no longer sufficient demand for that new state-of-the-art office building, it is often too late to stop the process. Some of this risk can be mitigated, however, by preleasing, that is, signing tenant leases for a substantial portion of the building's space before breaking ground.

Rental space and the prices that can be charged for it are, like most things, governed by the laws of supply and demand. During the 1990 and 1991 economic slump, net office space absorption nationwide was still positive, indicating an oversupply of space, not a lack of demand. Investors and lenders shut off the capital spigots, and there was very little development of new office buildings until office rents and occupancy rates firmed up in the mid-1990s. The moderate increase in supply of new buildings was readily absorbed by increasing demand, and the office markets were in equilibrium through the end of the decade. In a few hot markets, such as the San Francisco Bay Area, rents spiked in 1999 and 2000, stimulated in part by a flood of venture capital investments into fledgling technology and dot-com companies. However, absorption turned negative in 2001, for the first time, due to large job losses and the recession—the culprit this time was insufficient demand for office space, while existing lessees returned unwanted space back to the market in the form of sublease space. These adverse conditions remained in effect until 2005, when they began to stabilize.

The problem for office owners more recently was, again, not overbuilding but rather a contraction in space demand caused by the Great Recession. Unemployment nationwide rose to almost 10 percent, housing markets were collapsing, the credit markets seized up, and the commercial and investment banks were having to deal with soured loans and huge losses on derivative securities. As a result, companies that normally employ large numbers of office workers, such as investment banks, law firms, consulting companies, real estate brokers, financial analysts, and even insurers, simply needed less space. Demand for office space began to improve, however, in 2010, and the pace of leasing began to increase substantially. Today, an important issue for investors in office properties is whether office users still have more space than they need; if so, this "shadow space" will have to be re-leased before occupancy rates rebound to normal levels. "White-collar" job growth remains a key determinant of office owners' profitability.

There is often much debate over the issue of whether it's more profitable, on a long-term basis, to own low-rise suburban office buildings in rapidly growing "sunbelt" cities such as Dallas, Atlanta, and Phoenix, or whether the office owner will do better with large high-rise (or even trophy) properties in America's "24-hour" cities such as New York, Boston, or, perhaps, Washington, D.C. The costs of construction and operation are much lower for the first type, and cap rates are higher—so initial yields on investment will be higher also. And, with a steady influx of new businesses, perhaps seeking lower taxes and reduced employment costs, it's not been all that difficult to replace vacating tenants during stable economic conditions.

Proponents of major central business district (CBD) office buildings in America's most important cities claim, however, that the high land and construction costs and difficulty of obtaining building entitlements in these crowded urban areas make it less likely that owners of such assets will experience the oft-recurring problem of excessive development. They argue that this advantage, together with the preference of many companies for a presence in prestigious locations in "high-barrier-to-entry" markets, will ensure that rental rates and cash flows will grow at rates greater than those of their low-barrier peers over time. These proponents had the upper hand in this argument during much of the 1990s, due to rent spikes in several major metropolitan markets, but rents began falling sharply in many of them in 2001, as well as in suburban markets, as demand dropped suddenly. During the Great Recession, rents fell more sharply in these major markets, but seem to have been recovering more quickly in 2010.

Green Street Advisors' Mike Kirby has noted ("Heard on the Beach," November 30, 2010) that, despite lower cap rates and initial yields, "portfolios comprised of office buildings in high-barrier markets, such as Midtown Manhattan, DC, Boston, San Francisco and West LA, have delivered substantially better returns than those concentrated in all other markets." He attributes this to much better growth in net operating income in the high-barrier markets. Of course, there is no guarantee that this situation will remain in place in the future. The one thing that seems clear is that rental rates can be volatile in *any* office market, and owners' prospects will depend on location, new supply, the level of demand for space, macroeconomic issues, and other factors.

Office REITs comprise a significant portion of the REIT universe (approximately 12.2 percent at October 31, 2010), and they belong in every diversified REIT investor's portfolio. Although the sector can be volatile, as noted earlier, as well as being subject to deep and prolonged real estate cycles, a good-quality building located in a healthy business market will be attractive to tenants if it's well maintained and the owner provides the requisite tenant services. Long-term leases at fixed rental rates tend to act as a cash flow cushion during economic downturns, and can usually be renewed at higher rental rates upon expiration—assuming a reasonably healthy economy and a lack of overbuilding. Rental roll-downs do occur at times, but the long-term trend for office rents has been up. Rents may be expected to rise, on average, with inflation, which will generate reasonably good returns for the office owner, including, of course, the office REITs.

TIP

Investors should remember that because the office sector is quite cyclical, they should keep a close eye on current market fundamentals and future trends, as well as property owners' cash flows.

Lab Space and Data Centers   There are two specialized property sectors that can be categorized as office space but tend to march to their own drummers: lab space and data centers. Let's take a quick look at each of them, as their investment merits are substantial.

Lab space consists of what appears to be an ordinary office building but is configured on the inside as a combination of office space and lab benches and equipment with which research is conducted by the tenant. These buildings have higher ceilings, extensive ductwork, more environmental controls, and beefed-up heating, ventilating, and air conditioning (HVAC) systems. And, of course, they cater to a very specialized tenant base, consisting of large pharmaceutical companies, biotech firms, and government and private entities, such as research institutes, that do serious life science research. These properties, which constitute a small part of the office REIT universe, are located in very specific "clusters," often near universities, for example, Boston, Northern Virginia, and the San Francisco Bay Area. Alexandria Real Estate and Biomed Realty are two "pure play" REITs in this niche, and both have performed relatively well when compared with most REITs.

There are several dynamics that are likely to drive profit growth for lab space owners. Health care research has been a growing industry, and it is likely that research-and-development (R&D) budgets will continue to grow over time; this also provides for development opportunities that may create value for lab space REIT shareholders. And, of course, this business is not very sensitive to the ups and downs of the U.S. economy; indeed, many space users are nonprofit organizations. While some smaller, private companies lease lab space, tenant bankruptcies have been infrequent, and many space users are very well capitalized. Leases contain attractive terms for the owners and generally allow for the pass-through to tenants of the costs of tenant improvements. Competing developments are not likely to be a major issue for owners, as desirable space is confined to a few key geographic locations, and most developers often lack the close tenant relationships enjoyed by the existing players.

But, as in every commercial real estate sector, there are some concerns and risks. This is specialized space, requiring ample capital improvements, and vacant space created by a departing major tenant may not be easy to back-fill quickly. Some tenant improvements incurred by the building owner may become obsolescent and have to be written off. Because the industry is specialized, owners tend to have large lease exposure to just a few major tenants. Health care delivery in the United States is likely to incur substantial changes as a result of the Affordable Care Act of 2010, often referred to as "Obamacare," and the effects of this new legislation on health care R&D spending are still uncertain.

Data centers are a recent phenomenon, and REIT investors have been able to participate in this unique sector since 2004, when Digital Realty went public. Since then, two other REITs specializing in data centers, DuPont Fabros Technology and CoreSite Realty, completed initial public offerings (IPOs) in 2007 and 2010, respectively. Data centers are very specialized properties that provide power, cooling, and connectivity needs, including Internet gateways, to information technology and telecommunications companies and Internet enterprises. Some of these facilities are delivered to tenants with only the required power and network access, while others are delivered to tenants fully enabled, with full power, cooling, and other necessary capabilities (referred to by Digital Realty as "turn-key" facilities).

There are a number of positive attributes that may attract investors to this unique niche of the office sector. In preparing the following short discussion, I have relied heavily on an excellent and detailed Green Street Advisors report, entitled "Digital Realty Trust," dated January 23, 2009.

Those who want to invest in this industry are motivated by substantial growth expectations for Internet traffic, particularly the ever-increasing use of video transmissions. Demand is likely to be driven by corporate users with increasing power and connectivity needs. Competition has been limited, as building these facilities is capital and technology intensive; even major users have desired to "partner" with the developers and owners of these properties. This has created substantial barriers to entry to new competitors. There are long lease terms, which should provide for cash flow stability; for example, the average lease term at Digital Realty at the end of 2009 was in excess of 13 years. Demand for this space has grown, even during the Great Recession, and the investment yields on new developments—particularly when in the double-digit range, as they have been recently—are likely to be substantial enough to offset development risk.

But there is no free lunch in the investment world, and investors should consider certain risks in this sector. Information technology spending may slow, despite the increasing use of the Internet; a sustained slowdown in demand for this type of space would quite likely affect the share prices of these REITs and negatively impact development opportunities. Capital expenditures to build out these facilities are substantial, and it's not clear that some of the "latest and greatest" equipment won't become obsolete. Companies that lease these properties are generally technology and telecommunications firms, whose cash flows may be more volatile than those of most office tenants, and many of the lessees have less than an investment-grade credit rating. The high return on these properties could, despite the barriers to entry, bring in new competitors. Finally, due to the unique nature of these types of properties and the lack of a liquid trading market for them, it is difficult to value the shares of REITs that engage in this business on the basis of the values of their properties.

Lab space and data centers aren't the types of property investments that individuals—or even institutions—can easily make on their own, and those interested in the dynamics of these interesting property types should look closely at the REITs that have specialized in these sectors. The management teams of these REITs have substantial experience in these businesses and good track records, and the companies have built solid balance sheets.

Industrial Buildings An industrial building, whether a warehouse, a distribution center, "flex space," or a similar property type, can be free-standing or situated within a landscaped industrial park, and can be occupied by a single or multiple tenants. Estimates vary, but there is between 12 and 13 billion square feet of industrial space in the United States, a very substantial portion of which is owned by the actual users. The largest markets at the end of 2009, according to Collier's International "Highlights" (fourth quarter 2009), were Chicago, Los Angeles, and Dallas/Ft. Worth. Ownership is highly fragmented, and the public REITs own only about 1 percent of all industrial real estate. Industrial properties include:

- Distribution centers.
- Regular and bulk warehouse space.
- Light-manufacturing facilities.
- Research and development facilities.
- Small office, or "flex," space, for sales, or administrative and related functions.

Demand for this property type is driven by gross domestic product (GDP) growth, trade, U.S. manufacturing activity, growth in inventories and retail sales trends. Due to the growth in outsourcing and rising U.S. imports, global industrial production has become more important for this sector, and large distribution hubs, located at airports and seaports, may perform particularly well. Indeed, we have seen consolidation in the industry, with larger users and logistics companies seeking to upgrade and make their supply chains more efficient.

Ownership of industrial properties has generally provided stable and predictable returns, particularly in relation to office properties. Rents tend to be less volatile and have grown in most years. Rents declined in the early 1990s, when this sector had its own overbuilding problem, and in 2001 to 2004, when a fall-off in demand caused by a recession created an excess of space. However, even during cyclical lows, negative net absorption (the difference between space leased and space vacated) is not a common occurrence. This happened in the recession years of 2001 and 2002, and again in the 2008 to 2010 time period, as GDP fell during the Great Recession and global trade stalled. Long-term vacancy rates tend to be modest, about 8 to 10 percent, but spike during recessions. According to CBRE Econometric Advisors and Green Street Advisors, the vacancy rate for industrial space in the 2009 to 2010 time period was approximately 14 percent. If the U.S. economic recovery remains anemic, it may be several years before the industry-wide vacancy rate returns to its lower long-term averages.

TIP

The industrial property market has had a good track record of being able to quickly shut down the supply of new space as soon as the market becomes saturated.

One significant advantage of the industrial property sector is that, since it doesn't take long to construct and lease these types of properties, there is a faster reaction time than in some of the other sectors, and consequently there generally has not been excessive overbuilding. A significant portion of new space is built in response to demand from new or existing users and is therefore not an overhang on the market. "Built-to-suit" activity, that is, building an industrial property to meet specific design, location, and physical specifications pursuant to an agreement, has been an important contributor to a profitable development strategy among industrial property REITs.

Hamid Moghadam, CEO of AMB Property (now ProLogis) believes that speed and cost-effectiveness are becoming ever more essential criteria for industrial space users. He believes that goods will move from manufacturer to end user at much more rapid rates, and that distribution facilities, principally in major transportation hubs that offer the advantages of prime location and speed of movement, will be much preferred by space users. If this is indeed a long-lasting trend, some portion of the older industrial facilities in the United States—primarily warehouses used principally for storage—may become less attractive to existing and prospective tenants, thus affecting future rental and occupancy rates for these types of properties.

For a number of years in the last decade, two of the largest industrial property REITs, ProLogis and AMB Properties, allocated a significant portion of their capital to foreign investments, including Europe, Asia, and Mexico. Their objective has been to leverage customer relationships and to capitalize on increasing global trade and the need to modernize and consolidate distribution facilities. Although the Great Recession took a major toll on the business of each company, they have made appropriate adjustments to their business models. It is probably still too soon to know whether developing industrial properties overseas provides a significant long-term benefit for REIT shareholders. EastGroup Properties, a well-regarded industrial REIT, has not developed overseas, but its stock has performed well relative to its peers. Much will depend on the volume of global trade, and the REIT's relationships with large-space users here and abroad.

The industrial property business is, of course, cyclical, but the relatively low cost of building a state-of-the-art property, the short nature of industrial property cycles, and the ability—during most periods—to quickly lease new projects suggest that development of these properties can, in many cases, create value for shareholders. Thus, those REITs that pursue a well-conceived development strategy, whether here or in other countries, and that have a strong balance sheet and ample access to capital, for example, AMB Property and ProLogis, which merged in June 2011, should be looked at kindly by most REIT investors. But the timing of new developments is very important, and prospective profit margins must be high enough to more than offset the risk of new development. The devil is truly in the details.

Finally, another key advantage the industrial property sector owner enjoys is that, unlike the office, apartment, or retail sectors, this sector requires only modest ongoing capital expenditures to keep the buildings in good repair. Space demand has not been terribly volatile, and tenant retention rates have been high during most economic periods.

 TIP

REITs that specialize in industrial sector properties can be very good investments, particularly if their management teams have long-standing relationships with major industrial space users, and if they concentrate on strong geographic areas.

Principal risks in this sector include declining domestic or global economic and business conditions, periods of weak retail sales and imports, and, at times, overbuilding (it isn't prohibitively expensive to build a new industrial property, and many of them are built "on spec"). REITs that are active developers should be watched more closely. Development pipelines may be shut down relatively quickly, but if a REIT stock is priced on the basis of a very profitable development pipeline that doesn't come to fruition, shareholders are likely to suffer.

Health Care

Health care REITs specialize in various types of health care properties, including senior housing (primarily assisted- and independent-living properties), skilled nursing facilities, medical office buildings, hospitals of various types, and even, in a few cases, "life science" office and lab properties of the type discussed earlier. Health care REITs do not engage in the health care businesses that are conducted at these properties; rather, in most cases they lease them, on a "triple-net" basis, to companies that *are* in the health care business; for example, Brookdale Senior Living is among the largest tenants of many of the health care REITs. These leases are structured to provide for stable income and some protection from normal cyclical downturns in these businesses, and modest upside from rent growth when business is good.

The REIT Investment Diversification and Empowerment Act (RIDEA) enacted in 2008, as described earlier, enables health care REITs to lease properties to a taxable REIT subsidiary (TRS), as long as the property is managed by an independent company; this allows the REIT to participate more fully in the property's upside— but also in the downside. Ventas and Health Care REIT and, to a lesser extent, HCP, Inc., three of the leading health care REITs, have been particularly active in these strategies, but they still constitute only a minority of their operating income.

Thus, the great majority of health care REITs' revenues come from lease payments from independent lessees. The leases tend to be long term, have renewal options, and quite often contain provisions for additional rent at certain times specified in the lease or based on an inflation index such as the CPI. Many individual property leases entered into with a single lessee are bundled together under a "master lease," which makes it much more difficult for the lessee to "cherry pick" the best properties for renewal at the end of the lease term or to default on some leases but not others. Except for the 1998 to 2000 period, lease obligations have been adequately covered by the lessee's operating cash flows, and thus lease defaults have been modest.

TIP

Health care REITs were launched in the late 1980s and did well for many years until hitting a rough spot from 1998 to 2000.

Because of the structure of the leases and the lack of substantial participation in the growth of the lessee's profits, health care REITs tend to enjoy only modest internal cash flow growth (albeit, in most cases, with less risk than other REITs), and have traditionally sought to augment growth by acquisitions (and, to a much more limited extent, new development). This, of course, requires the REIT to have access to reasonably priced capital. This has not been a problem, except during the late 1990s, when their share prices tumbled due to financial problems experienced by many health care property lessees of skilled nursing facilities and assisted-living properties. These problems were due, in the former case, to government-mandated reductions in reimbursement for certain procedures performed for Medicare patients, and to overdevelopment, in the latter. Excessive debt leverage carried by many lessees exacerbated the problems.

Despite their modest internal growth prospects and the reliance of many of their tenants on government reimbursement in the skilled nursing and hospital subsectors, health care REITs have several key investment attributes that makes them attractive to investors. Perhaps the most important is that these properties tend to be recession resistant; demand for health services is relatively inelastic, and those who require a nursing home, assistance with daily living needs, or simply a doctor's visit are, for the most part, going to find a way to get what they need. Indeed, these REITs' shares have performed significantly better than their peers during periods of economic weakness, and vice versa. Health care REITs, and their stocks, performed quite well during the Great Recession.

Another favorable attribute of health care properties is that competition from new development hasn't often been an issue. Skilled nursing facilities are being built rarely, due to the difficulty in obtaining permits resulting from states' desire to control reimbursement costs for Medicaid patients; overbuilding had, at times, been a problem in the assisted- and independent-living sector, but new construction starts have been modest in recent years and are down considerably since early 2008; and while the supply of new medical office buildings is expected to increase, it is likely that favorable demographics will increase the demand for physician and nursing services and the usage of medical office space.

Finally, the shares of health care REITs have historically traded at lower multiples of free cash flow and at higher dividend yields than has been the case in other sectors; this is probably due to the perception of more modest cash flow and dividend growth, cost reimbursement issues among tenants, and the higher prevailing market cap rates for health care properties.

The long-term investment concerns in this sector include a heavy reliance on the capital markets to fund growth, risks of adverse changes in government reimbursement programs due to new

What to Look For in Health Care REITs

- Strong and conservative balance sheets (which facilitate access to equity and debt capital at a cost that will create value from new investments).
- An emphasis on stable sectors, such as skilled nursing facilities, assisted-living properties and medical office buildings.
- Diversification in operator-lessees and geographical location.
- Capable management teams who monitor their properties and lessees carefully.

What to Look Out For in Health Care REITs

- Adverse reimbursement legislation and regulations (mainly affecting skilled nursing facilities).
- Single-use facilities with questionable land values (can such properties be re-leased in the event the tenant leaves?).
- Overbuilding of assisted-living and other senior-oriented properties.
- Increasing competition from various private investors.

legislation or future cutbacks due to large budget deficits, reliance on a relatively small number of lessees within any particular REIT portfolio (many of which are private companies), and, particularly in the senior housing sector, the possibility of occasional overbuilding.

The following tip box may be of use to investors when considering a health care REIT.

Health care REITs have finally won respect and now represent a significant weighting (10.9 percent at December 31, 2010) within the FTSE NAREIT All REITs Index. There are risks for the investor, as noted earlier, but the merits of health care REITs are substantial; they deserve a place in every diversified REIT portfolio.

TIP

The long-term prospects for health care REITs depend on the stability and growth prospects for the U.S. health care industry, including demographics and, in particular, the segments served by their lessees. Government reimbursement programs will continue to be important, as will the pace of new developments in the assisted-living, independent-living, and medical office building segments.

Self-Storage

It wouldn't be surprising to learn that the Neanderthal man kept a lot of "valuable" items on a back shelf of his cave; perhaps it's merely human nature to save stuff. Even if we live in a small apartment, or when our collection of old lawnmowers exceeds our garage space, we have a solution: self-storage properties.

Originally built on the edge of town or near an industrial park, many newer self-storage properties are better located and nicely landscaped. Individual storage units normally range from 5 feet by 5 feet to 20 feet by 20 feet. These facilities were developed experimentally during the 1960s and have slowly but steadily increased in popularity. They are rented by the month, allowing renters to store such items as personal files, furniture, and even recreational vehicles and boats. Even businesses occupying expensive office space use them to store items not needed regularly. Marcus & Millichap, a large commercial real estate brokerage firm, has estimated that commercial use of self-storage space comprised about 16.5 percent of all such space in 2009. Most individual demand is driven by either major changes in a person's life, such as relocation, marriage, retirement, college enrollment, even death of a loved one, or by the desire to retain and store items for future use and enjoyment.

Self-storage has been a rewarding property type over the years, notwithstanding occasional periods of overbuilding and recessionary periods that depress occupancy rates. According to the Self-Storage Association, in 2009 there were approximately 46,000 self-storage owners in the United States, receiving total revenues exceeding $22 billion. Thus, ownership is fragmented among many small individual owners. According to Green Street Advisors, four REITs with substantial self-storage assets have a nationwide market share of just 10 percent. Fragmentation, however, may be less in larger markets. Ray Wilson, a pioneer in data gathering for the industry, notes that "most investment grade facilities are located in the nation's 50 largest markets, and ... the self-storage REITs control approximately 30 percent of the total net rentable area in those markets ... it is not as fragmented as everyone thinks."

There has been a rapid rise in the number of self-storage properties built over the past 30 years. According to a September 9, 2009, Green Street Advisors report, based on *Self-Storage Almanac* data (Figure 4.4), there were 3.3 square feet of available space per capita in the United States in 1995, and 7.0 square feet in 2008. Nevertheless, rising demand for the units has kept the industry profitable. The Green Street report notes that from 1994 to 2008, growth in same-property net operating income for self-storage REITs averaged 4.9 percent, compared with 2.9 percent for the major REIT sectors during that time period.

This property type is subject to the usual risks of commercial real estate ownership, including overbuilding and recessions, and is modestly cyclical. Average occupancy rates increased dramatically from 78 percent in 1987 to almost 90 percent in 1994. However, due in large part to more units being developed, national occupancy declined to 83 percent in 1998. The industry came through the 2000 to 2002 recession in good shape, but occupancy hasn't risen much above 85 percent since then. Nevertheless, owners have been able to trade lower occupancy for higher rents. According to R. Christian Sonne, Managing Director, Self Storage, at Cushman &

Wakefield, average rent per square foot has risen from $50 in 2000 to over $75 in 2008. The Great Recession caused a recent drop in owners' net operating income, but self-storage market conditions began to stabilize in 2010. Thus, it is fair to conclude that the self-storage industry is recession resistant but not recession-proof.

The investment merits of self-storage properties are numerous. As noted, the industry has delivered above-average operating income growth over the years, and it offers some downside protection in recessions as persons displaced or downsized often need a place to temporarily store their possessions. Due to the relatively fragmented nature of the industry, large and well-capitalized players, such as the self-storage REITs, often have favorable acquisition opportunities. These larger players are also in a position to capture market share through better economies of scale, brand-name recognition, sophisticated revenue management systems, and the use of call-in centers to capture new space users. Development, while substantial in prior years, has moderated, so new supply may be less of an issue at least for the near future.

TIP

There is a good case to be made for self-storage facilities' being recession resistant because, in a recession, individuals as well as businesses cut costs by reducing expensive occupied space. A reduction in living or office space often entails an increased need for storage space.

Still, as with any other investment, self-storage properties and the REITs that own them bear certain risks. Overbuilding has hurt this sector in the past, and barriers to entry are not formidable. Development costs vary widely and depend on location and building quality, but new properties often can be built for a few million dollars, and development financing often has been widely available from local banks. A legitimate question is whether the industry has excess capacity, due to substantial supply additions in the past. Aside from demand-dampening recessions, other risks include a possible long-lasting decline in consumer spending habits, the lack of long-term leases that can protect cash flows in market downturns, high tenant turnover rates, and frequent waves of rental rate discounting and free rent.

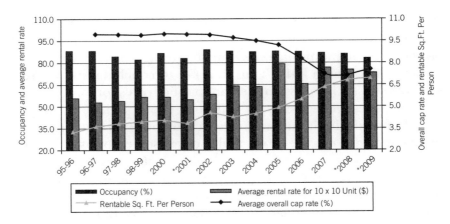

Figure 4.4   Self-Storage Data
Source: Cushman & Wakefield.

The self-storage REITs, benefiting from long-term positive trends in the self-storage industry, as well as sound and proven management teams, have delivered some of the best total returns in the REIT industry over multiyear periods and are obvious investment choices for well-diversified REIT investors.

Hotels and Lodging

Hotels and related lodging properties offer a wide variety of accommodations for business and leisure travelers, group meetings, and conventions. Upscale and luxury hotels, including those at convention destinations and vacation resorts, offer a full range of amenities for the business and leisure traveler and charge relatively higher rates; they are also expensive to build, due to higher land costs, longer building periods, and higher construction costs. Limited-service hotels don't offer dining, conference services, or other amenities, and charge modest room rates. Extended-stay inns offer more amenities than limited-service hotels, and often cater to the business traveler on assignment, who may need a room for extended periods. The relative investment performance of each of these properties will vary with changing market conditions, discretionary income, business conditions, room supply, and other factors.

The hotel and lodging industry is nothing if not cyclical. Room demand is very sensitive to prevailing economic conditions, and few hotel stays are consumer necessities. Even the more reliable business traveler becomes scarce when the economy softens. Overbuilding is often an issue, particularly in the upper upscale and luxury segments, where it can take several years between groundbreaking and completion—during which time the economy may have gone into reverse. But when market conditions are favorable, hotel owners have excellent pricing power.

Owners of these properties were beset with overbuilding issues from the mid-1980s into the early 1990s, then recovered strongly after 1993 to 1994. But a new wave of building caused occupancy rates to soften in the late 1990s, and the damage was greatly exacerbated by the September 11th terrorist attacks, when occupancy fell about 10 percent. Recovery began in 2003, and RevPar, a hotel industry metric combining occupancy and room rates, grew at close to double digits from 2004 to 2006. But the Great Recession and meltdown in the credit markets, worsened by a near shutdown in business conventions and business and leisure travel, again caused a major disruption in hotel stays. According to a PricewaterhouseCoopers analysis, occupancy fell by 760 basis points, from 63.1 percent in 2007 to 55.5 percent in 2009. RevPar declined by almost 18 percent. But room demand eventually began to recover, as it always does, and, beginning in mid-2010, RevPar was growing again.

Because we've experienced some fairly violent hotel industry cycles in recent years, this sector is not for the risk-averse or the faint of heart. It is also particularly subject to external and unpredictable geopolitical shocks that can disrupt all previous travel and room demand forecasts. Fixed and many variable operating costs cannot be pared back easily during periods of weak demand, so even modest downturns can create substantial income declines. And, of course, there are no long-term leases in this property sector to provide cash flow protection during those declines.

 TIP

Whether investors should consider a hotel or lodging REIT depends on their views of the economy, their forecasts for spending and travel patterns of businesses and consumers, and the levels of new and expected hotel construction in various markets—this sector is more economically sensitive than any other. Fortunately, the supply of new rooms will probably remain muted for a few years.

Investors in this sector often are treated to some wild rides, but when conditions improve, they can become very good indeed. Some may seek to avoid riding their investments though an entire hotel cycle by waiting to buy until the U.S. economy shows signs of accelerating growth. Because the fixed costs of maintaining high-end hotels, in particular, are substantial, owners have a great deal of operating leverage, and most of the benefits from higher room and occupancy rates can be brought down to the bottom line. The problem with such an investment strategy, of course, is that hotel stocks may have already moved up substantially before a recovery becomes clearly evident. Nevertheless, perfect timing will not be crucial to the extent that the next up-cycle lasts longer than some of those in the recent past.

Where are we in the cycle today? As this book went to press, the U.S. economy was growing—albeit modestly—and the hotel sector was clearly showing improvement. RevPar growth may be more muted in this recovery, depending on how long a "new normal" economy remains in force. One important positive is that new hotel supply is likely to remain muted for the next few years. RevPar growth may, yet again, approach the double digits, and perhaps the good fortunes of hotel owners can be sustained for several years into the future.

Other Property Sectors

There are also other, smaller property sectors that REIT investors might want to consider. *Triple-net lease,* sometimes referred to as *free-standing property,* REITs, own properties leased primarily to single tenants in separate buildings who pay for all maintenance expenses, property taxes, and insurance. These leases tend to have long durations. The internal cash flow growth for these types of REITs is likely to be lower than those in other sectors, but the risk is low if the properties are not built and configured for irreplaceable tenants and if the overall credit quality of the tenant roster is strong. The dividend yields on these shares have also been significantly higher than those of typical equity REITs. Because many view these shares as tantamount to bond proxies, they may be more sensitive to changes in interest rates than those of other REITs.

NAREIT often uses the term *specialty REIT* to describe those REITs that own properties that cannot be easily fit into the major property categories. These currently include timberland REITs, of which there are now four; a movie theater REIT; and a railroad track REIT. NAREIT has included data center REITs in the "specialty" category, but these were discussed earlier as part of the office sector.

The unique investment characteristics and operating dynamics of these unusual property types need to be carefully considered by the investor, along with such factors as strength of management, balance sheet quality, and growth prospects. Conservative REIT investors, particularly those looking for higher-than-average yields, will probably want to look closely at these REITs, particularly triple-net lease REITs, for a combination of good yields with modest risk. For example, Realty Income, a stalwart REIT organized in 1969, has compiled a very good and lengthy track record. As for specialty REITs of the future, I'm patiently waiting for the day when a cemetery REIT is organized, perhaps sold to investors on the basis of the aging of the U.S. population—the key attraction, of course, being that tenants will never leave!

How should REIT investors structure their investment portfolios to obtain exposure to each of the foregoing property types? Would investors benefit by "underweighting" or "overweighting" REITs that specialize in particular sectors? Let's defer this discussion until we arrive at Chapter 10, "Building a REIT Portfolio."

Summary

- With REITs, it's possible to invest in nearly every kind of real estate imaginable: apartment communities and other residential properties, retail properties, office and industrial buildings, a wide array of health care properties, self-storage facilities, and hotels. REIT investors can even own lab space, data centers, and timberland.
- The phases of the real estate cycle are depression, recovery, boom, and overbuilding and downturn, and these cyclical patterns, along with changes in capital flows, will affect REITs' performance and their stock prices.
- Real estate sectors often will have different cycles and behave differently from one another, and each must be considered separately.

- Apartment REITs tend to have stable cash flows, and their prospects are influenced by employment and wage growth, household formation, and the single-family home markets.
- Neighborhood shopping center REITs own properties frequently anchored by a supermarket or drugstore, which sell consumer necessities.
- Mall REITs dominate the mall sector of the retail industry; they are very much in the retail business and are not highly exposed to new, competing developments.
- Office properties have long cycles; cash flows tend to be stable, which lag changes in market conditions due to long-term leases.
- The industrial property market has had a good track record of reacting quickly and shutting down the supply of new space as soon as the market becomes saturated; overseas development may provide a good opportunity for some industrial property REITs.
- Health care REITs were launched in the late 1980s and have generally performed well; they are not economically sensitive, but investors need to monitor the financial strength of the lessees and changes in government reimbursement policies.
- Self-storage is a recession-resistant property type and, despite substantial new supply, has performed well over the years.
- Hotel REITs have had periods of both substantial strength and major weakness; they represent more aggressive investments because of their cyclicality and volatile room and occupancy rates.
- The author believes that the most recession-resistant property types are health care, self-storage, manufactured home communities, college housing, and lab space—and, to a lesser extent, apartment communities.

PART

HISTORY AND MYTHOLOGY

CHAPTER 5

REITs: Mysteries and Myths

"To suppose that the value of a common stock is determined purely by a corporation's earnings discounted by the relevant interest rate and adjusted for the marginal tax rate is to forget that people have burned witches, gone to war on a whim, rose to the defense of Joseph Stalin, and believed Orson Wells when he told them over the radio that the Martians had landed."

—James Grant, *Minding Mr. Market*

Despite a long and successful track record, increasing industry size, and growing investor acceptance, REITs have been plagued by lingering mysteries and myths that they haven't been able to shake off. This chapter addresses these misconceptions and seeks to dispel them.

Changing Attitudes toward REITs

For many years in the past, REITs were regarded as odd and uninteresting investments. They even had a strange name—REIT— that many investors couldn't even pronounce properly. Bruce Andrews, the former CEO of Nationwide Health Properties, noted that the term *trust*, as in real estate investment trust, implies that

REITs are oddities, that they are not like normal public corporations whose shares are traded on the stock exchanges. But, more substantively, one of the main reasons that REIT stocks were suspect for so long is that many people who traditionally invested in real estate didn't trust—or bother to understand—the stock market, while most people who invested in stocks were uncomfortable with, or had little understanding of, commercial real estate. REITs just didn't fit cleanly into either category.

But this confusion has been abating. In October 2001, Standard & Poor's (S&P) admitted the largest REIT at that time, Equity Office Properties, with an equity market cap of $12 billion, into the S&P 500 index. Equity Residential, the largest apartment REIT, was admitted soon thereafter, and at the end of 2010, there were 14 REITs in the S&P 500. Another form of investor acceptance is evidenced by the huge expansion of the REIT industry over the past 20 years. The equity market cap of all REITs was $8.7 billion at the end of 1990, but rose to $389.3 billion by the end of 2010.

Of course, the growth in the REIT industry will wax and wane from time to time, due to ever-shifting stock market trends, investor preferences, commercial real estate values, and differences between those values and REIT stock prices. And there are some valid reasons why some investors will want to own real estate directly, rather than an investment in a REIT. Nevertheless, because the advantages of property ownership through a REIT are so substantial, the size of the REIT industry will continue to grow, over time, with increasing investments by both individuals and institutions who appreciate REITs' professional management, liquidity, extensive information disclosure, and opportunity for wider diversification among property types and geographic locations.

It's even possible that changing attitudes toward REITs—and their wider acceptance—may eventually mute the volatile commercial real estate development experienced in previous cycles. The weakness in our space markets from 2001 to 2004, and from 2008 to 2010, resulted from recession and lack of space demand, not the overbuilding of many prior periods. Perhaps the greater scrutiny of public companies, combined with the alignment of REIT managers' interests with those of their shareholders, caused REIT organizations to exercise development restraint, particularly in recent years. And, because REITs now play a much greater role in the commercial real estate industry, their development discipline near cycle peaks may act as a damper on the "animal instincts" of private developers and their lenders.

The Bias of Traditional Real Estate Investors

Traditionally, most real estate investors have chosen to put their money directly into property—apartment complexes, shopping centers, malls, office buildings, or industrial properties—and not in real estate securities like REITs. In other words, investment in bricks and mortar, not stock certificates. Direct ownership historically has provided the opportunity to use substantial leverage, since lenders have traditionally been willing to lend 60 percent and more of the purchase price of a building. Leverage is a wonderful thing—when prices and rents are going up.

Since the Great Depression, real estate values have had a positive upward trajectory, notwithstanding cyclical dips along the way. Appreciation of 10 percent on a building bought with 25 percent cash down would generate 40 percent investment returns. In addition, owning a building directly provided the investor with a tax shelter, via depreciation expenses, for property operating income. Commercial real estate ownership has provided good returns over the years, even when not levered with debt, so most real estate investors tended to focus on what they knew—direct ownership.

Many individual real estate investors harbored a distrust for public markets (REITs included), which they saw as roulette tables where investors put themselves at the mercy of faceless fund managers—or worse, speculators and day traders whose income depended on volatility. These investors saw REITs as highly speculative and wouldn't touch them.

But what about institutional investment in real estate? Originally, pension and other institutional funds earmarked for real estate were invested in properties either directly (where their own property and investment managers were retained), or through "commingled funds" in which large insurance companies and others used funds provided by various institutional investors to buy portfolios of properties. Who managed these properties, supervised their performance, and answered for their results? The same sort of real estate investors who probably had no love for, nor experience with, the stock market—or, if they had no such qualms about equities, didn't believe that the performance of REIT shares would match that of direct real estate investments.

Furthermore, as REITs are traded as common stocks, the result was—catch-22—that a decision to invest in REITs could be made only by the *"equities* investment officer" rather than the *"real estate* investment officer" of the institution or pension fund. The institutions' common stock investment funds were placed and monitored elsewhere. Furthermore, various investment guidelines often precluded the equities investment officers from investing in REITs—even if they knew about them and wanted to pursue these oft-undervalued investments. And why should they bother? After all, REITs had always been a very small sector of the equities market and were not even included in the S&P 500 index until 2001.

A further discouragement has been volatility. Real estate investors have complained that REITs, even though less volatile, during most periods, than the broader stock market, nevertheless fluctuate in price. But they ignored the fact that *all* assets fluctuate in price—it's just that *some* prices are not revealed on a daily basis. Owning illiquid assets that are not traded every day (and by relying upon occasional appraisals), the private fund managers could maintain the illusion that the values of their assets were "steady as a rock," despite the continuous ebb and flow of the real estate capital markets. Owners are sometimes unaware of these changing valuations until they try to sell.

Finally, institutions buy and sell stocks in large blocks, and it's been only recently that REIT shares have had sufficient liquidity to attract institutional investors. In fact, one of the most oft-quoted reasons why pension funds have been reluctant to invest in REITs is their lack of liquidity. The REIT market was so thinly traded prior to 1994 that it would have been extremely difficult for an institution to accumulate even a modest position without disrupting the market for any particular REIT stock. But, since then, the size of the REIT industry has expanded dramatically, and now provides much greater liquidity for investors of all sizes.

And REIT stocks have performed! According to a 2010 National Association of Real Estate Investment Trusts (NAREIT) analysis, based on data compiled by that organization and the Townsend Group, REITs performed better (net of all expenses) than three different types of private real estate equity funds over the most recent entire 17-year real estate cycle that ended in the first quarter of 2007. Nevertheless, according to a 2010 study, by IREI/Kingsley Associates, only about 3.5 percent of $34.4 billion in new investment funds expected to be allocated in 2010 to commercial real estate by major institutional investors were earmarked for REIT stocks. (That figure, however, was increased to 7.4 percent in the IREI/Kingsley 2011 study.) Although REIT industry participants expect that this institutional mind-set will eventually change, and that more institutional funds will be deployed into REIT investments, it would seem that old habits die hard. We'll discuss institutional investment in REIT shares, as well as REITs' liquidity, in more detail in a later chapter.

The Bias of Common Stock Investors

Now that we've explored why *real estate* investors have been reluctant to embrace REIT investing, let's look at the other side. What has discouraged *common stock* investors from buying REITs? REITs' only business is real estate and, until fairly recently, stock investors haven't been comfortable with real estate; they focused primarily on product or service companies. Real estate was perceived as a different asset class from common stock and, in many ways, has its own language; this problem was, as suggested above, particularly acute in the institutional world.

Furthermore, the perception, until fairly recently, has been that REITs were essentially real estate mutual funds, and not active businesses—a perception precluding REITs from being admitted to the S&P 500 until 2001. An IRS ruling at that time confirmed that REITs are active businesses, but embedded perceptions don't change quickly.

In addition, there was a myth, accepted by many investors—wrong as it was—that REITs were high-risk but low-return investments. There were many investors who had bought construction-lending REITs and real estate limited partnerships in the 1970s and 1980s and were badly burned. These investors did not take the trouble to distinguish between these ill-fated investments and well-managed equity REITs.

Also, investors had been told for years that companies that paid out a high percentage of their income in dividends did not retain much of their earnings and therefore could not grow rapidly. Because, to most common stock investors, growth is the hallmark of successful investing, they didn't want to invest in a company that couldn't grow. Finally, some of the blame for lack of individual investors' interest in REITs can be laid at the feet of stockbrokers.

TIP

REITs for a long time were perceived as stocks by real estate investors, and as real estate by stock investors.

Until about 20 years ago, most major brokerage firms did not even employ a REIT analyst. And because individual investors generally bought individual stocks only when their brokers recommended them, the REIT story was never explored. Mutual funds have been popular for decades, but for many years only a handful of mutual funds were devoted to REIT investments—and those did not advertise or market widely. Many of those investors who did their own research and made their own investment decisions often felt that REITs were unknown territory into which they were reluctant to venture. Even income investors, for whom REITs would have been particularly suitable, invested primarily in bonds, electric utilities, and other higher-yielding stocks.

REITs, of course, given their favorable investment characteristics, were bound to be noticed sooner or later. They are gradually but inexorably becoming well known to real estate and common stock investors alike, and REITs' long period of neglect is now history. But be careful what you wish for! Increasing REIT industry recognition does have a downside. In 2007, before the implosion of Lehman Brothers, Merrill Lynch, and other major financial institutions, hedge funds began to short REIT stocks on the expectation that commercial real estate prices would tumble. They eventually were proven right—at least for a time—but their rapid-fire trades caused a major spike in REIT share volatility. Most of us REIT investors didn't enjoy those roller-coaster rides, but it was the increasing size and liquidity of the REIT industry that made these hedge fund trading strategies possible. REIT investors can't have it both ways;

if we want to play in the big leagues, we have to deal with bigger and more powerful competitors. Interest in REIT stocks will ebb and flow with changes in investor fads and preferences, but they are now firmly recognized as strong and stable investments, albeit cyclical, that help to diversify a broad-based investment portfolio.

Myths about REITs

In addition to—and sometimes because of—the obstacles REITs have had to overcome, as just discussed, some REIT and real estate myths exist—myths that in the past scared off all but the bravest investors. Although these myths were based on misunderstandings of the investment characteristics of REITs, they discouraged many would-be investors. Let's confront a few of them.

Myth 1: REITs Are Packages of Real Estate Properties

This myth, which probably sprang from investors' experience with the ill-fated real estate limited partnerships of many years ago, was certainly a contributing factor to REITs' failure in the past to attract a substantial investor following. Although most of the earliest REITs really were, in many respects, only collections of properties, or "real estate mutual funds," they are much more than that today.

 TIP

Today's REITs are not just portfolios of real properties; they are fully integrated commercial real estate organizations, capable of creating value in ways beyond passive property ownership.

Investment vehicles, in whatever form, that simply own, and have outside companies manage, a basket of properties must contend with several specific investment issues. Sponsors of these vehicles are often interested only in the fees, and may be less interested in superior performance. Similarly, sponsors often don't have their compensation directly linked to the success of the portfolio properties and therefore have no particular incentive to be innovative despite today's competitive environment. Often, there is no long-term vision or strategy for creating value and minimizing risk for the investors. Finally, attractively priced capital will often be unavailable, making it difficult for the entity to take advantage of "buyers' markets" for commercial real estate. An investment in such a passive fund or company, although perhaps providing an attractive dividend yield, offers little opportunity for growth or superior returns.

But the vast majority of today's REITs are vibrant, dynamic real estate business organizations first and "investment trusts" second. They are far more than collections of properties. Their management is highly motivated by their own ownership stake and other equity incentives. They plan intelligently for expansion either in areas they know well or in areas where they believe they can become successful players, and they frequently have access to the capital necessary for such expansion. They attempt to strengthen their relationships with their tenants by offering innovative and cost-efficient services. To categorize highly successful and entrepreneurial real estate companies such as AMB Property (now ProLogis), Acadia Realty, Alexandria Real Estate, American Campus Communities, and Avalon-Bay Communities—and I'm not even finished with the letter "A"—as just collections of properties, or "mutual funds of real estate," is to seriously underestimate and improperly categorize them. Yet this myth still persists, even among some institutional investors.

Myth 2: Real Estate Is a High-Risk Investment

It's amazing how many people believe that real estate is a high-risk investment that can decimate one's net worth due to declines in property values or tenant defaults. Recently, the problems of single-family home owners have probably reinforced that belief. And they surmise that if real estate investing is risky, then REIT investing also must be risky. But let's analyze real estate investment risk.

 TIP

Three key elements of real estate and REIT investing risk are debt leverage, lack of diversification, and the quality of asset or entity management (including the assets and property locations chosen for ownership).

- **Debt leverage**. Debt leverage in real estate, for an individual property or a large public REIT, is no different from debt leverage in any other investment: the more debt you use, the greater your potential gain or loss. When we buy stocks on margin, we are leveraging our investment returns with debt. And *any* asset carried on high margin, whether an office building, a blue-chip stock, or even a U.S. Treasury note, will involve substantial risk, since a small decline in the asset's value will cause a much larger decline in one's investment in it. And debt refinancing may not always be an option for the borrower, particularly if the owned asset falls substantially in value. However, because real estate historically has been bought and financed with substantial debt, many investors have confused the risk of debt leverage with that of owning real estate. (We'll discuss REITs' debt leverage in more detail in Chapter 8.)

TIP

Although real estate investments often have been highly leveraged with debt, it is the high leverage rather than the real estate that is the greatest risk.

- **Diversification**. Again, the same rule that applies to other investments applies to REITs: diversification reduces risk. People who would never dream of having a one-stock portfolio are happy to buy, individually or with partners, a single apartment building or shopping center. Unexpected and unwelcome events will occur—an earthquake, neighborhood deterioration, a local recession—and all of a sudden the building becomes a cash drain rather than a cash cow. Meanwhile, a similar apartment building or shopping center in another location may be doing well, or the office building owner upstate can be raking in cash. A lack of diversification produces real risk for a property ownership investment strategy, but that risk isn't due to real estate itself. Appropriate diversification should be the mantra of every investor, even within each asset class one owns.

One Common Misconception

When a single high-profile REIT encounters difficulty, investors sometimes rashly conclude that REITs as an asset class are very risky. Yet no one would condemn the entire stock market just because the price of one leading stock had collapsed.

- **Management issues**. Then, of course, there is the issue of management. Good property (and enterprise) management is crucial—but that is true not only in real estate. If you look around at major U.S. non-REIT corporations, you can see, for instance, the value of a Steve Jobs to Apple, or how Bill Gates' vision brought Microsoft to where it is today. Conversely, incompetent management can ruin a major corporation or a neighborhood candy store. Real estate, like all other types of investments, cannot simply be bought and ignored; it requires active, capable management. And good REIT management teams are able to select real estate for acquisition and ownership that is likely to appreciate, not depreciate, over time. Despite this, many otherwise intelligent investors have bought apartment buildings, small office properties, or local shopping centers, often in poor locations, and tried either to manage them themselves in their spare time or to give control to local agents who may have little incentive to manage the property efficiently or effectively. What happens? The apartment building or strip center does poorly, and the investor loses money and jumps to the wrong conclusion—that real estate is a high-risk investment. Rather, it's neglect—not real estate itself—that brings on greater risk.

Myth 3: Real Estate's Value Is Essentially as an Inflation Hedge

Real estate is really nothing more than buildings and land, and, like all tangible assets (whether copper, oil, gold, or even scrap metal), its value will ebb and flow. Expected inflation will affect prices of real estate. However, inflation is only one factor. Others are supply of—and demand for—space, national and local economic conditions, interest rates, prices of—and return expectations for—other assets and investments, replacement cost, the jobs market, consumer spending, levels of new personal and business investment, government policies, and even wars.

Part of the reason for the real-estate-as-inflation-hedge myth may have come from the fact that real estate happened to do well during the inflationary 1970s, while stock ownership during the same period was not as productive. This, quite likely, was simply a coincidence, or may have been driven by transitory investment psychology. According to *Stocks, Bonds, Bills, and Inflation 1995 Yearbook*, published by Ibbotson Associates, equities have been very good inflation hedges over many decades. So has real estate. But the reality is that neither the real estate market nor the equity market is substantially better or worse as an inflation hedge than the other, except, perhaps, during short-term periods when investor psychology drives prices.

Yes, there are times when inflation *appears* to help the real estate investor by boosting the replacement cost of real estate, but such inflation can also increase operating expenses such as property maintenance, other management costs, insurance and taxes, and thus restrain a property's net operating income growth—which could negatively affect its market value.

 TIP

The value of a commercial building is determined essentially by a number of factors, including property net operating income (current and prospective), location, replacement cost, prevailing interest rates, credit availability and its cost, age and condition, the expected supply of new competing properties, required capital expenditures to keep the property attractive, property occupancy, and the credit quality of the tenants. And these factors fluctuate in response to various market forces; the expected rate of inflation is only one of those forces.

High inflation can positively *or negatively* affect rental rates and net operating income. A positive influence resulting from inflation, at least in the retail sector, can come from the higher tenant sales that normally result from increased inflation and higher prices of goods sold to consumers; retail rents are substantially dependent on tenant sales levels and trends. Although these higher sales can translate into higher rents for property owners, this benefit will be short-lived if the retailers can't maintain their profit margins. If stores are not generating profits, it will be difficult for owners to raise rents. Similarly, higher inflation can help apartment owners by increasing tenants' wages and thus their ability to pay higher rents, but only if wages are rising at least as rapidly as the prices of goods and services.

When supply and demand for space are in balance, inflation may enable owners to raise rents because, as the cost of land and new construction rises, rents in new buildings will have to be high enough to cover these higher development costs. If the demand is sufficient to absorb the new units that are coming into the market, owners of seasoned properties often will be able to take advantage of the higher rents charged at the new properties by boosting their own rental rates. Real estate is not an effective hedge against inflation, however, when there is a large overhang of competing properties.

Higher inflation rates can also have a *negative* effect on the value of real estate, certainly over the short term. The Federal Reserve acts as a watchdog for inflation, and, when there is a perceived inflationary threat, the Fed will raise short-term interest rates. Higher interest rates are meant to slow the economy, but interest rates that rise too high can strangle it, causing a recession. Once a recession takes hold, a property owner will have difficulty maintaining rental rates and occupancy levels.

Now let's focus more closely on how inflation can affect the prices of real estate. The price of a property often is determined, in part, by applying a multiple to its existing or forward-looking annual net operating income (or by using its reciprocal, the cap rate), but the multiples (or the cap rates) fluctuate. Some will argue that buyers will pay more for, or accept a lower cap rate on, real property during inflationary periods. Since investors view real estate as a "hard asset," like oil and other commodities, they may be willing to pay a higher multiple for every dollar of operating income if they perceive that accelerating inflation will lead to higher rents.

The counterargument is that cap rates may indeed be influenced by inflation, but in the opposite direction. Higher inflation will often drive up interest rates, which in turn will increase the "hurdle rate of return" demanded by investors in a property, and have the effect of increasing the required cap rate and thus *decreasing* the price at which the property can be sold. Conversely, property values may rise even with no inflation whatever. Property values certainly rose from 2003 to 2005 when inflation was at a modest level, and began to rebound in 2010, when inflation was almost nonexistent. Consider the following example:

If the rental demand for apartment units in San Francisco exceeds the available supply of such units, rents will increase and the apartment building owner's net operating income will increase. Thus, one might think that the value of the apartment community would also rise. However, if this demand for apartment space was fueled by an overheated economy, which brings on higher interest rates to cool things down, the cap rate applied by a potential buyer of the property to the net operating income might also rise, perhaps even causing a *decline* in value of the asset.

However, if the supply of apartment units in San Francisco exceeds the demand by renters, as was the case from 2001 to 2004, rents and net operating income may weaken—but the value of the apartment community may nevertheless rise. This may occur as a lower cap rate is applied to that net operating income due to a buyer's willingness to accept a more modest return on his or her investment, perhaps goaded by lower prevailing interest rates. And all of this has little to do with inflation.

It is likely that replacement cost for a real estate asset will rise during inflationary periods, but this alone won't increase the property's market value if the profitability of the asset falls short of buyers' requirements; it means only that new competing properties are unlikely to be built until market values approach replacement cost. Properties can trade at prices well below replacement cost for substantial periods of time.

 TIP

Market factors such as supply and demand, along with interest rates and a host of other factors, are almost always more important than inflation in determining property value. REIT investors should focus more on market conditions, credit markets, cash flows, and management's ability to create value than on inflation.

Myth 4: REIT Stock Performance Is Anchored to the Performance of the REIT's Properties

Because REITs are all about commercial real estate, their performance and investment returns will, over time, be closely related to those of the broad commercial real estate markets. But it isn't always that simple.

The rapid industrialization and intense competition occurring globally today seem to be major and perhaps long-lasting phenomena. U.S. companies must now go toe-to-toe with foreign competitors virtually everywhere in the world. This, in turn, requires U.S. businesses to be very cost-efficient. Downsizings, restructurings, outsourcing of jobs, and layoffs have been the result. Companies find it difficult to raise prices, and employees are finding it equally difficult to get pay raises. Consumer spending has been subpar even after the end of the Great Recession. To the extent that these competitive trends persist, particularly if we become mired in a "new normal" environment, the growth in demand for space is apt to be muted, and returns to commercial real estate investors will be moderate. The real estate cycle may have bottomed in 2010, but medium-term growth in net operating income in most sectors may be limited to 2 to 3 percent after bouncing off of recessionary lows.

That kind of scenario shouldn't be terribly disappointing to REIT investors. If free cash flow can grow by an average of 2 to 3 percent when the economy is growing at a moderate pace, perhaps increasing to, say, 4 percent by using a modest amount of debt leverage, and if the average REIT dividend yield is close to 4 percent (yields for all REITs and for equity REITs averaged 4.23 percent and 3.54 percent, respectively, at the end of 2010, per NAREIT data), average annual total returns of about 8 percent are reasonable expectations. Those types of returns are likely to be very competitive with other investments bearing similar risks.

But it's not necessarily true that REIT investment returns are inextricably anchored to the returns on the properties they own. We have seen, in the history of the REIT industry and over the course of real estate cycles, that REIT performance and profitability are capable of transcending investment returns available in the vast commercial real estate markets.

REIT organizations have, at times, been able to take advantage of lucrative opportunities presented by challenging real estate environments. Smart REIT management teams view difficult conditions, and even tenant bankruptcies, as growth and value-creation opportunities. This occurred most dramatically in the early 1990s, when real estate markets were in disarray but many REIT organizations were able to buy quality assets at unusually cheap prices. Nationwide Health Properties and Health Care Properties (now HCP Inc.) were able to buy loans secured by nursing homes from the Resolution Trust Corporation at 16 to 18 percent yields, while some apartment owners, such as United Dominion (now UDR Inc.) went on a shopping spree and bought huge numbers of apartment communities from distressed sellers.

Many were expecting a similar event to unfold in 2010, due to the damage caused by the Great Recession and the huge volume of "underwater" loans resulting from the overly exuberant growth in the commercial mortgage-backed securities (CMBS) market in the middle years of the prior decade and very aggressive loan under-writing practices; however, due to very low interest rates and the desire of lenders to work with troubled borrowers (and not want-ing to write down the values of undercollateralized loans), coupled with ample capital waiting on the sidelines to take advantage of distressed real estate opportunities, this did not occur as expected. However, as this book went to press, it was still too early to know whether substantial buying opportunities may yet unfold.

TIP

The extent to which a well-managed REIT can avail itself of the opportunities pre-sented in weak markets depends on the amount and cost of capital available to it, the depth of the market weakness, and the extent of competition from other buyers.

Nevertheless, as we'll see in Chapters 7 and 8, many REITs, par-ticularly those with access to ample amounts of inexpensive capital, have often been able to create value for their shareholders through a wide array of initiatives, property acquisitions being just one of them. And when space markets are favorable, substantial value has been created, over time, by those REITs that are gifted property developers.

Thus, the return on one's investment in a REIT isn't limited to the actual performance of its properties. Although it is true that missteps by a REIT management team can destroy shareholder value and cause its stock to perform worse than its portfolio properties, the reverse has been true more often, as evidenced by the performance data provided by NAREIT and the Townsend Group (as noted earlier in this chapter).

A related issue for investors is the performance of REIT shares relative to the pricing of commercial real estate. We have seen many times in the history of the REIT industry that the price performance of REIT shares can be quite different, at least over shorter time periods, from pricing trends in commercial real estate. There are many reasons for this, but a key explanation is that REIT stocks, being real estate equities, look forward—as is the case in equities markets generally. Commercial real estate prices were firm throughout most of 2007, but REIT shares topped out in January of that year. Conversely, commercial real estate prices fell continuously from 2008 through 2009 (some fell even through much of 2010), but REIT shares bottomed very early in 2009. Those who were obsessed by the newspaper headlines and frightened by stories about declining commercial real estate prices were probably reluctant to buy REIT stocks and missed out on substantial price gains.

To summarize, although REIT stocks' long-term performance won't stray far from the performance of commercial real estate, they are not anchored to that performance, and can deliver superior returns to their investors—particularly during periods of unusual opportunity, for example, when REITs' access to capital gives them a competitive edge. And, unlike direct real estate owners, REITs enjoy external growth prospects in most environments. Finally, due to the somewhat different pricing cycles of commercial real estate and REIT shares, those who are willing to buy REIT stocks when others don't want to own them can garner some particularly good returns.

Myth 5: REIT Stocks Are Trading Vehicles

How often have you read in a financial magazine or the personal finance section of the local newspaper, "Is now the time to get into (or out of) REITs?" That question seems never to go away. Why is it asked so often? I believe this is due to the persistence of yet another myth that is often encountered with respect to REITs: that they are, like many commodities, best traded in and out of, stocks that must be market-timed if one is to make any money in them.

Although some speculators are probably capable of doing this on occasion, the belief that REIT stocks are best traded, rather than owned, is a dangerous myth. It is based on several assumptions, all of which are erroneous. These include: (1) REIT stocks, like commodity stocks, must be bought and sold at the right times if one is to do well with them; (2) real estate and REIT stock prices, market conditions, interest rates, capital markets, and investor psychology can be successfully anticipated and timed by astute investors; and (3) the objective of buying and selling these "risky little devils" is to score big wins and to avoid equally large losses. Wrong, wrong, wrong!

First, REIT stocks needn't be bought and sold frequently; indeed, they are the ultimate "buy-and-hold" investment. Their total return performance, over the past entire commercial real estate cycle beginning in the third quarter of 1989 and ending in the first quarter of 2007, a period of over 17 years, averaged 13.4 percent—certainly competitive with the broader equities markets. And over all meaningful time periods, REITs' total returns have averaged in the double digits. Depending on the time period examined, close to 50 percent of REITs' returns to investors come from dividend yields, so investors get paid to wait for the additional reward of stock price appreciation that comes, over time, with earnings, dividend, and net asset value growth. REITs are truly attractive investments for the patient, long-term investor.

Second, it is probable that the most wealth has been created by investors who buy and hold the stocks of excellent companies, for example, Warren Buffett. There is little evidence that traders or market timers have been able to make money consistently in the stock market. And this is certainly true in the REIT world. To successfully time the purchase and sale of REIT stocks, one must be able to forecast accurately the direction of interest rates (both long-term and short-term), real estate markets throughout the United States, capital flows of both institutions and individuals, rates of inflation and unemployment, and all the other factors that determine real estate and stock prices. This cannot be done consistently and, for 99 percent of all investors, isn't worth the effort.

Finally, most serious investors do not invest in REIT stocks for quick and sizable capital gains, as one might seek to do in technology, biotech, or natural resource stocks. REIT stocks are best suited to those seeking dividend income and modest price appreciation, over time, corresponding with increases in cash flows and asset values, and they have only modest correlations with other asset classes. The investors who do best with REIT stocks are those who have the most patience, are willing to ride out the occasional bear market, and are not expecting to hit home runs.

Thus, the claim that REIT stocks are best "played" is simply a myth. Intelligent financial planners and advisers should be telling their clients to decide on an appropriate allocation to REIT stocks within their diversified investment portfolios and to stick with them, perhaps rebalancing from time to time to maintain that allocation. We'll spend a little more time on this topic later in the book.

Summary

- For years, REITs have been shunned as "common stocks" by real estate investors and treated as "quirky real estate" by stock investors.
- REITs are real estate organizations, not just packages of properties or real estate mutual funds.
- Three essential determinants of long-term real estate risk are debt leverage, lack of diversification, and poor management of properties and portfolios of properties.
- Although real estate investments have often been highly leveraged, it is the high debt leverage, rather than real estate itself, that is the major risk.
- Real estate owners may, at times, benefit from inflation, but inflation is not a principal reason for owning real estate.
- Market factors such as supply and demand, interest rates, the existing and future strength of the economy, investors' preferences, expected returns, and available investment alternatives are almost always more important than inflation in determining property values.
- Well-capitalized REIT organizations have the ability, and often the opportunity, to deliver investment returns to their shareholders greater than what will be provided by the properties they own.
- REIT stocks are not "trading vehicles" and should be owned for dividend yields and modest capital appreciation over long periods of time.

A History of REITs and REIT Performance

"If past history were all there was to the game, the richest people would be librarians."

—Warren Buffett

As investors, we want to be equipped with as many analytical tools as possible. Knowing how a particular type of investment has behaved in the past may not be a sure predictor of the future. However, history can certainly help us to understand the investment merits and characteristics of particular asset classes.

How have REIT stocks behaved during the more than 50 years since they were conceived? Like a child, like a teenager, and like an adult, depending on which stage of their development we examine. We'll take a look at those developments—specifically, how REITs performed in their infancy, how they created havoc in their wild adolescent years, and how they've matured into solid citizens of the investment world. We will also consider how REITs have behaved during, and in response to, various real estate and economic environments.

The 1960s: Infancy

Congress authorized REIT organizations through legislation that was signed into law in 1960. The intent was to enable individual investors to invest easily in commercial real estate so that they might enjoy investment benefits similar to owning individual properties directly. Once the structure was created, the first REITs were quickly organized. However, most of these early REITs were not "pretty babies" by today's standards.

According to *The REIT Investment Summary* (1996), a report by Goldman Sachs, only 10 REITs of any significant size existed during the 1960s. Most of them were managed by outside advisers, and all property management functions were handled by outside companies. Many of these management companies were affiliated with the REIT's trustees, which created substantial conflicts of interest.

The REITs' portfolios were minuscule, ranging from $11 million for Washington REIT (one of the few survivors) to the "giant" $44 million REIT of America. Total assets owned by the entire REIT industry in the mid-1960s were very small, amounting to just over $200 million (by the end of 2010, REITs owned real estate assets estimated by the National Association of Real Estate Investment Trusts [NAREIT] at approximately $500 *billion)*. Directors and management of these early REITs owned very few shares—typically less than 1 percent .

Despite these weaknesses, the Goldman Sachs report shows that these early-era REITs turned in a respectable performance, aided by generally healthy real estate markets in the 1960s. Cash flow

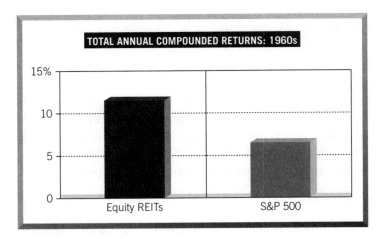

Figure 6.1   Total Annual Compounded Returns: 1960s

(the early version of today's funds from operations, or FFO) grew an average of 5.8 percent annually, and the average dividend yield was 6.1 percent. The multiples of per-share cash flow that investors were willing to pay for these early REITs didn't fluctuate much, and their shares provided investors with an average annual total return of 11.5 percent—quite a good performance, considering that from 1963 to 1970 the Standard & Poor's (S&P) 500's total annual return averaged only 6.7 percent. Thus, despite their many handicaps, these upstart investments performed quite well (see Figure 6.1).

The 1970s: Adolescence and Turbulence

The 1970s were tumultuous times for the economy, for the stock market, and for REITs. Inflation, driven by the OPEC-led explosion in oil prices, raged out of control. The Consumer Price Index (CPI) increased by 6.3 percent in 1973, 11 percent in 1974, 9.1 percent in 1975, and 11.3 percent in 1979.

As if those headwinds weren't enough, the REIT industry was busy creating problems of its own. Between 1968 and 1970, the industry spawned 58 new mortgage REITs. Most of these used a modest amount of shareholders' equity and huge amounts of borrowed funds to provide short-term loans to the merchant development industry, which, in turn, built hundreds of office buildings throughout the United States.

Stalwart banks such as Bank of America, Chase, Wachovia, and Wells Fargo, among many others, each sponsored their own REIT. Perhaps their belief was, "When the music's playing, you gotta dance"—sound familiar? Largely as a result of these new mortgage REITs, the REIT industry's total assets mushroomed from $1 billion in 1968 to $20 billion by the mid-1970s. But many of the development loans originated or bought by these REITs were very aggressively underwritten.

When the office markets—hammered by high interest rates deemed necessary to quash inflation—began weakening in 1973, the new mortgage REITs found that debt leverage worked both ways. Made vulnerable by questionable underwriting standards, nonperforming assets rose to a staggering 73 percent of invested assets by the end of 1974, and REIT share prices collapsed, falling 21.8 percent in 1973 and 29.3 percent in 1974.

TIP

As a result of their horrible experience with mortgage REITs, investors of the 1970s became disenchanted with the entire REIT industry for many years thereafter.

Ironically, aside from these mortgage REITs, nonlending equity REITs produced solid earnings growth during the decade of the 1970s, even as asset growth slowed; many real estate markets remained healthy. Federal Realty and New Plan, among others, made their first appearances; these retail REITs performed well for investors for many years. During that decade, 10 representative equity REITs charted by the Goldman Sachs study garnered an average annual 6.1 percent compounded cash flow growth rate, with negative growth in only one year. Not surprisingly, those REITs with more than 5 percent insider stock ownership did much better than the others. The 10 "representative" equity REITs charted by Goldman Sachs enjoyed average annual price appreciation of 4.2 percent. This, when added to their dividend yields, produced an average annual total return of 12.9 percent during the 1970s, which compared very favorably with the average annual total return of 5.8 percent for the S&P 500 index (see Figure 6.2).

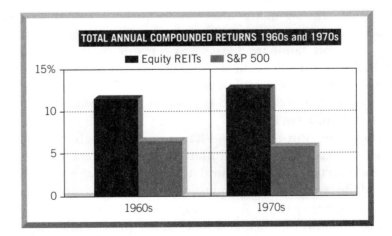

Figure 6.2   Total Annual Compounded Returns

Nevertheless, as the decade drew to a close, REITs were still not accepted by the investment community—perhaps due to the debacle of the mortgage REITs. By the end of 1979, the size of the REIT industry, as measured by its equity market capitalization (the stock market value of all REIT shares), was smaller than it was at the end of 1972. There was virtually no institutional money allocated to REITs during this time; they were unproven, illiquid, and still (in most cases) lacked internal and independent management. Further, with a few exceptions (notably Washington REIT, Federal Realty, and New Plan), they did not focus on specific property sectors in well-defined geographic regions. By the end of the decade, REITs were still young children, suffering growing pains, and were to be seen, not heard.

The 1980s: Overbuilding—The Troll Under the Bridge

The massive inflation of the 1970s had caused construction costs to skyrocket; these rising costs, together with only moderate rental rates, combined to discourage new property development. Thus, the new supply of property space was very modest, which favored property owners. Eventually, occupancy rates—and rents— rose. Property owners (including, of course, the REITs) were in pretty good shape.

 TIP

As the 1970s drew to a close, investors, reacting to high inflation, were searching for hard assets, such as gold, oil, and real estate.

Nevertheless, the extraordinarily high interest rates on mortgage loans in the early 1980s—ranging from 12.5 percent to 14.8 percent—substantially increased REITs' borrowing costs and negatively affected the space markets, eventually causing FFO growth to slow. According to the Goldman Sachs January 1996 *REIT Investment Summary*, per-share FFO growth rates for the firm's representative equity REITs declined from 26.1 percent in 1980 to 4.4 percent in 1983. However, overall FFO growth in the first half of the decade was surprisingly good, averaging 8.7 percent, due to higher rents and very modest new supply of real estate. During the six years from 1980 through 1985, the group's average annual total return to shareholders was truly outstanding, at 28.6 percent.

According to Ecclesiastes, "To everything there is a season," and the good times, having had their season in the first half of the decade, were not sustainable in the second half. Investors, both public and private, couldn't help noticing the outstanding returns achieved by real estate owners in the early 1980s; it was just too much of a good thing. Everyone just had to own real estate, and lots of it. What really inflated the real estate bubble, however, was the passage by Congress of the Economic Recovery Act of 1981, which created an attractive tax shelter for real estate owners. Authorizing property owners to use the vehicle of depreciation of their real estate assets as a tax shelter for other income prompted a real estate buying frenzy.

Almost immediately, major brokerage firms and other syndicators formed real estate limited partnerships and touted them as "can't-miss" investments, offering both generous tax benefits and rapid capital gains. The "law of unintended consequences" was proven valid again, as the tax incentives inflated property prices to unsustainable levels, not supportable by the basic economics of real estate ownership. REITs, offering greater cash flow stability but insignificant tax write-offs, were largely ignored.

As a flood of capital poured into real estate, several unfortunate events occurred. First, REITs had to compete for capital with limited partnerships and private investors, who, in creating tax shelters, didn't have to show a positive cash flow. There was no contest: The latter could afford to pay a lot more for properties than could the REITs, thus severely retarding REITs' external growth prospects.

Second, as a result of the buying frenzy, real estate prices spiked. Even if REITs could have raised the acquisition capital, properties were being priced at levels that precluded their earning an adequate investment return on acquisitions. And, back then, few REITs were willing to sell any of their properties to take advantage of inflated prices. Third, and worst of all, with real estate being priced well above replacement cost, the developers flexed their muscles and launched a huge wave of new construction. Virtually every developer who had ever built anything (and many who hadn't) visited his or her friendly banker, laid projections and budgets on the table, shouted "Construction loan time!" and walked away with 90 percent financing.

Small wonder that within a few years real estate markets, feeling the effects of overbuilding, weakened considerably. As if that weren't bad enough, Congress then decided to take away the tax-shelter advantage that had been such an impetus for investment, and passed the Tax Reform Act of 1986. Investors no longer even had those generous tax write-offs for consolation. By the late 1980s, real estate was becoming a very troubled investment.

TIP

During the 1980s, when investors were seeking the tax shelters offered by limited partnerships, real estate prices inflated to unsustainable levels.

By the second half of the 1980s, the average FFO growth rate for the representative group of REITs in the Goldman Sachs study dropped to only 2.5 percent. But REIT dividends rose faster than earnings, and the average FFO payout ratio for Goldman's group of REITs escalated from 72 percent in 1980 to 98 percent in 1986. But investors weren't paying attention—perhaps they were looking only at dividend yields—and, despite the problems encountered by the REITs in these difficult years, their stocks didn't do badly. Total annual returns for Goldman's REIT group ranged from a high of 29.4 percent in 1985 to a low of 3.7 percent in 1988. They slightly underperformed the S&P 500 in 1985, 1988, and 1989, but bested it in 1986 and 1987. Nevertheless, these high dividend payout ratios and slowing FFO growth, coupled with related problems in the real estate space markets, would eventually catch up with REIT stock prices in 1990 (see Figure 6.3).

The 1990s: The Modern REIT Era—Plus More Growing Pains

Emerging from the 1980s' real estate excesses, REITs did not begin the 1990s well. REIT shareholders suffered through a bear market in 1990 that cut their share prices down to bargain levels not seen since the 1970s. NAREIT statistics show that equity REITs' total return for 1990 was a negative 14.8 percent, making that the worst

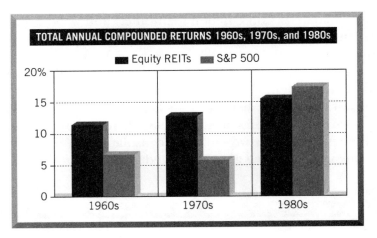

Figure 6.3   Total Annual Compounded Returns

year since 1974. This was quite a shock to REIT investors, who had perhaps become overconfident; from 1975 until 1990, equity REITs had experienced only one year of negative total return—1987—when the figures were in the red by a scant 3.6 percent.

The 1990 Bear Market

REIT stocks' very poor performance in 1990 resulted from several factors: the problem for owners of office buildings and apartment communities was overbuilding, causing rising vacancies and stagnating or reduced rents; in retail, it was the continued inroads made by Wal-Mart and other discounters on the turf of traditional retailers. Dividend cuts by a number of REITs, which had found their payout ratios too high during such tough real estate climates, certainly didn't help matters. And yet, although a general markdown in real estate securities prices was warranted, investors overreacted (as they often do), and share prices fell below reasonable levels.

 TIP

Excellent REIT bargains became available by the end of 1990, and these bear market lows set the stage for a major bull market that thrived from 1991 through 1993 and ushered in the great IPO boom of 1993 and 1994.

The opening of the decade had been rough for REITs, but the REIT industry itself by this time had nearly completed a metamorphosis. REITs in the late 1980s and early 1990s had come a long way from the REITs of the 1960s. Insider ownership increased and, thanks to the Tax Reform Act of 1986, which liberalized the rules pertaining to REITs, many of them terminated their outside investment advisory relationships—and the conflicts of interest that accompanied them—and internalized all their own leasing, maintenance services, redevelopment, and new construction. By the end of the 1990 bear market, a number of REITs, such as Health Care Property (now HCP Inc.), Washington REIT, and Weingarten Realty, could boast experienced management teams and good track records. The ranks of quality REITs were also augmented by the IPO of Kimco Realty in November 1991, although at that time few investors took much notice. But it would not be until 1993 that a large number of new, high-quality REITs would become available to investors.

1991 to 1993: The Bull Returns

A combination of factors caused equity REITs to perform exceedingly well from 1991 through 1993. According to NAREIT data, total annual returns for that period averaged 23.3 percent. This outstanding performance was ample reward for patient investors who had stuck with REITs through the bear market of 1990.

Why REIT stocks did so well from 1991 through 1993 is easy to explain in hindsight. For one thing, investors overreacted terribly when they dumped REIT stocks in 1990; some of the gain came merely from prices bouncing back to reasonable levels. Perhaps a more important reason, however, was the bargain prices at which REITs were able to pick up properties in the aftermath of the depression-like and overbuilt real estate markets of the late 1980s and early 1990s. By 1991, many REITs were once again able to raise capital. They bought huge volumes of properties at fire-sale prices from banks that had foreclosed on defaulted real estate loans, insurance companies that wanted to reduce their exposure to real estate, real estate limited partnerships that had crashed following the frenzy of the 1980s, and, last but certainly not least, the Resolution Trust Corporation, which had been organized by Congress to acquire and resell real estate and real estate loans from bankrupt and near-bankrupt lenders. REITs were once more able to pursue aggressive acquisition programs, raising funds from both equity offerings and additional borrowings, and investing them at very attractive rates of return.

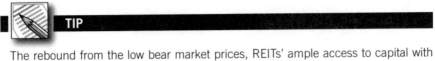

TIP

The rebound from the low bear market prices, REITs' ample access to capital with which to make attractive acquisitions, and lower interest rates were all factors in driving the REIT bull market of 1991 to 1993.

Between January 1991 and the end of 1993, the Federal Reserve Board incrementally lowered interest rates in an effort to ease what had become a shallow but long recession. In January 1991, the yield on three-month Treasury bills was 6.2 percent. By the end of 1993, it had fallen to 3.1 percent. REIT stocks, bearing substantial dividend yields and ramping up earnings growth, presented an irresistible lure to investors, who renewed their romance with them.

The Great 1993 to 1994 REIT IPO Boom

The REIT industry was transformed by a tremendous boom in REIT initial public offerings (IPOs) that began in 1993. That year, according to NAREIT, 100 REIT equity offerings were completed, raising $13.2 billion, including $9.3 billion by 50 new REITs and $3.9 billion by 50 existing REITs. An additional $11.1 billion was raised in 1994, including 45 new REIT IPOs raising $7.2 billion and 52 follow-on offerings by existing REITs raising $3.9 billion. The amount raised in 1993 alone surpassed the total amount of equity that REITs had raised during the previous 13 years, according to Merrill Lynch's August 1994 report, *Sizing Up the Equity REIT Industry.*

At the end of 1990, the estimated market capitalization of all publicly traded equity REITs was $5.6 billion. By the end of 1994, it exceeded $38.8 billion, thanks primarily to the REIT offering boom of 1993 and 1994. The level of activity abated in 1995, as $8.2 billion in fresh equity was raised; there were only eight IPOs, garnering just $900 million.

TIP

Although the REIT bull market took a breather in 1994, the IPO boom of the early 1990s had a revolutionary effect on the REIT world: it was largely responsible for a huge increase in the number of REITs and property sectors in which investors could participate.

Unlike many IPO frenzies that bring small speculative companies public from time to time, the REIT IPO boom brought to public investors some of the most solid and well-respected real estate organizations in the United States, including, to name just a few, Developers Diversified, Duke Realty, General Growth Properties, Kimco Realty, Post Properties, Simon Property Group, and Taubman Centers. Furthermore, the number of property sectors available to REIT investors expanded widely. As a result of the success of these IPOs, these new sectors now included regional malls, outlet centers, industrial properties, manufactured home communities, self-storage properties, and hotels, all in addition to previously available property types such as apartments, neighborhood shopping centers, and health care properties.

Why many of these companies went public has been the subject of much discussion. The cynics claim that, at many companies, insiders were taking the opportunity to cash out of some of their ownership interests at high prices at the expense of their new public shareholders. Although this claim undoubtedly had merit in some cases, there are more substantial reasons to explain the phenomenon. In the early 1990s, the banks and savings-and-loan institutions had been so badly burned by nonperforming loans resulting from the real estate depression that they stopped providing the kind of real estate financing they had once routinely given. Cut off from their historical sources of private capital, many of these real estate companies had good reason—some were forced—to seek access to *public* capital. Such public capital would provide substantially greater financing flexibility.

In addition, there was a growing perception in the minds of many management teams that the "securitization" of real estate through REITs was becoming a major new trend and would help them to become stronger and more competitive organizations. Another reason might have been the founders' desire to transform illiquid partnership ownership interests into publicly traded shares that could, from time to time, be more easily sold to diversify their investments, or used for estate planning purposes. In this respect, these new REITs were not any different from other thriving enterprises that go public as a way of solving financing, liquidity, and estate tax issues.

Many of the new REITs that were formed and went public during this era were taken over by, or have merged with, other REITs, while a few have been bought out by private companies or institutional investors. Although there have been mediocre performers among them, a large number of this new generation of REITs can make a legitimate claim to being outstanding real estate companies that should provide investors with excellent returns well into the future.

1995 to 2000: Supply/Demand Issues and the "Great Pie-Eating Contest"

Even before the end of the IPO boom of 1993 and 1994, the prices of many REIT stocks had cooled off considerably; REITs' average total return in 1994 was just 3.2 percent, and by the end of 1995 many, particularly in the apartment and retail sectors, were trading at prices well below their 1993 highs.

Nevertheless, the enthusiasm for REIT shares that was reflected in the IPO boom soon enjoyed a resurgence, and the shares delivered a very impressive 15.3 percent average total return in 1995. This was followed by a blowout year for REIT investors, as the stocks delivered an average total return of 35.3 percent in 1996. The next year, 1997, was almost as good; REITs scored a total return of 20.3 percent.

It's never easy to explain stock performance, even with hindsight, and looking for logic in relatively short-term stock market movements is often as productive as searching for a cuddly Tasmanian devil. Nevertheless, it's my view that the shares did so well from 1995 through 1997 for several reasons:

The stocks were cheap at the end of 1994; in November 1994, Green Street Advisors estimated that the REIT stocks in their coverage universe were trading at a free cash flow yield, based on forward-looking 1995 estimates, of 9.7 percent. The modest bond yields in those years and relatively strong performance by the broad equities markets made REIT stocks look inexpensive when compared with these other investments. Also, investors were anticipating well-above-average cash flow and dividend growth rates due to a target-rich acquisition environment, along with greater access to capital. It is also possible that they were expecting substantial appreciation in commercial real estate prices, perhaps due to milder real estate cycles, lower inflation and interest rates, and stronger property performance. Yet another reason might have been new interest from institutional investors due to greater REIT share liquidity and the huge expansion of REIT investment choices.

But the market often becomes excessively exuberant, which occurred at the end of the 1995 to 1997 period. A vicious bear market surfaced in 1998 and 1999, taking REIT stocks down 17.5 percent and 4.6 percent, (dis)respectively, on a total return basis, in those two years. Price-only declines were much greater. This was the first time since 1973 and 1974 that REIT investors suffered two consecutive down years. Even though this debacle occurred over a decade ago, let's explore what happened, as it may be helpful to today's investors. There were several culprits worthy of blame.

Lots of money was placed in REIT shares in 1996 and 1997 by investors and speculators, who hopped on board the "REIT express" simply because the shares were performing well. In this regard, the mid-1990s may have been the first time that REITs became a trading vehicle and thus perhaps was the precursor to the heightened volatility in REIT stocks that was to become so evident from 2007 to 2010. Near the end of 1997, when it appeared that the party was over, many of these new REIT investors exited in a hurry and hastened the drop in REIT share prices. Where did they go? It was not possible for even the most aggressive REITs to grow at the rates of bold new "dot-com" organizations and the tech companies that supplied them with infrastructure. Many who were speculating in REIT shares therefore cashed in their chips and moved them down the road to Casino Dot-com.

In addition to the evaporation of demand for REIT shares, there was a supply issue. According to NAREIT statistics, there were 318 equity offerings in 1997, raising a total of $32.7 billion; of these, only 26 were IPOs (raising $6.3 billion). Although the REIT bull market topped out in late 1997, a slew of offerings almost as large as in 1997 was completed in 1998, most of them early in the year. By the end of that year, REITs had raised an additional $21.5 billion in fresh equity via 314 offerings, of which 17 were IPOs. The total raised in both years—$54.2 billion—amounted to 69 percent of the equity market capitalization of all equity REITs at the end of 1996 ($78.3 billion).

 TIP

When the supply of anything greatly exceeds demand, prices fall; REIT shareholders learned that lesson in economics in 1998 and 1999.

Aside from those technical—but very important—supply-and-demand issues, investors overestimated REITs' ability to grow cash flows and, perhaps, were focusing on the wrong investment criteria. The buzzwords of 1996 and 1997 were *new era, thinking out of the box*, and *acquisition pipeline*, suggesting that many REITs would no longer be limited to their traditional growth rates of 4 or 5 percent annually. In their quest for rapid earnings growth, many REITs (and earnings-centric investors) were forgetting that value creation is much more important to long-term investment value, particularly if earnings growth is "bought" by the deployment of additional debt financing.

Late in 1997, many began to wonder whether REITs' huge acquisition volumes, funded by all that capital raising, were really doing anything other than expanding the size of their organizations. Were those acquisitions going to produce investment returns in excess of the REITs' cost of capital? Those who were skeptical began to call the REITs' acquisition spree the "Great REIT Pie-Eating Contest." As suggested above, growth in REIT cash flows can be "purchased" through deployment of cash raised from debt and equity sales, but no real value is created unless investment returns exceed the cost of that new capital. We'll spend more time on this crucial concept in Chapter 7. Meanwhile, some lessons learned from the REITs' 1998 and 1999 bear market are encapsulated in the following box.

Lessons from the 1998 and 1999 Bear Market

THE 1998 and 1999 REIT bear market was traumatic; for the first time since 1974 to 1975, equity REITs suffered two consecutive years of negative returns. Excluding dividends, REIT shares dropped 22.3 percent in 1998 and an additional 12.2 percent in 1999. In the preceding text, I have attempted to explain why the REIT bear market occurred. The philosopher and poet George Santayana once suggested, "Those who cannot remember the past are condemned to repeat it." So perhaps considering a few lessons might be helpful. Here are four of them:

1. A few months before the bear market began, in October 1997, the typical REIT stock traded at a 30 percent premium over estimated net asset value (NAV). Because REITs must pay out most of their earnings in the form of shareholder dividends and thus cannot retain more than a small portion of their earnings, and due to the capital-intensive (and often even commodity-like) nature of commercial real estate, very few REIT organizations are able to consistently grow their profits at very high rates. **Lesson: Investors should be reluctant to pay large NAV premiums for the shares of even the very best and fastest-growing REIT organizations**.

2. Hordes of new investors, both individual and institutional, embraced REIT investing in 1996 and 1997, creating unprecedented demand for additional REIT shares. This demand was satisfied primarily in the form of REIT secondary offerings. But a large number of these new investors were buying REIT shares only because they were rising—"momentum investing" was very popular in the latter part of the 1990s—and they exited quickly when the shares flattened out. **Lesson: Although REIT stocks are all about real estate, and their long-term returns will thus be very dependent on the profitability and values of quality commercial real estate, they are equities as well, and thus subject to the shifting fashions and investment styles that blow across the investment world from time to time—their popularity will ebb and flow. Corollary Lesson: Expect REIT prices to remain more volatile, over the short and medium term, than directly owned real estate**.

3. Many REITs bought huge amounts of real estate assets and expanded into many new markets as a result of the easy availability of equity capital from 1996 through early 1998, but these REITs frequently did not get bargain prices, nor did they bring anything to the table in their new markets. The decline in REIT shares during the bear market can be partially attributable to investors' disappointment with the REITs' prospective returns on these new investments. **Lesson: REIT organizations must generate investment returns**

(Continued)

that meet or exceed their long-term cost of capital, and understand that capital deployment decisions are among the most important that the REIT can make.

4. A number of well-regarded REIT organizations pursued some very aggressive acquisition strategies from 1995 through 1997, often making extensive use of short-term debt and exotic hedging techniques such as forward equity transactions. These REITs, which had been very popular with investors due to their high growth rates, became overextended and found themselves having to issue new equity at discounted prices in order to pay maturing debt. **Lesson: Conservative REIT investors should understand the risks of aggressive external growth strategies, particularly when short-term debt is used to finance long-term assets such as real estate. A sound and conservative balance sheet reduces risk. This lesson was apparently not learned very well, and came back to haunt a number of REITs and their investors in the 2007 to 2009 bear market.**

2000 to 2007: Credibility and Market Acceptance

Eventually, as a result of the deep and painful 1998 and 1999 bear market, REIT prices became extraordinarily cheap, in many cases trading at discounts of 20 to 25 percent below their estimated NAVs. Meanwhile, real estate markets were holding up well during that time-frame, as occupancy and rental rates moved higher in response to the strong economy, boosting REITs' FFO growth and asset values. Against this backdrop, dot-com and technology stocks had become exceedingly expensive, and were topping out; indeed, March 2000 was to be the high-water mark for the Nasdaq and most tech, dot-com, and telecommunications stocks. Value investing was about to become popular again, and REITs were quintessential values as the New Millennium dawned. Beginning in early 2000, REIT shares launched a major bull market that continued almost unabated until February 2007. Investment returns for equity REITs, including dividends, in the years 2000 through 2006, as reported by NAREIT, ranged from a high of 37.1 percent in 2003 to a low of 3.8 percent in 2002, and only in 2002 did REIT investment returns fail to reach the double digits.

Before looking for an explanation for such strong performance, it may be helpful to note that REIT stocks performed well even during 2001 through 2004, when most commercial real estate space markets struggled in response to the recession years of 2000 and 2001. Retail real estate was stable, but apartment owners, due to rising unemployment and the increasing popularity of single-family homes, were hit hard. Office owners suffered from substantial reductions in hiring and space needs by most U.S. businesses following the boom times of the late 1990s.

As a result, rents and occupancy rates in most commercial real estate sectors tumbled, and net operating income for most commercial property owners declined—in some cases significantly. Average apartment vacancy rates rose from 3 percent in 2000 to a peak of 6.8 percent in late 2003 and early 2004, and comparable community net operating income was negative from 2001 to 2004. Conditions were no better in the office sector, as same-property net operating income turned negative in 2002, worsened substantially in 2003, and remained weak, although improving, in 2004.

And yet, as noted above, REIT stocks performed very well during this time period, especially in 2003 and 2004; in each of those years, total returns exceeded 30 percent. Were investors just not paying attention? Did they simply fail to notice that, for most REITs, FFO growth was negative and dividend coverage was becoming very tight due to these challenging real estate markets?

Not at all. Students of the stock market know that stock prices do not necessarily correspond to current economic or business conditions, or even to the operating results of individual companies. Markets are often driven by factors that sometimes have little to do with near-term profits, and this phenomenon applies not only to REIT stocks, but also to commercial real estate generally. Let's speculate a bit on the causes for the apparent "disconnect" between REIT stock prices and real estate market conditions during that time frame.

I suspect that the fact that REIT stocks began their bull market in March 2000, the very month in which technology stocks peaked, was no coincidence. Indeed, 2000 marked the beginning of a period during which investing for current yield became very popular. This may have been a reaction to the horrendous investment losses in tech, telecom, and dot-com stocks, causing growth stocks to go out of fashion, or it may have been due to a "back to basics" philosophy in which investors wanted to be paid a substantial portion of their total return expectations in the form of current income.

In any event, REIT stocks, bearing some of the highest dividend yields in the equities markets (at the end of January 2000, the dividend yield on Simon Property Group's shares was 8.2 percent), certainly benefited from this trend.

As we have seen again, most recently in 2010, investors periodically shift their dollars into higher-yielding investments, and when that occurs, REIT stocks often benefit. Although it would be presumptuous to claim that there has been a secular shift in investor preferences toward such investments, it is certainly possible that such a shift is occurring. The large Baby Boomer cohort is approaching retirement age and may prefer to have a substantial portion of their retirement needs funded from current cash flows (in the form of dividend payments). And pension funds and other institutional investors are increasingly facing a similar problem, for instance, paying for pensions and other obligations to growing numbers of retirees. Capital gains in the stock market can't always be counted on, and so current income, either from real estate cash flows or REIT dividend payments, may become more highly valued in the future than in the past.

A related factor is that many of the REITs' investment attributes beyond substantial dividend yields also became popular during the 2000 to early 2007 time period. REIT stocks' movements haven't had high correlations with other asset classes, and these relatively low correlations probably attracted new investors who wanted to smooth out the fluctuations in their diversified investment portfolios. REIT cash flows, during most periods, are stable and predictable, and this attribute also may have found new favor with investors who became shell-shocked by negative "earnings surprises" and the market's oft-draconian reaction to them.

It is also likely, particularly from 2003 to early 2007, that investors were beginning to believe that commercial real estate markets were becoming more stable. Real estate market information has become more available and transparent, thanks to the Internet and the extensive compilation of property information, and this may have convinced investors that the risk of periods of excessive development has lessened. Financing for such assets, thanks to the burgeoning commercial mortgage-backed securities (CMBS) market in the middle years of the last decade (and prior to its collapse in 2008), was perceived as being much more available and efficient.

These factors may have been instrumental in causing risk perception to abate, commercial real estate prices to rise, and market cap rates to decline, all of which contributed to strong REIT stock performance until the bull market topped out in early 2007. Thus, a substantial portion of REIT stocks' superior performance during this time period was probably due to investors' beefing up their real estate/REIT allocations.

Investors also may have noticed that most REIT executives did a superior job of managing their companies throughout the downturn in real estate markets during the 2000 to 2001 recession. They also deployed their capital reasonably well, maintained investment discipline, and improved financial disclosure and corporate governance practices. Many were also selling assets as commercial real estate prices moved relentlessly higher until the market peaked in mid-2007. These enhancements in credibility, together with increased liquidity in REITs' shares, could have been a material contribution to rising REIT stock prices during this period.

It's also important to note that much of the rise in REIT stock prices during the 2003 to 2006 time frame was merely reflective of higher valuations for commercial real estate generally. We can expect that REIT stock prices will continue to be very sensitive to price changes in the vast commercial real estate markets, although the former have historically "led" the latter. According to Meredith Despins, Vice President of Investment Affairs and Investor Education at NAREIT (and as quoted in the *Financial Professionals' Post*, dated March 17, 2010), "Returns in the private real estate market lag behind returns in the publicly traded REIT market by an average of 15 to 18 months, although the lag is not constant at all phases of the market cycle."

2007 through 2010: REITs Survive the Great Recession

On February 7, 2007, REIT stocks had ascended to levels never previously experienced. That was the good news. The bad news was that the most horrendous bear market ever for REIT shares was about to unfold. The MCSI US REIT index (a price-only index) reached a closing high of 1233.66 on that date, and the ensuing bear market didn't end until REIT shares bottomed out on March 6, 2009, at 287.87. The mind-numbing peak-to-trough decline exceeded 76 percent in just over two years. REIT investors had never experienced anything like it. Some even worried about the very survival of the REIT industry, particularly when one of the largest and most widely respected REITs, General Growth Properties, filed for bankruptcy protection on April 16, 2009. Ironically, however, REIT stocks had already bottomed by then, and over the next 24 months they slowly recovered much of their bear market losses.

Much of the blame for this shocking bear market can be attributed to a "perfect storm," as almost everything that could go wrong with the U.S. economy, its space markets, and its credit markets did go wrong. Furthermore, commercial real estate was richly priced in 2007, a fact reflected in the prices of REIT shares. Some argue that the shares were in a "bubble" at that time; perhaps they were, but it is my belief that, as was true of all asset classes, they simply were priced as if global economies and space markets would continue to expand, with low inflation, and that nothing would go wrong.

But things *did* go wrong—and all at the same time! Stoked by ever-increasing problems in the housing market, and the discovery that the major U.S. investment banks had bet the ranch on derivative securities whose values were highly dependent on housing prices remaining stable and home mortgage default rates remaining low, credit markets began to quickly unravel. Thus began a run on the investment banks who were highly exposed to gigantic investment losses; Bear Stearns's collapse in the spring of 2008 was just the tip of the iceberg. By September 2008, Lehman Brothers had filed for bankruptcy, Merrill Lynch had to sell itself to Bank of America, and American International Group was on the verge of ruin. The net result was that credit was no longer available, the CMBS market—so important for commercial real estate financing—collapsed, Congress and the Fed concluded that they had to inoculate the large banks against failure through federal programs such as the Troubled Asset Relief Program (TARP), and a deep recession spread throughout the U.S. economy and its real estate markets.

As a result, commercial real estate prices, reflecting nonfunctioning credit markets and the expectation of rapidly rising vacancy rates and falling rents, began to plummet. But as credit markets were barely functioning and buyers had become exceedingly risk-averse, nobody really knew what commercial properties were worth. Eventually, liquidity improved and buyers began to emerge, beginning in late 2009 and into 2010. But commercial real estate prices were hit hard, as cap rates spiked. Green Street Advisors' Commercial Property Price Index reflects that firm's analysis that commercial real estate prices peaked in August 2007, and bottomed in May 2009 at a loss of 38 percent; Moody's Commercial Property Price Index (CPPI) declined 43 percent from peak to trough (and, as of February 2011, Moody's acknowledged a price rebound of only 0.8% off the cyclical low). CB Richard Ellis states that commercial real estate prices fell back to 2003 levels before bottoming. The declines in REITs' NAVs were, in most cases, even greater than the price declines in the private real estate markets, as REITs carry debt on their balance sheets—this debt magnifies declines in their property values.

And, of course, the Great Recession hammered space markets throughout the United States, as vacancy rates rose in virtually every sector. For example, Reis reported a Q3 2010 average national office vacancy rate of 17.5 percent, a 17-year high, and CB Richard Ellis, at approximately the same time, reported an industrial property availability rate of 14.1 percent, the highest since 1989. Markets began to stabilize in 2010, but the damage was substantial. As REIT stocks have been early indicators of pricing and operating trends in commercial real estate markets, it's not surprising that REIT shares began to weaken in early 2007.

REIT investors had to contend with yet another issue. REIT organizations, like most property owners, have always used debt to buy and finance their properties; while this magnifies risk as well as reward, debt leverage levels were not at worrisome levels (based on traditional yardsticks) as we headed into the 2007 downturn. With only a few exceptions, such as General Growth Properties, debt maturities were deemed manageable. As noted in a *REIT Portfolio* article, "How Will REITs Fare" (November/December 2008), REIT leverage ratios were then at levels close to those of 2003. At about 45 percent, this was consistent with recent norms, and within investors' comfort levels. However, ratios of debt to earnings before interest, taxes, depreciation, and amortization (EBITDA) had risen—perhaps a warning sign.

But previously acceptable leverage ratios are irrelevant during those rare times when commercial real estate prices are dropping like leaves in an early fall Nor'easter. When debt is compared with the value of the properties owned, and the latter declines by 40 percent, leverage ratios can become worrisome indeed. Owing $500,000 on a $1 million property is just 50 percent leverage. But if the value of that property falls to $600,000, the leverage ratio mushrooms to over 83 percent. This became a big problem for REIT organizations in 2008 and well into 2009, as it was quite unclear at that time whether the REITs' lenders would be willing to refinance debt when it was to come due over the next few years. Some REITs were being valued during that time period as though their very survival was in question.

There wasn't much the REITs could do about falling property prices or declining rent and occupancy rates, but they could certainly improve their balance sheets by reducing debt leverage. And so they did. They raised equity, sold or joint-ventured assets, addressed near-term debt maturities, reduced dividends (and/or paid them in shares, as noted later in this section), and otherwise preserved cash. The specific strategies used differed among REITs.

Beginning in mid-March of 2009, REITs began to raise large amounts of equity capital, led by Simon Property, Alexandria Real Estate, and AMB Property. These early stock offerings were done at low prices, and were generally dilutive to both NAVs and per-share cash flows; however, when the stocks traded well following these offerings—and confounded the bears, who expected dilutive death spirals—more REITs raised equity capital. By the end of 2009, 87 REIT secondary offerings were completed, raising $11.75 billion (per NAREIT data), and the REITs used almost all of it to reduce debt. Many REITs also disposed of assets to reduce debt leverage, either selling them outright or contributing them to new or existing joint ventures with institutional partners (a good example was Macerich, which found substantial institutional interest in its quality mall assets).

Debt was paid down to reduce overall leverage ratios, and debt maturing within one to three years was specifically addressed. Credit agreements were amended, unencumbered assets were mortgaged, and existing secured debt was refinanced—all to extend average debt maturities and to fund near-term maturities. This wasn't an easy task when lenders were so tight-fisted and nobody knew the value of commercial real estate, but most REIT organizations were strong enough, often benefiting from excellent long-term relationships with various lenders, to get it done. The terms of these early refinancings were almost such as to make a pawnbroker blush; for example, Simon Property, one of the most highly regarded REITs, had to pay 10.75 percent (including a substantial original issue discount) on new 10-year senior unsecured notes issued in March 2009; fortunately, later refinancings were done at much better terms as lending spreads over Treasury notes eventually narrowed.

Another strategy employed by many REITs, painful but necessary, related to the common stock dividend. According to SNL Financial, 35, 56, and 7 REITs cut or suspended their dividends in 2008, 2009, and 2010, respectively. Most of these actions were necessitated by sudden and substantial declines in free cash flow resulting from recession-induced contractions in property cash flows and per-share cash flow dilution caused by issuances of additional equity. In many cases, for example, Simon Property, REITs cut their dividends by substantially more than was absolutely required, due to an abundance of caution and to build a "war chest" to fund property acquisitions if the carnage in much of the commercial real estate markets would provide extraordinary buying opportunities.

Of course, some REITs didn't cut or suspend dividends at all. But, industry-wide, the dividend cutting was painful. In January 2011, a friend of mine (and fellow REIT investor) did an informal study of REIT dividend cuts and concluded that the median ratio of current dividend rates (in January 2011) to their previous peak dividend rates was 61.9 percent; and, he points out, at an assumed

Thoughts from Moody's

"REIT stocks are ahead of the underlying property market fundamentals, having done the "right" things in 2009 and 2010 (i.e., focused on internal growth), sold noncore assets, issued unsecured debt ($19.5 billion) and equity ($26.8 billion), and refinanced [and] joint-ventured, with some paying dividends with stock vs. cash."

—Merrie Frankel, Vice President and Senior Credit Officer, Commercial Real Estate Finance Group, Moody's Investors Services (quote from the May 2010 session of Hoyt Fellows–Weimer School of Advanced Studies in Real Estate and Land Economics).

5 percent growth rate, it would take 10 years just to get back to the high dividend water mark of 2006 and 2007.

In some cases, REITs took advantage of IRS Revenue Procedure 2008-68, issued in December 2008, which enabled them to pay their dividends partially in stock if certain conditions were met. This practice, although unpopular with many investors, preserved cash for debt reduction and delevering. By the end of 2010, only a handful of REITs were paying their dividends partially in stock.

Despite the huge and painful decline in REIT shares during the years of 2007 and 2008, they rebounded sharply in 2009 and 2010. And we should put that late bear market in perspective. REIT shares have certainly performed well over every reasonably long time period, as evidenced by the chart in Figure 6.4 covering the period 1990 through 2010.

Observations

Please permit me a few personal observations as an investor who was fighting bravely in the trenches during the chaotic and worrisome time period of 2007 through early 2009:

- REITs' equity raises in 2009, in particular, were painful but absolutely the right strategy for the times. The deployment of

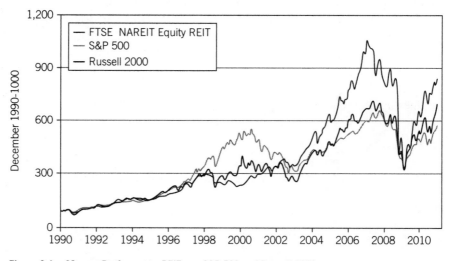

Figure 6.4   20-year Performance REITs vs. S&P 500 and Russell 2000
Source: NAREIT, *REITWatch,* January 2011.

this strategy, at a time when many private investors could not refinance their property loans, also proved the value of being a publicly traded REIT with so many sources of capital.

- The actions taken during the crisis also showed that REIT boards of directors and management teams have matured significantly since their early days and were willing to make hard but necessary choices.

- REITs' earnings are more stable and predictable than the earnings of most companies, protected as they are, in most cases, by multiyear leases, but real estate space markets have always been cyclical, and particularly violent cycles can negatively impact cash flows and even force dividend cuts.

- Debt has, perhaps since the Renaissance, been used to buy and own real state, but a long-term issue is whether real estate investors have been using too much of it. Mike Kirby, of Green Street Advisors, has studied this issue, and concluded that the positive impact of debt leverage in rising markets is not as conducive to growing cash flows as most have believed, and doesn't think that the use of debt creates any real benefits for REIT investors. Although moderate amounts of debt don't create unacceptable risks for REIT investors during the vast majority of the time, we never know when those "black swans" will fly into town. Most real estate owners continue to believe that they benefit from modest amounts of debt leverage; however, do these benefits offset the huge risks that arise when credit markets occasionally seize up? I am not sure; perhaps not. We'll talk more about debt in Chapter 8.

Some Lessons Learned

As suggested earlier in this chapter, in every crisis there is a learning opportunity. What lessons can we learn from the crisis encountered by REIT organizations and their investors during the 2007 to 2010 time period? Here are a few of them:

- Commercial real estate, as an asset class, is no longer priced on the basis of its own unique characteristics. It's now a widely recognized investment choice and will be priced to deliver satisfactory risk-adjusted returns relative to other asset classes such as stocks and bonds, as well as shifting levels of risk aversion.

Accordingly, its pricing will be more volatile than in the past. And because commercial real estate pricing is such a large driver of REIT share prices, which tend to adjust earlier and at a quicker pace, REIT stocks will be more volatile than they were during most of their history. We must learn to live with this. And we should never forget that real estate is a cyclical industry, although some cycles are more violent than others.

- Debt leverage and debt maturity schedules don't matter too much when economies are growing and credit flows freely. But we never know when some unforeseen event will suddenly arise and derail all preexisting assumptions. When that occurs—and it may occur more often—a REIT's balance sheet really matters. It matters a lot. Thus, a key component of a REIT stock's fair value should be its balance sheet. "Fat tails" *do* exist, and low debt levels will minimize their draconian effects.

- In 1995 to 1998, and again in 2004 to 2007, many REITs developed real estate–related businesses to generate above-average profit growth. Investors, quite reasonably, rewarded them with higher stock valuations; innovation with modest risk is often a good thing. But investors shouldn't assume that these businesses will always grow; they should value them conservatively, and perhaps sell any REIT whose management team is wearing rose-colored glasses, or if investors are pricing the REIT's shares as if its nonrental cash flows will grow to the sky.

- REIT organizations have survived the Great Recession in reasonably good shape, a tribute to the REIT as an investment vehicle and to REIT management teams. At the end of 2010, REITs were much healthier than their private real estate investment counterparts. The lesson here is that REITs enjoy many desirable investment attributes not available to other real estate investors, including a wide array of financing choices. Thus, REITs remain one of the best—and probably *the* best—way to own commercial real estate.

Recent Trends

Before leaving this chapter on REIT history, REIT share performance, and what drove that performance, let's quickly review some fairly recent trends in REITville.

Size Increases

The typical equity REIT has greatly increased in size (see Figure 6.5). At the end of 1994, there were only four REITs with equity market capitalizations of over $1 billion. Primarily due to a combination of increasing stock prices, merger activity, and equity offerings, there were 83 REITs with equity market caps of more than $1 billion by the end of 2010, and 20 equity REITs had equity market caps exceeding $5 billion. Simon Property Group, with an equity market cap of $29.1 billion as of December 31, 2010, was then the largest REIT. As we saw in Chapter 5, the increased size of the largest REITs, along with an Internal Revenue Service ruling to the effect that REITs are active businesses, led to the decision in October 2001 to include REITs within the S&P 500 index. This event, along with the increased size and liquidity of the entire REIT industry and its long-term performance, has dramatically enhanced REITs' credibility, and has caused many non-REIT equity investment managers to invest in REIT shares as part of their investment portfolios.

Capital Recycling

Capital recycling is another important and fairly recent trend; it began as early as 1998 to 1999 in response to the REITs' bear market at that time. With REITs losing the ability to raise equity capital, they needed a mechanism to take advantage of particularly attractive development—and even acquisition—opportunities. An intelligent method of financing these projects is to sell off portfolio

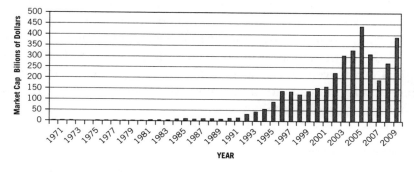

Figure 6.5   REIT Equity Market Cap Growth Over Time
Source: NAREIT *REIT*Watch January 2011.

properties with limited upside, or even to exit entire markets that are viewed as less attractive on a long-term basis, and to use the proceeds, net of debt repayment, to finance the new investments, at—it is hoped—much higher long-term returns than could be generated by the assets sold.

This capital recycling strategy was adopted by a large number of REITs and was a significant departure from the way in which most REITs had done business in the past; indeed, until the late 1990s, selling off any asset was viewed by most REIT executives as tantamount to selling off a firstborn child.

A second, although a bit different, phase of capital recycling occurred more recently. As commercial real estate prices rose rapidly beginning in 2003 and continuing into 2007, some REIT management teams decided—even though they were easily able to access capital for new investments—to sell some of their aggressively priced real estate. They were engaging in a bit of "market timing," believing that commercial real estate valuations had, in some cases, become a bit frothy. And they were right. Condo converters, in their effort to feed the quacking ducks demanding yet more residential property units, were making offers, for example, at 3 percent cap rates, that couldn't be refused, and some apartment REITs were happy to oblige them. It has been estimated by NAREIT (Special Report, May 2010) that REITs were net sellers of $86 billion in assets in 2006 and 2007, a period of peak pricing. Sometimes the capital received from these asset sales wasn't recycled into new acquisitions, and was distributed to shareholders in the form of a special dividend, for example, by Boston Properties in 2006 and 2007.

The significance of REITs' willingness and ability to sell or recycle assets should not be underestimated, as it constitutes part of a new business model by which REIT management teams can create value for their shareholders even without access to fresh equity capital. And, even assuming such access, REIT management teams increasingly understand that equity is precious and is the most expensive form of capital.

Institutional Joint Ventures

Another fairly recent trend, adopted by a number of REIT organizations, is the formation of joint ventures (JVs) with institutional investors to own, acquire, and/or develop investment-grade commercial properties. These JVs can take many forms, including the transfer of mature or recently developed properties to the JV, the acquisition of existing properties, and the development of new ones. These strategies have one thing in common: the opportunity for the REIT to leverage the talent of its in-place management, and sometimes its development expertise, to generate favorable returns on new investments by forming partnerships with institutions that have the capital and the desire to invest alongside the REIT.

These JVs allow the REIT to control more assets (and retain tenant relationships) and to generate somewhat higher returns by collecting management and development fees, often with additional incentive fees for particularly attractive returns to the JV. They can, however, be complex and make projections more difficult for the analyst, and can be destructive of value for the shareholders if not organized and implemented carefully. Furthermore, some investors worry that the REIT may be giving away too much upside, particularly in development projects. But if the JV is structured properly, the interests of the REIT and the institutional investor are properly aligned, there is sufficient incentive for the REIT to engage in the targeted activity, the debt incurred by the JV is not excessive in relationship to the REIT's own debt, there is a logical and mutually acceptable exit strategy, and there is a good working relationship on both sides, then the JV concept can be used effectively to create additional income streams and more value for the REIT's shareholders. JVs have been implemented successfully by a number of REITs, including AMB Properties, Developers Diversified, Kimco, Macerich, ProLogis, and Regency Centers, among many others.

Other—But Possibly Transitory—Recent Trends

I believe that the foregoing trends, for instance, the increasing size of many REITs, capital recycling, and JV strategies, will continue well into the future; they have benefited, and will continue to benefit, REIT shareholders. There have, however, been a few other REIT industry developments in recent years; we have not seen them since 2007, but they may eventually return. I'll mention them briefly.

REITs don't often acquire other REITs, but there have been times when merger-and-acquisition (M&A) activity has been substantial.

A number of these transactions occurred in 1996 and 1997, as rising stock prices provided acquiring REITs with cheap currency. Many more public-to-public mergers were completed from 1998 through 2000. Due to this merger wave, the number of equity REITs declined from 178 at the end of 1995 to 151 at the end of 2001, while the acquiring REITs grew larger in size. The number of such mergers has declined substantially over the past few years, but they may increase again; we'll discuss the likelihood of future REIT mergers in Chapter 13.

A phenomenon witnessed fairly recently—although not seen since the Great Recession—was a "going private" craze. In 2005 and 2006, according to *ChicagoBusiness*, 21 REITs were acquired by private commercial real estate investors and other private equity firms, for an aggregate of approximately $78 billion. This mini-trend was likely due to the rapid rise in commercial real estate valuations from 2004 through 2006, an event that, according to the acquirers' logic, wasn't reflected in REIT stock prices. The largest going-private transaction was Blackstone Group's February 2007 acquisition of Equity Office Properties, the largest REIT at the time, for $39 billion, including assumed debt. Many of these deals were highly levered with debt and ended badly with the collapse of real estate values as a result of the Great Recession. Although these types of deals were almost nonexistent in 2009 and 2010, they may return under the right—or, depending on one's perspective, the wrong—circumstances.

Another phenomenon that was popular in REIT world a little over 10 years ago was stock buybacks. Although long a staple of the public equities world, REITs don't ordinarily repurchase their own shares. REITs are capital intensive and must pay, as dividends, at least 90 percent of their pretax earnings each year; indeed, REITs are much more likely to *sell* new shares to raise capital than to *buy* them in. Nevertheless, stock repurchases can create value for shareholders if done at very attractive prices. According to a Merrill Lynch report at the time, from the beginning of 1998 through the end of 2000—during most of which time REIT stocks were experiencing a bear market—48 REITs announced stock buyback programs, and $4.1 billion in shares were repurchased. Although buybacks haven't been a focus of REIT management teams in recent years, investors shouldn't be surprised to see more of them—

at least among the well-capitalized REITs—the next time REIT stocks become unpopular and trade at prices significantly below their estimated net asset values.

Summary

- The first REITs, born in the early 1960s, ranged in size from about $10 million to $50 million; their property management functions were handled by outside management companies; and their combined assets were only about $200 million.
- As a result of their negative experience with mortgage REITs, investors of the 1970s became disenchanted with the entire REIT industry.
- During the 1980s, when investors were seeking the tax shelters offered by limited partnerships, real estate prices became inflated; this limited REITs' ability to grow through attractive acquisitions.
- REITs' performance improved substantially in the early 1990s as they were able to pick up properties at bargain prices resulting from the bear market in real estate that began in the late 1980s.
- The REIT IPO boom of the early 1990s had a revolutionary effect on the REIT world: it was largely responsible for a huge increase in the number of REITs and property sectors in which investors could participate.
- In 1996 and 1997, institutional money managers started to invest in REITs, and the trend of public securitization of real estate had become indelibly established.
- REIT investors suffered through a two-year bear market in 1998 and 1999, caused by excessive equity issuances, questionable allocations of capital, and the desertion of investors seeking more rapid capital appreciation in tech stocks—but the bull market returned with a vengeance in 2000 despite weak real estate "space" markets.
- REIT stocks performed quite well from 2000 through early 2007, driven by value- and income-oriented investors, and by rapidly rising commercial real estate prices.
- A devastating bear market trashed REIT shares, beginning in February 2007 and ending in early 2009, brought about

by the Great Recession, frozen capital markets, falling real estate prices, and weakening space markets—and even concerns about REITs' ability to pay or refinance their debt obligations.

- REITs responded quickly to the Great Recession and troubled capital markets, raising equity, selling assets, addressing debt maturities and positioning themselves well for the recovery.
- New trends seen in the REIT industry in recent years include capital recycling and joint venture (and investment management) strategies—which enable REIT management teams to increase shareholder value without raising excessive amounts of equity capital.

PART

III

INVESTING INTELLIGENTLY IN REITs

CHAPTER 7

REITs: Growth and Value Creation

"A public company should invest the money that shareholders trust them with at a spread to its cost of capital ... you really have to look at what your present cash flows are on a property and where you think they'll be over the next 10 years."
—Milton Cooper, Executive Chairman, Kimco Realty

Warren Buffett has famously said, "In the short run, the market is a voting machine, but in the long run it is a weighing machine." I think what he meant by this is that share prices are moved, in the short term, by transient investor psychology and insubstantial news, but over the long term a stock's price is determined by its intrinsic value. Thus, if a stock is to rise in price over time, the company's fundamental value must increase on a per-share basis. There are a number of ways to measure increases in company value, but measuring and valuing streams of income and cash flows is perhaps the most commonly used metric in the world of equities.

There are, of course, other metrics. Although not very popular today, book value has been used by some investors to determine the worth of a stock. But book value is based on historical cost, less depreciation, and thus doesn't reflect the *current* market values of company assets, many of which are worth much more—or less—today. And how can book value help to determine the fair values of intangible assets such as brand names, superior management teams, and customer goodwill? A number of countries outside the United States have adopted *fair value accounting*, which measures real-time estimates of the market value of certain types of assets. But fair value accounting has not yet been adopted in the United States. Accordingly, most investors here have generally continued to value stocks, even the stocks of companies owning commercial real estate, on the basis of net income, along with supplemental measurements such as earnings before interest, taxes, depreciation, and amortization (EBITDA) and, as we'll see shortly, funds from operations (FFO) and adjusted funds from operations (AFFO).

So investors have made earnings a key determinant of a company's share price. In the REIT world, steadily rising earnings normally indicate not only that a REIT is generating higher income from its properties, but may also suggest that it is making favorable acquisitions or completing profitable developments. And higher income is usually a precursor of dividend growth. In short, most REIT investors have assumed that a growing stream of cash flow means, over time, higher share prices, increased dividends, and higher asset values. This assumption is not always valid, however, as growth in income and cash flows can be "bought" through increases in debt leverage, and is sometimes fleeting. Conversely, a REIT can create value for its shareholders by investment activities that aren't immediately reflected in current income or cash flows. However, as income metrics are most easily quantifiable and are used by most equity investors—and remain important—let's consider them first.

The Significance of FFO and AFFO

Investors in common stock generally use net income as a key measure of profitability, but the custom in REIT world is to use FFO. The historical preference for FFO rather than net income relates to the concept of *depreciation*. The Securities and Exchange Commission (SEC), under federal securities laws, requires that all publicly traded companies file audited financial statements. On a financial statement, the term *net income* has a meaning clearly defined under generally accepted accounting principles (GAAP). Since most REITs are publicly traded companies, net income and net income per share can therefore always be found on a REIT's annual audited financial statements, and unaudited net income is reported quarterly.

For a REIT, however, these net income figures are less meaningful as a measure of operating success than they are for other types of companies. The reason for this is that, in accounting, real estate depreciation is always treated as an expense, but in the real world, not only have most properties retained their value over the years (at least those that are well maintained and competitive), but many have appreciated substantially. This is generally due to a combination of rising prices of land (on which the structure is built) due to inflation and increasing construction costs, steadily rising rental and operating income, and property upgrades. Thus, a REIT's net income under GAAP, reflecting a large depreciation expense, has been determined by most REIT investors to be less meaningful a measure of REIT cash flows than FFO, which adds back real estate depreciation under GAAP to net income.

TIP

Using FFO enables both REITs and their investors to analyze cash flows obtained from property ownership, either by looking at net income before the deduction of the depreciation expense or adding back depreciation expense to reported net income.

When calculating FFO, there are other adjustments that should be made as well, such as subtracting from GAAP net income any capital gain income recorded from the sale of properties. The reason for this is that the REIT can't have it both ways: in figuring FFO, it cannot ignore depreciation, which reduces a property's carrying costs on the balance sheet, and then include the capital gain from selling that property above the price at which it has been carried. Furthermore, GAAP net income is normally determined after "straight-lining," or smoothing out, contractual rental income over the term of the lease. This is another accounting convention, but, in real life, rental income on a multiyear property lease is not smoothed out; it will often rise from year to year. For this reason,

Funds from Operations (FFO)

Historically, FFO was defined in different ways by different REITs, which caused investor confusion. To address this problem, the National Association of Real Estate Investment Trusts (NAREIT) has attempted to standardize the definition of FFO. In 1999, it refined its definition of FFO to mean "net income computed in accordance with GAAP, excluding gains (or losses) from sales of property, plus depreciation and amortization, and after adjustments for unconsolidated partnerships and joint ventures. Adjustments for unconsolidated partnerships and joint ventures should be calculated to reflect funds from operations on the same basis."

some investors, when examining FFO, adjust reported rent revenues to reflect the actual contractual rental revenues received during the reporting period. Other investors deal with this issue by eliminating rent straight-lining when calculating AFFO, as we'll discuss later in this section.

Most REITs and their investors believe the concept of FFO is more useful than net income as a device to measure profits; nevertheless, although used almost universally in REIT world, there are a number of problems with it. For one thing, commercial properties can, in fact, slowly decline in value year after year, due to wear and obsolescence. Owners will have to invest in occasional improvements and structural replacements if a property's value is to be retained (e.g., a new roof or better lighting). Merely adding back depreciation, then, to net income, when determining FFO, can provide a distorted and overly rosy picture of operating results and cash flows; it fails to account for these major—but recurring—capital expenditures.

Also, items that investors should consider part of ordinary property maintenance, for example, an apartment building's carpeting, curtains, and dishwashers, are usually capitalized and depreciated, rather than expensed, for accounting purposes. But as the depreciation expense for these items is ignored when FFO is determined, FFO will be artificially inflated, giving a misleading picture of a REIT's real cash flow. Practically speaking, carpeting and related items, to use our example, really *do* depreciate over time, and the costs to replace them are real and recurring expenses.

Additionally, commissions paid to leasing agents when renting offices or other properties are usually capitalized, then amortized and written off over the term of the lease. But paying leasing commissions, while perhaps helping to stabilize or improve occupancy and thus supporting an owner's cash flow over the term of a lease, doesn't add anything to the property's value. Indeed, it is a *real* expense and, when ignored in the calculation of FFO, will overstate profits and cash flows. The same also can be said about tenant improvement allowances, such as those provided to office and retail tenants. These are owners' out-of-pocket costs and are often so specific to the needs of a particular tenant that they do not increase the long-term value of the property.

TIP

Many expenditures that are capitalized cannot be considered property enhancing, no matter how they are accounted for, and they should be subtracted from FFO to give an accurate picture of a REIT's operating cash flows.

Finally, despite NAREIT's efforts to standardize FFO, not all REITs capitalize and expense similar items in similar ways when their FFOs are reported each quarter. Some ignore noncash investment write-offs, for example, while others do not. Some REITs even include certain property sale gains in FFO. Simply put, there is a lack of consistency in FFO reporting.

But all is not lost. The concept of *adjusted funds from operations* (AFFO), which was coined many years ago by Green Street Advisors, Inc., a leading REIT research firm, can help to remedy some of the deficiencies of FFO.

Adjusted Funds from Operations (AFFO)

AFFO begins with a REIT's FFO, but is then adjusted for expenditures that, though capitalized, do not enhance the value of a property; it is also adjusted further by eliminating straight-lining of rents.

Although FFO as a measurement tool is more useful to REIT investors than net income under GAAP, a NAREIT white paper has correctly reminded us that FFO was never intended to be used as a measure of the cash generated by a REIT, nor of its dividend-paying capacity. But AFFO *is* a reasonable, albeit imprecise, measure of a REIT's operating performance; it's a fairly effective tool to measure free cash generation and the ability to pay dividends. Unfortunately, AFFO is not regularly reported by REITs due to the lack of one commonly accepted definition, and the investor or analyst must calculate it on his or her own by reviewing the financial statements and related footnotes and schedules. And even when AFFO is disclosed by a REIT, it is frequently calculated differently by each REIT. The following is an oversimplified, but perhaps useful, way of looking at this methodology.

1. All revenues (including capital gains), less operating expenses, write-offs, depreciation, amortization, interest expense and general and administrative expenses = **Net Income**.
2. Net income, less capital gain from real estate sales, plus real estate depreciation expense = **FFO**.
3. FFO, less normal and recurring capital expenditures, amortization of tenant improvements and leasing commissions, and adjusting to remove rent straight-lining and any gain or loss on the early extinguishment of debt = **AFFO**.

In addition, as AFFO is intended to measure current and recurring cash flows, noncash write-downs of property investments due to impairment charges are usually added back when calculating AFFO.

The problems encountered by investors in using FFO and its derivatives were discussed by George L. Yungmann and David M. Taube, Vice President, Financial Standards, and Director, Financial Standards, respectively, of NAREIT, in an article appearing in the May/June 2001 issue of *Real Estate Portfolio*. They note, "A single metric may not appropriately satisfy the need for both a supplemental earnings measure and a cash flow measure." They suggested using a term such as *adjusted net income* (ANI, which is GAAP net income prior to extraordinary items, effects of accounting changes, results of discontinued operations, and other unusual nonrecurring items) as a supplemental earnings measurement. Each REIT would then be free to supplement this ANI figure by reporting a cash flow measure such as FFO, AFFO, or other terms sometimes used by REITs and analysts such as *cash available for distribution* (CAD) or *funds available for distribution* (FAD). This is an interesting concept but, unfortunately, has not received the attention it deserves. Thus, we are left with GAAP net income, FFO and AFFO.

TIP

Although net income should not be ignored, AFFO—when properly calculated—is a reasonably effective tool for approximating a REIT's free cash flow.

Some analysts and investors, when determining AFFO, look at the actual capital expenditures incurred by a REIT during a reporting period, while others apply a long-term average to smooth out periods of unusually high or low capital expenditures. Still others try to determine a "normalized" figure, based on historical experience for the REIT over several years. There is no "right" or "wrong" approach, but it's important for the investor to compare apples to apples.

Now that we have established the differences between these important terms, we will refer to FFO more often than AFFO simply for the sake of convenience and because virtually all REITs report the former and only some report the latter, although FFO will be less meaningful to investors as a tool for tracking free cash flow.

When we discuss price-to-earnings ratios of REITs' shares in a later chapter, we will use either the P/FFO ratio or the P/AFFO ratio. P/FFO figures are simply more commonly used and more uniformly calculated. In any event, we must always be aware of how these supplements to net income reporting under GAAP are calculated by or for each REIT.

The Dynamics of FFO/AFFO Growth

One of the attractive attributes of a REIT, compared with other higher-yielding investments like bonds and preferred stocks, is their significant long-term capital appreciation potential and increasing dividends. If a REIT is viewed as having virtually no capacity to grow its FFO, AFFO, or dividend, its shares would be bought only for yield. Because of the ease with which the dividend can be cut or eliminated, the yields of growth-challenged REIT stocks would normally be higher than those of most bonds and preferred stocks, and their prices might be closely correlated with high-yield (or "junk") bonds.

We can sometimes find REITs that *do* trade as bond surrogates because of investor perception that they have very little growth potential. Some of these "bond proxies" can be of high quality because of the stability of their streams of operating income, while others can be compared to junk bonds because of their high yields but possibly unsustainable free cash flows. These "junk-bond" REITs may be traded, sometimes profitably, by bottom fishers and speculators, but we should understand that there is rarely a free lunch. High yield and high growth are not normally available together in one investment.

Investors looking for the best total returns, combining dividend yield with capital appreciation, will look for REITs whose dividends are not just safe but also have good long-term growth prospects. Wouldn't you rather own a REIT that pays a current return of 4 percent with an average annual growth rate of 5 percent than one that pays 7 percent but doesn't grow at all?

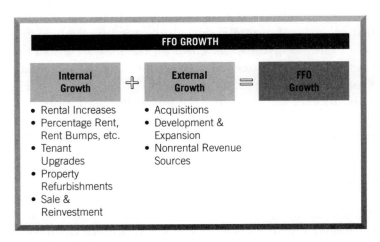

Figure 7.1   FFO Growth Formula

Before REITs had become widely followed, they were often priced so cheaply that it was possible to get the best of both worlds—a 6 percent yield *and* 5 to 6 percent annual growth; according to NAREIT statistics, the 30-year average annual total return for equity REITs, through 2010, was 11.87 percent. But REITs are now priced more efficiently, and today a REIT stock with a 7 percent dividend yield normally suggests that investors perceive very low growth or that the shares are particularly risky.

All right, then, how does a REIT generate growth in FFO and AFFO (collectively referred to in the balance of this chapter, for convenience, as FFO)? What should we look for? First of all, it is essential to look at FFO growth on a per-share basis. It does the shareholder no good if FFO grows rapidly because the REIT has issued large numbers of new shares. Such "prosperity" is meaningless—like a government printing more money in times of inflation. (In the following discussion, let's not forget that REITs must pay their shareholders at least 90 percent of their taxable net income each year, but, as a practical matter, most REITs pay out considerably more than this, as depreciation expense (which is not a cash outlay) is also normally taken into account when setting the dividend rate).

 TIP

FFO can be grown two ways: externally—by acquisitions, developments, and the creation of ancillary revenue streams; and internally—through increasing cash flows from a REIT's existing properties (see Figure 7.1).

REITs cannot retain much of their earnings for reinvestment; thus, if they want to achieve FFO growth through acquisitions or new developments, they will have to find the cash with which to make these investments. Where will it come from? REITs can generate cash from the sale of existing assets; the contribution, for cash, of some of their properties to new joint ventures; and retention of a modest portion of their free cash flows, all of which can be used for new investments. But most of their new capital for expansion comes from selling new shares to investors. And yet, such new equity capital isn't always available—and can, at times, be very expensive in terms of dilution to net asset values (NAVs). The bottom line is that *internal* growth, which can be accomplished without having to raise more equity or to take on additional debt, is very important to a REIT and its shareholders.

REIT investors and analysts need to understand how much of a REIT's growth is being achieved internally and how much is being achieved externally. External growth, through new developments, acquisitions, and the creation of ancillary revenue streams, may not always be possible because of a lack of available, high-quality properties at attractive prices, a scarcity of sufficiently profitable development opportunities, inability to raise capital, or the high cost of such capital. Internal growth, however, because it is "organically" generated through a REIT's existing properties, is more under management's control (though it is subject to real estate market dynamics).

But before we consider in some detail the ways in which REITs can grow FFO, it's important to make a very important point here. Measuring current cash flows, by using FFO or its variants, is an important exercise. But *when valuing REIT stocks*, many successful REIT investors place much less emphasis on measuring cash flow and pay more attention to estimated NAVs, including whether those NAVs have grown and will grow over time—on an absolute basis or in relationship to a REIT's peers in the same property sector. We'll consider the important topic of NAV analysis in some depth in Chapter 9 when we discuss REIT stock valuation; suffice it to say here that a single-minded focus on FFO, to the exclusion of NAVs, may often lead investors astray when valuing REIT stocks.

Internal Growth

When a REIT is able to increase profits from operating and managing its properties, through increased rental revenues (including higher rents and occupancy rates) and keeping expense growth under control, it is enjoying *internal growth*. Controlling corporate overhead expenses and interest expense are also very important; if these nonproperty expenses are rising faster than property net operating income, internal growth will be less than would otherwise be the case. As internal growth rates do not depend on acquisitions, development, or raising additional capital, they tend to be stable and reliable—albeit usually in the low to mid single digits—during most economic environments.

Before we examine the specific sources of REITs' internal growth, however, we should review one of the terms that analysts use in reference to internal growth. The term is *same-store*, or *same-community*, sales or revenues (or a related term, *same-store* or *same-community* net operating income)—a concept borrowed from the retail industry. For retailers, same-store sales refers to sales from stores open for at least one year, and excludes sales from stores that have closed or from new stores, as new stores characteristically enjoy temporarily above-average sales growth.

TIP

Although the term *same-store sales* was originally a retail concept, it and its companion, *same-store net operating income*, have been borrowed for use by REITs to refer to property income generated internally, rather than from new developments or acquisitions.

Let's see how this concept applies to the REIT industry. REITs report to their shareholders, on a quarterly basis, property rental revenues, expenses, and net operating income (NOI). These figures are compared with similar figures for the same period in the prior year, on a same-store—or, more accurately, a same-property—basis. These comparisons are very important and present a good picture of how well the REIT is doing with its owned properties in the recent quarter or year as compared to a previous period. And sometimes a REIT will report same-store revenues and NOI sequentially, for instance, compared with the immediately prior fiscal period.

Property owners, including REITs, use different tools to generate growth on a same-store basis. These tools include rental revenue increases, ancillary property revenues, upgrading the tenant roll, and upgrading—or even expanding—the property. Those REITs that are more aggressive, effective, and creative in their use of these tools are more likely to achieve, over time, higher internal growth rates. Of course, the strategic location of a property, and its location's demographics, are also highly important; a modest property in a great location can be very amenable to upgrading and retenanting, enabling the REIT to enjoy above-average NOI growth for a period of time. Let's now look more closely at some of these tools.

Rental Revenue Increases

TIP

The most obvious type of internal growth, the ability to raise rental rates and revenue, is probably a REIT's most important determinant of internal growth.

Rental rates can be increased over time if a property is desirable to tenants, and higher occupancy rates can lead to even higher rental revenues—high occupancy rates give owners greater negotiating leverage with existing and new tenants. Nevertheless, raising rents is not always possible, and there are periods in virtually every sector's full cycle when such revenues actually fall rather than rise. Anyone who owned office buildings in the early 1990s, in the first few years of the twenty-first century or during the Great Recession knows there's no guarantee that rent can be raised—or even maintained at the same level—when a lease comes up for renewal. Recessions are not friends of property owners. Even if the rent is raised slightly, if the tenant receives huge tenant improvement allowances as an inducement to lease the space, a new lease may not be very profitable. In addition, nominal rent increases received from some tenants can be offset by high vacancy rates, free rent or other rental concessions, and heavy marketing and advertising costs. These problems were faced, most recently, from 2008 to 2010 in virtually all property sectors, when high vacancy rates put existing and new tenants in the driver's seat when negotiating rents on new leases. Many factors, such as supply and demand for a particular property or property sector (including, of course, location and obsolescence), space market conditions generally, the current economic climate, the property's age and condition, and tenant amenities can enhance or restrict rental revenue increases.

Most retail shopping center owners have been able to raise rental rates at a healthy rate, even during the difficult real estate markets of 2001 to 2004, as leases have come up for renewal—despite the ever-present retailer bankruptcies, the challenges from Wal-Mart and others, and the rise of e-commerce. Mall tenants have signed new leases bearing higher rental rates to replace the leases signed during prior years when sales volumes were significantly lower. In the long run, however, rent increases will generally not be able to outpace the rise in tenant sales, as tenant occupancy costs as a percentage of sales have been fairly consistent over the years. Rental rate increases among neighborhood shopping center and outlet center owners have been slightly less favorable, due to the relative ease of entry of new competing centers and the inroads made by Wal-Mart and other large discounters. If the significant slowdown in consumer spending brought on by the Great Recession, high rates of unemployment, and slow consumer income growth continue, it is probable that even mall owners will not be able to increase rents or same-store NOI at the rates they have previously enjoyed.

Supply and demand in the apartment sector often has been in equilibrium. However, poor job growth in the early years of the twenty-first century, coupled with low interest rates that encouraged new construction and stoked demand for single-family housing, put renters in control. Apartment occupancy rates and net operating income declined; however, they started to grow again beginning in the latter part of 2004. The Great Recession and skyrocketing unemployment caused the same type of problem from 2008 to 2010, with a recovery commencing in the middle of 2010. Investors in this sector should expect long-term internal growth roughly in line with, and at times modestly exceeding, the rate of inflation.

Office rents suffered during the period of massive overbuilding in the late 1980s and early 1990s, but the cycle bottomed out earlier than most had anticipated. Rent growth was strong from the mid-1990s through 2000, but then a recession caused rents to decline substantially from 2001 through 2004. Rents rose again nicely from 2005 to 2007, but then declined again for the next few years as a result of waning demand resulting from the Great Recession. Rental growth cycles for industrial properties have been similar but, in most cases, less pronounced.

Self-storage facilities have enjoyed steady rental growth since the early 1990s, although growth slowed substantially from 2001 to

2004. Same-store NOI went negative during the Great Recession. The continuing popularity of these properties, despite rising supply until fairly recently, has enabled self-storage property owners to increase rents frequently; despite a recent slowdown in the pace of rent increases, self-storage property owners should be able to generate respectable same-store NOI growth over time.

The hotel industry is deeply cyclical; like the little boy in that old nursery rhyme, when market conditions are good, hotel owners' profits are very, very good, but when they are bad, room rates, occupancy, and RevPar (revenues per available room) are horrid. Hotel owners have experienced very wide swings in internal growth, which was excellent from 1994 to 2001, and horrendous from 2001 to 2004 (the shrinkage of the travel industry due to the September 11 terrorist attacks and the recession occurring at that time were the culprits). Profits accelerated again, beginning in 2004, and then again fell out of bed (no pun intended) commencing in 2008. But market conditions (and RevPar growth) began to improve, yet again, in 2010.

Health care REITs enjoy, in most of their subsectors, the protection of triple-net long-term leases, which also offer a bit of upside based on revenues generated by the operator or fixed rent bumps built into the leases. A key consideration here, as we saw in the late 1990s, is the financial strength of the lessees; defaulting tenants often are not easily replaced at the same, let alone higher, rents. Base rents for these facilities should remain fairly stable. The assisted-living market, however, will be somewhat more volatile, as barriers to entry are lower and these properties are more sensitive to the U.S. economy and to the prices of single-family homes.

Although it may be an oversimplification, most real estate observers seem to think that owners of well-maintained properties in markets where supply and demand are in balance will, on average and over time, continue to get rental revenue increases at least equal to inflation. We are talking here only about broad-based industry trends; some REITs will get better rental increases upon lease renewal than others, based on many factors related to supply and demand for specific properties in specific locations, as well as property quality and location. And, of course, management's leasing capabilities are also very important. Trying to determine which REITs and their properties have better-than-average potential same-store rental revenue and NOI growth is one of the challenges—and some of the fun—of REIT investing.

How to Build Internal Growth into a Lease

Many property owners have been able to obtain above-average increases in rental revenues by using methods that focus on tenants' needs and their financial ability to pay higher effective rental rates. These methods include percentage rent, rent bumps, and expense sharing and recovery.

"Percentage-rent" clauses in retail store leases enable the property owner to participate in store revenues if such revenues exceed certain preset levels. A retail lease's percentage-rent clause might be structured so that if the store's sales exceed, for example, $5 million for any calendar year, the lessee must pay the landlord 3 percent of the excess, in the form of additional rent. The extent to which lessees will agree to this revenue sharing depends on the property type and location, market conditions, negotiating leverage, the base rent, and the property owner's reputation for maintaining and even upgrading shopping centers to make them continually attractive to shoppers. This concept has been carried over into the health care sector, where REITs have sometimes been able to structure leases so that the owner shares in same-store revenue growth above certain minimum levels. In some cases, the potential rent increases are capped at predetermined levels.

Fixed "rent bumps" are contractual lease clauses that provide for periodic built-in rent increases. These are sometimes negotiated at fixed dollar amounts and sometimes based on an index of inflation such as the Consumer Price Index. Office and industrial property owners who enter into long-term leases are often able to structure them so that the base rent increases periodically, thus providing built-in same-store NOI growth. The rent-bump provision is also popular with owners of health care facilities, who use them in leases with their health care operators, and with retailers, who use them in an effort to offset increasing operating costs over time or simply to augment rental income.

"Expense sharing" or "cost recovery" is a practice whereby each lessee pays its pro rata share of property expenses incurred by the property owner. Owners have included "cost-sharing" or common area maintenance (CAM) recovery clauses in their leases to recover rising property maintenance, and sometimes even improvement, expenses. These might include items such as janitorial services, security, and even advertising and promotion expenses.

In the case of office buildings, the lessees may be required to pay their pro rata portion of increased operating expenses over a base year, including higher insurance, property taxes, and on-site management costs.

Many apartment community owners have put separate electric and water meters, or even separate heating units, into their apartments, with a twofold benefit. The owner is protected from rising energy costs, and the tenant is encouraged to save energy.

Cost-sharing lease clauses improve NOI, and thereby FFO, while tending to smooth out fluctuations in operating expenses from year to year. The degree to which they can be used depends on a property's supply/demand situation and location, as well as the property owner's ability to justify them to the lessee. The large mall REITs, such as Simon Property Group, may, on the basis of their size, market strength, and reputation for creative marketing, be able to get favorable cost-sharing lease provisions that are unavailable to a weaker mall owner.

Other Ways to Generate Internal Growth and Create Shareholder Value

Aside from favorable economic and space market dynamics, there are two principal ways in which a real estate owner can capture higher rental rates: (1) upgrading the tenant mix; and (2) upgrading the property, through renovation or refurbishment. Both can be effective.

Tenant Upgrades

Upgrading the tenant mix is primarily an opportunity available to retail property owners, who often have been able to increase rental revenues significantly by replacing marginal tenants with attractive new ones. Retailers who offer innovative products at attractive prices generate higher customer traffic and boost sales at both the store *and* the shopping center, and successful tenants can afford higher rents.

This ability to upgrade tenants is what distinguishes a truly innovative retail property owner from the rest. For example, Kimco Realty, which has one of the most respected management teams in the retail REIT sector, maintains a huge database of prospective tenants that might improve its centers' profitability. This resource, along with the strong relationships Kimco has with high-quality national and regional retailers, allows it to upgrade its tenant base within an existing retail center on a continual basis. Regency Centers, another well-regarded retail REIT, has been following a similar strategy, establishing long-term relationships with strong national and regional retailers. And many other neighborhood shopping center REITs, for example, Weingarten Realty, have been successful in the endeavor. Most mall owners have, for many years, been following this formula as well, and are always looking for opportunities to replace or downsize weaker tenants. For them, when a retail chain goes out of business (e.g., Mervyns) or stores close, rent may be lost temporarily, but opportunities for higher rental revenues from new tenants are often created.

Tenant upgrading is even more important during periods of weak retail demand. Late in 1995 and into 1996, a number of retailers, having been squeezed by sluggish consumer demand and inroads made upon them by Wal-Mart and other discount stores, filed for bankruptcy. Similar situations prevailed from 2001 to 2003 and from 2008 to 2010. Those mall owners who replaced poorly performing apparel stores with restaurants and other new and unique retailing concepts prospered; those who did not encountered flat-to-declining revenues, vacancy increases, and declining or stagnating rental rates upon lease renewal. A productive mix of retail tenants may be almost as important as a good location.

Property Refurbishments

Refurbishment is a skill that separates the innovative property owner from the passive one. This ability can turn a tired mall, neighborhood shopping center, office building—even an apartment community—into a vibrant, inviting property likely to attract new tenants and customers.

Successfully refurbishing a property has several benefits. The upgraded and beautified property attracts a more stable tenant base and commands higher rents and, for retail properties, more shoppers. The returns to the REIT property owner on such investments will often run into the double digits.

Federal Realty, another well-regarded retail REIT, has been generating outstanding returns from turning tired retail properties into more exciting, upscale, open-air shopping complexes. Acadia Realty, a smaller retail REIT, has accomplished some very innovative repositioning and refurbishment projects. Many apartment REITs, including Home Properties, Mid-America Apartment Communities, and UDR Inc., among others, have been buying apartment buildings with deferred maintenance problems or with significant upgrade potential at attractive prices, then successfully upgrading and refurbishing them with new window treatments and upgraded kitchens. Alexandria Real Estate, which focuses on the office/ laboratory niche of the office market and provides space for pharmaceutical, biotech, and other life science companies, has been successful with its redevelopment strategy, often earning double-digit returns. The lesson here for investors is that REITs with innovative management teams can create value for their shareholders through imaginative property refurbishing and tenant upgrade strategies.

Capital Recycling

Upgrading the tenant mix and refurbishing owned properties are not the only ways by which REITs can boost revenue and NOI growth. They can also sell properties with lackluster future income growth prospects, and then reinvest the proceeds elsewhere. These new opportunities might include the acquisition of properties that are likely to generate higher returns, initiation of new development projects, or other opportunistic deployments of capital such as stock repurchases, preferred stock redemptions, and repayment of high-cost debt. REITs should "clean house" from time to time and consider which properties to keep and which to sell, using the proceeds from the sale for reinvestment in more promising opportunities, or even returning it to shareholders in the form of special dividends. This strategy may still be regarded as producing internal growth—as no fresh capital is required. At other times, however, when sale proceeds are used to repurchase shares, to reduce expensive debt or even to pay a special dividend, there may not be a meaningful impetus to further cash flow growth, but value may nevertheless be created for the REIT's shareholders.

Truly entrepreneurial management teams are always looking to improve investment returns, and sale and reinvestment is a conservative and highly effective strategy. This practice, often referred to as "capital recycling," has become popular with REIT organizations ever since the capital markets slammed shut on them in mid-1998. Many REITs used it to sell properties as the market peaked in 2006 to 2007.

Here's an example of capital recycling. A property might be sold at a 6 percent cap rate, with a prospective long-term return of 7 percent annually, and the net proceeds invested in another (perhaps poorly managed) property that, with a modest investment of capital and upgraded tenant services, might provide a long-term average annual return of 9 percent or more, beginning within a year or two. Funds reinvested in well-conceived and well-executed development projects can be equally profitable, as we'll discuss below. Sometimes a REIT will decide to exit an entire market if it doesn't like its long-term prospects. This can create value without requiring a REIT to access fresh capital.

Thus, along with tenant upgrading and property refurbishing, capital recycling is an important tool by which investor returns can be enhanced. Most REIT management teams are always alert for new opportunities and should have no emotional attachments to a property just because their REIT has owned it for a while or because it's performed well in the past. For example, just in the apartment sector, AvalonBay, Camden, Equity Residential, Post Properties, and UDR have all been substantial sellers of mature assets in recent years. There may be a short-term cost in terms of temporary earnings dilution, as higher-quality assets that are acquired often trade at lower entry yields and cap rates than the lower-quality assets disposed of and as the sale proceeds are used temporarily to pay down debt, but the long-term benefits of this strategy will be substantial if executed with good judgment.

NOI and IRR

Before we leave this discussion, let's fill in our knowledge—and help us prepare for what follows—with a couple of very important concepts in real estate: net operating income, referred to briefly earlier in this chapter, and internal rate of return. The term *net operating income* (NOI) is normally used to measure the net cash generated by an income-producing property. Thus, NOI can be defined as recurring rental and other income from a property, less all operating expenses attributable to that property. Operating expenses will include, for example, real estate taxes, insurance, utility costs, property management and, sometimes, recurring reserves for replacement. They do not include "corporate" items such as a REIT's general and administrative expenses, interest expense, value-enhancing capital expenditures, or depreciation expense. Therefore, the term seeks to define how much cash is generated from the ownership and leasing of a commercial property. Investors might reasonably expect NOI on a typical commercial real estate asset to grow about 2 to 3 percent annually, roughly in line with inflation, during most economic periods.

The term *internal rate of return* (IRR) helps the real estate investor to calculate his or her investment returns, including both returns *on* investment and returns *of* investment. It quantifies the percentage rate of return from all future cash receipts, balanced against all cash investments and contributions, so that when each receipt and each contribution is discounted to net present value, the sum is equal to zero when added together. To put it more simply, an IRR is the real rate of return that an investor expects when making the investment or, with hindsight, the rate of return obtained from the investment.

For example, if the real estate investor requires a 10 percent return on an investment, he or she won't buy the offered property if it is believed that the net present value of all future cash receipts from that property, including gain or loss on its eventual sale, isn't likely to equal or exceed 10 percent. Of course, this requires some sharp-penciled calculations (done these days with Excel spreadsheets), including many assumptions concerning occupancy and rental rates, property expenses, growth in NOI, and what the property will be worth when sold at an assumed future date.

One of the reasons that so many real estate investors fared poorly in the early 1990s, and again in 2008 to 2010, is that the IRR assumptions they made when buying commercial real estate a few years earlier were too aggressive. Perhaps the *real* value of

IRR calculations for potential acquisition opportunities is not the resulting percentage derived from a single mathematical exercise. Rather, the value comes from requiring the prospective property buyer to test the sensitivity of percentage returns under differing sets of performance assumptions: "To what extent will my expected IRR be reduced if my NOI grows by only 2.5 percent rather than my expected 3.5 percent, or what if I must sell the property at the end of my holding period at a price 5 percent below my purchase price?"

As we've seen in this discussion, REITs' internal growth and value-creation opportunities are as numerous as their properties. In the hands of shrewd management, these options can be maximized so that results pay off for both the REIT and its investors. However, internal growth isn't the *only* way REITs can expand revenues, funds from operations, and dividend-paying capacity, as well as creating value for shareholders. There is another.

External Growth

Let's assume, for purposes of discussion, that a widely respected REIT can obtain annual rental revenue increases slightly better than the rate of inflation, say 3 percent, and that property expenses and overhead expense growth can be held to less than 3 percent. Let's further assume that with modest, fixed-rate debt leverage, such a REIT can increase its per-share FFO by 4 percent in a typical year. Finally, let's assume that the well-managed REIT can achieve another 0.5 percent annual growth in FFO through tenant upgrades, refurbishments, and other internal means. How do we get from this 4.5 percent FFO growth rate to the 6 to 7 percent

Acquisitions

REITs' acquisition opportunities are dependent on many factors, including access to the capital markets and the cost of the capital raised, the strength of the balance sheet, levels of retained earnings, and the prevailing cap rates and prospective IRRs of the type of property it wants to acquire. We investors would like the acquired properties to have meaningful NOI growth potential, which, together with the initial yield, will provide IRRs equal to, and hopefully in excess of, the REIT's weighted average cost of capital.

pace some REITs have been able to achieve quite often in the past? The answer is through *external* growth, a process by which a real estate organization, such as a REIT, acquires additional properties or engages in additional business activities, such as property development, that generate profits for the organization's owners. Let's look at the ways in which this can occur.

 TIP

External growth can be generated through attractive property acquisitions and developments, as well as activities such as property expansions, joint ventures, and initiating new real estate-related businesses.

Acquisition Opportunities

The concept of acquiring additional properties at attractive initial yields and with substantial NOI growth potential has been applied successfully for many years by a large number of well-regarded REITs.

For example, a REIT might raise $100 million through a combination of selling additional shares and medium-term unsecured notes, which, allowing for the long-term cost of the newly issued shares and the interest costs on the debt, might have a weighted average cost of capital of 7 percent. It would then use the proceeds to buy properties that, including both their initial yields and the additional growth from property income increases and some capital appreciation over time, might generate IRRs of 8 percent. The net result of such transactions would be a pickup of 100 basis points over the REIT's weighted average cost of capital. We must keep in mind, however, that near-term FFO "accretion" (obtaining initial yields on a new investment that will increase per-share FFO over the near term), while fairly easy to calculate, is much less important to investors than finding and acquiring properties able to deliver longer-term IRRs that equal or exceed the REIT's true cost of capital (this concept will be discussed more fully later in this chapter and in Appendix C). At certain times, this can be very difficult, making acquisitions of dubious value to shareholders.

An effective acquisition strategy will be difficult for a REIT to implement if it cannot raise either equity capital (perhaps because of unimpressive prior company performance, an unproven track record, or a history of poor capital allocation by management) or debt capital (when its balance sheet is already heavily leveraged or when capital markets are very tight). Furthermore, investors do not want their company to sell new equity if doing so would cause dilution to its FFO or estimated NAV. Dilutive acquisitions are not popular with REIT investors—and rightly so.

The early 1990s were a golden era of acquisitions for REITs, which is one reason why so many real estate companies went public during that time. The most seasoned apartment REIT in the early 1990s, United Dominion (now UDR), was able to raise equity capital at a nominal cost of 7 percent, and debt capital at 8 percent. It was able to acquire apartment properties at well below replacement cost in the aftermath of the real estate depression of the late 1980s, which provided it with entry yields of 11 percent or more and IRRs that were even higher. (The sellers were troubled partnerships, overleveraged owners, banks with repossessed properties, and the Resolution Trust Corporation.)

At first glance it may seem odd that properties could become available at such cheap prices and high investment returns; however, when markets are such that there are few willing buyers but lots of anxious sellers, the purchase price will be low in relationship to the expected cash flow from the property, and IRRs to the property buyer can be extraordinary. At the bottoms of property cycles we have seen such supply/demand imbalances because, under the threat of foreclosure, not only are owners anxious to cut their losses, but property refinancings are often unavailable, and confidence levels are low. And lenders are often anxious to dump foreclosed properties. This is not, however, always the case; in the early years of the twenty-first century, despite very weak real estate markets, owners were able to refinance assets at low interest rates, few of them were overburdened with debt, and there were lots of willing bidders for underperforming properties. And contrary to the expectations of many industry observers during the troubled real estate space and capital markets in 2009 and 2010, extraordinary buying opportunities were difficult to find.

The extent of REITs' acquisition opportunities thus depends on real estate pricing and prospects from time to time, including the prevalence or absence of competing buyers, as well as the

REIT's cost of capital—both equity and debt. Attractive acquisition prospects will be few when real estate prices are high and thus likely to offer poor returns relative to historic norms; this often results from an abundance of potential buyers waiting to snap up the next property coming onto the market, as well as overly rosy forecasts for rental and income growth. Perhaps because of wider acceptance of commercial real estate as an asset class and its role as a diversifier in an investment portfolio, there has been no shortage of buyers of quality assets in good locations in recent years; as a result, great bargains have been scarce.

Despite the challenges, investors want their REITs to patiently find the unusual acquisition opportunity at a bargain price— they believe that little value can be created when a REIT pays simply a fair price for an asset (unless it can manage it much more efficiently than anyone else or earn a substantially higher return through a joint venture strategy).

The Cost of Equity Capital

To create value from external growth initiatives, a REIT must earn a return on any new investment that exceeds the cost of the capital deployed. But what is the real cost to a REIT when it raises new capital from the issuance of shares?

There are several ways to calculate such cost of equity capital. "Nominal" cost of equity capital refers to the fact that a REIT's current cash flows (FFO or AFFO) and its asset values must be allocated among a larger number of common shares, while the "true" or "long-term" cost of equity capital considers such dilution over longer time periods and estimates shareholders' total return expectations on their invested capital. We need to keep in mind, moreover, that the cost of equity capital will rise as the REIT takes on more debt—investors will expect higher returns to compensate for higher risk.

And yet, despite the importance of this concept, there seems to be no general agreement among REITs and their investors on how the true cost of equity capital should be calculated. Nevertheless, what's most important for investors is that they focus not just on the initial accretion to FFO from an acquisition, but also on the probable longer-term IRR from an acquired property (or portfolio of them). Will the latter exceed the REIT's estimated weighted average cost of capital, which combines the cost of equity and the cost of debt? (For more discussion on cost of equity capital, see Appendix C.)

Even if reasonably attractive opportunities are available, a REIT cannot take advantage of them if its cost of capital exceeds the likely returns. To use a perhaps extreme example, let's assume that a REIT with an aggressive fast-growth business strategy (we'll call it *Gazelle REIT*) has an equity capital cost of 12 percent, and that Gazelle REIT wants to buy a package of quality properties that is expected to deliver an IRR of 7 percent. Even if the REIT finances the acquisition by borrowing 50 percent of the purchase price at a 4 percent interest rate, it's probably a "no-go" from the investors' standpoint.

Why? Gazelle REIT's weighted average cost of capital will be 8 percent (an equal blend of a 12 percent cost of equity capital and a 4 percent cost of debt capital), which exceeds the expected 7 percent return. However, if Gazelle REIT's cost of equity capital were 8 percent rather than 12 percent, the weighted average cost of capital would be 6 percent, and the deal would probably be deemed attractive.

 TIP

The importance of attractive investment opportunities to a REIT's FFO growth rate, investment value, and stock price cannot be overemphasized; buying high-return properties at cheap prices will create substantial value for shareholders. But each investment must be carefully analyzed by investors and a judgment made on whether value is likely to be created or destroyed.

We can thus see the importance of a REIT's estimating its cost of equity capital intelligently and conservatively. Fortunately, the cost of *debt* capital is fairly straightforward relative to the cost of equity capital—it is simply the interest that the REIT pays for borrowed funds. However, we should use long-term interest rates, since drawdowns under a credit line and other forms of short-term debt are temporary and must be repaid relatively quickly; furthermore, they are subject to interest rate fluctuations. Calculations should be based on rates for debt that will be outstanding for 5 to 10 years (perhaps a reasonable holding period for an acquired property), which will usually be higher than short-term interest rates. Using the short-term rate would distort the picture, making it seem that a REIT that borrows at 3 percent, on a short-term basis, and uses the loan proceeds to buy properties with 6 percent IRR potential—at a time when the cost of long-term debt is 6 percent—is making an attractive investment. This would certainly be a misleading analysis.

We should also note that when professional real estate organizations like REITs acquire a property, they often are able to operate and manage it more efficiently and profitably than the prior owner. Thus, REITs often can obtain above-average internal growth from acquired properties beyond the initial expected yield through better control of expenses, even assuming no change in rents. The largest apartment REIT, Equity Residential, often has been able to generate better profit margins than those selling apartment assets to it, and many other REITs have been able to do this as well.

I'd like to make two final points before we leave the topic of property acquisitions:

- A REIT's weighted average cost of capital will change often with changes in investor expectations, stock prices, borrowing costs and other factors. Thus we are all continually shooting at a moving target.
- A REIT whose shares trade in the market at a relatively high P/FFO ratio or substantial NAV premium can have a low *nominal* cost of equity capital but, at the same time, a high *true* cost of equity capital. An expensive REIT stock may trade on aggressive growth assumptions, and such REIT may be expected to find acquisitions with much better than average investment returns. If the long-term total returns on its acquisitions are not likely to meet these higher expectations, the shares will fall to the extent that disappointed investors punish the REIT for obtaining only average returns.

New Developments

 TIP

Some REITs have been able to increase external FFO growth, as well as NAV growth, by developing entirely new properties, whether apartments, malls, neighborhood shopping centers, office buildings, or any other property type.

Until the REIT IPO boom of 1993 and 1994, very few public REITs had the capability of developing new properties from the ground up. To do that requires specialized skill and experience. Today, REITs with those attributes are not uncommon, and we see them in almost every sector. A well-conceived development program requires capital as well as know-how. New developments require financing during the 12 to 24 months (and sometimes even longer) required to build them out and "stabilize" them by filling them with new tenants. Having development capabilities is a key advantage in many real estate environments, as they allow REITs to grow externally and to create value when tenant demand is expected to be strong and new competing developments will be modest; this may also be a time when finding good acquisitions is problematic due to high property prices.

Successful developments typically provide 7 to 9 percent initial unlevered returns on a REIT's investment when the property is stabilized, depending on the property sector, which will usually be significantly higher than returns on the acquisition of existing properties of comparable quality. Furthermore, the REIT's NAV will be enhanced because when lower cap rates are applied to newly developed and substantially leased properties, incremental value is created, which, over time, will also enhance the price of the REIT's stock. These development "spreads" often can approach 200 basis points. Some mall REITs, for example, have at times been able to develop new malls that provide 9 to 10 percent stabilized yields and could be sold at 6 to 7 percent cap rates; that's value creation!

Such development capability also allows a REIT to capitalize on unique opportunities. For example, many years ago, Weingarten Realty was able to obtain a parcel of property directly across the boulevard from Houston's Galleria, one of the premier shopping complexes in America, and it built an attractive new center in that location. In 2004, Macerich redeveloped the Queens Center in New York and obtained 11 percent returns on its investment. At times, a number of office and industrial property REITs have been able to get close to double-digit returns from developments and redevelopments, and Regency Centers' development pipeline of neighborhood shopping centers was very profitable until the Great Recession depressed stabilized returns.

Apartment development returns have declined in recent years along with cap rates, but AvalonBay and some of its peers have still been able, during many economic climates, to develop at up to 200 basis point spreads over prevailing cap rates. Finally, a few REITs, including AMB Properties, Kimco, ProLogis, and Simon, have even developed properties overseas, often forming partnerships or joint ventures with local real estate companies.

Although a REIT can contract with an outside developer to acquire joint ownership of a new project, it will not be as profitable because of the outside developer's need to generate its own profit. However, the REIT's risks will be lessened to the extent the outside developer assumes the risk of construction cost overruns and some of the lease-up risk. The prospective returns, and the risks, will be higher if the REIT fully develops its own projects, particularly when there is little or no preleasing.

TIP

Those investors willing to assume somewhat higher risk should consider REITs with successful track records of property development, which provides them with yet another avenue for increasing per-share FFO growth and NAV increases.

Property development certainly has a downside—the risks. What can go wrong? There are three principal areas of risk in development: construction risk, leasing risk, and financing risk. First, cost overruns during construction can significantly reduce investment returns. This can happen particularly when a builder lacks experience with a unique property type or develops in a new locality, or if the REIT relies extensively on unproven local contractors.

Second, leasing risk includes failing to bring the occupancy rate to projected levels, receiving lower-than-expected rents from new tenants or having to make substantial rental concessions; this is a particular risk if the development occurs when a favorable property cycle ends abruptly, as it did in 2001 and again in 2007. Overbuilding also will be a threat to rental and occupancy estimates, as it can quickly saturate the market with lots of competing space. Some apartment development projects in the San Francisco Bay

Area fell short of projected returns because of a sudden falloff in demand stemming from the reversal of fortunes of many high-tech and manufacturing companies in the national recession of 2001.

A third risk is that permanent debt financing is usually unavailable until a project is completed and substantially leased, which can take two or three years. Who knows what interest rates will look like that far down the road? A substantial increase in long-term interest rates can reduce the projected levered return on any development project.

The bottom line is that REIT investors and management teams alike should expect substantially higher returns from development in order to be compensated for taking greater risks. What is still unclear is whether development-oriented REITs that are capable of creating substantial value for shareholders via their development expertise, even when the extra risk is taken into account, will be given appropriate pricing premiums by investors. The jury is still out on that question; much may depend on the size of expected development profit margins and the anticipated shape and size of the development window from time to time.

A related method of external growth is the expansion and redevelopment of *existing* properties. Some development capability is required here, but the risks are significantly smaller for two reasons: the existing property has proven itself, and the cost of adding space is less than developing a new property from scratch. Furthermore, while the total profit potential from an expansion may be less than that from an entirely new "ground-up," or "greenfield," project, the percentage return on invested capital from the expansion is often higher. Successful expansions can be done in any property type, but strong and proven locations tend to bring more opportunities. Of course, the REIT must own or acquire the adjacent land.

Investors become enthused when a REIT announces that it's adding "phase 2" or "phase 3" to an existing successful property. This generally indicates that the existing property is doing well, that management has had the foresight to acquire adjacent land, and that the risk-return ratio is favorable. Many well-regarded REITs that are not generally known as ground-up property developers, such as Federal Realty and Macerich in the retail sector, have created substantial shareholder value with property expansions and redevelopments.

More External Growth Avenues

Although property acquisitions, developments, redevelopments, and expansions are the primary vehicles for a REIT to grow externally, they are not the only ways. As noted earlier, a number of REITs have been able to create joint ventures (JVs) with institutional partners to acquire, own, and, at times, even develop properties. Although these JV structures can make a REIT's business strategy and financial structure more complex and create risks not present when assets are owned outright, they will generate additional fee income streams for the REIT, and this can augment FFO growth and create extra value for shareholders. Each JV strategy should be examined on its own merit, of course, as investors will want the benefits to more than offset both the risks and the additional complexity in the REIT's business model and revenue sources.

REITs have other avenues for external growth as well. Thanks to the REIT Modernization Act, they can engage in real estate–related businesses that often can provide substantial additional revenues and net income. These businesses often are carried on in a taxable REIT subsidiary, and thus their profits are subject to corporate income tax. They can often create shareholder value, particularly if they can leverage off of the REIT's inherent real estate skills. For a number of years, Kimco Realty did very well in these businesses, including restructuring the leases of bankrupt tenants, providing financing for other retailers, and helping them to get rid of excess space. Some development-oriented REITs, particularly in the industrial sector, for example, AMB Properties, Duke Realty, and ProLogis, have developed properties for others on a fee basis.

And some REITs, such as Vornado Realty, have been making opportunistic real estate–related investments in which they do not own the underlying properties; in October 2010, Vornado announced that it had acquired a 9.9 percent stake in retailer JCPenney. A few REITs even make "mezzanine" loans, which can be risky but also potentially very profitable. SL Green, a leading office REIT, has long run a successful higher-risk lending business in the New York City office sector. In 2004 it organized a new mortgage REIT, Gramercy Capital, and took it public—but that business didn't fare well, becoming a victim of the Great Recession and the collapse of the credit markets.

There are certainly risks in these nontraditional businesses. They generate revenues from nonrental sources, and therefore they are less stable and predictable than rental revenues and can be more sensitive to changes in economic conditions. Investors should be careful not to value the income streams from these businesses as highly as they do income from property leases, as we were reminded in 2008 to 2010 when many of the former quickly evaporated. These nonrental businesses should be viewed as a tool for the creation of additional value and external growth for the REIT's shareholders, and any tool can be used well or misused. And some tools just don't work very well in hostile environments. Every such nontraditional business engaged in by a REIT should therefore be examined closely and judged on its own merits.

Summary

- The use of FFO and AFFO enables both REITs and their investors to estimate free cash flows by correcting for real estate depreciation expense, usually a noncash item.
- FFO and AFFO generally grow over time with growing economies and provide the means for dividend increases; however, measuring free cash flow isn't necessarily the best way to value REIT shares, as we'll address in a later chapter.
- AFFO is the most useful tool for estimating REITs' recurring free cash flows, but there is no uniform standard by which it is calculated.
- FFO and AFFO can be grown in two ways: externally, by acquisitions, developments, and engaging in joint ventures and other businesses; and internally, through a REIT's ability to improve the profitability of its existing properties.
- Investors should pay close attention to a REIT's value-creation capabilities, which are very important in determining a REIT's stock value, but the income from which isn't always reflected in FFO or AFFO.
- Internal growth is the most stable and reliable source of FFO growth because it does not depend on raising new capital or making acquisitions but only on controlling expenses, increasing occupancy rates, and raising rental rates at its properties.

- External growth can be generated through attractive property acquisitions, developments, and property expansions, as well as developing fee-related and investment management businesses.
- Investors should try to understand concepts such as *cost of capital* and *internal rate of return,* as they help us to understand how REITs can create—or destroy—value when making acquisitions or pursuing developments.
- The importance of attractive investment and development opportunities to a REIT's growth in free cash flows and enterprise value cannot be overemphasized, but the risk profiles of external growth strategies are higher and should be carefully monitored by investors.

CHAPTER

8

Searching for Blue Chips

"Gambling can be separated from investing not by the type of activity but by the skill, dedication and enterprise of the participant."

—Peter Lynch

Investment strategies of many types can be pursued in the REIT world, depending on our investment goals. We can look for companies of the highest quality, buy them, and hold them patiently over the long term. Or we can take more risk and go for large gains in more speculative REIT stocks, or focus on those selling at deep discounts to net asset value (NAV). We can try to pick up REITs that have stumbled and hope for a turnaround. We can buy high dividend yields, and pray that the dividend continues to be paid. It's also possible to search for little-known gems among the very small REITs. It's all a question of one's investment preferences, return requirements, and risk aversion.

Investment Styles

Some non-REIT investors have done well by buying and owning the large, steadily growing companies with excellent long-term track records, such as Coca-Cola, Exxon, or Wal-Mart. Peter Lynch called these stocks "stalwarts." Other investors have looked for companies growing at very rapid rates, such as Apple, Baidu, or even some biotech companies. "Contrarian" or "value" investors buy shares whose prices are temporarily depressed by bad news that they expect will eventually dissipate, or where hidden asset values will soon surface. Some investors like to buy "small-cap" shares in growing companies most people have never heard of. All of these approaches can work—for REITs as well as for other stocks—if the investor is disciplined and patient and exercises good judgment. There is no consensus as to which investment style or preference works best, and a Warren Buffett–type guru of the REIT world has yet to emerge (although the "Sage of Omaha" himself has reportedly bought REIT shares on occasion).

The most conservative investors are likely to emphasize blue-chip REITs, which I will try to define in this chapter. Those seeking quality and safety above all else certainly will. And it is vital for *all* REIT investors to know what makes a blue-chip REIT different from the rest, as it's the blue chips that set the standards by which all others should be measured. Before we look for the blue chips, however, we'll examine a few of the other choices.

Growth REITs

Some believe that the term *growth REIT* is an oxymoron; by their very nature, REITs cannot grow per-share earnings at rapid rates. A real estate business is a higher-yielding but slower-growth enterprise, and REITs must, by law, pay out most of their free cash flow to shareholders and thus cannot retain much of their earnings to plow back into the business to generate growth. Yet there have been times in the past when some REITs have been viewed as growth stocks, and such periods will undoubtedly occur again.

Growth REITs, then, are those viewed by investors as having the ability to increase their funds from operations (FFO) at rates much faster than historical norms of 4 to 5 percent annually, perhaps at times even at rates exceeding 10 percent. The reason for this growth potential may be that a specific sector is enjoying the boom phase of its property cycle, when rental rates and occupancies are rising rapidly, or their business strategy is to implement a very aggressive acquisition or development program or to generate rapid growth from fee-based businesses. This type of growth in a REIT often requires substantial regular infusions of new equity and debt capital to expand the business and property portfolio. If the newly raised capital is used to acquire properties that are cheaply priced and offer strong rental and net operating income (NOI) growth prospects, management will be perceived as smart and opportunistic, and the share price will rise quickly. Another approach to rapid growth is through a strategy of building a number of new properties and selling them to others or to a captive joint venture. If, however, acquisition or development opportunities abate, such a REIT's earnings growth will slow; the REIT will be hard-pressed to meet investors' lofty expectations, and its stock price is likely to decline substantially. Much, of course, depends on the premium accorded to a growth REIT's shares and the extent of the disappointment.

TIP

As long as a growth REIT can stay one step ahead of investors' expectations, it can deliver exciting returns—but it's very important to estimate when that growth rate may slow significantly.

Several hotel REITs were in a high-growth phase in the mid-1990s. Starwood Hotels and Patriot American Hospitality, for example, enjoyed above-average internal growth, while acquiring billions of dollars in new hotels. Their FFOs increased rapidly. Those who bought into these stocks in 1995 and 1996 enjoyed hefty gains for a while, but those who jumped on board later or held on too long saw most or all of their gains dissipate in later years. Starwood recovered, but Patriot American, now Wyndham International (and no longer a REIT), was a disaster for shareholders, having overextended its balance sheet with an excessively aggressive acquisition strategy. More recently, industrial REITs AMB Property and ProLogis were growing very rapidly by developing properties overseas until the Great Recession suddenly impeded their growth prospects. Even mortgage REITs can be growth REITs at certain times, raising huge amounts of capital and making large volumes of new loans. Growth-oriented REIT investors can, for a period of time, do quite well; but they need to figure out when a REIT's unusually rapid growth phase will begin to slow and avoid paying a rich price for transient growth.

Value or "Turnaround" REITs

If you're a value investor, there are often a number of depressed REITs from which to choose—these are REITs that are selling for low valuations relative to their peers or at large discounts to NAV. Perhaps they're below the radar screens of most investors, they own poorly performing properties, or they've been banished to investors' doghouse due to management's miscues. Or maybe their balance sheets are frightfully ugly. The stocks of these REITs might be excellent short- or even long-term investments if they're cheap enough or if we buy them just prior to a turnaround in their operating prospects or financial condition.

Carr America Realty (which was taken private in 2006) is a good example. This office REIT was languishing shortly after it went public and had no access to capital to take advantage of acquisition opportunities in recovering office markets. The stock was selling at cheap prices despite a good management team. However, a short time later, Security Capital Group, a large real estate investment organization, agreed to acquire a controlling interest in Carr America, and those who bought before the Security Capital Group transaction were extremely well rewarded. More recently, a number of REITs were selling at very low prices in the wake of the Great Recession and credit crunch because many doubted their ability to survive. When they completed new debt and equity financings, their shares doubled, even tripled, in price.

 TIP

Investors can do very well buying a depressed REIT in hopes of a turnaround—but it's usually very difficult to know when a REIT's stock price fully discounts its current and prospective difficulties.

Most REIT stocks that are very cheap are that way for good reason. Problems may include declining cash flows, weak properties or markets, high debt leverage, and suspect management teams. These stocks can be compared to junk bonds—high risk *sometimes* brings high rewards, but sometimes just brings further woes.

It is possible for investors to do very well with a turnaround REIT, but it's important to remember that some of these investments will never make a comeback if inept management has been the problem—it may continue to destroy shareholder value. It's particularly important to do extensive homework before venturing into these REITs, including detailed balance sheet and property analysis. Investors should know *why* the stock is cheaply priced before buying in.

Bond-Proxy REITs

Another type of REIT that often appeals to some investors is one that I refer to as a *bond proxy*. It is perceived as having a relatively slow FFO and dividend growth rate, but, because of its moderate debt and stable properties, it has a reasonably secure dividend with a yield that is usually higher than that of most REITs. Adjectives like *reliable* and *consistent* describe these REITs, which do not have aggressive external growth strategies and often own properties with long-term leases. Those seeking bond proxies should look for conservative, capable, and dedicated management teams, moderate debt levels, and a substantial, well-covered dividend. Growth and capital appreciation, of course, are likely to remain modest. Bond-proxy REITs often own health care or other properties leased to a single tenant on a "triple-net" basis.

 TIP

Bond-proxy REITs provide high dividend yields, often in the range of 6 to 7 percent, but they have less well defined growth prospects compared with other REITs. Investors are trading higher prospective total returns for higher current income.

Many of these REITs might be quite suitable for those investors to whom stable, high income is more important than capital appreciation. However, it is likely that most investors will do better, over time, if they pass up the reward of high current dividends in favor of the higher-potential, long-term total returns offered by blue-chip REITs.

The Virtues of Blue-Chip REITs

So far, we've discussed growth, value, and bond-proxy REITs. Now I'll introduce the stalwarts of REITdom—the blue-chip REITs. But first, a caveat: There is no objective or commonly accepted definition of "blue-chip REIT," so you will have to accept mine until you develop your own. Blue-chip REITs are, like all REITs, subject to the ups and downs of their sector's cycles but should, over reasonably long time periods, deliver consistent, rising, long-term growth in FFO, dividends, and asset value. Because they are financially strong and widely respected, they will, in most periods, have access to the additional equity and debt capital that can fuel above-average growth. They will rarely provide the highest dividend yields or even, in many years, the best total returns, nor can we frequently buy them at bargain prices—but they should provide years of 7 to 8 percent total returns, on average, with only modest risk.

TIP

Blue-chip REITs have certain qualities that set them apart from most REITs. These qualities include:

- Outstanding proven management, familiar with the demands of both real estate ownership and operation and the quirks of public markets.
- Access to debt and equity capital, and a track record of effective deployment of that capital to create shareholder value.
- Balance sheet strength and flexibility.
- Sector focus and deep regional or local market expertise.
- Conservative and intelligent dividend policy.
- Good corporate governance.
- Meaningful insider stock ownership.

A blue-chip REIT doesn't have to exhibit *all* of these attributes, but it will have most of them. Let's discuss them in detail.

The Supreme Importance of Management

 TIP

Smart and capable management is the single most important attribute of blue-chip REITs.

Smart and capable management is what separates mere collections of properties from superior businesses whose stock-in-trade just happens to be real estate. Even if its management team is mediocre, a REIT will do reasonably well when its property sector is doing well—a rising tide lifts all boats. The rapidly rising rents and occupancy rates enjoyed during a sector's boom cycle will generate strong internal growth for the entire sector, such as was the case for apartment REITs throughout much of the 1990s, office REITs from 1995 through the end of that decade, and retail REITs from 2000 through 2007.

But the true test of quality comes when difficult property markets return, often bringing excellent buying opportunities as well as pain in their wake. That is when excellent property management, superior asset location, admirable leasing skills, and strong access to capital make a difference. When real estate space markets are soft, strong companies do a better job of retaining their tenants, thus minimizing cash flow erosion. At such times, real estate prices may be softening, and some overextended property owners may be anxious to sell at discount prices. Strong REITs often are able to take advantage of this situation by picking up sound, well-located properties cheaply—properties that can, with effective and imaginative management, be put back on track and produce excellent returns for shareholders. Excellent management teams should be able to guide their REITs through the downside of real estate space and capital market cycles and emerge even stronger.

When shopping for solid blue chips, it's important to focus on REITs whose management teams have been able to build sound portfolios with only a modest amount of debt, who have been able to invest shareholder capital wisely, who know how to measure risk, and who can raise reasonably priced capital to take advantage of acquisition or development opportunities when they arise. These are REITs whose management teams have also been able to achieve internal growth by upgrading properties and tenant rolls, while maximizing rental revenues and controlling operating and administrative expense growth. But we need to learn how to recognize them.

Creating Value in All Types of Climates

We've discussed buying opportunities in depressed real estate markets. But there are other advantages that superior management teams offer: they know which tenants are looking for space and in which locations. They make sure that in-place lease rates in acquired properties are supported by underlying real estate values, which enables them to find replacement tenants who can afford equal or higher rents if the original tenants leave or go bankrupt. Superior management of retail and office properties includes close monitoring of tenant rosters, and always looking for opportunities to replace the weak with the strong and reducing the risk of tenant defaults. Defaults are disruptive to cash flow, not only because of lost rent and "down time" but also because changing tenants mid-lease might require that expensive space improvements be made for the new tenants.

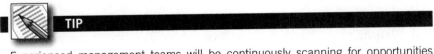

TIP

Experienced management teams will be continuously scanning for opportunities that they can use to their advantage.

One example of a REIT that's been able to take advantage of challenging retailing environments is Kimco Realty, a neighborhood shopping center REIT with an excellent long-term reputation among REIT investors. Retailers are engaged in a very competitive business, and some of them who own their own stores need extra capital when business trends deteriorate. Capitalizing on such difficulties, Kimco bought a number of retail stores in early 1996 from Venture Stores, a retailer that was trying to restructure its business. The stores were bought at prices well below market and leased to Venture at an estimated yield to Kimco of almost 13 percent. Investors should look for blue-chip REITs that have the ability to do well even in difficult environments by making unusually attractive acquisitions, upgrading properties and tenant quality, and pursuing business opportunities that create value for shareholders.

Extra Growth Internally

There are times when attractive acquisitions are not available to a REIT, for example, when expected rates of return would be below the REIT's weighted average cost of capital, and often there just aren't many development opportunities that are likely to provide an acceptable risk-adjusted return. This occurred, perhaps most notably, from 1998 through 2000. Not only were real estate markets very competitive and very late in their cycles, but REIT stock prices were such that raising equity capital was prohibitively expensive. Robert McConnaughey, managing director and senior portfolio manager of Prudential Real Estate Securities at the time, stated, "The low-hanging fruit has already been picked. We are no longer in an environment where anyone can find bargains, as we have been in a recovery mode for five years now."

During such periods, value creation is difficult and challenging, and obtaining better-than-average internal growth is one way for a blue-chip REIT to excel. For example, creative apartment REITs have been able to provide useful services for tenants, such as concierge services, educational and enrichment programs in a community setting, and cable and Internet services, and have managed their properties in a highly efficient manner. Many quality retail REITs, including Kimco, Regency, and Weingarten, have been able to build and maintain an extensive database of tenants' space requirements. As a result of their long-standing relationships with hundreds of national, regional, and local retailers, they have been able to refer to this database to fill vacant space quickly, whether in established properties or at newly acquired properties. A number of mall REITs also have this capacity. In the office and industrial sectors, look for REITs that have been able to keep their vacancy rates at levels well below U.S. averages.

We discussed earlier how a REIT often is able to charge higher rents for enhanced properties. There is no guidebook written on how to improve the appearance and desirability of specific properties most effectively, nor on how to reduce operating costs, but innovative management will always find a way to generate above-average NOI growth at their REITs' properties; over time, this creates shareholder value.

Another key advantage of blue-chip REITs with respect to internal growth is that their properties tend to be situated in strong "in-fill" locations, where it often is difficult for competing properties to be developed. Excellent management teams figure out ways to build or acquire in these locations, as apartment REIT AvalonBay has done for many years. This, too, enables the REIT to provide long-term returns to its shareholders that exceed those of its peers.

TIP

External growth opportunities are important, but internal growth is more stable and dependable.

The "One-Off" Deal

We'll discuss the broad topic of property acquisitions in some detail later in this chapter in the context of effective deployment of capital. However, here I would like to note that one unique characteristic of a high-quality management team is that it demonstrates, from time to time, its ability to make the unusual but very profitable real estate deal. An early example of this is Vornado's acquisition of Alexander's in 1995. Alexander's was a department store chain in the New York City area that filed for bankruptcy in 1992. It owned seven department store sites and a 50 percent interest in an adjacent regional mall. According to a Green Street Advisors' March 17, 1995, report, these sites were very valuable, including a full square block in Midtown Manhattan. In March 1995, Vornado bought a 27 percent stock interest in Alexander's from Citicorp for $55 million, a purchase price estimated at 20 percent below the prevailing market price. Vornado structured the deal to earn fees for managing, leasing, and developing Alexander's real estate. This not only enabled Vornado to increase its FFO significantly, but also to increase its per-share NAV.

Another instance of value creation through deal-making was the 2002 acquisition of the Westcor portfolio of shopping malls in and near Phoenix, Arizona, by Macerich Company. Many investors at that time argued that Macerich was overpaying for these quality assets, but their return on the capital invested in them has been outstanding. Kimco Realty has earned widespread investor respect on the strength of many such favorable deals, including both large property portfolios such as the Albertson's grocery store transaction in 2006 and "one-off" smaller deals. In August 2010, Simon Property Group, the largest mall REIT, announced that it had closed an acquisition of Prime Outlets at a cost of $700 million (excluding assumed debt). Green Street Advisors stated in February 2011 that Prime was acquired at a cap rate of approximately 8 percent, but that "the public market would likely value [the Prime assets] in the high–5 percent [cap rate] range today."

Commercial real estate markets are both broad and deep; during most periods, there are many buyers competing for bargains. But a blue-chip REIT with an excellent management team can sometimes find a great deal by buying a vacant property in an excellent location and filling it with tenants. For example, in mid-2010, Boston Properties acquired a new but unleased building at 510 Madison Avenue in Midtown Manhattan from Harry Macklowe for approximately $320 million, a price that Green Street Advisors estimated to be below replacement cost and 33 percent below the price paid for a similar building on Madison Avenue in 2007. The firm estimated that Boston Properties might, when the property becomes substantially leased, obtain an IRR in the mid–7 percent range. That would be an excellent return for such a quality building in a great location, especially at a time when the 10-year Treasury note was yielding well below 3 percent.

Blue-chip REITs have management teams that can add value by finding and making unusually attractive deals—particularly those that are not widely marketed. Anyone with the capital can buy real estate at market prices; only a few can steal it.

Attracting the Best Tenants

A well-managed REIT should not be entirely at the mercy of the creditworthiness of its tenants. Even in difficult environments, it should be able to take back space vacated by a financially troubled tenant and re-lease it at rates comparable to or better than before. Retailers have a habit of closing stores and even going out of business. However, except during those unusual times when market rents have declined precipitously, high-quality retail REITs have generally been able to protect their cash flows from the effects of store closings even in difficult environments, for example, during the waves of retailer bankruptcies in 1995 to 1996 and 2000 to 2001. Even the Great Recession, while putting dents in retail REITs' cash flows, had less of an impact on quality retail REIT organizations than most observers had expected. Same-center NOI for blue-chip mall REITs was flat to only slightly down even in the aftermath of the Great Recession (2009 and 2010). Office and industrial REITs with strong underwriting standards and assets in excellent locations should also be able to "back-fill" vacant space relatively quickly in most economic environments.

Regardless of retenanting skills, a REIT's ability to attract a roster of high-quality tenants is very important, particularly in retail sectors such as malls and neighborhood shopping centers. In a shopping center, having productive tenants means higher traffic, which means higher sales—for all the stores located there. For the owner of the center, such retail prosperity means that the tenants will be able to pay the rent bumps built into their leases, as well as provide additional rent to the property owner when sales overage provisions are contained in the leases. It also justifies higher rental rates when it's time to renew them. The bottom line is that highly productive centers mean higher operating profits and higher asset values for their owners.

 TIP

A blue-chip retail REIT's management team will figure out ways to boost traffic at its centers. More traffic means more sales, and more sales means less tenant turnover and higher lease revenues.

Better-quality tenants, whether in retail space, industrial properties, or office buildings, will often be looking to expand, and if the REIT enjoys good relationships with these tenants, they will turn to the REIT when they're ready for additional space. For example, industrial REITs AMB Properties and ProLogis (which merged and became ProLogis in mid-2011) have been cultivating long-term relationships with America's major users of logistics space, and this, over time, leads to the development of additional properties for expanding tenants both here and abroad. As these two REITs have significant overseas development capabilities, the merger is likely to give the combined company a competitive edge in meeting the needs of many large industrial space users.

TIP

A REIT with an excellent management team can perform well even when some of its tenants are struggling.

Cost Control

It has always been axiomatic in business that the low-cost provider has an edge on the competition. That has never been more true than in today's highly competitive business environment, and running a commercial real estate business is no exception. Outstanding REITs are able to manage their properties very efficiently, while also keeping overhead costs—administration, legal services, accounting, and so forth—under tight control.

We spoke about REITs' availing themselves of buying opportunities in a depressed market, but what about buying properties in a healthy market? Well, rich or poor, it's nice to save money. If it can keep property operating costs low, a REIT will be in a position to outbid competing buyers and still generate highly satisfactory returns on the acquired properties. Saving just 2 percent on annual property management expenses amounts to a total cost savings of $200,000 annually when a portfolio of properties generates $10 million of rental revenues.

But it isn't only property management expenses that need to be kept under control; overhead must be kept down as well. Let's consider a hypothetical REIT that owns $500 million of properties (at current market value) that generate unleveraged NOI of 9 percent, or $45 million per year, and has no debt. If the overhead costs amount to 1 percent of assets, or $5 million per year, the REIT's FFO (excluding interest expense—remember, we're assuming no debt leverage) will be $40 million, or 8 percent of current asset values. Compare this with a second REIT whose overhead costs amount to only 0.5 percent of assets, or $2.5 million. The second REIT will generate $42.5 million in FFO, providing an 8.5 percent return, and saving $2.5 million annually.

Controlling costs and operating with a low-cost structure are often overlooked factors when evaluating REIT management teams, but, over a significant period of time, the REIT that can contain its costs will provide greater long-term returns to its shareholders.

Track Record of Value Creation

Patrick Henry famously said, "I have but one lamp by which my feet are guided, and that is the lamp of experience." One of the most obvious but often neglected methods of determining the quality of a REIT management team is to review the REIT's historical performance. Does the REIT have a long and successful track record of increasing per-share FFO and NAV? Does it have a history of steady and rising shareholder dividends? How long has the REIT been a public company, and how has it weathered various real estate cycles? Has its management team found ways to protect cash flows even when its real estate markets have been depressed or when it's encountered stiff competition from new developments? How has it invested the capital that's been entrusted to it by shareholders and new investors? How does it truly create value for its shareholders?

These are questions that must be asked and answered in our quest for blue-chip REITs; a REIT with a successful track record in these areas—some of which can be measured objectively—will be highly esteemed by most REIT investors.

But we need to be realistic. The U.S. economy and its space markets are cyclical, and recessions—which cause market rents and occupancy rates to decline—will certainly impact REITs' cash flows. And when recessions are particularly severe (as in 2008 to 2009), dividends may have to be cut in recognition of difficult times. So even the bluest of the blue-chip REITs won't emerge from all recessions unscathed; even Boston Properties, Simon Property Group, and Vornado Realty, three of the largest and most respected REITs, cut their dividends during the Great Recession.

Nevertheless, today's REIT investors are fortunate. Many of the REITs that have gone public since 1993, and even some that were public before then, are blessed with management teams that are dedicated, highly experienced, and battle-tested in all sorts of space and capital market environments. By closely examining their track records of total returns (on an absolute basis and in relationship to their peers specializing in the same sector) over a long period of time, and by using some of the other criteria suggested in this chapter, we can, with diligence, ferret out those that meet the requirements of blue-chip REITs.

Today's REITs have finally proven that they can maintain successful long-term track records as public companies throughout entire real estate cycles. Certainly the evidence, at least over the past 10 years, has been impressive. Most REITs were less aggressive on the development front prior to the most recent economic and cyclical downturns, and they were net sellers at the top of the market in 2006 and 2007. They have also been more active in pruning their portfolios, at attractive prices, and have been disciplined with respect to acquisitions. And they have reacted quickly and effectively to the multitude of problems caused by the Great Recession. Thus, there are now more blue-chip REITs than ever before.

Access to, and Effective Deployment of, Capital

In determining which REITs deserve the "blue-chip" label, we also need to look at access to capital and how that capital is deployed. As we've seen earlier, access to capital to fund external growth such as acquisitions and developments is very important in determining a REIT's potential long-term returns to shareholders. Likewise, how a REIT chooses to allocate its precious capital is vital to shareholders' assessment of a REIT's long-term value as an investment.

Access to Capital—and Its Benefits   A REIT with a good track record, which has earned shareholders' respect, will have greater ability to raise new capital upon which a satisfactory return can be earned. Although most REITs could raise equity capital from 1996 through early 1998, very few were able to do so from then until 2001. REITs were put in the penalty box because many of them were perceived as having done a poor job of allocating the capital that was given to them in prior years. Even though a substantial number of REITs were able to raise equity during the credit crunch of 2008 and 2009, raising capital is not a God-given right of a REIT.

When markets are in equilibrium, it would be reasonable to expect that a REIT, as the owner of a portfolio of commercial properties, will enjoy NOI growth at or slightly above the rate of inflation, say

2 to 3 percent. Using debt leverage might enable the REIT to obtain 3 to 4 percent FFO growth. However, if it has access to additional equity capital, it often will be able to buy additional properties, hopefully at prices that will deliver returns in excess of its cost of capital, or pursue new developments. This type of external growth potential can enable a REIT to grow its free cash flow at above-average rates (while also creating value for its shareholders). Simply put, this is one of the principal reasons why many outstanding REITs will, over many years, be able to report FFO growth of 5 to 6 percent per year, on average.

TIP

Both access to capital and investing capital wisely are key factors in separating the blue-chip REITs from the rest.

The Importance of Allocating Capital Wisely

But obtaining capital is one thing. Using it effectively is quite another. A blue-chip REIT won't squander that capital by making investments at returns less than its true cost. Rather, it will create value for its shareholders by investing it effectively, in property acquisitions, new developments, or in other ways. And it is the *spread* between the investment return and the cost of capital, adjusted for risk, that's most important for investors, not just the absolute levels of capital costs or investment returns.

Some REIT investors use the term *franchise value* to refer to the ability of a REIT to generate returns on new opportunities that exceed its cost of capital. There are times, such as in the early 1990s, when franchise value is easy to accumulate, due to REITs' ease in obtaining outsized returns; this may be due to an abundance of

Value Creation

Value creation can be defined as the positive difference between the true cost of capital and the long-term return obtained from the use of that capital, discounted to net present value. It can be manifested in higher income and/or greater net asset values. This concept is appropriate for *all* business enterprises.

buying opportunities in the real estate markets. Conversely, there have been other times, as in the late 1990s and the early years of the twenty-first century, when few REITs could avail themselves of such opportunities. And there are yet other times when only some REITs, operating in specific sectors, have been able to do so.

But blue-chip REITs, due to imaginative management and multiple strategies for creating value (along with a strong balance sheet), often have better value-creating opportunities than other REITs regardless of the status of the economy or the real estate markets. And they allocate and invest their capital wisely—they build lasting franchise value. How do they do so?

Capital can be allocated by a REIT in various ways, including acquisitions of single properties or entire portfolios, the purchase of real estate–owning companies (such as other REITs), engaging in new property developments or joint ventures, repurchasing its own stock, paying down debt, or even, at times, launching a new real estate–related business or investing in an operating company. Sometimes these investments are made through a taxable REIT subsidiary (TRS). For example, Ventas, a widely respected health care REIT, has been able, through its TRS, to more directly participate in income increases from its assisted-living community business.

The overriding issue for investors is to determine whether capital thus invested or otherwise deployed will generate strong returns for its shareholders, particularly when risk is factored into the equation. Was that recent acquisition done at a market price, or did the REIT get a great deal? What's the upside potential—and prospective IRR—from the acquisition? Is the new development likely to succeed, and to what extent—and is it worth the risks? Is management stepping outside of its field of expertise? As a Clint Eastwood movie character once noted, "A man's gotta know his limitations," and that admonition certainly applies to REIT management teams. Buying entire companies is often problematic. Does the REIT have a good reason for doing so? Is it growing just for growth's sake? Or to create property geographic diversification that REIT investors can get on their own by buying an assortment of REITs? What kind of premium is being paid, and how long will it take for the REIT to earn back that premium in the form of cost savings, more efficient property management, greater negotiating power with tenants, or a higher growth rate? How is it being financed? Is it a good time to retire debt, or should the balance sheet be "expanded" to take advantage of an apparent abundance of real estate opportunities? Did management plan conservatively when it launched that new business activity, and will it augment the growth rate of its core business? Is raising new equity even necessary—can growth be financed more cheaply through capital recycling or a joint venture strategy?

These are the kinds of difficult questions that investors need to ask themselves when trying to determine whether a REIT is effectively deploying its capital and creating value for its shareholders. Blue-chip REITs will do this well and consistently. Of course, most of these questions can be answered only in hindsight, and sometimes it can take quite some time before the answers are known. Nevertheless, to the extent that a REIT proves that it can be trusted to allocate and invest its capital wisely and effectively, it will not only be able to access additional capital, if needed, with which to generate higher growth rates but will also be accorded a higher stock market valuation by investors.

Balance Sheet Strength

A third factor that can help to ferret out blue-chip REITs is the balance sheet. Property owners like to use debt to partially finance their acquisitions. At certain times, such as when an individual buys a single-family residence, the amount of debt has greatly exceeded the amount of equity put into the property. Developers, too, have sometimes been able to obtain 90 percent, even 100 percent, financing, and loan-to-value ratios for commercial real estate buyer-borrowers have, at times, been very generous.

TIP

Debt leverage increases both the risks and rewards of owning real estate—and may not create any meaningful shareholder value.

Most investment advisers discourage buying stocks on margin; doing so, of course, magnifies both gains and losses but, perhaps even more important, sometimes forces an investor to sell at temporarily low prices when markets are seized with fear. So why is real estate so often bought partially with debt, which is like buying stocks on margin? The long-accepted theory is that the stability and predictability of real estate cash flows, as well as the low volatility of real estate prices, justify a moderate amount of debt leverage to buy and own quality real estate. The debt leverage is intended to improve investment returns.

But perhaps it's time to question that belief, for several reasons. Recessions—and credit crunches—are not predictable, and seem to have been arriving with greater regularity. Real estate prices may fluctuate more in the future than in the past, due, perhaps, to greater concentrations of short-term capital looking for the best risk-adjusted returns globally; falling prices can wreak havoc upon leveraged owners. The REIT industry experienced a huge and frightening margin call during the Great Recession. Using debt leverage may create substantial value for a REIT's shareholders only when available properties are unusually cheap or cash flows and property values are rising enough to more than offset the added risks inherent in debt leverage. But both of those situations can be known only with hindsight. Great market-timers are as scarce in the world of real estate as they are in the stock market.

Although a modest amount of debt leverage is not terribly dangerous to property owners in normal economic environments, using debt may not add a lot of value over time—and having too much of it simply isn't prudent. Says Green Street Advisors' Mike Kirby, quoted in a *Wall Street Journal* story dated January 6, 2010, "At its core, commercial real estate should be an income-oriented investment. But when you overlever you take away those merits."

Perhaps the bottom line is that modest debt leverage is acceptable when it doesn't compromise the strength of a REIT's balance sheet. It may enable a REIT to capture greater investment returns when good investment opportunities are abundant. Conversely, even a REIT with strong management, presented with the best development or acquisition climate in the world, will nevertheless be shut out of the capital markets and find itself unable to take advantage of opportunities if it has a weak balance sheet, perhaps marred by excessive debt leverage.

Debt Ratios and Interest Coverage Ratios   What does a strong balance sheet look like? First, a modest amount of debt relative to a REIT's total market cap, to the total market value of its assets, or to earnings before interest costs, income taxes, and depreciation and amortization expenses (EBITDA); second, strong coverage of the interest payments on that debt, and other fixed charges, from operating cash flows; and third, a manageable debt maturity schedule.

Debt Ratios   Suppose a REIT has 100 million shares of common stock outstanding (including partnership units convertible into shares), and its market price is $10 per share, for a total equity capitalization of $1 billion. It also has $100 million of preferred stock outstanding, and indebtedness of $600 million. The debt/market cap ratio can be determined by dividing debt ($600 million) by the sum of the common equity cap ($1 billion), the preferred stock ($100 million), and the debt ($600 million), resulting in a debt/market cap ratio of 35.3 percent. Here's the formula:

Debt/Market Cap Ratio = Total Debt/(Common Stock Equity
+ Preferred Stock Equity
+ Total Debt)

Some analysts, such as Green Street Advisors, prefer using a ratio based on the estimated asset values of a REIT, instead of the debt/total market cap ratio. For example, if a REIT had $100 million in debt and total asset values (an estimation of the fair market values of its properties) of $300 million, its debt/asset value ratio would be $100 million divided by $300 million, or 33 percent. This method, which focuses on the *asset value* of a REIT rather than its *share valuation* in the stock market, has two advantages: it is more conservative (as REITs have generally traded at market valuations modestly in excess of their NAVs), and it avoids rapid fluctuation in debt ratios (a REIT's share price is usually more volatile than the value of its assets). Advocates of this formula believe that a REIT's leverage ratio should not be subject to a temporary rise or decline in its stock price if the price movement has nothing to do with operations or property values. Nevertheless, the debt/asset value ratio is less frequently utilized than the debt/total market cap ratio as the former involves a subjective factor (estimated asset values).

Debt/Asset Value Ratio = Total Debt/Estimated Value of All Assets

How much debt leverage is acceptable in a blue-chip REIT? First, let's look at some historical averages. At the end of 1995, Robert Frank, who has followed the REIT industry for many years, estimated that REITs' historical debt/total market cap ratio averaged, up to that time, 34 percent *(Barron's, December 18, 1995)*. According to SNL Securities and National Association of Real Estate Investment Trusts (NAREIT) data, this percentage has increased moderately since then, rising to an average of approximately 43 percent by the fourth quarter of 2003, falling briefly to a low of 36.6 percent in the fourth quarter of 2006 (when REIT stock prices were high), and then moving back up to 44.8 percent in the second quarter of 2008 as REIT stocks declined. Debt leverage ratios rose even further into 2009 as REIT prices were victimized by a bear market; as a result, debt had to be reduced with new equity offerings and asset sales in 2009 and 2010. At the end of the third quarter of 2010, NAREIT data reflected an average debt ratio of 41.1 percent for equity REITs.

Today, even though some seasoned observers, such as Mr. Kirby, argue that debt leverage should be reduced even further, most REIT management teams and REIT-dedicated investors seem comfortable with leverage ratios in the low 40 percent range. Regardless, REIT investors should never forget that debt increases investment risk, and the amount of debt carried by a REIT should be taken into account when determining fair market value for any REIT stock. Blue-chip REITs will reflect modest debt ratios, for instance, generally no more than 40 to 45 percent in most environments. This

Debt/Market Cap Ratio Guidelines

Here are some general guidelines regarding a debt/market cap ratio:

- Anything over a 55 percent debt/total market cap ratio makes many REIT investors uncomfortable, particularly in the more volatile sectors, such as hotels, where cash flows are not protected by long-term leases.
- A ratio under 40 percent is almost always regarded as conservative and is an important indicator of a strong balance sheet, subject to the other yardsticks described in this chapter.
- When real estate prices are unsustainably high, or markets are softening, even a 50 percent debt ratio might create concern.

provides added investor safety and allows the REIT greater balance sheet flexibility.

Even though they have been utilized throughout REITs' history to determine leverage levels, debt/market cap and debt/asset value ratios can be misleading at times, and may provide an overly rosy picture when REIT stocks or property prices are at lofty levels. This lesson was learned in 2008 and 2009, when REIT stock prices and the values of their properties fell dramatically in response to the Great Recession, causing debt/market cap and debt/asset value ratios to spike. A "reality check" can be made by comparing a REIT's indebtedness to its expected EBITDA over the preceding or following 12 months. This enables the investor to look at a REIT's debt in the context of its free cash flow, before interest payments; the ratio of debt to EBITDA will, quite often, be more stable than its stock price or even its aggregate property value. Using this metric, a debt/EBITDA ratio of 5× to 7× may be considered acceptable, while a ratio of 4× or less will be quite conservative; a ratio above 8 to 9× may make conservative REIT investors uncomfortable.

The REIT sector averages in Table 8.1, provided by NAREIT at the end of the third quarter of 2010, provide a fairly recent reference point. Note the high debt/EBITDA ratios in many of the sectors, caused by falling rental revenues and NOI resulting

Table 8.1 Debt Ratios at Q3 2010

REIT Sector	Debt/EBITDA Ratio	Debt/Market Cap
Apartments	8.2×	44.6%
Neighborhood Shopping Centers	7.4×	45.6%
Malls	8.2×	52.3%
Health Care	5.0×	28.2%
Lodging	7.3×	50.0%
Office	7.2×	47.1%
Industrial	8.6×	44.8%
Self-Storage	4.8×	31.3%
Diversified	7.3×	54.0%

from the Great Recession. Fortunately, these ratios are expected to improve with the stabilization of space markets that began in mid-2010.

Interest Coverage Ratios   A different way to determine whether debt levels are reasonable or excessive is to look at the extent to which the REIT's EBITDA exceeds interest payments on its indebtedness. This relationship is often referred to as an *interest coverage ratio*. Sometimes analysts consider, in addition to interest expense, other recurring financial commitments such as dividend payment obligations on outstanding preferred stock or scheduled debt repayments ("fixed charges"). That ratio, so defined, is referred to as the *fixed-charge coverage ratio*, and is a more conservative test than the interest coverage ratio.

For example, if Trophy Office REIT has annual EBITDA of $14 million and carries debt of $100 million, which costs it $7 million in annual interest expense, then its interest coverage ratio would be $14 million divided by $7 million, or 2.0×. An interest coverage ratio significantly below 2.0× will often be cause for some concern.

Like the debt/EBITDA ratios discussed previously, many analysts prefer to measure debt leverage this way instead of looking at the debt/total market cap ratio or the debt/asset value ratio, since the former measurement provides a picture of how burdensome the debt service is in relation to current EBITDA. In other words, if the REIT is doing very well with its properties at a particular time and can obtain fixed-rate financing at reasonable rates, it may have little difficulty servicing the debt, even though debt leverage may be higher than desirable. As noted earlier, using interest coverage ratios, fixed-charge coverage ratios and/or debt/EBITDA ratios avoids the difficulty of assessing leverage during periods of rapidly changing stock prices and fluctuating property values. However, it does penalize those REITs that hold temporarily non-revenue-producing assets, for example, land or properties under development. And it may also unduly reward REITs that are enjoying unusually high—but temporary—rates of return on their assets. Accordingly, it is best to examine *all* of the foregoing formulas when making a judgment as to the strength and health of a REIT's balance sheet.

TIP

A careful REIT investor will look at debt/total market cap (or debt/asset value) ratios, debt/EBITDA ratios and interest coverage or fixed-charge coverage ratios in order to determine whether a REIT might be overleveraged.

Under adverse economic conditions or when property prices are falling, high debt levels in relationship to market cap, asset values or EBITDA, and low interest or fixed-charge coverage ratios, can be a time bomb waiting to explode. Yesterday's reasonable leverage and manageable debt might become tomorrow's overly aggressive leverage and crippling debt. There is no "magic number" that will enable REIT investors to be comfortable at all times, and no universally appropriate debt level or coverage ratio that, if exceeded, would make a REIT overlevered. Much depends on conditions in the space and capital markets, capital availability, stability of existing and prospective cash flows, and other factors—even a REIT's relationships with its lenders. Suffice it to say, however, that a hallmark of a blue-chip REIT will be a conservative and strong balance sheet—on an absolute basis and in relationship to its peers.

Variable-Rate Debt   But there is yet another balance sheet issue to consider: variable-rate debt. Variable-rate debt subjects the REIT and its shareholders to significantly increased interest costs in the event of rapidly rising interest rates. REIT investors invest in a REIT for its business and real estate prospects and don't want to see their expectations dashed because a REIT's management team guessed wrong on the direction of interest rates. Some variable-rate debt is appropriate, but it should be used sparingly. As a large portion of a REIT's total expenses is comprised of interest expense, substantially higher interest costs could cause a significant reduction in FFO and even, on occasion, result in a dividend cut. Conversely, fixed-rate debt is a positive, since it improves FFO stability and reduces exposure to changes in short-term interest rates.

Hotel REIT executives occasionally argue that some variable-rate debt is appropriate for them, as interest rates tend to rise when the economy is strong, and vice-versa. Hotels generally do quite

> ### Fixed-Rate Debt
>
> The advantage of fixed-rate debt is that it sets a specific interest rate for the entire duration of the debt instrument. In addition, if the borrower is allowed to prepay the debt should interest rates fall substantially after the debt is incurred, the borrower will have the opportunity to reduce interest costs. In recent years, many REITs have borrowed at a variable interest rate, but also entered into contracts by which the interest rate is capped at a level somewhat higher than the current short-term rate of interest. These caps can be expensive, their price depending on the duration of the cap and the width of the interest rate band. Generally, in spite of the cost, capped variable-rate debt is worth paying for because it is an insurance policy against the possibility of interest rates spiking due to higher inflation or an overheated economy. However, all such caps, and related "swaps," have termination dates.

well in strong economies, so variable-rate debt can serve as a hedge against weak economies, that is, lower hotel receipts can be partially offset by lower interest expenses.

Some REITs have, at times, inflated FFO growth by using cheaper, variable-rate debt to finance property acquisitions. The economics of a property acquisition should be analyzed on the basis of its being financed with equity and fixed-rate debt, as near-term "accretion" from variable-rate debt is usually meaningless. Thus, the *quality* of a REIT's FFO and its growth rate are suspect when the REIT relies heavily on variable-rate debt, and this issue should be recognized in the multiples of earnings that investors are willing to pay for REIT shares. Fortunately, the levels of variable-rate debt at most of today's REITs are modest, particularly the blue-chip REITs.

Despite the negatives, REITs, which often seek additional capital for external growth initiatives, will often find it advantageous to use *some* variable-rate debt. The typical pattern is for a REIT to establish a line of credit that can be used, with flexibility, on a short-term basis and then paid off through either a stock offering, the issuance of longer-term, fixed-rate debt, or the sale of assets. Credit line debt is usually at a variable rate. The key is the *amount* of such variable-rate debt in relation to enterprise value such as the REIT's estimated gross asset value or its entire market cap.

TIP

To the extent that variable-rate debt exceeds 10 to 15 percent of the value of a REIT's assets, a REIT may be exposed to earnings disappointments should interest rates escalate.

Maturity of Debt   It's axiomatic that real estate, being a long-term asset, should be financed with long-term capital.

An excessive amount of short-term debt (which must be repaid within one or two years) exposes the borrower to substantial risk. If for any reason a lender is unwilling to renew a significant loan to the REIT borrower when it comes due, and if no other source of refinancing can be found, the REIT will be forced to sell off assets at whatever price is offered, raise new equity at very dilutive prices, or even, on occasion, file bankruptcy proceedings. This issue was well more than of academic interest to many REITs during the credit crunch that accompanied the Great Recession. The mere threat of a failure to extend financing can cause a severe drop in the REIT's stock price, thus making fresh equity capital prohibitively expensive—if available at all.

Nationwide Health Properties, a well-respected health care REIT that was acquired by Ventas in 2011, experienced this problem in its early years. Under its original management team it took on substantial short-term debt, which the lender was unwilling to roll over at its due date. The REIT (then known as Beverly Investment Properties) was required to sell off a significant number of assets and to reduce its dividend. General Growth Properties (GGP), a major mall REIT, amassed large amounts of short-term debt when it acquired Rouse Company in 2004. Although management believed that this debt would be manageable, the capital markets froze in 2008 and 2009, and it found that there was no practicable way to refinance its maturing indebtedness. Although the value of GGP's assets exceeded its liabilities, it was forced to file for bankruptcy in April 2009 in order to prevent creditors from seizing its mall assets. Although it was able to exit the bankruptcy court in 2010 and arrange for the payment or refinancing of its debts, many shareholders lost a great deal of money.

Accordingly, REIT investors must be mindful of the maturity dates of a REIT's debt. Some analysts look at the average debt maturity, and intelligent investors prefer that most of a REIT's debt not mature for at least several years. A modest amount of short-term debt is certainly acceptable, but the bulk of the debt should not be due for a number of years and should be at fixed interest rates. Blue-chip REITs stagger their debt maturities intelligently.

TIP

Wise REIT management teams will refinance expensive debt well before maturity, if this can be done with modest prepayment penalties, and seek a wide range of debt maturities.

The Importance of Sector and Geographic Focus

Many, many years ago, during the infancy of the REIT industry, it was believed important for a REIT to be well diversified by property sector and geographic location. Such diversification was deemed important for the reduction of investment risk. But that concept is no longer valid for two reasons. First, the major expansion of the REIT industry has allowed investors to create their own diversified property portfolio by owning a substantial number of REITs, each operating in a different location and owning a different property type.

Second, local market knowledge is a very important key to success in the property investment business. Let's consider this second point in more detail. There are many idiosyncrasies in local real estate markets relating to demand for space in the "best" locations, the nature and identity of the strongest tenants, the number of amenities required to make space competitive, and, with respect to property development projects, a whole host of zoning and entitlement procedures. And each property sector has its own unique set of operating and investment characteristics. To buy, manage, and develop properties well requires a deep familiarity and extensive experience with a property sector and specific markets.

TIP

The investor should indeed diversify—by buying shares in a number of REITs, each doing business in a different sector and location, not by trying to buy one REIT that tries to be all things to all investors.

A good example of a specialized REIT is AvalonBay Communities, an apartment REIT created from a 1998 merger of Bay Apartment Communities and Avalon Properties. Bay went public a number of years ago, after having been an active developer and owner of apartments in northern California since 1970. It never owned other types of properties. Management survived the depression-like conditions in California in the early 1990s and built an excellent track record in developing and refurbishing high-quality apartments. Avalon Properties, with which Bay merged, successfully owned, managed, and developed apartment communities in the Northeast and mid-Atlantic states for many years. Today, AvalonBay remains a strong competitor on both coasts, having a deep knowledge of local markets.

Local, specialized knowledge gives a REIT several advantages in its markets. Its management will be more likely to hear of a distressed seller who must unload properties, or the availability of a great development site. It will therefore be able to take advantage of unusual opportunities, and similarly, it may be able to close a deal before it's put out for competitive bidding. If it has development capabilities, it will know the best and most reliable contractors and will be familiar with the challenges and politics of getting zoning permits and variances. It will be very much aware of local economic conditions and which local markets are becoming more desirable. If it is a retail REIT, it will have good access to the up-and-coming regional retailers. The bottom line is that, in most real estate sectors, REITs that focus intensively on specific geographic regions have a significant competitive edge.

TIP

If it's important for a REIT to concentrate on a specific geographic area, it is even more important to specialize in one property type.

Real estate ownership and operation is as competitive as ever. Each type, or sector, of commercial real estate has its own peculiar set of economics, and it's far more likely that a management team familiar with one particular sector's idiosyncrasies and supply/demand issues will be better able to navigate through rough waters—and take full advantage of unusual opportunities—than a management team that tries to adjust to the shifting economics of several different property types. Only a very few, such as Washington REIT and Vornado Realty, have managed to do well consistently with multiple asset types.

For all these reasons, most blue-chip REITs will specialize in both sector and location. Examples in the apartment sector include BRE Properties and Essex Property; the former has limited itself to only the West Coast, Arizona, and Colorado, while the latter is focused only on California and Washington.

There are, however, some exceptions. Health care REITs that own nursing homes, for example, may find geographic concentration a negative; nursing home operators depend on state Medicaid payments and are subject to various other regulations—having too high a percentage of total assets in one state means excessive exposure to the vagaries of that state's reimbursement policies. Mall REITs also have less need for geographic concentration, and their lack of geographic focus shouldn't be a significant issue with investors. Indeed, a wide-ranging presence can improve a mall owner's negotiating position with its larger retail tenants. Mall economics are similar in most areas of the United States, and a large percentage of mall tenants are national retailers, for example, Gap Stores. And self-storage REITs, such as Public Storage, have benefited from national marketing strategies and brand-name recognition across the United States.

Many blue-chip REITs have been expanding their businesses into additional regions, some even becoming national players. It can be advantageous for a retail, health care, or even an apartment, office, or industrial REIT, to have locations in several neighboring states because of the importance of size, market dominance, and tenant relationships. Duke Realty is a good example. It operates in a number of Midwest and Southeast states, and because of its relationship with strong regional companies needing industrial and warehouse space, its geographical reach has provided a wider range of prospective tenants.

In other cases, blue-chip REITs simply outgrow their home base. For many years known as the dominant neighborhood shopping center owner in Houston, Weingarten Realty has frequently entered new markets in Sunbelt states. Another well-respected retail REIT, Regency Centers, has expanded well beyond its origins in Florida, while Camden Properties and UDR Inc., strong apartment REITs, have greatly expanded their footprints. EastGroup, a well-respected industrial property REIT, has expanded successfully into several Sunbelt locations. Some veteran REIT investors may decry such wanderlust, but at some point many well-run and growing real estate companies like those just mentioned will look for promising new markets. If the REIT applies the same degree of innovation and foresight to its new markets, investors need not be overly concerned—but it must have experienced local management in place and seek to become a strong local player.

Finally, we are now seeing the presence of powerful national REITs, with assets in major markets throughout the United States; Equity Residential, the largest apartment REIT, is national in scope and has performed well. Others, such as AMB Properties and Boston Properties, have developed a very strong local presence in selected regional markets. AMB, which merged with ProLogis in 2011, owns productive logistics and distribution properties at major transportation hubs, while Boston Properties owns important office assets in four key markets—New York City; Washington, D.C.; Boston; and San Francisco. The key to the continuing success of these REITs will be their competitive position and management strength in each of their local markets, together with the ability of corporate headquarters to walk the fine line between providing adequate guidance and allowing for local initiative and creativity.

It's therefore not necessary that a REIT limit itself to only a few markets if it wants to earn the designation of "blue chip." However, I believe that the smaller the REIT, the more it should focus its limited resources on only a few markets that it knows well and where it can obtain a competitive advantage through local contacts and other relationships. And the small REIT has one important advantage: one or a few excellent opportunities captured can really "move the needle" with respect to earnings growth and NAV accretion.

TIP

REIT investors should put the burden of proof on those REITs with a presence in many different geographic locations to show that they have become market leaders in each of them.

Conservative and Intelligent Dividend Policy

Another criterion for separating REIT "haves" from REIT "have-nots" is the dividend policy. Is it well designed in the context of the limitations on a REIT's ability to retain earnings, prospects for the space markets in which the REIT holds properties, external growth opportunities such as acquisitions and developments, and its cost of debt and equity capital? Is it conservative enough to withstand unexpected adverse market conditions but not so conservative as to alienate income-oriented investors?

One key issue for investors is the REIT's payout ratio of dividends to adjusted funds from operations (AFFO). As new equity capital is so often expensive, the best-managed REITs prefer to retain a substantial slice of their operating income for acquisitions, developments, and other opportunities that invariably arise from time to time. Using retained capital is cheaper than raising debt capital or selling additional shares.

TIP

A modest dividend payout ratio, for instance, dividends to AFFO or free cash flow, allows the REIT to retain some cash for external growth.

A modest payout ratio is also good insurance against unexpected events that might cause a temporary downturn in free cash flow. Although it would be nice if their earnings climbed higher each and every year, REITs operate in a cyclical industry and are subject to such surprises as recessions, rising vacancy rates, tenant defaults, lower rents due to overbuilding or other supply/demand imbalances, or higher-than-anticipated operating expenses. If a REIT pays out too much of its AFFO in dividends, it may create investor concern about the possibility of a dividend cut, which could negatively affect the stock price and raise credibility issues regarding the management team.

Traditionally, REIT investors have been attracted to REITs, in substantial part, for their stable and gently rising dividends, and a significant dividend yield remains important to most real estate investors. However, with the recent increase in REITs' popularity among equity investors looking for strong *total* returns, together with the recognition of the importance of creating value through the deployment of retained earnings, conservative payout ratios (consistent, of course, with REITs' statutory dividend payment requirements) are a very desirable REIT trait.

 TIP

REITs with low payout ratios will generally have better growth potential, as well as better investor perception of dividend safety.

Just what should we be looking for in payout ratios? Let's begin with the premise that AFFO is superior to FFO in determining a REIT's free cash flow. If a REIT claims to have earned $1.10 per share in FFO but uses $0.15 of that for recurring capital expenditures each year, it really has only $0.95 available for dividend distributions. Further, if it pays out the full $0.95 in dividends, it will have retained absolutely nothing with which to expand the business or to reserve against the effects of occasional stormy weather. Accordingly, the wise investor will look at a REIT's ratio of dividends to AFFO, not FFO. If AFFO is $0.95 and the dividend rate is $0.85, the payout ratio would be $.85 ÷ $.95—or 89.5 percent. Or we can reverse the formula, with the $0.95 AFFO divided by the $0.85 dividend; this is known as the *dividend coverage ratio*, in this example approximately 112 percent ($0.95 ÷ $0.85).

NAREIT regularly publishes the average payout ratios of REITs over time, using FFO rather than AFFO, as the former measure is

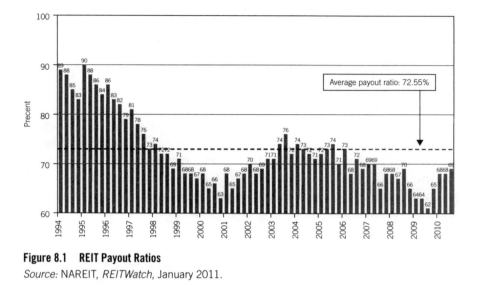

Figure 8.1   REIT Payout Ratios
Source: NAREIT, *REITWatch*, January 2011.

calculated by each REIT on a quarterly basis and is thus more read-ily available. See, for example, Figure 8.1. As of the end of the third quarter of 2010, the average payout ratio as a percentage of FFO was 69 percent. This ratio fluctuates over time, and tends to increase dur-ing periods when cash flow is weak, for example, in the aftermath of recessions. The long-term average going back to 1994, as of late 2010, was 72.6 percent, and has generally reflected a modestly declining trend. When NAREIT first began to compile these ratios, in 1994 and 1995, the average payout ratio was in the 85 to 89 percent range. Of course, there are wide differences from REIT to REIT.

Equity Residential, a large and well-respected REIT in the apart-ment space, announced in 2010 that it would pay a very conservative regular dividend during the first three quarters of its fiscal year. But for the fourth quarter, "the company intends to pay a dividend that will bring the total payment for the year to approximately 65 percent of FFO as adjusted for certain non-comparable items." This interesting concept balances investors' desire for steady dividend income with a REIT's need to size its annual dividend rate to existing cash flows. We may see other REITs emulate this type of flexible dividend policy.

High payout ratios do not necessarily mean dividend cuts. Most REITs will keep their dividends intact when they can anticipate a near-term improvement in their cash flows due to strengthening real estate markets. Furthermore, many REITs have been able to fund a significant portion of any shortfall out of property sales at substantial profits. But paying out more than warranted by free cash flow over an extended period of time isn't smart and amounts to slow liquidation by a REIT.

A few last words about payout ratios. There may be times in the REIT sector's business cycle when acquisition or development just doesn't make sense. At such times, a higher payout ratio might be the most efficient use of the REIT's free cash flow. A REIT may even sell properties and distribute the net proceeds as a special dividend, as Boston Properties and a few others have done on occasion. Growth shouldn't be force-fed, and sometimes the best deployment of retained earnings is to return it to the shareholders.

Although some REIT investors—whose primary investment objective is income rather than substantial capital gain—may prefer relatively high dividend payout ratios, most blue-chip REITs tend to have lower dividend payout ratios, which are likely to contribute to better long-term growth and, hopefully, greater total returns. Again, there's no free lunch!

Good Corporate Governance

Corporate governance is a nebulous and squishy—but very important—concept in the world of publicly traded stocks. I think of it as describing (1) how well a public corporation is governed internally by its stewards (the board of directors and executive management team); (2) to what extent these stewards adopt bylaws, rules, regulations, and policies that are likely to result in sound decisions being made and outside shareholders being treated fairly; and (3) whether these rules and policies are enforced honestly and impartially. A blue-chip REIT will be strong in each of these areas.

There are many aspects of good corporate governance, and books can be—and have been—written about it. Let's briefly review some of the more important governance issues that can arise in the REIT world.

Many years ago, conflicts of interest were a key issue for REIT investors. At times, the conflicts were blatant, for example, the sale of an insider's property to the REIT he manages. Conflicts abound when a public REIT is managed by an outside adviser, which is paid a fee based not on the profitability of the REIT or its returns to shareholders but on the dollar value of its assets. This can give the outside adviser an incentive to increase the amount of the REIT's assets simply as a basis for increasing the fees—decisions not necessarily for the long-term benefit of the REIT or its shareholders. Today, fortunately, the vast majority of REITs are internally administered and managed, and managements' interests are aligned much more closely with those of the shareholders. Of course, substantial stock ownership by management can also alleviate any concerns.

Although a few potential conflicts still remain, they are more subtle. On occasion, a key executive officer of a REIT may not be a full-time employee and thus not fully involved in the business. Executive officers may own operating partnership units, rather than stock, and thus (due to adverse tax considerations) may not want to sell an asset when such a transaction would benefit shareholders. Some compensation plans motivate the executive officers to emphasize short-term FFO growth rather than long-term value creation, while others are simply too generous for the size of the company or are based on easily met or inappropriate bonus criteria.

There is another form of conflict of interests, sometimes reflected in charter documents or bylaws, which entrench management by giving insiders the ability to block unfriendly merger or buyout proposals.

The public markets have witnessed many instances when an attractive buyout offer at a premium price is rejected by the board of directors, sometimes at the insistence of the CEO or a major insider shareholder. The motivation of the directors and management team might be to continue running the company for as long as possible, for monetary or even psychological reasons; however, the motivation of the public shareholders is usually to obtain the best price possible for their stock, particularly if it has not been a good performer in the past and has uncertain prospects going forward.

REIT boards of directors seeking to ward off unwelcome suitors have one particular advantage over those of non-REITs. The laws pertaining to REITs require that "five or fewer" individuals cannot own more than 50 percent of the value of a REIT's stock. This enables REIT organizations to insert in their charter documents a provision prohibiting any person from acquiring more than, say, 10 percent of the stock of the REIT without prior approval of the

REIT's board of directors. Accordingly, hostile takeover offers are very rare in REITdom, and established management teams and their boards have been able to discourage merger-and-acquisition offers—no matter how attractive.

This strategy may be bolstered by other defensive tactics such as poison pills, "staggered" boards of directors, different classes of stock (each with different voting rights), super-majority voting requirements and other anti-takeover devices used to entrench management.

An issue that's not strictly a conflict of interests but that affects good corporate governance is the composition of a REIT's board of directors. Is the vast majority of directors truly independent, willing and able to reject inappropriate executive compensation programs or other policies unfriendly to public shareholders? And have these independent directors invested personal funds in the stock of the REIT, so that they have "skin in the game"? If so, how much have they invested? Finally, the attitude of the REIT's insiders toward public shareholders can sometimes be gleaned by what it's done in the past: how has it resolved potential conflicts, and does it have a track record of treating shareholders fairly?

All public companies, including REITs, must deal with these issues, but the lesson for us is that we want to see REIT boards of directors and management teams create structures to protect, and to act in the best interests of, *all* the shareholders.

The extent to which significant conflicts of interest or a less-than-ideal corporate governance impacts a stock price is unclear. But I believe that these issues will be important to many investors and should not be discounted. Of course, this doesn't mean that we should never own a REIT with poor governance. The fact that there is an opportunity for a decision that could adversely affect public shareholders doesn't mean that such a decision will in fact be made. But this is an area investors need to watch, and it is probable that poor governance does affect a REIT's stock price. The blue-chip REITs, as a group, tend to have few or no conflicts between management and shareholders, along with good corporate governance.

Insider Stock Ownership

After having fought the investment wars for many years, it's my belief that significant stock ownership in a company by its board of directors and management team will be an important contributor to the company's long-term success.

TIP

That profit is the best incentive is basic capitalism, and a management team that has a substantial ownership position in the REIT it manages will be making money for shareholders while it's making money for itself.

Why this is true is certainly no puzzle. What better incentive for success can there be than for the manager of the company to be an owner? REIT management teams that have a large equity stake in their company are more likely to align their personal interests with public shareholders' interests and look for long-term appreciation rather than the fast buck. They will sacrifice faster, short-term FFO growth, if necessary, in order to reach a long-term goal or create better shareholder value. They will avoid "goosing" FFO by taking on too much short-term, variable-rate debt and will not buy properties with limited long-term growth prospects just to increase FFO in the current fiscal year. Furthermore, REIT management teams with high insider ownership are likely to be more conservative about new development projects, as their net worth will be negatively affected by poorly conceived or poorly executed development strategies.

REITs historically have had a much higher percentage of stock owned by their own management teams than most other publicly traded companies. This was due, in large part, to the substantial number of REITs that went public in 1993 and 1994; most of them had been very successful private companies and, as they became REITs, the owners continued to hold large stock positions in the public entity. However, due to the passage of time, the large number of secondary stock offerings by REITs over the years, and the addition of younger professional managers by the REIT, the percentage of ownership of REIT shares by their management teams has declined. In assessing insider ownership, therefore, it is important to look at the number of shares (and stock options) owned by each member of the management team, and their market values, rather than the percentage of the REIT's outstanding shares that they own. We investors would like to see large stock positions held by key management personnel (with only occasional share sales); that is yet another hallmark of a blue-chip REIT.

TIP

For most REIT investors, owning a portfolio consisting of blue-chip REITs—those with management teams that use good judgment, that have access to capital with which to create shareholder value, a strong balance sheet, an intelligent dividend policy, and good corporate governance—will provide the most worry-free and the best route to long-term financial success in this asset class.

Summary

- The shares of *growth REITs* might appreciate quickly during certain time periods, and tend to trade at lower dividend yields; but because of their aggressive business strategies and high shareholder expectations, there's more risk in owning them.
- Shares of *value*, or *turnaround*, REITs often bear high dividend yields and have a higher risk factor. Sometimes they do manage to turn themselves around and appreciate in value, but these REITs must be watched closely, as it's difficult to know whether the perceived problems will be resolved.
- Bond-proxy REITs provide high dividend yields—in the range of 6 to 7 percent—but they have less well-defined growth prospects compared with other REITs. It's a trade-off.
- Blue-chip REIT stocks may appear more expensive than those of other REITs, but, when purchased at reasonable prices, they are usually the best long-term investment for conservative REIT investors.
- Qualities to look for in blue-chip REITs include experienced management with good judgment, access to capital when necessary to fund value-creating opportunities, balance sheet strength, sector focus and strong regional or local management, an intelligent and conservative dividend policy, and good corporate governance.

- The shares of REITs run by the very best management teams tend to perform well relative to their peers when measured over reasonably long time periods.
- Difficult economic periods frequently bring opportunities to those REITs with the resources available to take advantage of them.
- Access to capital—and the intelligent and profitable deployment of that capital—is a key factor in separating the blue-chip REITs from the rest.
- A REIT with a relatively low dividend payout ratio has more capital available for opportunities and has better protection against economic downturns and other stress factors.
- Look for strong corporate governance, including minimal conflicts of interest between management and public shareholders; substantial stock ownership by insiders is also a favorable attribute.
- For most investors, owning a portfolio of mostly blue-chip REITs is likely to provide the best total returns with the least risk and volatility.

The Quest for Investment Value

"The combination of precise formulas with highly imprecise assumptions can be used to establish, or rather to justify, practically any value one wishes, however high, for a really outstanding issue ... calculus [gives] speculation the deceptive guise of investment."
—Ben Graham, *The Intelligent Investor*

Successful REIT investing is a marathon, not a sprint. The wise REIT investor will buy quality merchandise at reasonable prices, and hold on despite often annoying volatility and the ups and downs of commercial real estate cycles. Nevertheless, our returns will be higher if we are able to add new stocks to our REIT portfolios (and cull them occasionally), taking advantage of overvalued or undervalued situations. In this chapter we'll look at some yardsticks for determining the investment value of a REIT's stock.

The Investor's Dilemma: Buy-and-Hold versus Trading

One school of thought is that the key to investment success is to purchase shares of stock in the largest, most solid companies, or to buy mutual funds (actively or passively managed), and to hold those stocks or funds indefinitely. The only time to sell, say the buy-and-hold advocates, is when you need capital for other uses. Advocates of buy-and-hold have been bruised by the volatile stock markets of the recent past, including two significant recessions in the past 10 years, but they continue to believe that it's impossible to consistently and accurately time the markets, that economies will expand over time, and that profits of well-run public companies will grow—rewarding the patient and determined investor.

The other school of thought—a more hands-on approach—says that, with hard work and good judgment, an intelligent investor can beat the market or the broad-based averages, either by astute stock picking or by clever market timing. Some advocates of this approach, which rejects the theory that markets are normally quite "efficient," might point to investors such as Warren Buffett and Peter Lynch as examples of what a talented stock picker can accomplish, while others in this group believe that certain signs— technical or even astrological— can indicate when either the entire market or specific stocks will rise or fall.

Advice for the buy-and-hold crowd with respect to REITs is simple: assemble a portfolio of blue-chip REITs or buy a managed or indexed REIT mutual fund or REIT exchange-traded fund (ETF). Then, if you've chosen wisely, you can spend your time on the golf course, pocket the dividend income, enjoy long-term price appreciation, and not worry about price fluctuations, beating the competition, or any other such irrelevancies.

Advice for the active REIT trader who desires to perform better than the REIT market is somewhat more complicated. First, you must have a way to determine when a REIT stock is overpriced or underpriced, given its quality, risk profile, underlying asset values, and growth prospects. Second, you must have a way to judge when REIT stocks *as a group* are cheap or expensive. Valuation of any stock is never easy, but there are guidelines and tools that can help determine approximate values.

But before we delve into REIT valuation methods, which will be of interest primarily to those who want to actively manage their REIT portfolios or want to try timing the REIT market, let's quickly summarize the buy-and-hold strategy. (Those who want to invest in REITs passively, particularly through mutual funds or ETFs—and even those who simply have a very long investment horizon—might want to read the following short section, then skip ahead to Chapter 10).

The Buy-and-Hold Strategy

TIP

The buy-and-hold strategy has a number of advantages. Investors don't need to worry about real estate cycles, occupancy or rental rates, or even REITs' asset values. Rather, they will simply place their faith in experienced REIT management teams and be patient.

Also, since these investors are not active traders, commission costs and capital gains taxes will be much lower. Furthermore, if the efficient market theory is correct, it's not possible to beat the market anyway, and a buy-and-hold REIT portfolio should slightly outperform a heavily traded portfolio or an actively managed mutual fund.

However, buy-and-hold has some disadvantages. If mutual funds are used—particularly if actively managed—investors will pay an annual management fee and other expenses and, in some cases, a marketing or sales charge. Mutual fund investing often involves extensive record keeping, especially when dividends and capital gains are reinvested. And, on occasion, entire property sectors may underperform for a number of years; buying and holding forever may not generate the best returns.

Buy-and-hold aficionados who don't want to go with a REIT mutual fund or ETF (we'll cover ETFs in Chapter 10) should be careful to construct a portfolio consisting primarily of a broadly diversified group of blue-chip REITs that have most of the characteristics we discussed in the previous chapter. These REITs are likely to grow in value over time, notwithstanding occasionally difficult real estate markets, and will have management teams that can be counted on to avoid serious blunders. They can be compared to blue-chip, non-REIT stocks such as Caterpillar, Coca-Cola, or Exxon. But the blue-chip REIT of the type we discussed in the previous chapter isn't always large in size; there are a number of excellent smaller REITs that qualify as blue chips and that can be owned for diversification. The investor may also want to include some "growth," "value," or "turnaround" REITs for additional diversification.

Of course, not all blue-chip REITs will deliver the expected returns, since *any* public company is subject to management mistakes and challenging economic conditions, as well as a slew of other potentially negative developments. Furthermore, all stocks, including REITs, are subject to periodic bear markets, sometimes having little to do with how the company itself is performing.

REIT Stock Valuation

 TIP

Active REIT investors will want to spend time analyzing and applying one or more valuation methodologies to seek maximum investment performance for their portfolios.

Investors who are not content with a buy-and-hold strategy and who want to buy and sell REIT stocks more actively and take advantage of undervalued situations will need to know how to determine value.

Can we really determine what a REIT stock is worth on an absolute basis or relative to its peers? And can we make intelligent decisions as to whether REITs as a group are cheap or expensive? Professional REIT investors and analysts each have their own approach; there is no general agreement on which one works best. But, although there is no Holy Grail of REIT valuation, there are commonly used methods and formulas that can provide helpful insight into a REIT's merit as an investment at any particular time, bands of reasonable values based on historical precedent, and even assessments of the fairness of pricing of all REIT stocks as a group.

Real Estate Asset Values

Until the past few decades, analysts and investors in the wide world of equity investing have thought it important to look at a company's "book value," which is simply the net carrying value of a company's assets (after subtracting all its obligations and liabilities), as listed and recorded on the balance sheet. But that method of valuation has serious drawbacks. Plant, equipment, and inventory usually comprise only a small part of a company's value. Furthermore, "intellectual capital," brand-name recognition, and "franchise value" are now generally deemed more important than the book value of physical assets. Although some analysts and investors may examine "private market" or liquidation values rather than book values, most of them focus on earnings and earnings growth. Indeed, with very few exceptions, stocks generally trade at prices well above their book values.

Furthermore, book value has never been a satisfactory way to value real estate companies because office buildings, apartments, and other such properties do not necessarily depreciate at a fixed rate each year, as suggested by generally accepted accounting principles (GAAP), while land is carried at cost but tends to increase in value over time.

And yet, although the vast majority of today's REITs are operating companies that focus on growing their cash flows and dividends, and will rarely be liquidated, they do own real estate whose values *can* be assessed and approximated through careful analysis. Furthermore, these assets are much more liquid than, say, the fixed assets of a manufacturing company, a distribution network, or a brand name, and thus the market values of REITs' assets are much less difficult to determine than those of non-REIT companies.

TIP

REITs are significantly more conducive than other companies to being valued on a net asset value (NAV) basis, and many experienced REIT investors and analysts consider a REIT's NAV to be very important in the valuation process, either alone or in conjunction with other valuation models.

One of the leading advocates of using NAV to help evaluate the true worth of REIT shares is Green Street Advisors, an independent REIT research firm that has a well-deserved reputation in the REIT industry for its excellent in-depth analysis. Green Street's primary approach is first to determine a REIT's NAV. This is done by reviewing the REIT's properties by segment and location, determining an appropriate cap rate for each group of properties, and applying the cap rate to a 12-month forward-looking estimate of net operating income (NOI). It then adds the estimated values of land, developments in process, equity in unconsolidated joint ventures, and an approximate value of fee income streams, nonrental revenue businesses, and other investments. Then, debts and other obligations are subtracted, and adjustments are made for government-subsidized financing and situations where market interest rates are significantly higher or lower than the rates the REIT is currently paying. Finally, the dollar amount of outstanding preferred stock is deducted. A per-share NAV is then calculated, which takes into account "in-the-money" options, operating partnership units, and convertible securities.

Green Street recognizes that REIT stocks shouldn't be valued merely at their NAVs at any point in time. Accordingly, it derives a "warranted share value" by taking into account a number of factors that the firm believes will have an impact on where a REIT stock should trade in relationship to its NAV. These include franchise value, or "the ability of a management team to create value" for shareholders; balance sheet strength; corporate governance; share liquidity; and corporate overhead expense ratios.

The net result, under Green Street's methodology, is the price at which the REIT's shares "should" trade when fairly valued. The firm uses a *relative* valuation approach, weighing one REIT's attractiveness against another's. It does not decide when a particular REIT's stock is cheap or expensive on an absolute basis, although it does provide general guidelines on REIT sector valuations.

An NAV-based approach to determining value in a REIT stock has a great deal of merit, notwithstanding its being difficult and often imprecise. It combines an analysis of underlying real estate

Finding Net Asset Value

Unfortunately, a REIT's NAV is not an item of information that can be obtained easily. REITs themselves don't appraise the values of their properties, nor do they hire outside appraisers to do so, and very few provide an opinion as to their NAV. Thus, NAV is not a figure you will find in REITs' financial statements. However, research reports from brokerage firms often do include an estimate of NAV. Also, investors who want to take the time to do so can estimate NAV on their own by carefully reviewing the financial statements, asking questions of investor relations personnel, and talking with commercial real estate brokers (or reviewing their web sites) to ascertain prevailing cap rates. Nevertheless, intelligent and useful NAV analysis is difficult and time consuming, and perhaps explains why it is given less attention than it deserves.

value with other factors that will affect the price investors should be willing to pay for a REIT's shares at any particular point in time. Since REITs are rarely liquidated, investors should ordinarily be reluctant to pay even 100 percent of NAV (or more) for a REIT's shares if the REIT has a habit of destroying shareholder value, excessive balance sheet risk, and/or poor corporate governance. Indeed, the history of REITdom has shown that the shares of some REITs *deserve* to trade at an NAV discount.

Conversely, investors should be willing to pay more than 100 percent of NAV for a REIT's shares if the strength of its organization and its access to capital, coupled with a sound strategy for external growth and value creation, make it likely that it will increase its funds from operations (FFO), NAV, and dividends at a faster rate than a purely passive, buy-and-hold commercial real estate investment strategy. This approach to valuation has worked well for Green Street and its clients, as the firm's track record of forecasting relative performance of specific REIT stocks has been excellent.

At any particular time, the premiums or discounts to NAV at which a REIT's stock may sell can be significant. Much depends on the particular REIT, and investors' perceptions from time to time as to its ability to grow earnings and create value (or vice versa), as well as the risks inherent in owning that stock. Another key factor, of course, is the market's perception of the future values of a REIT's properties; if the market value of its assets is expected to rise, perhaps because of generally rising commercial real estate values, the stock price, and its NAV premium, will rise in anticipation of those more favorable circumstances. REIT shares were trading at significant NAV premiums in 2009 and 2010 due, in large part, to investor expectations of a recovery in property prices following their crash during the Great Recession. Equities markets do, indeed, look forward.

Investors who use NAV analysis should develop their own criteria for determining an appropriate premium or discount to NAV, taking into account not only the rate at which the REIT will grow its NAV, FFO, or adjusted funds from operations (AFFO) relative to its peers and to a purely passive investment strategy, but all the other blue-chip REIT characteristics we have discussed in the prior chapter. Perceived risk, of course, should play a key role in this process.

An important advantage of NAV analysis is that it may keep investors from becoming excessively optimistic during periods of extraordinary but unsustainable FFO growth that occur from time to time. Let's look at the apartment sector. From 1992 to 1994, apartment REITs enjoyed incredible opportunities for FFO growth through attractive acquisitions, as capital was inexpensive and there was an abundance of good-quality apartment communities available for purchase at cap rates north of 10 percent. Furthermore, occupancy rates were rising and rents were increasing, since in most parts of the country few new units had been built for several years. As a result, FFO was growing rapidly. But analysts using valuation models that ignored NAV analysis might have valued the stocks of acquisitive REITs at excessively high prices—perhaps not realizing that unusually attractive acquisition environments tend to dissipate relatively quickly.

As was bound to happen, growth slowed substantially in 1995 and 1996 as apartment space and capital markets returned to equilibrium. Investors who bought stocks of apartment REITs trading at the then-prevailing high multiples of projected FFO never saw FFO growth live up to projections, and, consequently, saw little appreciation in their share prices for quite some time. A similar situation occurred in 1998 and 1999, when external growth slowed substantially for most REITs, and investors who ignored very high NAV premiums in 1997 experienced significant stock price declines.

Using an NAV model may also restrain an investor from giving too much credit to a REIT whose rapid growth in FFO results merely from levering up the balance sheet with debt. Interest rates on debt are usually lower than cap rates on real estate, making it easy for a REIT to "buy" FFO growth by taking on more debt, especially low-cost variable-rate debt. If only price-to-FFO (P/FFO) models are used, such a REIT might be assigned a high FFO multiple, based on expected rapid growth, without taking into account that such growth was bought at the cost of an overleveraged balance sheet.

As suggested earlier, perhaps the principal negative in NAV analysis is simply that, to be effective and meaningful, it must be done carefully and requires extensive research of various property markets and real estate cap rates. If the cap rates used to determine NAVs are off by as little as 1 percent, the derived NAV will bear little resemblance to reality. Investors who want a life outside of REITs should hope that the "fair value" accounting practices that are used in Europe, which provide for company reporting of estimated current real estate values, will eventually be brought to the United States. And this may happen. Although the winds of change blow slowly in the world of accounting, in May 2011 the Financial Accounting Standards Board (FASB) announced that it had reached some tentative conclusions regarding the reporting of investment properties at fair market value under U.S. GAAP standards, and that it would issue an exposure draft of the new requirements in June. It is impossible to know when REITs will be required, under these pending accounting rule changes, to report the fair market value of their properties–but this prospect is closer to reality now than ever before.

To summarize, a valuation model that focuses on NAVs is an excellent way to determine value in a REIT stock; also, if used intelligently, it can help the investor avoid overvalued REITs. We must, of course, remember to apply an appropriate premium or discount to NAV—*appropriate* being the significant word here—in order to give credit to the REIT's value-creating ability (or tendency to destroy value). The ability of smart and opportunistic management teams to add substantial value and growth beyond what we'd expect from the properties themselves can, at times, significantly exceed the REIT's real estate values. Some REITs, including Boston Properties, Kimco Realty, Regency Centers, and Vornado Realty, to name just a few, have been able to accomplish this at various times, but it is very difficult to create substantial excess value consistently. Accordingly, these premiums and discounts should fluctuate in response to economic conditions applicable to the sector, to real estate in general, and to the unique situation of each REIT.

It's my belief that a solid management team, an intelligent and well-executed business strategy, reasonably good access to capital, modest debt leverage, and substantial share liquidity are sufficient to warrant a modest (e.g., 5 percent) NAV premium during most market cycles, and that significant value-creating opportunities may entitle a REIT to an NAV premium of as much as 15 to 20 percent at times. Investors should, however, be wary of valuations in excess of that unless they believe that commercial real estate prices are poised for a significant increase or that a particular REIT has unusually attractive external growth or value-creation opportunities that will endure for several years.

P/FFO Models

Some REIT investors reject NAV analysis and consider it flawed because a REIT's true market value isn't based only on its property values. They argue that an NAV approach ignores the REIT's value as a business enterprise. These investors believe that, because REITs are rarely liquidated, their NAVs are not terribly relevant. If investors wanted to buy only properties, they say, they would do so directly. These REIT investors share a philosophy with common stock investors, who want to determine a business enterprise value. If we use price-to-earnings (P/E) ratios, or multiples, to value and compare regular common stocks, the argument goes, we should use P/FFO or P/AFFO ratios, or multiples (these terms will be used interchangeably), to value and compare REIT stocks.

This argument has some appeal—much more now than it did many years ago—because today many more REITs are truly businesses and not just portfolios of real estate. This view was confirmed by Standard & Poor's (S&P) when it decided, in 2001, to admit REITs into its S&P 500 index and related indices. Furthermore, most brokerage firms today make extensive use of P/FFO ratios (and P/AFFO ratios) when discussing their REIT recommendations. Nevertheless, P/FFO ratio analysis, if it's to be useful in REIT valuation, must be applied very carefully, and will be based on some very arbitrary assumptions. This makes it problematical to use as a stand-alone valuation tool. Although it may be somewhat helpful in comparing *relative* valuations among REITs, it is less helpful as a measurement of *absolute* valuations. Let's explore it now.

TIP

As various types of REIT valuation models do not always agree with one another with respect to their conclusions of value, they should be used in combination with one another. Furthermore, as predicting the future is more than challenging, we should keep in mind that *all* valuation models will be imprecise.

The P/FFO ratio approach might work something like this: If we estimate Sammydog Properties' FFO at $2.50 for the next 12 months, and we think that it should trade at a P/FFO multiple of 15 times the next 12 months' estimated FFO, then its stock would be fairly valued at 15 times $2.50, or $37.50. If it trades below that price, it's undervalued; if it trades above that, it's overvalued. Simple, huh? No, not at all!

But before we discuss how this simple-sounding formula is fraught with difficulties, let's take a couple of steps back. First, let's take a look at REITs' average price/FFO multiples for the principal property sectors, based on NAREIT data, as of December 2010 (these figures exclude one office REIT bearing a negative P/FFO):

Property Sector	2011 P/FFO Multiple
Office	13.4×
Industrial	18.3×
Retail: Shopping Centers	15.3×
Retail: Regional Malls	13.5×
Apartments	19.1×
Lodging/Resorts	16.3×
Health Care	14.1×
Self-Storage	16.5×
Diversified	13.2×
Timber	16.5×

As we discussed in a prior chapter, AFFO is a better indicator of a REIT's free cash flow than is FFO, but, unfortunately, AFFO figures are not reported by most REITs. The investor has the choice of either digging through various disclosure documents to construct a quarterly or annual approximation of AFFO, or obtaining AFFO data from a brokerage firm or another source. Most brokerage firms follow REITs and issue research reports on them. Industry publications such as those of SNL Securities are other good sources, and NAREIT provides substantial data on its web site. AFFOs may be approximated from these and other sources.

Now let's look at some of the practical difficulties in applying P/FFO or P/AFFO multiple analysis; we'll return to Sammydog Properties. How do we decide that Sammydog's P/FFO ratio should be 15 and not 12 or 20? Sammydog's price history may be a good starting point. We need to look at Sammydog's past multiples. Let's

The Relevancy of Past Statistics

Let's take a brief detour. When constructing valuation models based on statistics that may go back many years, some have made the point that the "Modern REIT Era" did not begin until 1992. Before then, there were few institutional-quality REITs. And yet, statistics from pre-1992 still have relevance for investors. They provide an accurate picture of the returns available to most investors who bought shares in such widely available and well-respected REITs as Federal Realty, New Plan Realty, United Dominion, Washington REIT, and Weingarten Realty, all of which were public companies for many years. One might argue that, because of the higher quality of today's REITs, future returns could be even better than they were prior to 1992. Much, however, depends on the prices at which REIT shares are acquired, as richer prices in relation to current cash flows usually mean lower future returns for *any* investment.

assume that between 2000 and 2010, the average P/FFO ratio for Sammydog Properties, based on expected FFO for the following year, was 12. Let's assume further that Sammydog's management team, balance sheet, and business prospects have improved and that the prospects for its sector are better than what they had been earlier. That might justify a P/FFO ratio of 14, 15, or 16 rather than 12. But we need to do more.

If we think that the market outlook for REIT stocks as a group is more or less attractive than it has been, we can use higher or lower multiples. We also need to factor in interest rates, which have historically affected the prices of all stocks. Perhaps a 1 percent increase or decrease in the yield on the 10-year Treasury note might equate to a similar adjustment in the ratio. But that's still not enough. We should adjust our warranted P/FFO ratio in accordance with prevailing price levels in the broad stock market; if investors are willing to pay higher prices for each dollar of earnings for most other public companies, they should likewise be willing to pay a higher price for each dollar of a REIT's earnings, adjusted for growth rates and risk levels of REITs versus other equities.

We must also compare the P/FFO ratio of Sammydog REIT to the P/FFO ratios of other REITs in the same sector and to the P/FFO ratios of REITs in other sectors. And, of course, we have to adjust for debt. Shares of REITs with higher debt levels must trade at lower P/FFO and P/AFFO multiples to account for greater risk; other aspects of a REIT's debt, for example, variable rate versus fixed rate, maturity schedules, and other relevant debt information also need to be factored in.

Furthermore, we should take into account the cap rates of Sammydog's properties; a REIT, such as Boston Properties, that owns 5 percent cap-rate assets should trade at a higher P/FFO ratio than a REIT in the same property sector that owns 7 percent cap-rate properties. And we must take qualitative factors into account as well. A strong, lower-risk blue-chip REIT should trade at a higher P/FFO ratio than a weaker one, as risk is an important factor in determining any stock's appropriate valuation.

There are also forward-looking, and even "macro," issues to consider, particularly with respect to REIT stocks in general. To what extent are past P/FFO ratios relevant to the period ahead? Where are prices for commercial real estate headed? What's the direction of short-term and long-term interest rates? In months and even years to come, how will individual and institutional investors perceive the virtues of REIT stocks relative to other common stocks? These are all factors that will affect the "warranted" P/FFO or P/AFFO ratio for Sammydog Properties, as well as for other REITs. But can these attempts at determining "appropriate" P/FFO or P/AFFO ratios be more than just wild guesses?

Despite the difficulties, getting appropriate P/FFO and P/AFFO multiples right can be helpful in REIT stock valuation. An example from many years ago is still relevant today. On October 31, 1997, the shares of Boston Properties, a widely respected blue-chip office REIT, were trading at $32 (an above-average P/AFFO multiple of 18.6 times the estimated 1997 AFFO of $1.72). Boston Properties has always been a fine company and has owned high-quality assets. Yet, although the REIT delivered outstanding AFFO growth over the next few years, its growth rate would slow with the office market recession. Boston's increasing AFFO from 1997 to 1999 was offset by a lower P/AFFO ratio, and the stock price stagnated, trading at $31.13 at the end of 1999. Investors who had bought at the relatively high P/AFFO multiple over two years earlier received nothing more than the dividends.

Those who determined that Boston's P/AFFO multiple was too high in 1997, despite the quality of the company and its growth prospects, avoided a very mediocre investment over the following two years. It's also important to note, however, that in October 1997 it might have been easier to conclude that Boston's stock was overvalued by looking at its NAV premium—which was a huge 39 percent!

More recently, the shares of most REITs were trading at lofty P/AFFO multiples in 2010 relative to historical norms. This may have been due to very low interest rates then prevailing, or an expectation for nicely rising earnings as property markets were poised to recover from their cyclical bottoms, or because of perceived substantial external growth opportunities through property acquisitions at very attractive prices. Were these lofty P/AFFO multiples warranted? As this book went to press, there was no clear answer to this conundrum; we'll know only with the benefit of hindsight (and even then we'll just be guessing).

These difficult issues involving P/FFO or P/AFFO models shouldn't cause us to discard them entirely as useful tools, but we must understand their limitations. A prevailing multiple that appears "too high" may merely be reflective of improving asset values and rising cash flows—and vice versa. Furthermore, we need to avoid the trap of justifying ever-higher "appropriate" multiples as stocks rise.

The bottom line is that P/FFO or P/AFFO valuation models are most helpful as *relative* valuation tools, determining whether one REIT is a better investment value than another at any given time. If we think one REIT has a stronger balance sheet, better management, more valuable properties, a less risky business strategy, and better growth prospects than another within its peer group, but the two trade at equal P/FFO or P/AFFO ratios, that's when this valuation tool can be useful—by helping us to choose between the two. Concluding, however, that a REIT stock is overvalued because it sells at 20 times estimated 2011 AFFO when our P/AFFO model says it should sell at only 18 times—well, don't bet the farm on that one. Yet another valuation tool might be helpful.

Discounted Cash Flow and Dividend Growth Models

Another useful method of REIT share valuation is to discount the sum of expected future free cash flows, or perhaps AFFOs, to arrive at a "net present value." If we begin with current or 12-month forward AFFO, estimate a REIT's AFFO growth over, say, 10, 20, or 30 years, and discount the value of all future AFFOs back to the present date at an appropriate interest (or discount) rate, we can obtain the approximate current value of all future free cash flows. Discounting AFFO this way somewhat overstates value, as investors don't receive *all* future AFFOs as early as implied by this method. Shareholders receive only the REIT's cash dividend, with the rest of the AFFO retained for the purpose of increasing future growth. Nevertheless, this tool can be helpful in suggesting a fair price for a REIT on an absolute basis, not just in relation to its peer group of REITs.

Several methods can be used to determine the all-important assumed interest or discount rate by which the aggregate amount of future AFFOs is discounted to arrive at current value. One way is to use the average cap rate of the properties contained in the REIT's portfolio, adjusted for the debt leverage used by the REIT. If the cap rate on a REIT's portfolio of properties averages 7 percent, and if the REIT uses no debt leverage at all, we might apply a 7 percent discount rate. The use of debt, of course, will require us to increase the discount rate applied; the greater the debt leverage, the higher the discount rate. This method has the advantage of applying commercial property market valuation metrics to companies that own commercial properties, and allows a drop or rise in cap rates to translate into a higher or lower current valuation for the REIT.

A variation of this method might be to use a mix of (1) private market cap rates applicable to the REIT's properties and (2) the current yield of a very low risk benchmark such as the 10-year U.S. Treasury note plus a "risk premium." The risk premium, under capital asset pricing model (CAPM) theory, is intended to reflect the extent to which REIT stocks are riskier than a riskless security, for example, 10-year Treasuries. There are various ways to determine an appropriate risk premium, but if one considers that REITs' average annual investment returns since 1972 have exceeded those of long-term Treasury bonds by approximately 330 basis points, then it is reasonable to expect that REIT investors will expect similar return spreads over U.S. Treasuries in the future. Thus, the analyst might set this portion of the discount rate formula at 10-year Treasuries + 330 basis points (technically, such risk premium should incorporate a "beta" factor, which is based on each REIT stock's price changes relative to a broad market index). This CAPM-based figure could then be averaged with the prevailing private market cap rate applicable to the REIT's properties to determine an appropriate discount rate— assuming the REIT is free of debt (a higher discount rate would be applied to adjust for the REIT's indebtedness).

Another approach toward ascertaining an appropriate discount rate is to assess the different types and degrees of risk inherent in each particular REIT stock and then decide what kind of total return we demand from our investment dollars when adjusting for that risk. If, for instance, we feel that we need an 8 percent total return in order to be compensated properly for the risk of owning a particular REIT stock, we'll use 8 percent as the discount rate. Investing in a higher-risk REIT, such as one with a very aggressive business strategy, or one using large amounts of debt leverage, would dictate a higher total return requirement. This method may produce more consistent valuations, but will be less sensitive to property cap rate fluctuations.

Each discount rate we use will produce very different results. For example, a REIT with an estimated first-year AFFO of $1 that's expected to increase by 5 percent a year over 30 years will have a net present value of $18.56 if we use a 9 percent discount rate. But applying an 11 percent discount rate will give us a net present value of only $15.01, while a 7 percent discount rate would suggest a present value of $23.23.

Because of the peculiarities of compound interest, there is little point in trying to estimate growth rates for very long periods of time; indeed, the contribution to net present value from incremental future earnings begins to taper off substantially after even just 5 years. Fortunately, although forecasting earnings is difficult, it's somewhat less difficult to forecast earnings for the first 5 years than it is for the next 30! Thus, a variation of this model might be to estimate the AFFO that will be earned over the next 5 years and obtain its net present value by applying an appropriate discount rate; we would then add a "terminal value," or "residual value," by estimating AFFO in the fifth year, applying a long-term growth factor to it, such as 2 to 3 percent (which may be slightly higher, depending on expected debt leverage), and then applying the discount rate to arrive at a net present value for these longer-term cash flows.

Another type of model, although similar in many ways, is the discounted dividend growth model. It begins with the dividend rate over the past 12 months, rather than current or 12-month forward estimated AFFO, and projects the current value of all future dividends over, say, 30 years, based on an assigned discount rate and an assumed dividend growth rate. A problem with this approach is that it can penalize those REITs whose dividends are low in relation to AFFO, unless the lower payout ratio is given extra credit with a higher assumed long-term dividend growth rate. Alternatively, a model can be created that assumes faster dividend growth only over the near term. A benefit of this method is that it values only cash flow expected to be received in the form of real money—dividend payments.

Both discounted cash flow and dividend growth models have their limitations. The net present value estimate is only as good as the accuracy of future growth forecasts and the wisdom of our assigned discount rates. As to the former, if we forecast 6 percent growth and get only 4 percent, our entire valuation will have been based on defective assumptions and therefore will be much too high (and, of course, we will undervalue a REIT stock if using excessively pessimistic forecasts).

We should also remember that, when assigning an appropriate discount rate, we need to take into account factors—even "qualitative" and subjective factors—beyond just the REIT's debt. These might include the quality of the management team (and its reputation and track record), business strategy, debt structure (including coverage ratios, fixed- versus variable-rate debt and maturity schedules), corporate governance, stock liquidity, and even insider stock ownership. Remember, there is as much art as science in all of these valuation tools.

Valuing REITs as a Group

Now that we've seen how individual REITs can be valued based on NAV analysis, P/AFFO ratios, and discounted cash flow and dividend growth models, can we also assess whether REITs, *as an asset class*, are cheap or expensive at any particular time?

Investors who bought heavily into REITs in the fall of 1997 or the spring of 2007 learned, to their regret, that sometimes *all* REITs can be overvalued—although that insight normally comes only with hindsight. Future stock price performance can be poor indeed following periods of overvaluation. Although, fortunately, REITs pay meaningful dividends while we wait, it can be very discouraging to watch the stock prices languish—or even drop sharply—for a couple of years.

We should expect REIT stocks to perform poorly in the event of a significant and unforeseen recession, or a major decline in property values, as occurred from 2007 through 2009. However, periods of REIT stock overvaluation can be followed by flat or declining prices even when earnings grow and REITs' property values are stable.

For example, in October 1997 Equity Residential, the largest apartment REIT, was trading at $50, or 13.6 times estimated FFO of $3.68 for 1997. Three years later, in October 2000, Equity Residential's stock was selling at $47, or only 9.5 times its estimated FFO of $4.97 for 2000. FFO growth was significant, but the stock price stagnated. "Multiple compression" hurt those shareholders who bought REIT shares at prices that we know, with hindsight, were "too high" in 1997.

 **TIP**

We should be aware of the importance of recognizing unsustainably high REIT stock prices—even though this is much easier said than done.

Is there any reliable way to determine whether REITs are expensive (or cheap) at any particular time? If we use P/FFO ratios as our principal valuation method and a high-quality apartment REIT like Equity Residential is selling at, say, 12 times expected FFO, and one of comparable quality, such as AvalonBay is selling at 10 times expected FFO, we may conclude that AvalonBay is undervalued relative to Equity Residential. But this doesn't tell us whether they're both cheap or both expensive. Similarly, one may be trading at a premium of 15 percent and the other at a premium of 5 percent over their respective NAVs, but this tells us nothing about what premiums over NAV these REITs—or any other REIT—*should* sell for. Is there any way out of this dilemma? Is there a way to determine how the *entire REIT industry* ought to be valued?

The use of an intelligently crafted discounted AFFO growth or dividend growth model may be of some help here. When the entire REIT market is cheap, the current market prices of *most* REITs will be significantly lower than the "warranted" prices indicated by such a model, assuming our projected growth and discount rates are reasonable. For example, if 60 of the 70 REITs that we follow come out of the "black box" of our discounted AFFO or dividend growth models as significantly undervalued, this could mean that REIT stocks, as a group, are being undervalued by the market. Nevertheless, these valuation models need to take into account possible future changes in the U.S. economy, and space and capital markets; perhaps when they are telling us that there are scores of cheap REIT stocks, they are failing to recognize impending negative developments in the real estate space markets or the economy. Financial markets are, indeed, complex systems.

We should thus understand that, as no one can predict the future with any degree of reliability, determining intrinsic values for any equity (or group of equities) will be merely an educated guess at best. No model is any better than the validity of the assumptions and forecasts we have put into them. Yet all is not lost—we do have history as a guide, imperfect though it may be.

If we know, for example, that REITs have historically provided dividend yields modestly above that of a low-risk bond benchmark such as the 10-year Treasury note, we have at least one useful tool by which to measure current REIT valuations. This data point is available from NAREIT. Its *REITWatch*, available on its web site (www.reit.com), periodically provides a graph that enables us to track that information (see Figure 9.1). As of the end of 2010, the graph shows that during the previous 20 years the average equity REIT dividend yield has been approximately 100 basis points higher than the yield of the 10-year Treasury.

Of course, this should be just a starting point. When REIT dividend yields are well above or substantially below the 10-year Treasury yield, suggesting cheap or expensive valuations, respectively, we will also need to discern the *reasons* for this apparent discrepancy; for example, perhaps REIT dividends are unsustainable or the Treasury note is priced to reflect temporary and unusual conditions in the credit markets, such as extreme risk aversion. If we cannot find any evidence to explain a pricing discrepancy, then this tool may help us to form a conclusion as to whether REIT stocks are cheap or expensive at the time of measurement.

Another method would be to compare REITs' current average P/FFO or P/AFFO ratios to their historical norms. At the end of

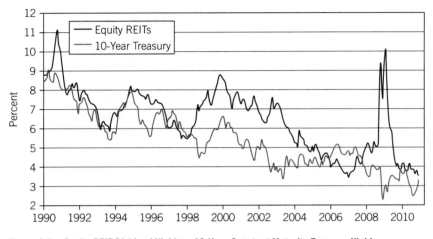

Figure 9.1   Equity REIT Dividend Yield vs. 10-Year Constant Maturity Treasury Yield
Source: NAREIT, *REITWatch*, January 2011.

2010, these multiples were well above those of the past, suggesting that REIT stocks were then overvalued. However, P/AFFO multiples were also unusually high at the end of 2009, and that didn't prevent REIT stocks from delivering total returns in excess of 20 percent in 2010. Thus, investors should look for *reasons* for high or low multiples; a higher-than-average multiple might be indicative of pending unusually rapid AFFO growth over the next few years, or even the market's view that NAVs are about to rise in reflection of lower cap rates and higher prices in the vast private commercial real estate markets.

It might also be helpful to know whether, and to what extent, REITs have historically traded at prices above (or below) their NAVs, and to compare that information with current NAV premiums (or discounts). Often, large NAV premiums or discounts as compared with historical norms simply reflect investors' perceptions of future changes in commercial real estate prices; in other words, large REIT NAV premiums may not be evidence of excessive pricing in REIT shares but, instead, merely reflect investors' reasonable expectations that commercial real estate prices are due to rise significantly.

Let's look briefly at a few historical examples. In 1998 (the year following the year in which REIT stocks were priced at a very lofty 27.4 percent premium above their NAVs), REIT stocks performed very poorly indeed, suffering a *negative* 17.4 percent total return. Thus, the high NAV premiums of the prior year may have been reflective of REIT stock overvaluation. But this approach doesn't always work. REIT stocks traded at an average 30 percent NAV premium in December 1996 (an unusually large premium) but they still managed to perform well in the succeeding year (+20.3 percent on a total return basis in 1997). A bit further back in time, REIT stocks delivered outstanding total returns in 1993 and 1994 despite selling at double-digit NAV premiums. And REITs' modest NAV premiums in early 2007, generally below 5 percent, didn't prevent a major bear market for REIT shares—the low NAV premium was, in hindsight, merely a reflection of unusually rich and unsustainable pricing in the private markets. So, while large NAV premiums or discounts should never be disregarded and often can be helpful in forming a broad-based assessment, they cannot be relied upon as sure and accurate predictions of the future direction of REIT stock prices (see Figure 9.2).

Another useful tool to determine whether REITs are cheap, expensive, or priced appropriately at any particular time is one used by Green Street Advisors in its *Real Estate Securities Monthly* reports to clients (see Figure 9.3); perhaps variations of this tool are used by other investors as well. This chart compares unlevered return expectations in the private real estate markets (based on

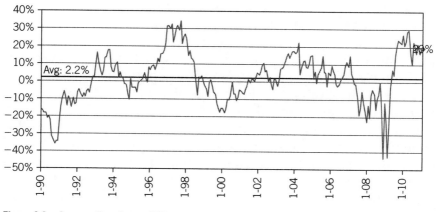

Figure 9.2   Average Premium to NAV
Source: Green Street Advisors.

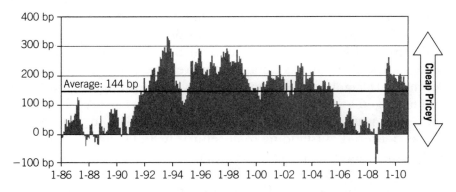

Figure 9.3   Return Premium on Real Estate Unlevered IRR Expectations Minus Baa Rate
Source: Green Street Advisors.

existing prevailing cap rates and cash flow growth expectations) with yields on a bond index, for example, the Moody's Baa-rated long-term bond index, to determine whether, using historical comparisons, private real estate markets are pricing commercial real estate appropriately. Then, REIT NAV premiums are examined in order to determine whether the prices of REIT shares have already discounted (or haven't discounted enough) expected movements in commercial real estate prices. Thus, for example, if it looks as though the private markets are underpricing commercial real estate in relationship to long-term intermediate-grade bonds, and if REIT stocks are not trading at large NAV premiums in reflection of those prospects, REIT stocks may be deemed cheap.

The conclusion we might draw from this discussion is that all of these models can help us to form an educated guess as to whether REIT stocks are cheap or expensive at a particular time, on the basis of their dividend yields versus the 10-year Treasury note, their earnings multiples, their NAV premiums or discounts relative to historical norms, or their prices relative to expectations for commercial real estate prices generally. But a very healthy dose of skepticism and caution is warranted; these tools may be helpful as general guidelines or indicators, but some canny crystal ball gazing will be necessary to determine whether the observed spreads, premiums, and multiples, no matter how high or low relative to historical norms, are appropriate in light of anticipated conditions in the U.S. economy, space markets, and credit markets. Let's remember, too, that commercial real estate and REIT stocks are no longer priced in a vacuum, and the prices and values of bonds, non-REIT stocks and other asset classes will affect the pricing of REIT shares.

There will never be a substitute for detailed factual investigation and thoughtful analysis, on both a quantitative and a qualitative basis, and historical metrics tell us only where we've been, not necessarily where we are going. While it's rarely, if ever, "different this time," we should also heed the advice of Peter Lynch: "You can't see the future through a rear view mirror."

Summary

- Buy-and-hold investors desire to own REITs for portfolio diversification and attractive total returns over time, and should have relatively less concern regarding quarter-to-quarter data such as FFO growth rates, occupancy and rental rates, or even asset values.
- Performance-oriented REIT investors will need to spend a fair amount of time analyzing and applying historical and prospective valuation methodologies in an effort to achieve maximum investment performance for their portfolios.
- There are a number of tools to help us evaluate REIT stocks. These include NAV-based models, P/FFO or P/AFFO models, and discounted cash flow and dividend growth models—all of which have their strengths and limitations.
- Because REITs own liquid–and often commodity-like–assets, their shares are more conducive than the shares of other public companies to being valued on a net asset value basis, and many experienced REIT investors and analysts consider a REIT's NAV to be very important in the valuation process, either alone or in conjunction with other valuation models; performing intelligent and useful NAV analysis, however, is difficult and time consuming.
- Because the various valuation tools do not always agree, they are best used in conjunction with one another and only as a general indication of whether the shares of any particular REIT are cheap or expensive. These models are best used to value one REIT stock against another.

- Similar tools can help to address the question of whether REITs, as an asset class, are cheap or expensive at any particular time. These include REITs' dividend yields in relation to an appropriate high-grade bond benchmark, the NAV premiums or discounts at which they trade versus historical norms, and their pricing relative to return expectations in the vast private real estate markets and to bond yield indices—and, perhaps, even to equities markets.
- Historical norms and patterns are often a useful tool in stock valuation, but must be tempered with careful inquiry and analysis—and even forecasts—regarding the economic, space, and credit market outlooks; future growth prospects; perceived risks; and even the relative attractiveness of other asset classes.

CHAPTER

Building a REIT Portfolio

"As a state of mind, Wall Street is no different from Main Street. Lazy and avaricious, prejudiced and easy to panic, it can believe in anything and just as readily shed its belief."
—Martin Sosnoff, *Humble on Wall Street*

If you've read this far, you're definitely interested in REITs. You may already have some idea of the types of REITs that are likely to meet your investment objectives, and perhaps even which sectors you favor. But, before you place buy orders, let's take a step back and seek some perspective on REITs as investments.

How Much of a Good Thing Do You Want?

Almost every book on financial planning and investing discusses asset allocation: how much of one's portfolio should be in stocks (domestic and international, large-cap and small-cap, growth and value), how much in bonds, how much in real estate, and how much in cash. And let's not forget commodities and other "alternative investments." Some experts say that as we get older we should shift more into bonds and put less in stocks in order to reduce risk, while others recommend that our asset allocation be adjusted according to the economic, interest rate, and investment environments—or even one's tolerance for risk and volatility.

I don't know if there is a "right" answer, but my personal belief is that the proper asset mix should depend on one's financial objectives, ability to absorb losses in portfolio value, and tolerance for risk. These criteria may help you decide how much of your investment portfolio you should be putting into REITs. This isn't a book about financial planning. However, I'll express a few thoughts about the role of REIT stocks in a diversified investment portfolio.

TIP

Before you make any decision on precisely *what* to invest in, you need to determine *why* you're investing—you need to define your investment goals.

If you have substantial spending needs over the next year or two, keeping enough cash to meet these needs is highly important—even when bank savings and certificate of deposit (CD) rates are embarrassingly low. At least you'll have it when you need it. Investing—whether in stocks, bonds, or REITs—is always an uncertain venture, particularly over the short term. Stock prices are affected by such variables as interest rates, inflation, corporate profits, budget deficits, the strength of the dollar, world geopolitics and wars, global trade—and other situations we haven't even conceived of. And, of course, investment styles shift constantly; if your favorite stocks aren't currently in favor, perhaps nothing will get them to perform well for a period of time.

Let's assume you have $20,000 or $100,000 that you don't think you'll need for several years, and you already have something set aside for known future spending requirements, as well as a "rainy day" fund. Or perhaps you have $50,000 sitting in cash in a 401(k) plan. The way you should allocate these investment funds depends on your answers to questions such as:

- How aggressive an investor are you? Does your pleasure from gains more than offset your pain from losses?

- How comfortable are you with market volatility and fluctuating portfolio values?
- How depressed would you feel if your investments suffer substantial declines, and could your lifestyle be adjusted in the event of a possibly permanent loss in value?
- How much will you need to withdraw annually from your portfolio investments to supplement your salary, pension, or Social Security payments? And when will you need to do so?
- How important to you is a steady stream of dividend income?

Aggressive Investors Should Have Modest Exposure to REITs

TIP

Aggressive investors seeking large returns, for example, 12 to 15 percent annually, should not normally put a high percentage of their assets into REITs.

Despite the fact that, on a long-term, total-return basis, REITs have been quite competitive with the Standard & Poor's (S&P) 500 index, REIT investors should expect only moderate capital appreciation on an annual basis, consistent with moderate REIT cash flow and net asset value (NAV) growth. Although REIT stocks have, in some years, appreciated by 20 percent or more, this should *not* be expected. Real estate is capital intensive, and there are no "newest new thing" technologies that can propel earnings at warp speed. So, despite what many people believe, real estate ownership—as long as one avoids excessive debt leverage—is a low-risk, modest-reward investment, and shareholders of even the fastest-growing REIT organizations should not expect double-digit average annual total returns. Thus, investors who wouldn't be happy with 7 to 8 percent returns shouldn't put much of their funds into REITs.

Modest Risk of Major Price Declines

An important aspect of REIT investing is that, in the absence of very unusual circumstances—such as deep and sudden recessions coupled with collapsing credit markets, as we saw in 2008 and into 2009—REIT stocks tend not to suffer precipitous declines.

According to the National Association of Real Estate Investment Trusts (NAREIT), equity REIT stocks suffered negative total returns of more than 20 percent in only 2 of the 40 years from 1971 to 2010, and of more than 15 percent in only 6 of those 40 years. Even when a particular REIT is afflicted by poor space markets, a weakening balance sheet, or management miscues, a decline in the REIT's stock has normally been gradual, giving investors a chance to take defensive measures.

Probably the greatest contributor to a sudden price decline is a very weak balance sheet, but this risk can normally be quantified, and is usually avoidable by the conservative investor. And often there are other signs of risk, such as a very aggressive business strategy. Be careful of an exceptionally high dividend in relation to the company's free cash flows. If it's too good to be true, it won't be true for long. And yet, even dividend cuts aren't lethal if investors view them as temporary; responding to the Great Recession, office REIT SL Green slashed its dividend in May 2009, but the stock has performed well subsequently. As we've often seen, non-REIT common stocks have been far more sensitive to negative news, particularly during the past few years. It's not at all unusual for an earnings shortfall, lower revenue "guidance," a product liability claim, a rejected new drug application, or a new competing technology to decimate the price of a non-REIT stock overnight.

Of course, as we learned in 1998 to 2000, and from 2007 to early 2009, REIT stocks can decline substantially if REITs as an asset class become disliked by, or fall out of favor with, investors, or when

When Stability Is What You're Looking For . . .

"I do believe REITs are unique," says Geoff Dohrmann, CEO of Institutional Real Estate. "No other sector of the stock market enjoys cash flow based on a diversified portfolio of relatively stable, predictable, contractual revenues (rents) that in most cases are essential components in the ability of the customer (tenants) to continue to do business. Consequently, even though as subject to the business cycle as any other corporation, REIT cash flows will tend to be more defensive than most other cash flows. REITs, therefore, offer relatively high, stable yields that—because of their stock market effect—adjust well to inflation, but that also tend to be defensive on the downside."

sudden and deep recessions occur. But that is far different from a 10 to 15 percent price decline overnight due to sharply reduced profit guidance for next year.

REITs Provide Relatively High Current Income

Some financial planners advocate a large common stock weighting even for people near or in retirement. They argue that bonds don't protect retirees—who are living much longer now—from inflation and, over any significant period of time, common stocks have provided more appreciation than virtually all other types of investments.

It's hard to criticize the wisdom of investing in common stocks, but the problem with many investment theories is that they are based on long-term averages—and, as we know, a person can drown in water that *averages* 3 inches in depth. The years up through 1999 were excellent years for most equities, but the broad stock market indices have gone nowhere since then. Bear markets arrive when we least expect them. Many investors at or near retirement must live off their investments; selling off a piece of one's portfolio isn't enjoyable during a bear market and can wreak havoc even on carefully crafted retirement strategies. Owning REIT stocks, however, provides a relatively high level of current income, with dividend yields that are fairly competitive with investment-grade bonds, as well as potential dividend increases and long-term price appreciation prospects. The higher current yield of REITs versus non-REIT equities makes the investor less dependent on ever-increasing stock prices to fund living expenses.

Looking for the "Holy Grail": The Perfect REIT Allocation

There are two parts to the question of asset allocation in the context of REIT investing. First, how should REITs be weighted in a diversified investment portfolio relative to other investments such as non-REIT equities, international stocks, bonds, and cash? And, second, how should REIT investments themselves be balanced in order to obtain adequate diversification within the REIT space?

Addressing the first issue of overall diversification, investors' responses to the five questions suggested earlier should help work out the optimal allocation of REITs within a portfolio; they help to define comfortable risk levels. Unfortunately, there are just too many variables to suggest a rigid formula, and doing so is beyond the scope of this book. But I will offer a few thoughts.

TIP

REIT allocation within a broadly diversified investment portfolio will be different for each investor, depending on the investor's financial goals, age, risk tolerance, and desire for current income.

Even if, because of all their unique qualities, you find REIT stocks highly attractive, you still shouldn't make them a vast majority of your investment portfolio. A fundamental principle of investing is that, over time, diversification is the key to stability of performance and preservation of capital. You *might* have outstanding results if you put a huge portion of your assets in REITs, but nobody can foretell the future. Occasionally even Warren Buffett has zigged when he should have zagged, and real estate has, in the past, been a somewhat cyclical investment.

Thus, investors should structure an investment strategy and asset allocation mix consistent with the principles of diversification, as well as their specific needs and investment goals. However, I can suggest some general guidelines for your consideration. If you're a fairly conservative investor looking for steady returns with a modest degree of risk and volatility, where capital appreciation is not paramount, a REIT allocation of somewhere between 20 and 25 percent of your portfolio should suit you. If the stock market seems overpriced but REITs look reasonably priced, you might feel comfortable moving up toward 25 percent—and down toward 20 percent, or even 15 percent, if you believe the opposite market conditions exist. But if you are more aggressive and looking for higher returns, and are psychologically suited to handle more risk and volatility, then perhaps a modest 5 to 10 percent allocation to REITs would be appropriate. Of course, these are only very general guidelines—in investing, it's rare that "one size fits all."

That said, and based on both logic and historical precedent, I believe the following conclusion is supportable and applicable to *most* investors: to the extent that one believes that REIT stocks can continue to deliver total returns equal to those of other asset classes—and with fairly low correlations with those other asset classes—adding a REIT component of 15 to 20 percent to a diversified investment portfolio should reduce portfolio volatility and may even increase overall investment returns.

Diversification among REITs

Assuming you've decided what percentage of your portfolio should be allocated to REITs, let's now address the second part of the allocation question. Within your REIT allocation, what would be an appropriate sub-allocation among the different property sectors, investment characteristics, or even geographic locations that REITs offer?

Basic Diversification

Much depends, of course, on the absolute level of cash you have to invest. One easy way for individual investors to diversify is through REIT mutual funds and exchange-traded funds (ETFs), which we'll discuss later in this chapter. Obtaining diversification through such funds and ETFs is easy and virtually automatic. But first, let's look at ways to diversify if the investor prefers to invest in *individual* REIT stocks.

 TIP

For most investors, an absolute minimum of six or eight REITs is necessary to achieve a basic level of diversification.

Six different REITs would provide a minimally acceptable level of sector diversification (perhaps one in each major sector—apartments, retail, office, and industrial—and one each in two smaller sectors), but 8 or 10 REITs would be preferable. If you're in a position to buy 10 different REITs, a good allocation would be 2 each in residential, retail, and office (the major sectors), and 1 each in industrial, health care, self-storage, and lodging. With more available investment funds, you might seek to add subsectors, for example, lab space, data centers or college residences, or a timberland or triple-net lease REIT. Or you may also want to widen your geographic diversification within each sector, adding an apartment REIT focused on the West Coast, for example, to one that's national in scope. The same approach can be applied in other sectors, such as neighborhood shopping centers, offices, and industrial properties. A handful of REITs, such as Vornado Realty and Washington REIT, own more than one property type, so it may be logical to get additional diversification in that manner.

TIP

With 10, REITs, a reasonable diversification might be 2 REITs in residential, retail and office, and 1 in industrial, health care, self-storage, and lodging.

Overweighting and Underweighting

One of the key diversification issues for REIT investors is how to allocate holdings among particular property sectors. There are differing opinions on this topic, even among institutional REIT investors. Some REIT asset managers don't try to adjust their portfolios in accordance with how much they like or dislike a sector but simply use "market weightings." For example, if mall REITs make up 12 percent of all equity REITs, such investors, using a market weighting approach, will make sure that mall REITs comprise approximately 12 percent of their REIT portfolio. Similar to what many professionals do in the broad world of equities, these investors try to add value by owning the most attractive stocks within

Diversification with REITs

According to Roger C. Gibson, CFA, CFP, a nationally recognized expert in asset allocation and investment portfolio design, "The investment diversification achievable with REITs is of particular value to investors. Unlike the case with direct real estate ownership, a REIT investor can easily diversify a relatively small sum of money both geographically and across different types of real estate investments, such as shopping centers, office buildings, and residential apartment complexes."

each market sector, without making large sector bets. Advocates of this approach might argue that REITs, like other stocks, are usually efficiently priced, and it's unrealistic to assume that anyone can forecast with any accuracy and consistency which property sectors will perform better than others.

Other investors, frequently those oriented toward maximum short-term performance, believe they *can* figure out the best sectors or property locations to own at any particular time. They will closely examine the fundamentals across all commercial real estate markets—and overweight or underweight their sector allocations accordingly. They will pursue those markets and property types where demand for space exceeds the supply, where rents and occupancy rates are rising fastest, where profitable acquisition or development opportunities abound, or where some other factor seems to make the outlook for one or a few sectors particularly favorable. Or they might merely emphasize those REIT sectors where REIT stock prices look the cheapest. Kenneth Heebner, a well-known fund manager, seems to have used this approach at CGM Realty Fund, and many others use a similar strategy.

A final point on REIT sector weightings: Overweighting the "right sectors" is tricky because if other investors have the same (and accurate) perceptions, that will already be factored into the stock prices, and we won't have gained anything at all. Over- and underweighting effectively requires that we know more than the market does—often a tall order!

Author's Choice

The investment style I prefer is to put most of my REIT investment dollars in blue-chip REITs, along with some that seem underpriced, misunderstood, or not widely followed, and then add a few more that look as if they'll enjoy rapid growth. Although I own them on occasion, I'm careful about mortgage REITs—they've often been badly hurt by rising interest rates and other gyrations pertaining to the credit markets. Fortunately, the REIT industry is now so vast that our choices are very wide. More personal thoughts on REIT portfolio management are contained in Appendix D.

TIP

Unless investors believe that they can determine which sectors will perform appreciably better than others over the next year or two, a portfolio in which each sector is weighted in line with its share of the REIT industry makes the most sense.

Diversification by Investment Characteristics

Another approach to diversification is not to worry too much about sectors or property locations, but instead to own a package of REITs with different investment characteristics. This approach would have the investor assemble one group of REITs with high-quality assets in major real estate markets, led by widely respected real estate executives, offering very predictable and steady growth; another group of "value" REITs with low valuations based on a substantial discount to estimated NAV or a low price-to-adjusted funds from operations (P/AFFO) multiple; a group of REITs that appear to offer above-average growth prospects; and, to round out the portfolio, a few bond-proxy REITs having high yields, low volatility, and modest growth prospects. Such an approach may help to insulate the portfolio from major price gyrations as institutional investors shift their REIT funds from one style of REIT investing to another.

Toward a Well-Balanced Portfolio

Which approach toward diversification is best? By property type? By geography? By investment characteristics? Or by all of the above? I'm not aware of any definitive statistical evidence suggesting that one approach is better than another. As the significant expansion in size of the REIT industry has been fairly recent, there's not enough history to guide us, nor are there, to my knowledge, any academic studies regarding this issue. And few REIT mutual funds are willing to place themselves in a particular style box. While there's no agreement on *how* to diversify, there is almost universal agreement on the *need* to diversify.

Although REIT investors shouldn't ignore the concerns expressed by industry observers from time to time with respect to particular sectors, for example, a Kiplinger story, dated January 2011, entitled "Why You Should Sell Health Care REITs Now," neither should they take them too seriously. REIT investing is, for most investors, a long-term strategy; the prospects for any particular sector will fluctuate, but there's no reason to think that one sector will perform better or worse than others on a long-term basis. REIT investors thus needn't become terribly concerned if they find themselves overweighted in a currently unpopular sector, such as retail REITs in 2009, as long as the long-term prospects for that sector appear to be stable. Real estate, like stock investments, always seems to revert to the mean.

Also, investors need not be terribly concerned with geographic diversification with respect to mall REITs, health care REITs, and self-storage REITs, as most of these REITs are widely diversified by property location, and detailed knowledge of the conditions and opportunities peculiar to local markets isn't quite as important in these sectors.

Table 10.1 provides just a sample of the kind of diversification that can be obtained within certain major sectors. Areas of major geographic focus are included. The table includes many of the largest REITs as of September 2010.

Table 10.1 Property Types, REITs, and Primary Locations

REIT	Principal Locations
Apartments	
Apartment Investment and Management	Nationwide
AvalonBay Communities	Northeast, mid-Atlantic, West Coast
BRE Properties	California, western United States
Camden Property Trust	Sunbelt
Equity Residential	Nationwide
Essex Property Trust	California and Seattle
Home Properties	East Coast, mid-Atlantic
Mid-America Communities	Sunbelt
UDR Inc.	Nationwide
Retail: Neighborhood Shopping Centers	
Developers Diversified Realty	Primarily power centers, nationwide
Equity One	Southeast
Federal Realty	D.C. Metro, Los Angeles, New York, Philadelphia
Kimco Realty	Nationwide, Canada, Mexico

(Continued)

Table 10.1 Continued

REIT	Principal Locations
Regency Centers	West and East Coasts, Sunbelt
Tanger Factory Outlet Centers	Nationwide
Weingarten Realty	Sunbelt
Retail: Malls	
CBL & Associates	Southeast, Midwest
General Growth Properties	Nationwide
Macerich	Nationwide, esp. California and Arizona
Pennsylvania Real Estate	East Coast
Simon Property Group	Nationwide
Taubman Centers	Nationwide
Health Care	
HCP Inc.	Nationwide
Health Care REIT	Nationwide
Nationwide Health	Nationwide
Ventas	Nationwide
Office	
Alexandria Real Estate	Lab space, coastal markets
Biomed Realty	Lab space, coastal markets
Boston Property	New York; Boston; Washington, D.C.; San Francisco
Corporate Office	Government/defense tenants, mid-Atlantic
Douglas Emmett	Los Angeles, Hawaii
Duke Realty	Southeast, Midwest
Highwoods Property	Southeast
Kilroy Realty	Southern California
Liberty Property	Mid-Atlantic, Southeast, Midwest
Mack Cali Realty	East Coast, mid-Atlantic
Piedmont Office Realty	Nationwide
SL Green Realty	Midtown Manhattan
Industrial	
AMB Property	Coastal "hub" markets, Europe and Asia
DCT Industrial Trust	Atlanta, Houston, Dallas
Eastgroup Properties	Sunbelt
ProLogis	California, Japan, eastern Europe

Table 10.1 Continued

REIT	Principal Locations
Self-Storage	
Public Storage	Nationwide, Europe
Extra Space Storage	Nationwide
U-Store-It	Nationwide
Hotels	
DiamondRock Hospitality	Nationwide, upper upscale
Hospitality Properties	Nationwide, extended stay, upscale
Host Hotels	Nationwide, upper upscale, luxury
LaSalle Hotel	Nationwide, upper upscale
Sunstone Hotel Investors	Nationwide, upper upscale
Diversified REITs	
Cousins Properties	Office and retail, Southeast
Lexington Realty	Nationwide, net-leased properties
Realty Income	Nationwide, net-leased retail properties
Vornado Realty	Office and retail, New York City; Washington, D.C.
Washington REIT	Several asset types, Washington, D.C.

How to Get Started

We REIT investors can choose from three basic and very different approaches toward building a REIT portfolio: we can do the research ourselves; we can rely on a professional, such as a stockbroker, financial planner, or investment adviser; or we can buy a REIT mutual fund or ETF. Let's examine what's involved in each approach.

Doing It Yourself

The tools required to build and monitor your own REIT portfolio include a willingness to spend at least a few hours a week following the REIT industry and monitoring your REIT portfolio. It will also help to have a subscription to a REIT newsletter and/or access to REIT research reports.

The do-it-yourself approach is the most difficult and time-consuming method, but many investors find it satisfying and possibly the most rewarding. There are several ways to stay informed of what's happening in the world of REITs. For example, SNL Financial covers the entire REIT industry thoroughly, providing vital REIT data, dividends, and earnings estimates. Most retail brokerage firms also provide research reports on REIT sectors and individual REITs. More information than ever before can be obtained online, and virtually all individual REITs, as well as NAREIT, have established their own web sites. The Motley Fool, REIT Café, and other sites also provide REIT information, and sometimes offer real estate discussion boards.

Commercial real estate isn't terribly complicated once we've mastered the lingo. And REITs' business prospects do not change quickly. REIT investing is thus perhaps less data and research intensive than most other common stock investing. With access to a database such as that provided by SNL Financial and NAREIT, a willingness to listen to quarterly conference calls and Webcasts (or to read the conference call transcripts available on sites such as Seeking Alpha), and the discipline needed to review the information publicly available—such as quarterly supplemental data packages available on REITs' web sites, annual reports, 10-Qs, and various other filings with the Securities and Exchange Commission—most diligent investors can do a good job managing their own REIT portfolios.

The do-it-yourself approach has several advantages. First, it saves on management fees and brokerage commissions because without the need for outside advice, you can use a discount broker for at least some of your trades. Second, the realization of capital gains and losses can be tailored to your own personal tax-planning requirements. Third, a significant portion of many REITs' dividends is treated as a "return of capital," and is not immediately taxable to the shareholder, while another portion is often treated as capital gains. Owning REIT stocks directly ensures that you can take advantage of these tax benefits, which are more fully described in Appendix A. Finally, the knowledge and experience gained from managing your own portfolio may well lead to good investment results and a great deal of personal satisfaction.

Do-it-yourself investors can obtain a list of every public REIT, with links to their web sites, at www.reit.com/IndividualInvestors/ PubliclyTradedREITDirectory.aspx. Another useful tool, among many at NAREIT's web site, is *REITWatch*, which is available each month. It contains a great deal of current information on publicly traded REITs; go to www.reit.com, click on "NAREIT Statistical Publications," and then on "REITWatch."

Table 10.2 provides a general description of some sources of information for REIT investors, but this list is certainly not exhaustive; note that Web addresses can change from time to time. If you exhaust all of these sources and are still hungry for more information, just do a Web search on the word *REIT*.

Table 10.2 Sources of Information for REIT Investors

Sources for the Do-it-Yourselfer	Where to Find It	General Description
CB Richard Ellis	cbre.com	News and reports on real estate markets globally
Colliers International	colliers.com	Reports and reviews regarding global real estate conditions
Green Street Advisors	Greenstreetadvisors .com	REIT investment research
Institutional Real Estate	irei.com	Information on commercial real estate
Investment and brokerage firms	Contact your registered representative at a major or regional firm	Research reports on REITs and REIT property sectors
Motley Fool REIT Board	http://boards.fool.com/ real-estate-inv-trusts-reits-100061.aspx	Message board discussions on REIT investing, and regarding specific REITs
NAREIT	reit.com	Gold mine of REIT industry data and information (and videos)
NCREIF	ncreif.org	Data and investment returns on commercial real estate
Real Capital Analytics	rcanalytics.com	Information on commercial real estate space and capital markets
REIT Café	www.iirealestate.com/ ReitCafe_Home.aspx	Information, interviews, and commentary on the REIT industry
ReitNet	reitnet.com	Online tools for the REIT investor
SNL Financial	www.snl.com/Sectors/ RealEstate/Default .aspx	Newsletters, data, and information on REITs and real estate
Wall Street Journal	Subscription or on newsstand; online, wsj .com	Periodic updates on commercial real estate and REITs
Web sites and home pages	Virtually all REIT organizations have web sites	Individual REIT data, including press releases, financial and other information

Using a Stockbroker

TIP

Investors who don't enjoy poring over annual and quarterly reports and calculating NAVs and AFFOs may want to look for a stockbroker who is familiar with REITs and who has access to the research reports published by his or her brokerage firm.

Perhaps most investors would rather not spend their leisure time managing their own portfolios when they could be playing golf, taking the kids to a baseball game, or gardening. Not too many years ago, however, individual investors had no alternative; it was difficult to find a broker who knew much about REITs. Today, such brokers are easy to find. REITs are continuing to grow in popularity. We can read about them in personal finance magazines, on the Internet, and in the business/finance sections of major newspapers; and most brokerage firms employ one or more experienced REIT analysts. You should have no problem finding at least one REIT-knowledgeable registered representative at most brokerage offices.

Assuming that you find a good broker, the advantages of this approach include personal attention, the ability to decide when you want to take capital gains or losses, and the relief of not having to research and worry about such issues as NAV, AFFO, same-store NOI, debt leverage, and other REIT essentials. The brokerage commissions will be higher than for the do-it-yourself investor, but, if you're careful to avoid excessive trading and you buy only those REITs consistent with your investment objectives, higher commissions may be a small price to pay for the service provided. Some brokerage firms even offer "wrap accounts," allowing the client to have that portion of his or her funds allocated to REITs invested by a professional REIT portfolio manager.

Financial Planners and Investment Advisers

Today, with the advancing years of the Baby Boomer cohort, there are more people concerned about investing for a longer life expectancy and a retirement free of financial worry.

Financial planners can act in different capacities. Some manage and invest their clients' funds directly in specific stocks and bonds; others prefer to use well-researched mutual funds. Still others do the financial planning but refer the client to an investment adviser for the investment process. Some are paid on the basis of commissions from the sale of insurance or other investments, while others charge only on a fee basis.

Pure investment advisers generally do little or no financial planning and specialize in investing client funds in stocks, bonds, and other securities. Their only compensation is, in most cases, an annual fee of between 1 and 2 percent of the assets they manage. Thus, the adviser's fee will vary with the value of the investment portfolio. Some advisory firms provide a great deal of personal attention and hand-holding, while others do not. Some take great care to individualize a portfolio, taking into account their clients' personal tax situations before making buy-and-sell decisions, and others buy and sell solely on the basis of maximizing their clients' investment gains.

Many investors have found that using a financial planner or investment adviser has definite advantages, including the personal attention given to clients and the customizing of clients' portfolios based on their financial objectives and tolerance for risk. Until fairly recently it was difficult to find financial planners or advisers who knew enough about REITs to help clients wanting to invest in them. Today, however, REIT stocks are well known in the investment world, and I would be surprised if anyone reading this book is unable to find a financial planner or adviser who doesn't have at least a working knowledge of REITs as investments.

REIT Mutual Funds

As recently as 20 years ago, only a handful of mutual funds specialized in real estate–related securities such as REITs. Today, there are more than 76 fund sponsors that offer funds that invest in REIT stocks, some of which offer more than one REIT fund. A list of these funds can be found at the NAREIT web site (www.reit.com/IndividualInvestors/ ListofREITFunds/MutualFunds.aspx). More information is available regarding REIT and real estate mutual funds through Morningstar (www.morningstar.com). Let's take a quick look at these fund choices.

TIP

REIT mutual funds provide an excellent way for individuals to obtain sufficient REIT diversification with just one or two investments.

To take a purely arbitrary number, if we assume that a REIT investor wants to put 20 percent of a $50,000 investment portfolio into REIT stocks, the total REIT investment would be just $10,000. It would be difficult to obtain substantial diversification with that relatively modest amount. In contrast, with the same or even a smaller REIT budget, much more diversification can be obtained through a REIT mutual fund—most such funds own at least 30 different REITs.

Perhaps even more important, in a REIT mutual fund the investor gets the benefit of professional fund managers who, when they make their investment decisions, have access to REITs' management teams as well as extensive research materials and proprietary valuation models. Most of these funds have performed pretty well relative to their benchmarks. Even do-it-yourself investors might want to invest in a few of these mutual funds in order to benchmark their personal REIT investment track records against the results of the professional fund managers.

Despite their significant advantages, REIT mutual funds are not without drawbacks. Although no brokerage commissions are payable when investing in no-load funds, management and other fees can be sizable, typically ranging from 1 to 1.5 percent of total assets annually. Fund investors do not receive individual attention, and their tax-planning ability is limited. A fund that actively trades REIT stocks may present its investors with a large capital gains tax bill following a REIT bull market, as the gains or losses realized by the fund during the year are simply passed on to the individual investor. Finally, investors who reinvest dividends and capital gain distributions in additional fund shares and who trade in and out of the same fund may find it very time consuming to keep current and accurate records of their cost basis and tax gain or loss information.

REIT investors who decide to go with a mutual fund have a wide array of choices today. Most funds are actively managed, and each utilizes a somewhat different investment strategy. Some focus almost exclusively on the large REITs, while others try to add value by focusing on the smaller names. High current yields are important to some, but total returns drive the decisions of others. Some invest in non-REIT real estate companies. One fund might keep real estate sectors roughly in line with the benchmarks, while another will ignore these market weightings. If you have read this far in the book, you have enough knowledge to analyze a wide variety of real estate funds to ascertain their preferences and strategies and to pick one or a few that best coincide with your investment objectives.

Investors can also invest in indexed REIT funds designed to perform in line with a REIT stock index. Perhaps the most well known is the Vanguard REIT Index fund (symbol: VGSIX), which is indexed to, and will closely track, the MSCI US REIT Index, less a relatively small management fee.

A Mutual Fund Alternative: ETFs

Another type of indexed fund that is fairly new on the investment scene and has become widely popular with the investment community is the exchange-traded fund (ETF). An ETF is essentially an indirect ownership interest in a basket of stocks put together by a sponsoring organization and traded as a single stock on a major stock exchange. ETFs seek to track a specific index or basket of stocks, and thus lack an active portfolio manager; their objective is to replicate the performance of the targeted group of stocks. Because they are traded as stocks, ETFs can be bought and sold during the trading day, even on margin. And because they don't employ active fund managers, management expense ratios tend to be very low.

According to NAREIT, there were eight sponsors of REIT ETFs in October 2010, most of which make more than one ETF available, and they track different indices; some are limited to specific property sectors, others are indexed to non-U.S. benchmarks (e.g., Asian and European indices), and yet others use leverage to magnify performance. Two funds, sponsored by ProShares, take short positions in REIT stocks (one of which uses leverage to magnify performance). A listing of these ETFs is available on NAREIT's web site.

As previously noted, expense ratios for ETFs are low; for example, according to ETF Database, the expense ratio for the Vanguard

REIT ETF is only 0.15 percent annually. All of them are worthy of consideration if one's objective is a low-cost, index-oriented approach to REIT investing. The MSCI US REIT Index excludes mortgage REITs and REITs that don't generate most of their revenue and income from rental and leasing, as well as REITs below a minimum size. These exclusions mean that this index could modestly outperform or underperform a broader REIT index.

Another type of fund that has drawn REIT investor interest in recent years is the closed-end REIT fund. Some of these own only REITs, while others own REITs along with other income-oriented stocks such as utilities—and, in some cases, preferred stocks. There are many types of these closed-end funds, each with different capital structures and investment strategies, but two of their common characteristics are that they trade as stocks and do not, unlike conventional "open-ended" mutual funds, allow for shareholder redemptions or reinvestment at net asset value. These features allow the shares of these closed-end funds to be bought and sold quickly, and shareholders won't need to be concerned about their fund's having to liquidate assets in a bear market when less patient fellow shareholders bail out. (Cynics will note, however, that these funds are rarely liquidated, even when trading at substantial discounts to their NAVs, as they generate income for their sponsors even when they perform poorly.)

Investors need to look closely at the structures of these closed-end funds, as many of them use investment leverage by issuing preferred stock or borrowing in the credit markets to boost investment returns. Those that do this are investing on margin, and leverage, of course, is a two-way street. While returns can be enhanced in strong markets, they are likely to perform very poorly indeed in REIT bear markets, such as in 2007 through 2008. Leverage, of course, will also increase the share volatility of the closed-end fund that uses it. And, as rising interest rates may have a greater impact on a closed-end fund that uses debt leverage, its shares may perform particularly poorly when interest rates are rising. Investors also need to be aware of the amount of leverage being used, how it is structured, and whether the preferred component of the fund's capital structure or the amounts borrowed are at fixed—or variable—rates of interest. The latter, of course, creates yet more risk for investors in these funds, particularly if exposure to rising interest rates is not hedged.

For investors who don't want to invest on their own or don't have the resources to diversify REIT holdings adequately, do the advantages of a fund, an ETF, or closed-end fund outweigh their disadvantages? Clearly, they do—especially if the investor refrains from trading in and out of these shares. REIT mutual funds are especially attractive in individual retirement accounts and 401(k) plans, where neither tax gains and losses nor cost bases are relevant.

Summary

- Before we make any decision on precisely *what* to invest in, we should determine *why* we're investing—and define our investment goals and risk tolerances.
- The aggressive investor seeking very large returns over short time periods should not put a high percentage of assets into REITs; they are a singles-hitter's game.
- Allocations to REIT investments will be different for each investor, depending on his or her age, financial goals, risk tolerance, and desire for current income, but I believe that a 15 to 20 percent allocation to REITs is appropriate for most investors.
- An absolute minimum of six or eight REITs is necessary to achieve a basic level of diversification when investing in individual REIT stocks.
- Unless an investor is very confident about which sectors will do best over the intermediate term, a portfolio allocated according to market weighting makes the most sense.
- Those who want to participate in the long-term benefits of REIT investing but who don't want to worry about frequent monitoring of their REIT investments can utilize the services of a knowledgeable stockbroker, financial planner, or investment adviser.
- Investors who prefer not to do any individual REIT research can invest passively through REIT mutual funds—either actively managed or indexed—or even a REIT ETF. These alternatives provide an excellent way for individuals to obtain sufficient REIT diversification and with minimal expenditure of time.

CHAPTER

11

Investing in Global REITs and Property Companies

Steven D. Burton and Kenneth D. Campbell*

The world of investing in real estate is flattening with each passing day, to paraphrase *New York Times* columnist Thomas Friedman. Technology has transformed the movement of capital into real estate from a local, hit-or-miss affair, often depending on which cocktail party you attended, into a fast-paced global business you can manage from your desktop.

Investors today live "in a world in which technology provides instantaneous connections among markets and allows just about anyone to do just about anything, anywhere," says James Glassman, writing in the *Wall Street Journal* recently to explain why his book *Dow 36,000* was wildly off the mark.

Moreover, investors in global REITs and property companies today have more information at their fingertips than can scarcely be imagined. Information sources are discussed in this chapter's section on the practicalities of investing overseas.

Not too many years ago, investing in commercial real estate was a local business. Equity money was generally raised locally by a local

---

*Contributors Burton and Campbell are senior investment professionals at CBRE Clarion Securites, a global investment adviser with approximately $23 billion under management.

real estate entrepreneur or developer, and a local or regional bank provided the construction and/or permanent mortgage financing. The system worked because all parties in the transaction knew—or thought they knew—the local market demand for the space being built, be it office, retail, industrial, or residential.

All that began to change in the 1950s and 1960s with the rise of larger regional banks and multicity developers specializing in specific property types. In the United States, flamboyant New York City developer William Zeckendorf Sr. pioneered real estate's quest for capital in public markets in 1952 by taking over a small utility investment trust, then listed on the Curb (American) Stock Exchange, in a reverse merger and renaming it Webb & Knapp Inc. Throughout the 1950s Zeckendorf's W&K captured headlines by successfully developing visionary projects such as Roosevelt Field Mall on New York's Long Island in 1955 and Denver's Mile High Center in 1956, one of the nation's first truly successful urban renewal projects.

But as the calendar turned into the 1960s, realty values peaked in most cities, imperiling Zeckendorf's full-throttle development style. Place Ville Marie in Montreal, begun in 1960 almost entirely on spec, cost nearly double the original estimates and tenants proved elusive. Groundbreaking for Century City in Los Angeles was staged in 1959 but full-scale construction didn't begin until much later. Newer Zeckendorf projects were pinched: Freedomland, conceived as an East Coast Disneyland and opened in 1960, struggled, and a planned chain of Zeckendorf hotels never got beyond an empty foundation. A rescue effort by a British financier failed in summer of 1963, forcing Zeckendorf to choose between liquidating assets or refinancing those that retained value. When Zeckendorf began mortgaging assets at rates up to 20 percent, he famously remarked, "I'd rather be alive at 18% then dead at the prime rate." Tight financing ultimately caught up with the highly leveraged W&K and the company filed for bankruptcy in May 1965.

The challenging 1960s economic landscape spelled opportunity for other, more risk-averse developers. In Indianapolis, Indiana, Melvin Simon founded Melvin Simon & Associates in the 1960s and launched a career of building suburban shopping centers. Simon Property Group went public in 1993 and today is among the world's largest regional mall owners with an equity market capitalization approaching $30 billion at the end of 2010.

In Australia, at about the same time, the Lowy family began building shopping centers to serve burgeoning suburban populations and, in September 1960, listed their Westfield Development Corporation on the Australian Stock Exchange. Today, Westfield Group owns malls in Australia, New Zealand, the United States, and the United Kingdom and its combined $29.0 billion equity market cap regularly vies with Simon Property for the mantle of world's largest regional mall owner. These two companies have one element in common: both have turned to public securities markets for the capital needed to expand their businesses to worldwide prominence.

Nor are Westfield and Simon the largest companies in the global real estate firmament. That title goes to Sun Hung Kai Properties, Ltd. (SHK) of Hong Kong, with $42.7 billion equity market cap as of December 31, 2010. SHK was formed by Kwok Tak Seng and two partners, Fung King-hei and Lee Shau Kee, in 1963, about the same time the Simon and Lowy families were setting up shop elsewhere. Today, the Kwok family controls approximately 42 percent of SHK shares with the rest being available for regular trading. SHK listed on the Hong Kong Stock Exchange in 1972.

Around the world CBRE Clarion counts 29 companies with over $10 billion equity market capitalization. While these 29 giants comprise only about 3½ percent of the global real estate company universe by number of companies, they account for about 28% of total equity market capitalization and free-float market value. The United States is home to 11 of these companies, while nine are domiciled in Hong Kong. Three are located in Japan, while Australia, India, Korea, Singapore, France, and Spain each host one global goliath.

And while the Simon/Westfield rivalry captures the headlines, hundreds and thousands of real estate builders, developers, operators and owners have over the last half-century competed for real estate riches in their cities, regions, and nations. A growing proportion of these entrepreneurs and the organizations they have built have turned to the public markets as the most reliable source of equity and debt capital, good times or bad.

This chapter introduces this vibrant and expanding global marketplace for real estate capital. But this bustling and expanding marketplace may not be for everyone. Individual investors may encounter two impediments to constructing a global portfolio:

1. **Real estate differences around the globe.** Every element of real estate varies in each nation: lease structures and ownership patterns, laws and regulations, tax structures, and so on. Hence, it is crucial that the investor carefully weigh input from skilled analysts in each nation to determine with some certainty what can be forecast or expected.
2. **Securities differences around the globe.** Many attractive non-U.S. real estate companies do not have American Depositary Receipts (ADRs) available in the United States, and hence their stocks must be bought in local currencies on their local stock exchanges. Custody of these securities had historically been a challenge. Happily, a number of global investment banks over the past decade have dedicated significant analytical firepower to make available comparable and meaningful cross-country company data. As discussed in this chapter, these firms can also provide execution and custody services that were not within reach just a few years ago.

For the individual investor, then, global real estate investing can be complex and time consuming—but is now within reach.

How the U.S. REIT Revolution Spread around the Globe

Younger readers may not appreciate the seismic changes that have turned the world of real estate investing on its ear, creating not one but two revolutions over the past half-century. This section examines in some detail the rationalization and expansion of real estate financing in the United States. The parallel experiences of real estate investors in Australia are summarized for their commonality with the United States. But similar stories could be told about virtually every nation where investors now can purchase shares of public real estate companies. The story unfolded in two phases in the United States, and then spread around the globe as REITs attained success.

1960 to 1990: A Difficult First 30 Growing-Up Years for U.S. Equity REITs

The first revolution began in September 1960 when the U.S. Congress passed legislation creating real estate investment trusts (REITs). REITs were created with the stated goal of making professionally managed portfolios of commercial real estate (i.e., not single family homes) available to smaller investors. To achieve that goal, Congress exempted REIT operating profits from income taxes to the extent the REIT distributed 90 percent of its REIT taxable income to shareholders. This is the same tax treatment enjoyed by U.S. mutual funds since 1940. To ensure that no single individual or group could control the REIT, Congress required that U.S. REITs have only one class of shares, must have 100 or more shareholders, and no more than five shareholders may own over 50 percent of the shares.

REITs were envisioned as long-term holders of equity ownership in investment income–producing properties and hence the statute exacted a penalty tax of 100 percent of gains from any property sold less than four years after its purchase. Since construction of a new building is often the riskiest part of real estate investment, development options for the new REITs were debated. Ultimately, lawmakers permitted REITs to improve and redevelop properties, and even construct new buildings for long-term ownership from the ground up. In practice, equity REITs have generally limited new construction to about 10 percent of total assets, enhancing the image of equity REITs as "Steady Eddie" owners of income properties able to generate reliable dividend streams.

Before that time, "access to the investment returns of commercial real estate equity as a core asset was available only to institutions and wealthy individuals having the financial wherewithal to undertake direct real estate investment," in the words of the U.S.-based National Association of Real Estate Investment Trusts (NAREIT). Before then, the only large-scale real estate investment organizations available generally to large groups of investors were syndications, or limited partnerships in which groups of limited partners (LPs), put up the equity needed to buy a single building or small group of buildings and relied on a general partner (GP) to manage the properties. The GP was usually an experienced real estate developer or broker acknowledged to have real estate "smarts," while the LPs supplied the capital. (A joke of that era reveals a cynic's view of syndications: the LPs started with money and wound up with the experience, while the GPs started with experience and wound up with the money.) In other words, the syndication structure itself embedded a conflict between money sources and managements.

The success or failure of such single- or small-property investments inevitably rises or falls on the success of one or a few buildings. The only way a pre-1960 investor could create diversification was to buy stakes in several syndications, in effect creating a customized portfolio.

A few 1960s-era syndications were large enough that a public market developed for their units, thanks to a 1961 New York State law requiring syndicators to issue prospectuses telling investors how they planned to use proceeds. Louis J. Glickman, a prominent syndicator, helped organize a trade association to prevent syndicator abuses and widen the market for syndication units. But the vast majority of syndication units had one major drawback: lack of liquidity. Syndicate investors were generally told they must hold their units for a stated period of time—5 to 10 years was common. Only in extreme cases, say to settle an estate or tax claim, would the general partner consent to repurchase a unit from an original investor, and then only if the GP had the cash.

Although the advent of the REITs in 1960 eventually stole the show from the syndication cottage industry, two events combined to extend the life of the syndicates.

Slow Early Acceptance of REITs by Investors   The new REIT structure was not initially widely accepted by investors, owing partly to unfamiliarity with the new animal and partly to a nasty stock market crash in May 1962 that effectively killed the plans of over 25 REITs then trying to go public. Not until 1967 and 1968 did REITs receive any investment notice when the focus turned to mortgage REITs. Thanks to a 1961 IRS ruling that mortgages were an "interest in real estate," this new breed of mortgage REITs became popular. These mortgage REITs loaned money, mainly for short-term construction and development (C&D) loans for real estate. Despite their higher risk, short-term mortgage lending REITs became prominent because of their relatively high dividend yields. These REITs loaned construction-and-development money to developers and thrived until the 1973 to 1975 recession, which was then the deepest since the Great Depression of the 1930s. That recession stilled nearly all real estate construction cranes and effectively ended the C&D mortgage REITs by the late 1970s. Unhappily, this 1970s stock market debacle soured a generation of investors on "REITs." Investors, most of whom suffered price declines but survived financially, paid little attention at this time to equity REITs.

Tax Policy Changes Favored Syndicates over REITs   National tax policy began tilting toward promoting additional real estate investment as a way of combating the 1973 to 1975 recession, culminating in legislation in the early 1980s under President Ronald Reagan letting individuals use losses from real estate syndications to reduce taxable income from other sources. Depreciable lives were also shortened, effectively increasing the amount of noncash depreciation charges available to shelter cash flow. Net result: a revived syndication industry raised an estimated $100 billion in equity from 1980 to 1985. This equity was then leveraged to an estimated 4 to 1, unleashing about $500 billion into new real estate investments. New investment in REITs languished because REITs could not compete with the tax-advantaged returns offered by syndicators.

By 1986, many syndicator investment return forecasts turned out to be wildly optimistic, and the resulting overbuilding pushed all commercial real estate into recession in the second half of the 1980s. REIT shares flattened in 1987 and 1988, then fell steadily for nearly two years, from 1988 through October 1990. This decline caused most syndicators to disappear as effective real estate owners and operators. And the savings-and-loan (S&L) associations that had been heavy lenders to syndicates were effectively taken over and liquidated by the U.S. Resolution Trust Corporation in the second half of the 1980s and early 1990s. Equity REITs, however, again survived these traumatic setbacks for real estate and set the stage for a resurgent second act.

1990s: Modern Equity REITs Emerge as Battle-Tested Investment Favorites

By the beginning of 1991, virtually all large U.S. real estate organizations were on the verge of bankruptcy. Most owed more to the banks than their properties were worth, and owners' equity had been either depleted or lost. The only real estate investment vehicle to withstand these ravages was a relatively small group of equity REITs. While their shares had fallen sharply in the late 1980s, most were not highly leveraged and their capital remained largely intact.

But how to match the severely wounded private realty operators with the viable REIT structure? The private owners were so severely wounded that some wondered if they could survive. It was a dark time for private companies, faced with the stark choice of "going public or going broke."

A small circle of creative investment bankers in New York City, including Richard Saltzman, then head of Real Estate Corporate Finance for Merrill Lynch (now Bank of America/Merrill Lynch), theorized that the moribund private operators could be revived as viable public REITs with public equity financing *if* principal owners would agree to three conditions:

1. Limit future debt leverage to about 50 percent of total market value, well down from the 75 to 90 percent leverage ratios common in precrash real estate.
2. Eliminate all personal conflicts by putting *all* their real estate assets into one pot so investors could gauge their investability from a single balance sheet.
3. Give up their competitive penchant for secrecy in return for public transparency in rents, occupancy, other portfolio operating metrics, and financial statements.

There were few takers initially because these promising strategies still had to deal with two nitty-gritty realities embedded within the portfolios of potential public companies. Solving those two sticking points would require trailblazing deal structuring. Over the next two years, two real estate companies stepped forward with pioneering transactions that provided templates for the rise of the modern REIT industry in the United States.

How to Put Portfolios Containing Both "Good" and "Bad" Properties under One Umbrella?   The reality of that time was that virtually all private real estate portfolios held a mix of both "good" properties with strong income and cash flow, and "bad" properties whose lack of earnings dragged down consolidated earnings so much that the entire portfolio was unsalable to investors. To resolve such situations, the investment bankers turned to a "good bank, bad bank" strategy, forged in the prior S&L crisis, to split the baby, Solomon-style, so the "good bank" portion was attractive to investors.

An example of how the bankers dealt with the inherent conflict between owners of "good" and "bad" properties can be seen in the first workable initial public offering (IPO), that of Kimco Realty Corporation, in November 1991. Kimco, located in New Hyde Park on Long Island, New York, went public with an offering that split the company's portfolio into two parts:

1. About 126 Kimco shopping center properties with positive cash flow were included in the proposed newly public company.
2. Another 46 centers with vacant anchors or other cash constraints, or about 27 percent of the total portfolio, were placed in a *separate* entity that continued to be owned by management. The newly public company was granted an option to buy these 46 laggards if and when they became profitable. Directors of the "New Kimco" were charged with deciding if, and when, Kimco would buy these losing properties from Kimco's managers, and at what price. Until these losers were purchased, prior owners bore the burden of improving their cash flow and eating their losses.

This decision solved a common problem for struggling companies: how to get access to public equity capital without dumping bad properties onto public investors. The Kimco template thus let other companies with similar situations gain access to public equity capital.

How to Deal Fairly with Conflicting Ownership Goals in Jointly Owned Properties? Joint or common owners of commercial properties often have conflicting goals because of differing taxable cost bases in their ownership interests. These differing goals can be one of the great hidden dangers for public investors in a real estate company. A joint or common owner with a high cost basis will generally be indifferent to the timing of a property sale because he or she would have little or no taxes to pay. But a low-basis owner will generally resist selling because he or she would face a hefty tax bill when the taxable transaction closes.

In October 1992, less than a year after the Kimco IPO, Taubman Centers, Inc., a Detroit-area shopping center operator, sought to bridge this gap when it prepared for its IPO. Taubman owned a portfolio of enclosed regional malls whose founders had provided initial equity in the properties, then later sold a large stake in the portfolio to a major pension fund at a much higher price. As a result, the pension fund could be expected to be indifferent to any future sale of one or more malls, while management might be inclined to avoid future sales, even those that would improve or maximize portfolio profits.

To bridge that gap, Taubman adopted a new corporate structure that revolutionized the tax treatment of owners of struggling and underwater commercial properties. The structure creates an "umbrella partnership REIT" (referred to as an *UPREIT*) that owns all of a REIT's properties, directly or through a controlling interest in a partnership. Public shareholders would invest in this UPREIT with cash at current market prices, while managers and other prior investors whose tax basis in the properties was very low or negative were allowed to swap their ownership interests for operating partnership units (OPUs) in the UPREIT. These OPUs are exchangeable for shares at the holder's option.

This swap was a nontaxable transaction under U.S. tax rules and enabled these legacy owners to retain their original tax basis and defer taxable gains until a future time of their own choosing. Without this OPU option, these owners would have been hit with hefty tax bills upon the formation of the new REIT. Since the Taubman IPO, dozens of REITs in the United States have used the UPREIT structure to permit investors with differing cost bases for their shares or units to invest side by side with public shareholders in an individual REIT.

As of December 2010, the value of OPUs was estimated at $20.2 billion, or about 5.3 percent of the $379 billion implied market capitalization of all U.S. REITs. The owners of this $20.2 billion in OPUs have thus turned over control of their properties to public REITs but, at the same time, essentially postponed any taxes on their holdings until such time as they decide to dispose of those units. The compromise lets REIT managers have full say in deciding when and if properties should be sold.

Changing Tax Rules to Facilitate Wider Institutional Ownership   Effective in January 1994, Congress changed REIT laws to end most tax-related reasons causing many tax-exempt institutions to shy from investing in REITs. Specifically, Congress modified an arcane application of the "Five or Fewer" rule to many tax-exempt investors. Prior to 1994, many tax-exempt investors, including stock bonus, pension or profit-sharing plans, had been limited in their REIT investing because the tax law treated them as a single "individual" for purposes of the IRS "Five or Fewer" rule. That rule required that a REIT not be "closely held," meaning that five or fewer individuals could not own more than 50 percent of a REIT's stock. The change modified this rule so that it applies by looking at the stock owned indirectly by plan beneficiaries in proportion to their interest in the trust.

Helped substantially by these two pioneering IPOs and the 1994 tax ruling, the market value of equity REITs soared in the United States, as shown in Figure 11.1.

Specifically, industry-implied market capitalization rose slightly over 10-fold, from $42 billion in the 16 years from November 1994, the first month in which NAREIT reported the value of OPUs as part of total market capitalization, to a peak $453 billion in January

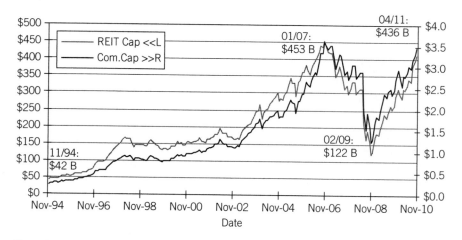

Figure 11.1   REIT Industry Market Cap and Average Company Cap, Nov. 1994 to April 2011

2007. From that point, market value fell sharply during the global recession to $122 billion before recovering smartly to $436 billion in April 2011.

Average company size has followed a similar trajectory, rising from $0.24 billion in 1994 to a peak $3.60 billion in January 2007. Four plus years later in April 2011 the average U.S. REIT had a $3.62 billion market cap, slightly exceeding its former peak.

This market recovery reflected ability of U.S. REITs to raise about $65 billion new common equity, including $6 billion in IPOs from January 2009 to April 2011. Through that date, share prices have rebounded to about 75 percent of their previous peak. The rapidity with which investors bid REIT stock prices back to near their previous highs is strong evidence that U.S. investors were willing, even eager, to provide capital quickly to fund REITs during the 2008 to 2009 credit crunch. Indeed, REITs were able to tap a broad menu of capital sources that were not available to most private operators whose financing options, being nonpublic by choice, were more limited. This experience is strong evidence that public markets have evolved into a deep and ready source of real estate capital. This constitutes the strongest vote possible for a strong future for equity REITs.

This half-century of gradual growth in acceptance of U.S. REITs as the preferred public property investment vehicle is playing out in similar fashion in nearly three dozen nations around the globe. Most have followed the U.S. experiences of significant ebbs and flows in investor enthusiasm, but the general trend has been up.

Australia: A Parallel Investment Story

The U.S. experience is mirrored in some respects in Australia. As noted, public real estate investment in real estate dates from 1960, when mall company Westfield listed on the Australian Stock Exchange (ASE). In 1971, General Property Trust was organized and listed on the ASE, becoming the first property-owning trust formed in Australia. A number of property entities followed suit, and the listed property trusts (LPTs) became a dominant form of real estate ownership in Australia. This prominence increased when Australian pension contribution laws were changed in 1985, and by the years 2000 to 2005 the Australian REITs, or A-REITs as they are now called, were estimated to own about 40 percent of all institutional grade commercial property in Australia. A-REIT growth has been aided by a national pension scheme that forces all Australians to pay 9 percent of income to the country's superannuation plan, which then invests approximately 10 percent of pension assets into real estate.

Because A-REITs owned an estimated 40 percent of the nation's commercial properties by the mid-2000s, many A-REITs began buying properties overseas. Many of them became major owners of properties in the United States, United Kingdom, and New Zealand. This trend accounted for the aggressive move of Westfield into overseas markets, because Westfield's growth exceeded the company's ability to invest efficiently entirely within Australia. Westfield has focused on the United States and the United Kingdom in its international expansion.

The A-REIT industry's move abroad had some unintended consequences, as most such forced moves ultimately do. Centro Properties Group, once a major Australian retail property trust that expanded aggressively into the United States, became so heavily indebted that it tumbled into lender-supervised restructuring in December 2008 during the worldwide financial crisis. Lenders ultimately pushed Centro to liquidate most of its holdings, and in February 2011, Blackstone Group, a major U.S. hedge fund, acquired substantially all of Centro's U.S. properties for approximately $9.4 billion. Net proceeds will be used to reduce debt in Centro Properties and Centro Retail Trust, its listed property vehicle.

Westfield also rearranged its corporate structure to adjust for the unequal ratio of home versus overseas investment opportunities, and in December 2010 spun off approximately half of its Australian properties into a separate entity, Westfield Retail Trust. The intent was a combination of creating a cleaner Australia-only vehicle, improving the company's balance sheet, and enabling potentially higher growth for the remaining portfolio, most of which is outside Australia.

The favorable United States and Australian experiences with raising real estate investment funds from a liquid and growing global capital market have given the REIT format a significant impetus as the "vehicle of choice" for much real estate investing around the globe.

As a result, REIT-like tax regimes have been embraced by 35 nations, according to a September 2010 survey by the European Public Real Estate Association (EPRA). Based in Brussels, Belgium, EPRA is supported by most financial organizations active in real estate investment, securities, development, and finance. EPRA provides significant index services to institutional investors in real estate, in addition to its authoritative annual survey of REIT regimes and regulations.

Table 11.1 is a summary of EPRA's September 2010 survey of REIT-like tax regimes around the world. EPRA's survey found 597 entities operating under REIT-like regimes in 22 nations. Some of these REITs appear to be smaller entities, and a parallel survey by CBRE Clarion Securities finds only 327 REITs of institutional market size as of December 31, 2010. REITs in the United States account for 53.1 percent of the global market capitalization of REIT structures in the EPRA survey. Other nations with significant shares of REIT global market cap are: Australia, 11.2 percent; France, 9.6 percent; United Kingdom, 5.4 percent; Japan, also 5.4 percent; and Canada, 4.3 percent.

In the context of the global marketplace, REITs now account for approximately 51 percent of real estate securities available to investors, based on CBRE Clarion data with 49 percent attributed to non-REIT real estate operating companies (REOCs) based on free-float equity market cap. The data are shown in Table 11.2.

Mapping the Size of Global Property Stock Markets

In 1990, scarcely two decades ago, there were no readily available measurements of the global market for property-linked stocks. Investors with a yen to buy property stocks "across the pond" had to rely on methods that are primitive by today's standards. An individual investor in New York City, for instance, who wanted to buy a property stock traded on the London Stock Exchange (LSE) had first to find a local broker willing and licensed to execute a trade on the LSE. Information on that distant investment or company operations was difficult to come by, often arriving by slow telex or fax.

From an institutional investor's standpoint, an intelligent allocation to real estate securities outside the institution's home nation would have been almost unheard of because there were no widely

Table 11.1 Status of Global REIT Regimes, September 2010

Country	Designation	Year Enacted	Year Modified	No. of REITs	% of Global REIT Mkt.	Citation of Enabling Legislation	EPRA Data	UBS Data
ACTIVE REIT REGIMES								
Australia	A-REITs (LPTs)	1971	1985	60	11.2%	Managed Investment Trusts	1985	1971
Belgium	SICAFI	1995	NA	14	1.0%	Societe d'investissement en immobilier a capital fixe	1995	1995
Brazil	FII	1993	NA	95	NA	Fundo de Investmento Imobiliario		
Bulgaria	SPIC	2004	NA	19	0.0%	Special Investment Purpose Companies Act	2004	2005
Canada	REIT/SIFT	1994	2007/09	35	4.3%	"Specified Investment Flow-through Entity"	1994	1993
France	SIIC	2003	NA	44	9.6%	Societes d'invertissement immobiliers cotees	2003	2003
Germany	G-REIT	2007	NA	2	0.1%	German Real Estate Investment Trust	2007	2007
Greece	REIC	1999	NA	2	0.1%	Real Estate Investment Companies	1999	
Hong Kong	HK-REIT	2003	2005	7	1.7%	Real Estate Investment Trusts	2003	2004
Italy	SIIQ	2006	NA	1	0.1%	Societa d'Investimento Immobiliare Quotate	2007	2008
Japan	J-REIT	2000	NA	36	5.4%	Investment Trust Law	2000	2001
Malaysia	Unit Trust	2005	NA	14	0.5%	Malaysian Islamic REIT	2005	2005
Netherlands	FBI	1969	NA	7	1.8%	Fiscale beleggingsinstelling	1969	1969

(Continued)

Table 11.1 Continued

Country	Designation	Year Enacted	Year Modified	No. of REITs	% of Global REIT Mkt.	Citation of Enabling Legislation	EPRA Data	UBS Data
New Zealand	PIEs/Unit Trusts	1960	2007	8	0.4%	Portfolio Investment Entity	1960 and 2007	
Singapore	S-REIT	1999	2002	21	3.7%	Property Fund Guidelines	1999	2002
South Africa	PUT and PLS	2003	NA	5	0.7%	Property Unit Trust (PUT) or Property Loan Stock Ciompany (PLS)	2003	
South Korea	REIC	2001	NA	6	0.1%	Real Estate Investment Company Act	2001	2001
Taiwan	REIT/REAT	2003	NA	8	0.4%	Real Estate Securitization Act		
Thailand	PFPO	1992	2006	6	0.1%	Property Fund for Public Offering	1992	2005
Turkey	REIC	1995	NA	15	0.3%	Real Estate Investment Companies	1995	1999
United Kingdom	REIT	2007	NA	19	5.4%	Finance Act 2006	2007	2007
United States	US-REIT	1960	Various	173	53.1%	Real Estate Investment Trusts	1960	1960
22				597	100.0%			
REIT REGIMES APPROVED								
Chile	FII	1998	2001	0	0.0%	Fondos de Inversion Inmobiliario	1998 (M2001)	
Costa Rica	REIF	1997	2009	0	0.0%	Real Estate Investment Fund (Act. #7732)		
Dubai	REIT	2006	NA	0	0.0%	Investment Trust Law No. 5		

Country	Type	Year			%	Description	
Finland	REIT	2009	NA	0	0.0%	Act on Tax Incentives for Certain Limited Companies	
India	REMF	1996	NA	0	0.0%	Real Estate Mutual funds	
Israel	REIT	2006	NA	0	0.0%	Secs. 64A2 to 64A11 Israeli Tax Ordinance	2006
Lithuania	REIT	2008	NA	0	0.0%	Law on Collective Investment Undertakings	
Luxembourg	SIF	2007	NA	0	0.0%	Specialized Investment Fund	
Mexico	FIBRAS	2004	2007	0	0.0%	Fideicomisos de Inversion de Bienes Raices	
Pakistran	REIT	2008	NA	0	0.0%	Real Estate Investment Trusts	
Philippines	REIT	2009	NA	0	0.0%	Real Estate Investment Trusts	
Puerto Rico	REIT	1972	2000/06	0	0.0%	Real Estate Investment Trusts	
Spain	RECII	2009	NA	0	0.0%	Sociedades Anonimas de Inversion en el Marcado Immobiliario	

13

Costa Rica: Law also establishes Real Estate Development Investment Funds (REDIF), which differ from REIF by the type of assets in which they are allowed to invest.
Germany: Six other entities are in pre-registration as pre-REITs.
Greece: Four qualified REICs are managed by banks.
Malaysia: The Securities Commission (SC) had issued Guidelines on "Property Trust Funds" in 2002, which were superseded by the issuance of REIT Guidelines in January 2005. Further updates were issued by way of Guidance Notes issued in 2005, 2006 and 2007. The above were further superseded by the revised Guidelines on REITs issued by the SC on August 21, 2008.
South Africa: PUTs were introduced in the market in 1969 and the Collective Investment Schemes Act was enacted in 2003.
Source: Eruropean Public Real Estate Association, Brussels, Belgium, "epra.com"; Global REIT Survey, September 2010; and UBS Global REIT Analyzer, November 18, 2010.

Table 11.2 Global Real Estate Securities: REITs and REOCs, December 31, 2010

Companies	Total	Market Cap	Free-Float Cap	Percent	Avg. Co.
REITs	327	$683 B	$607 B	51%	$1.86 B
REOCs	492	$1,015 B	$581 B	49%	$1.18 B
TOTALS	819	$1,698 B	$1,188 B	100%	$1.45 B

recognized global benchmarks available, let alone in real time. Few individual investors are concerned about availability of benchmarks, but the flow of institutional capital depends intimately on availability of recognized benchmarks, because benchmarks let an institution make three critical decisions:

1. Examine how the sector represented by an asset class has performed over time and under varying market conditions, assess its total return, standard deviation, and correlation with other asset classes.
2. Determine how that asset class might fit into the entity's overall portfolio and its likelihood of providing above average, or excess, returns over time.
3. Measure how any manager or managers the entity may hire perform relative to this benchmark.

In the institutional world, steps 1 and 2 take place at glacial speed, almost always guided by a real estate consultant hired to advise the institution on how best to structure its portfolio for maximum return and risk aversion. In the 1990s, the reality was that global benchmarks were still being developed and without global benchmarks, few institutional investments were made.

In the intervening two decades, several organizations have stepped into this vacuum and today provide institutional-grade index and other services to institutional investors, asset managers, custodians, consultants, and others involved in the global real estate securities markets. Two of the major benchmark providers are:

1. **Standard & Poor's (S&P) Corporation,** an internationally known provider of securities indices and other related services since the 1930s. The S&P Global Property set of indices

was introduced by a predecessor provider about 1992. S&P subsequently divided the Global Index into a Developed Property Index and an Emerging Property Index. It benchmarks base prices back to July 1989.

2. **European Public Real Estate Association, or EPRA,** was formed in 1999 to encourage greater investment in listed real estate companies through provision of better information to investors, improvement of the general operating environment, encouragement of best practices and the cohesion and strengthening of the industry. It seeks to establish best practices in accounting, reporting, and corporate governance; provide high-quality information to investors; and create a framework for debate and decision making on key issues. EPRA is a member of the Real Estate Equity Securitization Alliance (REESA) and works with NAREIT in the United States and the Asian Public Real Estate Association (APREA) in Asia. Its Global Real Estate Index—officially known as the FTSE EPRA/NAREIT Developed Index—was introduced in October 2001. The European portion of the index was introduced in June 2000.

Benchmark providers focus on the "free float" of companies in their respective databases. Put simply, free float is the market value of shares available for normal open market trading, as distinguished from the value of shares held by management and other insiders whose holdings are not expected to trade regularly.

Additionally, each index provider has varying guidelines for inclusion of companies in their indices; hence, specific companies may or may not be included in any given index. In general, the index providers focus on larger and more liquid companies. Hence, the average size of the 399 companies in the S&P Developed Property Index weighs in at $2.08 billion free market float at the end of 2010, for a total market cap of $828 billion. The EPRA Index contains only 282 companies, but its $795 billion total cap works out to $2.82 billion market cap per company. An expanded data set maintained by CBRE Clarion totals $1.18 trillion free market cap, and the 819 companies have $1.44 billion in average value.

Global portfolios are typically thought of by investors as containing the stocks of companies from four distinct regions. Each region has distinct economic and financial metrics that must be weighed in selecting portfolio weights. These regions are:

- **The Americas**, including both North and South America.
- **Asia/Pacific**, containing stocks from nations stretching northward from Australia and New Zealand to China, Japan, and westward to Singapore.
- **Europe**, containing the European Community nations plus some Baltic nations.
- **Middle East and Other**, embracing Israel, Turkey, United Arab Emirates, and South Africa, smaller nations with emerging REIT markets.

Investors in global real estate securities typically look beyond the benchmark names for investment opportunity. Countries currently not included in the indices include:

- **Americas**: Argentina, Brazil, Chile, and Mexico.
- **Asia/Pacific**: India, Indonesia, Korea, Malaysia, Philippines, Taiwan, Thailand, and Vietnam.
- **Europe**: Luxembourg, Poland, Russia.
- **Middle East and Other**: South Africa, Turkey, and United Arab Emirates.

The names of major companies in these nations and regions will generally be unfamiliar to U.S. investors. To acquaint readers with the largest companies in each nation, we provide, in Appendix E of this book, an extensive listing of the 175 largest and most recognizable global real estate companies as of December 31, 2010. Readers are advised to spend some time with that listing because it contains important data about these major companies and their standing within their countries' markets.

We also present, in Table 11.3, a comprehensive view of investment opportunities in global real estate securities by country. It's important to note that all measurements of the size of the global real estate marketplace must be qualified by source and date. With these qualifications, the following is a comparison of basic data from both S&P and EPRA indices, plus an expanded real estate securities universe as developed by CBRE Clarion.

Table 11.3 Mapping the Global Real Estate Securities Market, December 31, 2010

	Number of Companies			Free Float Market Cap in Th. USD			Index Weight		
	CBRE	EPRA	S&P	CBRE	EPRA	S&P	CBRE	EPRA	S&P
Americas	204	126	137	$489,278	$357,492	$347,148	41.6%	45.0%	41.9%
Argentina	1			$346			0.0%		
Brazil	24			$33,355			2.8%		
Canada	29	20	23	$56,995	$34,147	$19,193	4.8%	4.3%	2.3%
Chile	1			$357			0.0%		
Mexico	4			$3,758			0.3%		
United States	145	106	114	$394,468	$323,345	$327,954	33.5%	40.7%	39.6%
Asia/Pacific	383	73	158	$481,803	$313,987	$350,331	41.0%	39.5%	42.3%
Australia	35	15	30	$77,958	$68,261	$76,295	6.6%	8.6%	9.2%
China	16	3		$11,341	$12,410		1.0%		
Hong Kong	96	19	40	$170,093	$108,937	$112,022	14.5%	15.4%	13.5%
India	20			$9,477			0.8%		
Indonesia	13			$4,732			0.4%		
Japan	64	20	50	$106,959	$82,623	$112,081	9.1%	10.4%	13.5%
Korea	3			$5,367			0.5%		
Malaysia	26			$10,430			0.9%		
New Zealand	5	1	4	$2,371	$760	$2,099	0.2%	0.1%	0.3%
Philippines	12			$8,774			0.7%		

(Continued)

Table 11.3 Continued

	Number of Companies			Free Float Market Cap in Th. USD			Index Weight		
	CBRE	EPRA	S&P	CBRE	EPRA	S&P	CBRE	EPRA	S&P
Asia/Pacific	383	73	158	$481,803	$313,987	$350,331	41.0%	39.5%	42.3%
Singapore	50	15	34	$53,524	$40,997	$47,834	4.6%	5.1%	5.8%
Taiwan	24			$11,440			1.0%		
Thailand	17			$8,312			0.7%		
Vietnam	2			$1,026			0.1%		
Europe	198	82	90	$182,897	$122,584	$126,604	15.6%	15.4%	15.4%
Austria	10	2	5	$10,819	$2,546	$8,195	0.9%	0.3%	1.0%
Belgium	17	6	4	$5,350	$4,137	$3,516	0.5%	0.5%	0.4%
Denmark	3		2	$483		$302	0.0%		
Finland	3	3	3	$2,066	$2,547	$1,823	0.2%	0.3%	0.2%
France	31	9	8	$48,406	$31,899	$33,045	4.1%	4.0%	4.0%
Germany	15	8	9	$6,033	$5,584	$5,393	0.5%	0.7%	0.7%
Greece	3	2	2	$236	$215	$168	0.0%		
Italy	5	2	3	$1,484	$1,047	$1,322	0.1%	0.1%	0.2%

				Market Cap (Th. $)			%		
Luxembourg			1						
Netherlands	11	7		$15,218	$13,201	$12,075	1.3%	1.7%	1.6%
Norway	3	1		$1,232	$888	$888	0.1%	0.1%	0.1%
Poland	6			$1,815			0.2%		
Russia	7			$10,025			0.9%		
Spain	11	1	2	$12,769	$250	$703	1.1%	0.0%	0.1%
Sweden	15	6	10	$11,614	$8,897	$9,712	1.0%	1.1%	1.2%
Switzerland	7	4	6	$9,066	$7,948	$8,933	0.8%	1.0%	1.1%
United Kingdom	51	31	27	$46,281	$43,427	$40,528	3.9%	5.5%	4.9%
Mideast/Other	34	1	14	$22,008	$975	$4,049	1.9%	0.1%	0.5%
Israel	14	1	14	$4,272	$975	$4,049	0.4%	0.1%	0.5%
South Africa	14			$14,247			1.2%		
Turkey	3			$1,186			0.1%		
United Arab Emirates	3			$2,302			0.2%		
Grand Total	819	282	399	$1,175,985	$795,039	$828,133	100.0%	100.0%	100.0%
Average Company Market Cap - Th. $				$1,436	$2,819	$2,076			

Source: Compilation of CBRE Clarion

Managing a Global Real Estate Securities Portfolio

Managing a portfolio of global real estate securities comes with extra layers of risks compared to a portfolio drawn from securities representing only one country.

Currency Risks and Benefits

An investment in equities outside an investor's home currency brings with it exposure to currency risk, which may either help or hinder overall total return, depending on the net changes in aggregate currency relationships. For a U.S.-based investor, currency risk comes in the form of ownership of companies whose shares are denominated in currencies other than the U.S. dollar or currencies that are pegged to the U.S. dollar. Since the United States represents approximately 42 percent of the benchmark (FTSE EPRA/NAREIT Developed Index), and since Hong Kong (whose dollar is pegged to the U.S. dollar) is approximately 14 percent of the global real estate universe, currency exposure exists on less than half of the global portfolio (the United States and Hong Kong comprise 56 percent of the portfolio, so there is currency exposure on the remaining 44 percent). A look at the benchmark by currency, derived from the FTSE EPRA/NAREIT Developed Index, puts into sharper relief what the world looks like for real estate securities in terms of currency (see Figure 11.2).

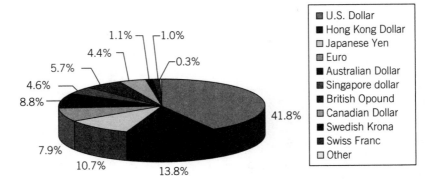

1.1%   1.0%
4.4%
5.7%   0.3%
4.6%
8.8%
41.8%
7.9%
10.7%   13.8%

- U.S. Dollar
- Hong Kong Dollar
- Japanese Yen
- Euro
- Australian Dollar
- Singapore dollar
- British Opound
- Canadian Dollar
- Swedish Krona
- Swiss Franc
- Other

Figure 11.2   Global Currency Weights (as of 2/24/11)

Currency relationships are a more significant opportunity or threat for investors who have a base currency other than the U.S. dollar, where currency exposure typically may exceed 80 percent or more of the overall portfolio. Non-U.S. investors, therefore, have perhaps been more traditionally attuned to the vagaries of currency risk and are accustomed to addressing it. Some investors may take the view that currency risk is simply part of the overall investment proposition and that currencies should not be hedged. Other investors may decide to hedge currency, perhaps in acknowledgment that forecasting currency movements is beyond the investment objective at hand, or not a core differentiating strength of the investor. It is important to note that a 100 percent hedged portfolio simply creates a structure that ensures that total returns will approximate those in stated respective local currencies, without gain or loss from currency movements. Hedging currencies avoids a directional bet on currencies except to the extent that the hedge is not 100 percent for each particular currency represented in a portfolio (the bet would be on whatever is not perfectly hedged). The ability to hedge currencies is an expertise that appears to be in higher demand as investors increasingly consider a global real estate securities investment strategy.

Currency Hedging

Currency hedging may take many forms. One common strategy for a large, sophisticated institution is a currency overlay program, wherein the overall currency exposure of an investor with many investments is taken into account. A currency overlay program attempts to take into account the overall currency exposure of an investor, for example, a pension fund, which may have many investments in many asset classes in various currencies, in an effort to limit the risk from adverse movements in exchange rates within the portfolio as a whole. Or, if the investor has an opinion as to the direction of exchange rates, the overlay program may be structured with a directional bias in an effort to capture incremental total return, with net exposure to certain currency relationships.

A portfolio-specific hedged portfolio, however, is a hedge on an identified portfolio, which tends to be a focused investment strategy. For example, an investor might select a global listed real estate securities strategy, hedged to the U.S. dollar. The hedging typically consists of forward contracts of shorter duration (typically one- to three-month forward contracts), which are continually rolled upon maturity so that returns remain hedged within the bounds as defined by the hedging strategy. The forward contracts simply provide an offset to the currency exposure of the underlying investments. For example, if a U.S.-based global real estate securities fund invests in a French property company at a 1 percent position, then this fund is now "long the euro" by a magnitude of 1 percent. The underlying investment in the property company will be affected by currency movements of the euro versus the U.S. dollar in addition to other investment merits. To offset this, a hedging strategy might be to enter into a one-month forward currency contract that goes "short the euro, long the U.S. dollar" in an amount that exactly offsets the size of the investment in the euro. Any appreciation of the euro versus the U.S. dollar in the underlying investment (in the property company) will be exactly offset by a loss of value in the forward contract, and vice versa, thus providing the desired hedge. When the forward contract matures, the investor simply puts a new contract in place. The cost of doing this is nearly immaterial assuming professional foreign exchange trading execution.

Hedging is typically defined with some degree of latitude in the overall portfolio, for example, a 5 percent tolerance level. This means that the overall currency exposure must stay within 5 percent of the value of the portfolio, which means that currency exposure should at most be 5 percent (so hedges could range from 95 percent to 105 percent of the portfolio).

Trading and Execution in Global World

Global investment execution requires trade execution that is available as the sun circles the globe. The underlying securities of property company investments are largely bought and sold on the local exchanges of each country, including, for example, London, Amsterdam, Hong Kong, Tokyo, Sydney, New York, Toronto, and Singapore. While some of the larger non-U.S. companies may have ADRs, most of the action is on the local exchanges, not in the U.S. ADRs. An effective execution strategy must include using trade desks that can find order flows and execute trades on local exchanges.

This includes communicating with the trade desks of major (and at times minor) banks, as well as knowing how to execute on electronic exchanges, which are of increasing importance to investors in equities in general. Electronic exchanges enable traders to find buyers or sellers in an anonymous fashion at a fraction of the cost of full-service brokerage firms (the difference in the United States is paying one cent per share for electronic trading versus four to five cents per share for a full-service firm; outside the United States the difference is approximately 4 basis points a share for electronic trading versus 15 to 20 basis points for a full-service firm). Commissions in the United States are still quoted on a cents-per-share basis versus, and outside of the United States as a percentage of the trade amount.

A trade desk must prove adept at finding blocks of stock when available, and at bargaining effectively to achieve discounts. An experienced trader will be in sync with the portfolio management team and know when to execute trades opportunistically, often when there is not much time to discuss the trade. Trade desks are often the first point of communication on capital-raising activities of a property company, some of which occur quickly. For example, many U.S. REITs raise follow-on equity "overnight," which means the company lets the world know what it is doing after the market closes at 4:00 p.m. on a given day, with orders due at the latest the next morning before the market opens (or even earlier, depending on demand). The trade desk is often the first point of communication for such deals.

Liquidity of global real estate securities is generally good. It is estimated that nearly US$7 billion in volume trades on a daily basis, on average. A new mandate of US$200 million could easily be invested within several days without affecting market prices. With the increased size and liquidity of the global real estate securities universe comes the ability of larger institutions to allocate significant funds to the sector. Large pension funds, including sovereign wealth funds, are increasingly looking to real estate securities as an effective way to invest in real estate.

The Practicalities of Investing Overseas for the Individual Investor

As indicated earlier, global investing in real estate stocks is dominated by institutional investors. This leaves the individual investor with two realistic choices, discussed next.

Investment Mutual Funds

While open-end mutual funds may be anathema to some iconoclastic investors, for many investors the sheer complexity of the global real estate securities (GRES) market makes the investment fund route the choice for many, if not most, individual investors. This choice seems reasonable, regardless of the sum an individual may wish to commit.

As with all mutual fund investments, investors should consider carefully the information contained in the fund prospectus, keeping in mind that past performance is no guarantee of future performance. In Table 11.4, we list summary data for 51 U.S. mutual and exchange-traded funds that were invested, as of March 2011, to some extent in global real estate companies. This is not a complete tally of the 350-plus funds active in global real estate securities, but rather a sampler of U.S. funds with wide varieties of investment objectives and minimum initial investment requirements. A similar menu of funds could be compiled for nations outside the United States.

Funds are grouped in three major groups of investment targets as follows:

1. **Global.** The 22 global funds listed seek investments in all parts of the world where real estate securities are available. Total mutual fund assets of $14.5 billion are a tiny fraction of the relevant market, indicating that funds in this category have ample room for growth. This group includes retail funds requiring minimum initial investments, ranging from $1,000 for several funds to $2 million for high-end institutional funds (Alliance Bernstein). The group also includes two exchange-traded funds (ETFs) active in the space, First Trust FTSE EPRA/NAREIT (symbol: FFR) and SPR DJ Wilshire Global RE (symbol: RWO). Annual management fees average 0.76 percent for this group, and annual expenses average 1.14 percent.
2. **International.** The 11 international funds shown generally invest in real estate companies in all parts of the world *except* the United States. Total mutual fund assets of $5.5 billion are also small compared to related market capitalization. The

underlying concept for these fund sponsors is that an investor can form a global portfolio by selecting one U.S. domestic fund and one international fund. Minimum investment varies from $1,000 for a retail product to $1 million for the three institutional funds in this group. The group also includes two ETFs active in the space, SPDR DJ Wilshire International ETF (symbol: RWX) and WisdomTree International Real Estate Fund (symbol: DRW). Annual management fees in this group average 0.83 percent, and annual expenses are 1.11 percent.

3. **United States.** The 18 domestic funds generally seek investments from among companies operating in the United States or listed on U.S. exchanges. Total mutual fund assets of $26.9 billion are about 8 percent of available market cap, a smaller penetration than for many other sector funds. Minimum investment ranges from relatively small retail funds with $500 minimum (Virtus RE Securities) to institutional funds with a $3 million entry (Cohen & Steers Institutional). Two ETFs are listed: iShares Dow Jones Real Estate Index (symbol: IYR) and Vanguard REIT Fund (symbol: VNQ). Annual management fees average 0.69 percent for this group, and annual expenses average 0.96 percent.

Table 11.4 generally shows data for Class A or the most widely held class of shares of the open-end mutual funds, although investors should be mindful that nearly all funds offer multiple classes of shares with varying front-end and back-end loads, early withdrawal fees, and minimum investments.

The attributes of each class of shares also should be considered carefully because they may have significant bearing on total return over time. There are many experienced advisers skilled in selection of mutual funds, and investors would be wise to consult one or more such advisers before making a final choice.

The mutual fund investor thus has a wide variety of choices, ranging from open-end to exchange-traded funds, offering a variety of load and no-load formats, wide ranges of minimum investment, and management fees and expense ratios reflecting significant competition among fund advisers and sponsors. These offering can be expected to grow in quantity and diversity as the GRES expands over time, all to the benefit of the mutual fund investor.

Table 11.4 Representative Investment Funds Available to Global Real Estate Investors

Fund Sector	Ticker - C Ticker	Net Assets (Mil.$) - D	Inception Date	Load % Front End	Load % Back End	Early With.	Mgmt. Fee	Expense Ratio	Minimum Invest.	Asset Date	Yrs. Track. Record
Global Funds											
Alliance Berstein Global RE Fund II	ARIIX	$885.7	12/9/1997	0.00%	0.00%	0.00%	0.55%	0.62%	$2,000,000	3/9/2011	5
Cohen and Steers Global Realty Shares (A) - B	CSFAX	$58.8	9/30/2004	4.50%	0.00%	2.00%	0.90%	1.56%	$1,000	10/31/2009	5
Delaware Pooled Trust-Global RE Secur. Port.	DGROX	$58.2	1/10/2007	0.00%	0.00%	0.00%	0.99%	1.25%	NA	3/9/2011	3
DFA Global RE Securities Portfolio	DFGEX	$724.1	7/31/2008	0.00%	0.00%	NA	0.35%	0.41%	NA	3/15/2011	1
DWS RREEF Global RE Secur. Fund (Cl. I)	RRGIX	$1,026.8	7/5/2006	0.00%	0.00%	2.00%	1.00%	1.00%	$1,000,000	3/9/2011	5
EII Global Property Fund-IN	EIIGX	$90.4	2/1/2007	0.00%	0.00%	1.50%	0.75%	1.00%	$1,000,000	6/9/2009	3
Franklin Global RE Fund - Cl. A	FAGRX	$76.0	6/16/2006	5.75%	0.00%	2.00%	0.80%	1.35%	NA	2/28/2011	3
ING Global Real Estate Fund - A	IGLAX	$3,490.5	11/5/2001	5.75%	0.00%	0.00%	0.72%	1.39%	$1,000	3/9/2011	5
Invesco Global RE Fund (A)(AIM)	AGREX	$889.9	4/29/2005	5.50%	0.00%	2.00%	0.74%	1.59%	$1,000	3/15/2011	5

Fund	Ticker	Assets	Inception						Min. Invest.	Date	Rating
Janus Global Real Estate Fd.-Cl. I	JERIX	$69.3	11/28/2007	0.00%	0.00%	2.00%	0.80%	1.32%	$1,000,000	2/28/2011	3
Morgan Stanley-Global RE Port. Cl. I	MRLAX	$1,527.3	8/30/2006	0.00%	0.00%	2.00%	0.85%	1.01%	$500,000	3/9/2011	3
Northern Global RE Index Fd	NGREX	$639.2	8/7/2006	0.00%	0.00%	2.00%	0.35%	0.65%	$2,500	3/9/2011	3
PACE Global Real Estate (UBS) - Cl. A	PREAX	$99.3	12/19/2006	5.50%	0.00%	1.00%	0.70%	1.45%	NA	2/28/2011	3
Principal Global RE Secur.-Cl. A	POSAX	$146.4	1/17/2007	5.50%	1.00%	1.00%	0.90%	1.45%	$1,000	3/9/2011	3
Prudential Investment Portfolios 12	PURAX	$671.7	5/5/1998	5.50%	1.00%	0.00%	0.75%	1.07%	$1,000	3/9/2011	5
Russell Global RE Securities-Cl. S	RRESX	$1,739.7	7/28/1989	0.00%	0.00%	0.00%	0.80%	1.09%	NA	3/15/2011	5
T. Rowe Price Global Real Estate Fund	TRGRX	$42.6	10/28/2008	0.00%	0.00%	2.00%	0.71%	1.05%	$2,500	2/28/2011	1
Third Avenue RE Value Fund - Cl. IS	TAREX	$1,873.9	9/17/1998	0.00%	0.00%	1.00%	0.90%	1.14%	$10,000	3/9/2011	5
Transamerica Clarion Global RE Secur.-I (IDEX)	TRSIX	$284.4	3/1/2003	0.00%	0.00%	2.00%	0.80%	0.91%	$1,000	3/9/2011	1
Universal Global RE Fund-Cl. II (Morgan Stanley)	UGETX	$95.7	4/28/2006	0.00%	0.00%	0.00%	0.85%	1.40%	NA	3/9/2011	5

(continued)

Table 11.4 Continued

Fund Sector	Ticker - C	Net Assets (Mil.$) - D	Inception Date	Load % Front End	Load % Back End	Early With.	Mgmt. Fee	Expense Ratio	Minimum Invest.	Asset Date	Yrs. Track. Record
First Trust EPRA/NAREIT Global RE Index Fund	FFR	$67.0	NA	NA	NA	NA	0.60%	0.60%	NA	3/15/2011	3
SPR DJ Wilshire Global RE ETF	RWO	$236.1	NA	NA	NA	NA	0.50%	0.51%	NA	3/15/2011	3
Total/Averages Mutual funds	**20**	**$14,489.9**					**0.76%**	**1.14%**			
Totals/Averages ETFs	**2**	**$303.0**					**0.55%**	**0.56%**			
International Funds	**Ticker**										
Alpine International Real Estate Equity Fund	EGLRX	$550.3	2/1/1989	0.00%	0.00%	1.00%	1.00%	1.20%	$1,000	3/9/2011	5
Cohen & Steers Intl. Realty Fund, Cl. I	IRFIX	$1,400.0	3/31/2005	0.00%	0.00%	2.00%	0.95%	1.26%	$1,000,000	9/30/2010	5
DFA International Real Estate Sec. Port.	DFITX	$1,010.7	5/3/2007	0.00%	0.00%	NA	0.35%	0.41%	NA	3/9/2011	3
EII International Property Fund-Cl. I	EIIPX	$631.4	7/1/2004	0.00%	0.00%	1.50%	0.75%	1.00%	$1,000,000	3/9/2011	5
Fidelity International Real Estate Fund	FIREX	$378.5	9/8/2004	0.00%	0.00%	1.50%	0.71%	1.14%	$2,500	2/28/2011	5

Fund	Ticker	Assets	Date						Minimum	Date	
Goldman Sachs International RE Fund-Cl. I	GIRIX	$396.7	7/31/2006	0.00%	0.00%	2.00%	1.05%	1.13%	$1,000,000	2/28/2011	3
ING International Real Estate Fund-Cl. A	IIRAX	$655.4	2/28/2006	5.75%	0.00%	0.00%	0.94%	1.50%	$1,000	3/9/2011	5
JP Morgan International Realty Fd.-Cl. A	JIRAX	$82.3	12/1/2006	5.25%	0.00%	2.00%	0.90%	1.40%	$1,000	3/9/2011	3
Morgan Stanley-International RE Port.-Cl. I	MSUAX	$394.7	10/1/1997	0.00%	2.00%	2.00%	0.80%	0.98%	$500,000	3/9/2011	5
SPDR DJ Wilshire International RE ETF	RWX	$1,696.0	NA	NA	NA	NA	0.59%	0.60%	NA	3/15/2011	3
WisdomTree International Real Estate Fund	DRW	$120.2	NA	NA	NA	NA	0.58%	0.58%	NA	3/15/2011	3
Total/Averages Mutual funds	**9**	**$5,499.9**					**0.83%**	**1.11%**			
Totals/Averages ETFs	**2**	**$1,816.2**					**0.59%**	**0.59%**			
US Only Funds	**Ticker**										
Alpine Cyclical Advan. Prop. Fd.-Cl. Y	EUEYX	$63.3	9/1/1993	0.00%	0.00%	1.00%	1.00%	1.30%	$1,000	3/9/2011	5
Amer Century RE Fund-Cl. Inv.	REACX	$1,075.5	9/21/1995	0.00%	0.00%	0.00%	1.15%	1.16%	$2,500	3/15/2011	5
CGM Realty Fund	CGMRX	$1,515.8	5/13/1994	0.00%	0.00%	0.00%	0.80%	0.89%	$2,500	3/15/2011	5

(continued)

Table 11.4 Continued

Fund Sector	Ticker - C	Net Assets (Mil.$) - D	Inception Date	Load % Front End	Back End	Early With.	Mgmt. Fee	Expense Ratio	Minimum Invest.	Asset Date	Yrs. Track. Record
Cohen & Steers Inst. Rlty. Shs.	CSRIX	$610.3	2/14/2000	0.00%	0.00%	0.00%	0.75%	0.75%	$3,000,000	10/31/2009	5
Columbia RE Equity Fund-Cl. Z	CREEX	$384.1	4/1/1994	0.00%	0.00%	0.00%	0.75%	1.02%	NA	3/15/2011	5
Davis RE Fund-Cl. A	RPFRX	$301.7	1/3/1994	4.75%	0.50%	0.00%	0.55%	1.11%	$1,000	3/15/2011	5
DFA RE Securities Portfolio	DFREX	$2,874.3	1/5/1993	0.00%	0.00%	0.00%	0.30%	0.33%	$2,000,000	3/15/2011	5
DWS RREEF RE Secur. Fd.-Cl. Inst.	RRRRX	$1,109.6	12/1/1999	0.00%	0.00%	2.00%	0.41%	0.63%	$1,000,000	3/9/2011	5
Fidelity Real Estate Invest. Port.	FRESX	$3,507.8	11/17/1986	0.00%	0.00%	0.75%	0.56%	0.90%	$2,500	2/28/2011	5
ING Real Estate Fund - Cl. I	CRARX	$671.8	12/31/1996	0.00%	0.00%	0.00%	0.70%	0.90%	$250,000	3/9/2011	5
Invesco Real Estate Fd.-Cl. Ins.	IARIX	$1,941.5	4/30/2004	0.00%	0.00%	0.00%	0.73%	0.90%	NA	2/28/2011	5
Invesco Van Kampen RES Fund-Cl. A	ACREX	$343.3	6/9/1994	4.75%	0.00%	0.00%	0.80%	1.46%	NA	3/9/2011	NA
Morgan Stanley-US RE Port.-Cl. I	MSUSX	$992.1	2/24/1995	0.00%	0.00%	0.00%	0.77%	0.98%	$500,000	3/9/2011	5
Natixis AEW Real Estate Fd.-Cl. Y	NRFYX	$303.5	8/31/2000	0.00%	0.00%	0.00%	0.80%	1.25%	$100,000	3/9/2011	5

Fund	Ticker										
Vanguard REIT Index Fund	VGSIX	$10,446.2	5/13/1996	0.00%	0.00%	1.00%	0.22%	0.26%	$3,000	3/10/2011	5
Virtus RE Securities Fund-Cl. A	PHRAX	$718.5	3/1/1995	5.75%	0.00%	0.00%	0.75%	1.48%	$500	3/15/2011	5
iShares Dow Jones U.S. Real Estate Index Fd.	IYR	$3,136.0	NA	NA	NA	NA	0.47%	0.47%	NA	3/10/2011	5
Vanguard REIT ET Fund	VNQ	$8,499.7	NA	NA	NA	NA	0.12%	0.12%	NA	3/15/2011	5
Total/Averages Mutual funds	**16**	**$26,859.2**					**0.69%**	**0.96%**			
Totals/Averages ETFs	**2**	**$11,635.7**	k				**0.30%**	**0.30%**			
GRAND TOTALS/AVGS. MUT. FUNDS	**45**	**$46,849.0**					**0.76%**	**1.07%**			
GRAND TOTALS/AVGS. ETFs	**6**	**$13,754.9**					**0.48%**	**0.48%**			

Notes: A - Funds managed by the employer of the authors. B - Transitioned from U.S. to global fund during 2000s.
  C - Five-letter tickers denotes open-end mutual funds; Three letters denote exchange-traded funds. D - Net assets as of early March 2011.

Source: CBRE Clarion compilation from Bloomberg. Track record is number of years compiled by Bloomberg (maximum five).

Closed-end real estate funds (CEFs) were quite popular in the early 2000s in the United States because of their above-average dividend yields achieved by leveraging assets with auction-rate preferred shares. Their popularity waned, however, during the 2008 and 2009 financial crisis when leverage vanished as the auction-rate preferred market disappeared. At this writing, only two CEFs operate in the global real estate sphere, with $2.0 billion net assets. At their peak popularity at the end of 2007, 19 U.S. CEFs with $14.5 billion assets pursued both global and domestic strategies. Today, the main investment attraction for CEF investors is as a vehicle offering an income priority strategy and access to portfolios investing in instruments such as preferred stock not widely available in open-end actively managed mutual funds. The global CEFs sometimes also trade at a discount to NAV, ranging from 8 percent to 15 percent at this writing. Some also use modest leverage via bank borrowings, providing additional yield and value.

Individual Management

Sophisticated and self-reliant investors may desire to assemble a portfolio of global real estate securities of their own choosing. Several academic studies over the years have demonstrated that individual investors can and do "beat the averages" by keeping expenses as low as possible and hewing to personalized investment strategies that may not be followed by mutual funds and other institutional investors.

Mutual fund investors may be vulnerable to volatility in their shares during sharp downturns because the mutual fund's portfolio managers may be forced to sell strong stocks to meet redemption requests. The individual investor is not subject to these pressures and can hold through such panics—unless, of course, personal circumstances or preferences dictate selling holdings.

Because the individual investor is somewhat isolated from these temporary market pressures, he or she can potentially execute a chosen strategy without interruption. For instance, if an individual chooses to follow a deep value strategy of buying stocks when they fall out of market favor and holding for a longer-term recovery in value, he or she avoids institutional impediments.

The individual choosing this course must, however, face two technical hurdles:

1. Executing trades in many different stock markets around the globe. A decade ago the simple execution of trades in foreign lands, and custodying these holdings was a major impediment to global investing by an individual. Today, thanks to the flowering of the Internet, an individual can easily open an account with any one of a dozen or more global investment banking firms and get good executions around the clock. Such firms also will hold the securities purchased and provide monthly statements of market value, income, and other attributes. Most large investment banks also provide clients with income tax–friendly annual documents that investors can incorporate into their tax returns or turn over to their tax preparer. Either way, much of the paperwork disincentive to follow a global investment strategy is now removed.
2. Obtaining timely information about global stocks and local real estate markets. Again, the global investment banking houses now are equipped to meet most investment information needs. All large banks deploy from one to two dozen security analysts in most world-class cities overseas (e.g., London, Paris, Tokyo, Hong Kong, Sydney) who generate an ongoing stream of reports covering most major companies in most major markets.

Their output is back-stopped and enhanced by the thinking of global and regional economic analysts who sift the changing economic fortunes for their impact on real estate in nations, regions, and the global economy. The individual clients of these firms can receive as much of this prodigious output as they can use or digest.

Several of these firms have begun producing weekly or monthly research reports addressing the specific needs of the global real estate investor. These reports range from summaries of company and economic news from each major country or region, to model portfolios that help guide an individual investor. An investor should check with individual firms for their current offerings, which can and do change over time.

In addition, the individual investor will wish to monitor the web sites of the three major real estate securities associations. They are:

NAREIT—REIT.com. The U.S. National Association of Real Estate Investment Trusts maintains a web site offering a rich array of data on property stock markets in the United States. Of note are its monthly Investment Performance for the FTSE NAREIT US Real Estate Index Series, found in "Industry Data"; Investment Performance by Property Sector and Subsector; and the monthly publication *REITWatch*, under "NAREIT Statistical Publications."

EPRA—epra.com: The European Public real Estate Association issues a number of reports to members. Nonmembers may, however, receive their *Monthly Market Review*, which contains much useful information.

APREA—aprea.asia. The Asian Public Real Estate Association web site makes a series of news reports available to nonmembers. Research reports and other publications are available only to members.

Finally, an investor may wish to follow global markets through any one of several recognized financial web sites. Yahoo Financial. com is one such potential information source, as are Bloomberg. com and several others. These mainstream sites generally provide timely content for price quotes, earnings releases, and other general news for stocks in the United States, Australia, Hong Kong, and London, but are somewhat less useful for stocks in venues such as Japan, China, and smaller European markets.

A Summary: Stocks for All Investment Seasons

The global real estate securities market is dynamic and ever changing, offering a wide variety of securities for almost every investment objective. This chapter introduces the investor to the potential opportunities existing in real estate securities around the globe. Today's investor may select from a global real estate securities universe divided about equally between real estate investment trusts (REITs) and real estate operating companies (REOCs). These two very large groups of public real estate entities have such differing investment attributes that an institutional or individual investor may construct portfolios able to achieve a wide variety of investment goals.

REITs, as described in this chapter, mainly focus on owning income-producing commercial properties. They are generally prized for above-average and usually stable income because REITs are required to distribute their operating profits to shareholders. From an investment standpoint, most REITs are thus viewed as income vehicles with modest but not inconsequential growth potential.

REOCs, however, tend to focus on developing and selling new properties, with a strong focus on residential properties. Their merchant-building activities thus tend to impart more volatility to earnings and share prices, and dividend income is not a major consideration for investors. From an investment standpoint, REOCs offer potentially higher growth balanced against higher earnings and price risk.

As discussed earlier, public real estate entities now have access to a deeper and more varied menu of public capital, ranging from long-term debt to equity, than substantially all private operators. Through joint ventures, their managers have become the funnels through which billions in institutional capital is directed into real estate each year.

It has been observed that no entrepreneurial, capital-intensive industry has ever turned back once it has come to rely on public capital. That is the underlying fundamental of global real estate securities. Real estate, once a bastion of self-reliant local entrepreneurs building local properties, has in little more than half a century emerged as a global marketplace in which capital can be mobilized to finance worthy real estate projects. During 2010 and into 2011, about a half-dozen real estate companies each were able to raise $1 billion or more in overnight offerings on the major stock exchanges of the world; such capital-raising prowess was unheard of five years ago.

Technology has put information on the activities of any company operating anywhere at the fingertips of any investor with a keyboard and reading time. That same technology and the emergence of global investment banking firms now make possible investment in any company operating in any nation with a stock traded on any exchange.

A final word about risk: Public real estate securities historically have suffered one major market correction during each decade.

Some have been relatively short, while others have dragged on a bit longer. The U.S. average decline is 22.3 months. These corrections have averaged 46.9 percent price declines, with the 2007 to 2009 slump of 70.4 percent being the deepest of all. The individual investor is urged to be alert to the beginnings of such declines and take defensive measures accordingly.

One of the best defenses is to hold the stocks of public companies whose track records during past downturns set them apart. Managers of these companies know full well the potential for such downtimes and reduce debt leverage, scale back development and take other precautions whenever they spy a storm on the horizon. By their track record they become the most prized securities in the global real estate securities universe, and in a sense their past performance in downturns provides some assurance they will come through such episodes in the future.

Five or ten years from now, the current balance between REITs and REOCs almost surely will shift, but the authors are confident that both REITs and REOCs will be alive and well around the globe, representing a much larger slice of commercial real estate. Global real estate investing's time has come.

The Long-Term Evidence Supporting Investments in Global Real Estate Securities

[This section was circulated as a White Paper by CBRE Clarion in June 2010 and appears here because it consolidates the statistical and academic evidence supporting investment in global real estate securities. All data are updated through December 31, 2010.]

An allocation to global real estate securities in an otherwise mixed-asset portfolio provides investors with liquid, transparent, well-benchmarked access to institutional-quality real estate that increases diversification and the potential for attractive risk-adjusted returns.

Long-Term Performance of Global Real Estate Securities

Global real estate securities have generated competitive returns over time. Over the nearly 20-year period covered by this analysis, global listed real estate securities provided the second-highest per annum

Table 11.5 Average Annual Total Returns and Spread over Risk-Free Rate, 1991 to 2010

	FTSE EPRA/NAREIT Developed Index	MSCI World Equity Index	JP Morgan Global Bond Index	NASDAQ	Private Real Estate
Total Annualized Return	10.9%	8.2%	7.5%	13.7%	7.4%
U.S. 10-Year Treasury Yield	5.2%	5.2%	5.2%	5.2%	5.2%
Risk Premium	5.7%	3.0%	2.3%	8.5%	2.2%

Sources: FTSE EPRA/NAREIT, Bloomberg, NCREIF, IPD, CBRE Clarion Securities, as of December 31, 2010. Average annual total returns are for the period 1Q 1991 through 4Q 2010. Private real estate returns are a weighted average of the U.S. NCREIF Index, the U.K. IPD Index, and the Australian IPD Index.

total return within a universe of five major asset classes. In addition, global real estate total returns provided the second-highest risk premium relative to the yield from U.S. 10-year Treasury bonds. This suggests that investors have been, to some degree, compensated for the higher volatility in listed property stocks in recent years. Table 11.5 examines the difference between annual average yields from the 10-year U.S. Treasury bond and the annual rate of total returns from the five asset classes included in this universe.[1]

Competitive Dividend Yields

Yield remains a critical element for investors in global real estate companies. Recent dividend yields offered in key listed real estate markets globally have been generally higher than the yield for respective government bonds (see Figure 11.3). Additionally, the spread between real estate dividend yields and long-term government bond yields has generally been above long-term average spreads in major geographies, suggesting relative value.

Also, an analysis of dividend coverage ratios within the major listed real estate markets suggests that there is sufficient cash flow for companies to pay out dividends, as shown in Figure 11.4.

---

1. There is no robust global index that measures commercial private real estate total returns as of yet. Therefore, we have created a synthetic weighted index utilizing annual total return data from Australia, the United Kingdom, and the United States. These three countries were chosen specifically for the quality and depth of data available, the size of the markets, and the reliability of the data.

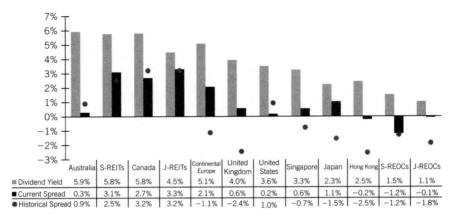

Figure 11.3   Attractive Dividends Relative to Historical Spreads

Sources: CBRE Clarion, FactSet, and Bloomberg as of December 31, 2010

Diversification Benefits

Global listed real estate securities help to diversify a portfolio in two ways: through lower correlation across different markets as well as through lower correlation to other asset classes. Since 1990, the local listed real estate equity indices in major markets across the world have generally displayed low to moderate correlation levels with each other, as shown in Table 11.6. This modest correlation across different markets makes intuitive sense, as real estate remains an inherently local business with different and distinct economic and property cycles.

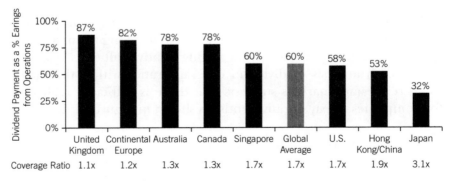

Figure 11.4   Dividend Payout and Coverage of Earnings from Operations

Source: CBRE Clarion

Table 11.6 Correlation of Annual Total Returns, Major Markets, 1990 to 2010

	U.S.	Hong Kong	Japan	U.K.	Australia	Singapore
U.S.	1.00					
Hong Kong	0.41	1.00				
Japan	0.45	0.34	1.00			
U.K.	0.71	0.33	0.41	1.00		
Australia	0.59	0.33	0.43	0.55	1.00	
Singapore	0.47	0.70	0.37	0.40	0.39	1.00

Source: FTSE EPRA/NAREIT, CBRE Clarion as of December 31, 2010. Total return calculations in U.S. dollars.

Global real estate companies also offer low to moderate correlation to other asset classes, particularly to fixed income securities. See Table 11.7.

Generally, low correlation, along with a solid return profile, enables an allocation to global real estate companies to improve the efficient frontier of returns for an otherwise diversified mixed-asset portfolio. An allocation of global real estate companies to a portfolio including global equities, global bonds, U.S. technology stocks, and private real estate with a 15 percent constraint on global listed real estate and private real estate shows improvements in risk-adjusted portfolio returns (see Figure 11.5). Specifically, a 15 percent allocation to global real estate securities in an otherwise diversified portfolio would have led to an additional 10 basis points (0.10 percent) in annual total return while reducing portfolio risk

Table 11.7 Correlation of Annual Total Returns, Major Asset Classes, 1991 to 2010

	FTSE EPRA	JPM	MSCI	NASDAQ	PRIVATE RE
FTSE EPRA	1.00				
JPM	0.02	1.00			
MSCI	0.68	−0.03	1.00		
NASDAQ	0.38	−0.03	0.85	1.00	
PRIVATE RE	0.25	−0.23	0.28	0.02	1.00

Sources: FTSE EPRA/NAREIT, Bloomberg. NCREIF, IPD, CBRE Clarion as of December 31, 2010.

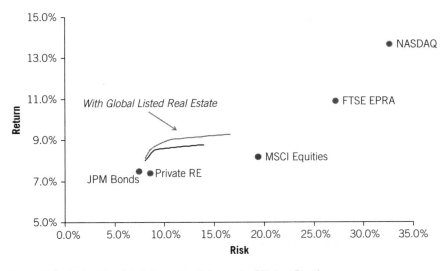

Figure 11.5   Global Real Estate Securities Enhance the Efficient Frontier
Source: FTSE EPRA/NAREIT, Bloomberg. NCREIF, IPD, CBRE Clarion Securities as of December 31, 2010

by approximately 50 basis points (0.50 percent). A portfolio including global real estate securities produces a Sharpe ratio of 0.53 compared to a Sharpe ratio of 0.50 for a portfolio without global real estate securities. Although the improvement in the efficient frontier is not as dramatic as studies that predate the global financial crisis, diversified portfolios nevertheless continue to benefit from an allocation to global real estate companies.

The Power of the Capital Markets: A Case Study in the Recapitalization of Global Real Estate during the Credit Crisis of 2008

Access to capital is a clear differentiator between private and public sponsors of commercial real estate. Public real estate companies successfully raised over $90 billion in equity capital globally coming out of the recessionary credit crisis during the time period October 2008 to December 2010 (see Figure 11.6). This occurred at a time when refinancing and loan originations to privately held real estate from financial institutions were often unavailable. The reopening of the capital markets was the catalyst behind a dramatic recovery in market values in listed real estate and has helped alleviate some issues regarding debt rollovers. In addition, the fresh capital raised

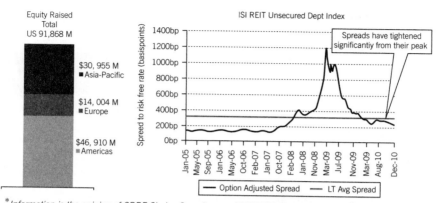

Equity Raised
Total
US 91,868 M

$30, 955 M
■Asia-Pacific

$14, 004 M
■Europe

$46, 910 M
■Americas

ISI REIT Unsecured Dept Index

Spread to risk free rate (basispoints)

1400bp
1200bp
1000bp
800bp
600bp
400bp
200bp
0bp

Spreads have tightened
significantly from their peak

Jan-05 May-05 Sep-05 Jan-06 May-06 Oct-06 Feb-07 Jan-07 Oct-07 Feb-08 Jan-08 Nov-08 Mar-09 Jul-09 Nov-09 Mar-09 Aug-10 Dec-10

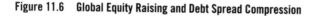

—— Option Adjusted Spread   —— LT Avg Spread

*Information is the opinion of CBRE Clarion Securites as of 12/31/2010, which is the subject to change and is not intended to be a forecast of future events, a guarantee of future results, or investment advice. Forecasts and any factors discussed are not necessarily indicative of future investment performance. Equity raised is from the time period October 2008 to December 2010. The ISI REIT Unsecured Debt Index is an inded of 30 unsecured bonds with an average amount outstanding of $370 million and an average maturity of 6.1 years. ISR REIT Unsecured Debt Index data is of Decemeber 31, 2010.

Figure 11.6   Global Equity Raising and Debt Spread Compression

helped provide investors visibility and confidence in the steps being taken to address the debt maturities that real estate companies will need to meet over the coming years.

The recapitalizations accomplished a number of objectives, depending on the company. For some companies, raising equity represented a "defensive" move to reduce leverage ratios and improve interest coverage ratios. For other companies, raising fresh equity represented an "offensive" move to bolster capacity to take advantage of potentially attractive pricing in future property acquisitions. The magnitude and success of new capital raised demonstrates the ability for listed property companies to raise significant capital quickly, even in challenging capital market environment. The capital raised led to declining leverage across global listed real estate securities. Globally, leverage levels have declined from 48 percent at the end of 2008 to 38 percent at the end of 2010 (see Table 11.8).

Access to capital has emerged as an important differentiator between public and private sponsors of commercial real estate in the recovery cycle thus far. Listed real estate companies, having lowered leverage on their balance sheets and with access to equity and debt capital, are well positioned to benefit from any investment opportunities that may arise. Looking back, there is historical evidence of

Table 11.8 Leverage of Global Real Estate Securities

	World	U.S.	U.K.	Continental Europe	Hong Kong	Japan	Australia
12/31/2006	30.9%	35.0%	30.0%	32.6%	14.3%	28.1%	27.0%
12/31/2007	35.5%	42.8%	47.4%	42.3%	11.5%	42.5%	27.1%
12/31/2008	47.9%	51.9%	63.4%	50.8%	26.1%	60.6%	41.7%
12/31/2009	40.5%	46.8%	48.4%	47.9%	20.0%	53.2%	35.4%
12/31/2010	38.2%	41.6%	46.2%	45.8%	20.2%	51.0%	34.7%

Source: CBRE Clarion Securities, as of December 31, 2010.

listed real estate companies' taking advantage of superior access to capital relative to private sponsors of real estate. In the early 1990s, the U.S. commercial real estate market was severely distressed, with values having fallen sharply and the credit market in a state of disarray—very similar conditions to those that have existed since 2008. Listed real estate companies, however, were able to access the public markets as the real estate cycle showed signs of improvement and the mid-1990s witnessed the emergence of the modern REIT era in the United States. As Figure 11.7 shows, listed real estate companies delivered positive earnings growth and strong total returns coming off the deep real estate crisis of the early 1990s.While historical patterns may not necessarily be repeated this time, the early to mid-1990s' experience of the U.S. REITs provides some indication as to how listed real estate companies can grow during the early stages of the next real estate cycle.

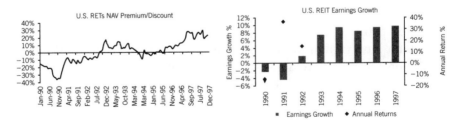

Figure 11.7   U.S. REIT Market Post S&L Crisis and Recession
Sources: Green Street Advisors, NAREIT, Goldman Sachs, and CBRE Clarion Securities

PART IV

RISKS AND FUTURE PROSPECTS

What Can Go Wrong?

"[The world] looks just a little more mathematical and regular than it is; its exactitude is obvious, but its inexactitude is hidden; its wildness lies in wait."

—G. K. Chesterton

I have written this book in an effort to help you understand the REIT industry and the dynamics pertaining to REIT investments. I have also tried to explain why REIT stocks have been very good investments during most of the past 50 years. But the book would be incomplete if it didn't also dedicate a chapter to what can go wrong from time to time. Alas—no investment is risk free (except perhaps T-bills, which often don't provide any meaningful return).

In general, the risks of REIT investing fall into two broad categories: those that could affect *all* REITs, and others that have to do with *specific* REITs. First, we'll address the broader REIT industry issues.

Issues Affecting All REITs

A condition where there is an excessive amount of real estate space offered to prospective tenants is often referred to as a "renters' market"—supply and demand are not in balance. In such a market,

TIP

All REITs are subject to three principal risks: weak space markets, rising interest rates, and declining commercial real estate prices, as well as other less important risks. I'll briefly touch on each of the first three, then discuss them in more detail.

---

tenants are in the driver's seat and can negotiate very favorable rental rates and lease terms with property owners. An excess supply of space can be a result of more new construction than can be readily absorbed or a major fall-off in demand for space, perhaps due to a recession; but as the old saying goes, it doesn't matter whether you get killed by the ax or by the handle. Either way, weak space markets, at least in the short term, mean difficulties for property owners.

Rising interest rates can also dampen property owners' profits. When interest rates escalate, borrowing costs increase; real estate is usually financed with debt. Higher interest rates can also impact the funds from operations (FFO) of a REIT as well as the profits of a property owner. But there is often another issue here. Those rising interest rates can slow the economy, which in turn may reduce demand for rental space. Furthermore, as we'll discuss in some detail later in this chapter, rising interest rates will often have negative implications for REIT stock prices.

REITs are all about commercial real estate. Although, over the short term, their stock prices are influenced by many factors, at the end of the day their intrinsic values will be very heavily dependent on the values of the properties they own. Accordingly, a third major risk for REIT investors is that the values of commercial real estate assets decline—this occurred most recently during the Great Recession.

Although weak space markets, rising interest rates, and declining commercial real estate prices aren't the only problems that can vex REITs and their investors, I believe they are the most critical and merit further discussion.

Weak Space Markets

Earlier, we discussed how real estate investment returns can change through the various phases of a typical real estate cycle. Rising rents and real estate prices early in the cycle may eventually result in significant increases in new development activity and excess amounts of space. We also discussed how overbuilding in a property type or geographic area can influence and exacerbate the real estate cycle by causing occupancy rates and rents to decline, which in turn may cause property prices to fall. Over time, of course, demand catches up with supply, and markets ultimately recover.

TIP

Whereas a recessionary economy sometimes results in a temporary decline in demand for space, the excess supply that is brought on by overbuilding often will be a larger and longer-lasting problem.

Overbuilding can occur locally, regionally, or even nationally; it means that substantially more real estate is developed and offered for lease than can be readily absorbed by tenant demand. If an overbuilt situation exists for an extended period, it will put substantial pressure on rents, occupancy rates, and operating income. It will increase ownership risk and decrease profitability, both of which are likely to negatively impact commercial real estate prices. This reduces the values of REITs' properties—and, most likely, their stock prices. Accordingly, if most of a REIT's properties are in a location affected by overbuilding, or it specializes in an overbuilt property type, the REIT's shareholders may sell their shares in anticipation of declining FFO and a reduction in net asset value (NAV). In extreme cases, a REIT may even be unable to renew its credit line or refinance its secured debt. Not a pretty picture.

Similarly, when the economy is weak and tenants are seeking to vacate underutilized space, rather than sign new leases, insufficient space demand will cause occupancy and rental rates to decline, and tenant improvement allowances to rise. This also will tend to put downward pressure on REIT stock prices. The share prices of most office REITs lagged the REIT market in the early years of the past decade, due in large part to rising vacancy rates and falling market rents for office properties. This resulted not from overbuilding but rather from softening demand and an increased amount of space offered for sublease by busted dot-coms and other shrinking businesses.

Of course, problems caused by supply-and-demand imbalances, whether from excessive new developments or weak space demand, vary in degree. Often, the problem is modest and temporary, creating minor concerns in just a few markets. Sometimes the problem is devastating, wreaking havoc for years in many sectors throughout the United States. We saw the effects of severe overbuilding in the late 1980s and early 1990s on virtually all property owners and their lenders. The problem for most real estate owners from 2001 to 2004, and from 2008 to 2010, was not due so much to overbuilding, but to a significant weakening in demand for space. But, either way, when supply greatly exceeds demand, real estate owners suffer. A mild imbalance will work itself out quickly, especially where job growth is not severely curtailed. In these situations, investors may overreact, dumping REIT shares at unduly depressed prices and creating great values for investors with longer time horizons.

 TIP

Investors must try to distinguish between a mild and temporary condition of excess supply or insufficient demand and one that is much more serious and protracted; in the latter case, a REIT's share price may decline and stay depressed for a year or two.

Overbuilding, as opposed to a shrinkage of demand for existing space, arises most often from overheated markets. When operating profits from real estate are very strong because of rising occupancy and rental rates, property prices can escalate quickly. Everybody "sees the green" and wants a piece of it. REITs themselves have occasionally been a significant source of overbuilding, responding to investors' demands for ever-increasing FFO growth by continuing to build even in the face of weakening absorption rates or unhealthy levels of construction starts. Today, many REITs have the expertise and access to capital to develop new properties, and those that do business in strong markets will normally be able to flex their financial muscles and put up new buildings. However, it's usually very difficult to time markets well, and even the most highly

Too Many "Big Boxes"?

"Big-box" discount retailers, such as Wal-Mart, Target, and Costco, attract shoppers looking for big discounts; at times, investors have thrown a lot of money at them in order to encourage continued expansion. Some investors are now questioning whether, perhaps due to weak consumer spending in the wake of the Great Recession, the supply of big-box space exceeds demand. Rental rates for big-box space have declined significantly during the past few years. Can America's consumers support all of today's big-box discount retailers?

regarded REITs often fail to throttle back their development pipelines early enough.

While the investment banks are essential in helping REITs raise capital that can be invested at attractive rates of return, these same firms can sometimes raise too much development capital for REIT organizations. When a particular real estate sector becomes very popular, Wall Street is always ready to satisfy investors' voracious appetites. But investment bankers are often reluctant to stop, and they are inclined to feed the quacking ducks. REITs often may be unwilling to resist the urge to raise new capital to develop more properties. Some retail REITs raised ample funds and developed too many properties in 2005 to 2007, when the housing market crested. It is encouraging, however, that capital allocation strategies by most REITs in recent years have been reasonably conservative, and the recent space market problems have been due to shrinking tenant demand rather than excessive development—on the part of REITs or anyone else.

Strangely, even when it has become obvious that we are in an overbuilding phase, the building may continue. An inordinate amount of office construction was done in the late 1990s by private developers, particularly in "high-tech" markets, even as many observers and lenders realized that the pace of absorption was unsustainable. Although some would explain this by the long lead time necessary to complete an office project once begun, it's more likely that there were some large egos at work among developers—each believing that *his* project would become fully leased—and that lenders were too myopic to detect the problem early enough.

Just as dogs will bark, developers will develop—if provided with the needed financing. REITs may be innocent bystanders, but can suffer collateral damage.

Looking forward, and particularly if capital remains less available to many private players in the future, REITs may eventually become the dominant developers within particular sectors or geographic areas, as is largely true today in the mall sector. Should this happen, new building in a sector or a market may be limited by investors' willingness to provide REITs with additional equity capital or by the REITs' own discipline. The mall sector, dominated by large REITs, has not suffered from overbuilding in recent years. In view of the fact that management teams normally have a significant ownership interest in their REITs' shares, they will have no desire to shoot themselves in the foot by creating an oversupply. Of course, it's important to remember that none of this prevents the occasional supply-and-demand imbalance created when demand for space cools because of a slowing economy and weak or negative job growth.

Today, excessive new development is not a significant issue, and one may dare to hope that perhaps major real estate developers and their lenders have become more intelligent and circumspect. The tax laws no longer subsidize development for its own sake. Lenders, pension plans, and other sources of development capital that were "once burned" are now "twice shy" and wary about making development loans for projects without significant preleasing commitments. Says real estate maven Sam Zell, quoted in Reuters on December 14, 2010, "We're now approaching three and a half years of no development, and I see little prospect for new supply over the next 12 to 36 months except multifamily."

The key point is that weak space markets, whether caused by excessive new development or simply anemic demand for space, is a risk for commercial real estate and REIT investors.

Rising Interest Rates

When investors talk about a particular stock or a group of stocks being interest rate sensitive, they usually mean that the price of the stock is heavily influenced by interest rate movements. Stocks with high yields are interest rate sensitive because, in a rising interest rate environment, many owners of such stocks will be lured into safer T-bills or money market funds when their yields become competitive with higher-yielding stocks, adjusted for the latter's higher risk.

The stocks of some companies might also be interest rate sensitive for reasons other than their dividend yields. Homebuilders are but one example; they pay very low dividends, but rely on reasonably low mortgage rates, the availability of credit, and housing affordability. Also, the profitability of a business might be very dependent on the cost of borrowed funds. In a rising interest rate environment, the cost of doing business for such companies will rise. If increased borrowing costs cannot immediately be passed on to the buyers of the product or service offered, profit margins shrink, causing investors to sell the stocks.

 TIP

Whether correct or not, if investors even *perceive* that rising interest rates will negatively affect a company's profits, then the stock's price will vary inversely with interest rates—rising when interest rates drop, and dropping when interest rates rise.

How, then, are REIT shares perceived by investors? Are they interest rate–sensitive stocks? Is a significant risk in owning REITs that their shares will take a major tumble during periods when rates are rising briskly? Before we try to answer these questions, let's take a quick look at why REIT shares are bought and owned by investors, and how rising interest rates affect REITs' expected profitability.

Traditionally, REIT shares have been bought by investors who are looking for attractive total returns with modest risk. "Total return" is the total of what an investor would receive from the combination of dividends received plus stock price appreciation. Yields have historically made up about one-half of REITs' total returns. For example, a 4 percent dividend yield and 4 percent annual price appreciation (perhaps resulting from 4 percent annual FFO or NAV growth and assuming a stable price-to-FFO [P/FFO] ratio or NAV premium) results in an 8 percent annual total return. Because the dividend component of the expected return is so substantial, REITs must compete in the marketplace, to some extent, with such income-producing investments as bonds, preferreds, and even utility stocks.

For example, let's assume that investment-grade "long bonds" (with maturities of up to 30 years) yield 4 percent and the average REIT stock yields 4 percent as well. If the long bond drops in price in response to rising interest rates and inflationary pressures, driving the yield to 6 percent, the average REIT's price may also drop, causing its yield to rise so that it remains competitive with bonds. That's pure logic. However, it's interesting to note that, historically at least, REIT prices haven't correlated very well with bond prices. According to the National Association of Real Estate Investment Trusts (NAREIT), REIT stocks' correlation with a domestic high-yield corporate bond index for the period December 2000 through December 2010 was a modest 0.63, and the correlation with a Merrill Lynch corporate/government bond index was a very, very low 0.10. These historically modest correlations could have been due to the fact that rising interest rates often occur when the U.S. economy strengthens—which can improve space markets and benefit the REITs as property owners.

Nevertheless, the reality remains that a substantial segment of REIT stock owners invest in them for their substantial yields, which have provided a significant part of their total returns. And, just as important, rising interest rates will tend to increase real estate cap rates, thus depressing REIT NAVs. Furthermore, some large investors will sell, or even short, REIT stocks before interest rates rise if they believe that rates will increase in the near future. As a result, investors should assume that REIT stock prices, like the prices for almost any investment, won't react well to higher interest rates.

A related issue is whether a rise in interest rates might also cause concern among REIT investors that FFO growth will decelerate, along with falling asset values. This is a multifaceted issue, and much depends on the individual REIT, its sector, and the location of its properties. Let's consider the possibilities.

TIP

Higher interest rates are generally not good for any business, as they depress customers' purchasing power and can eventually lead to recession.

Apartment and retail REITs, both of which own properties dependent on consumer incomes and spending patterns, may be adversely affected by higher interest rates if they slow the economy and reduce available consumer buying power. However, even office and industrial REITs, which lease properties to businesses, will be adversely affected, as their lessees will also be influenced by rising interest rates and a slowing economy. Property owners in most sectors enjoy longer-term leases, which provide some cash flow protection during a slowing economy. However, if the slowdown becomes severe, property owners will suffer from occupancy declines and prospective rent roll-downs as leases expire. For apartment owners, rising rates are a mixed blessing. They will slow the migration of tenants to single-family residences (a big problem for apartment owners in 2001 to 2004); however, if rising interest rates slow the economy enough to cause job losses, that will obviously impact their cash flows.

Interest is usually a significant cost for a REIT because, like other property owners, REITs normally use debt leverage to increase their investment returns and will frequently borrow to fund a portion of property acquisition and development investments. The concept of variable-rate debt is that it allows the lender to adjust the rate according to the interest rate environment. When interest rates rise, a substantial amount of variable-rate debt carried by a REIT can impact its profit margins and FFO. But even with fixed-rate debt, REITs must be concerned with interest rates—when they are rolling over a portion of their debt and when they are taking on new debt. And new developments often will be funded with short-term variable-rate debt, then permanently financed upon completion with long-term fixed-rate debt. Rising interest rates can significantly impact the investment returns from these new developments.

Even when a REIT chooses to raise capital through equity offerings rather than debt financing, higher interest rates can have an adverse effect if they depress REIT share prices; this will raise a REIT's nominal cost of equity capital, and perhaps its long-term cost as well.

As noted briefly earlier, another negative aspect of rising interest rates relates to the value of a REIT's assets. Commercial real estate prices are influenced by many factors, and two of the most important are borrowing costs and required investment returns. A substantial increase in interest rates will usually impact these key variables, and thus put downward pressure on property values. Generally speaking, property buyers will insist on higher real estate returns when interest rates have moved up, which will affect the asset values of the properties owned by REITs. Asset values are very important in determining a REIT's intrinsic value, as we saw in Chapter 9 and as we'll discuss briefly below, and thus weakening asset values will often have an impact on REIT share pricing. Jeffries & Company, in a January 2011 research report, stated that "our analysis has found that REIT stock performance has had an 85 percent negative correlation with rising cap rates since the birth of the new REIT regime in the early 1990s."

The foregoing discussion shows how rising interest rates can negatively affect a REIT's operating results, balance sheet, asset value, and stock price. However, we might also note that in one important respect REITs may actually be *helped* by rising interest rates. This relates to the overbuilding threat. The construction of new, competing projects, whether apartments, office buildings, hotels, or any other type of property, must be financed. Clearly, higher interest rates will increase borrowing costs and make developing new projects more costly or, in some cases, prohibitively expensive. Higher rates may also affect the "hurdle rate" demanded by the developer's financial partners, again causing many projects to be shelved or canceled. Obviously, the fewer new competing projects that get built, the less existing properties will feel competitive pressure. Threats of overbuilding can fade rapidly when interest rates are rising briskly.

We should keep in mind, of course, that we are speaking in generalities here, and the extent to which rising interest rates will affect a particular REIT's business, profitability, asset values, and financial condition will vary. On balance, however, rising interest rates are unfavorable for most REITs most of the time. Combined with the tendency of all companies' shares, including REITs', to decline in response to rising interest rates, REIT investors need to be aware of the interest rate environment and to expect some stock price weakness when interest rates look as though they will be moving higher.

Declining Real Estate Prices

TIP

Any significant decline in the value of its underlying real estate properties is likely to negatively affect the share price of a REIT.

Finally, although rising interest rates may, as we discussed, put downward pressure on commercial real estate and REIT prices, we should also note that commercial real estate prices may decline at times for other reasons. Pricing is determined by a host of factors, as mentioned earlier in the book, and interest rates are just one of them.

Unlike the situation in years past, commercial real estate is now a widely followed asset class, and prices are now more fluid and respond quickly to changing global capital flows. REIT investors should try to monitor the reasonableness of the prices at which commercial real estate assets are being traded at any particular time, perhaps by checking the web sites of real estate data providers, for example, Real Capital Analytics (some of this information is free), or even keeping an eye out for newspaper stories on pricing trends. If commercial real estate prices look unsustainably high, perhaps a reflection of very low required rates of return, REIT investors should take note, and might want to do some portfolio trimming—particularly if REIT stocks have run up in expectations of yet higher property prices.

Hostile Capital-Raising Environments

Let's now consider a few other risks that REIT investors should keep in mind.

REITs must distribute to their shareholders at least 90 percent of their taxable income, but most pay out more than that because "net income," under generally accepted accounting principles (GAAP) and U.S. tax code requirements, is determined after a noncash property depreciation expense. This normally leaves a REIT, at the end of each year, with more free cash flow than is suggested by net income measurements. Nevertheless, because of REITs' dividend requirements and payout policies, they are unable to retain much cash for new acquisitions and development and are, therefore, dependent to a substantial extent on raising funds in the capital markets if they want to grow their FFOs at rates higher than what can be achieved from net operating income (NOI) growth at the properties they own.

As a result of these inherent limitations, investors must be mindful that even the most highly regarded REIT may not, during most economic and real estate climates, be able to grow its FFO at a pace beyond a mid-single-digit rate unless it has access to additional equity capital for property acquisitions and developments. There will always be another bear market, and when it comes, many REITs will find it difficult or costly to sell new shares to raise funds for these new investments. The equity market for REITs slammed shut in early 1998 and reopened only in 2001. The capital markets froze again during the Great Recession and didn't open until the spring of 2009. These occasional contractions in the capital markets will, while they last, affect virtually all REITs.

In addition, individual REITs with lackluster growth prospects, excessive debt, or poor credibility with investors will have problems attracting fresh equity capital, as will REITs that are perceived as being unable to earn returns on new investments that exceed the REIT's cost of capital. Although some REITs, due to recent "asset recycling" and joint venture strategies, have been able to substantially reduce their dependency on new equity offerings, attracting additional capital remains a very important tool for most growing REIT organizations. External, and perhaps even internal, events over which management may have little or no control may cut a REIT off from this essential new capital and thus affect its rate of FFO growth, which in turn affects investor sentiment and the REIT's stock price. Investors should be more willing to pay a premium price for the shares of those REITs—because of their track records of balance sheet management, strong capital allocation skills, and growth prospects—that are most likely to attract additional equity capital, as needed, on favorable terms, or that have reduced their dependency on external capital raising.

Legislation

If the cynic's view that "no man's life, liberty, or property is safe when Congress is in session" is correct, we must recognize that

Congress giveth, but Congress can also taketh away. As this book went to press, a few observers have questioned whether Congress might decide to tax non-corporate entities, such as partnerships, master limited partnerships and even REITs, as regular corporations in order to offset tax revenue loss resulting from a possible reduction in corporate tax rates. Although the risk exists, it is highly unlikely that Congress would enact legislation to rescind REITs' tax deduction for the dividends paid to their shareholders, thus subjecting REITs' net income to taxation at the corporate level.

There are several public policy reasons for this. First, because of REITs' very substantial—and required—dividend payments to their shareholders, they may generate as much income for the federal government as they would if they were conventional real estate corporations that could shelter a substantial amount of otherwise taxable income by boosting debt and deducting from income larger interest expenses. Second, property held in a REIT most likely provides more tax revenues than if held, as it historically has been, in a real estate partnership. And, perhaps most important, unlike most private real estate owners, REITs use only moderate amounts of debt leverage. This puts real estate into the hands of more stable owners. Excessive debt, as we have learned repeatedly, can be a very destabilizing force in the U.S. economy, and it's unlikely that Congress would want to contribute to that.

 TIP

Encouraging greater debt financing of real estate could substantially exacerbate the swings in the normal business and real estate cycles, harming the economy over the long term.

A proposal made a number of years ago would have tightened the restrictions on the ability of a REIT to own controlling interests in non-REIT corporations; the rules at that time were designed to prevent a REIT from indirectly generating impermissible non–real estate income through controlled subsidiaries. However, this proposal was modified significantly and was ultimately incorporated into the REIT Modernization Act (RMA), discussed earlier in this book. Indeed, the RMA, as well as the REIT Investment Diversification and Empowerment Act (RIDEA), also previously discussed, contain many benefits and flexibilities for the REIT industry, as well as acceptable limitations.

Over the years, thanks in large part to both the efforts of NAREIT and simple common sense, Congress has, if anything, liberalized laws to expand the scope of REITs' authorized business activities. Furthermore, the quick and effective response of the REIT industry to the debt crisis of 2008 and 2009 has enhanced REITs' credibility and has proven the soundness of Congress's decision 50 years ago to authorize REIT organizations. Thus, the risk of adverse legislation, while always present, deserves to be ranked low on REIT investors' worry lists.

Loss of Investment Popularity

As discussed in an earlier chapter, REIT stocks' investment peculiarities cause them to be regarded, among many investors, as a separate and distinct asset class, and are still not widely understood. Perhaps due to this uncertain status and the many misconceptions about REITs, REIT stocks have, at times, been unpopular with investors despite their stable and predictable cash flows during most economic conditions and their outstanding total return performance. In 1998 and 1999, despite rising cash flows and strong real estate markets, investors didn't seem to want any part of them (although valuation issues and excessive capital raising also may have played a large role in the bear market of those years). That difficult cycle for REITs was followed by a very different one, from 2000 through 2006, in which REIT stocks could do no wrong—despite weak real estate markets early in that period. They were hated again, from 2007 to early 2009 (this time for pretty good reasons), but welcomed back into investors' portfolios later that year and in 2010.

This perversity should teach us REIT investors an important lesson: we need to be prepared for periods in which REIT stocks are simply unpopular and won't perform well even when all the commercial real estate and equity market stars are properly aligned. This means that one additional risk in owning REIT shares is that these investments may, at times, decline in price for reasons having little to do with their intrinsic valuations or growth prospects.

How can we protect ourselves from this risk? Simply put, we cannot. However, our best defense is a simple one: we must think of REIT stocks as permanent investments and, aside from those who are stock traders, own them over long time horizons as an integral part of our investment portfolio. We know that over all meaningful time frames REIT stocks have delivered outstanding returns, generally in line with our expectations, and there's no reason why that will change.

Problems Affecting Individual REITs

It's axiomatic that any public company can stumble, causing its stock to perform poorly; after all, it's a very competitive and complex world, and companies are led by fallible human beings. A REIT organization is no different. Let's look at some types of risks that can affect the enterprise values and stock prices of *specific* REITs.

Local Recessions

We discussed recessions earlier in the context of problems that may affect the entire REIT industry. But *local* recessions can also impact specific REITs. Such recessions can hurt real estate owners even when supply and demand for space in a particular market had previously been in equilibrium—or even unusually strong. A retail property, for example, located in a healthy property market may be 95 percent leased, but its tenants' sales might decline in response to a severe local recession. This will result in lower "overage" rents (additional rental income based on sales exceeding a preset minimum), lower occupancy rates, and even tenant bankruptcies. Apartment communities, especially those recently built, may be slow to lease, perhaps because of declining job growth in specific local markets. During recessionary conditions, both consumers and businesses are likely to cut back on their spending and investment plans. In this situation, rents cannot be raised without jeopardizing occupancy rates.

We've mentioned that, for many property types, REIT investors prefer their REITs to focus on a specific geographic area to maximize the value of local expertise; however, the downside is that local or regional recessions can be more damaging for a geographically focused REIT. Despite nationwide recessions that take place from time to time, such as those beginning in March 2001 and in December 2007, we've learned that economic conditions in the United States aren't always the same everywhere, and local recessions are not uncommon. We can have an oil-industry depression in the Southwest, while the rest of the country is doing fine. Or Florida and California can be suffering from housing busts, while the midwestern economy is riding a wave of high agricultural prices. In the early years of the prior decade, problems in the technology sector hit some markets particularly hard, such as the San Francisco Bay Area and Seattle. These types of issues can have a negative effect on the shares of REITs with heavy concentrations in those markets, due to anticipated declines in FFO growth and general shareholder angst.

Changing Consumer and Business Preferences

Investors also must watch for trends and changes in consumer and business preferences that can reduce renters' demands for a property type, causing existing supply to exceed demand and reducing owners' profits.

Today, for example, because of our increasingly mobile population, self-storage facilities are popular. Will they always be so, or will storing things become less important? In 2010 and 2011 apartment owners were doing well because of the single-family housing bust; but will falling home prices increase housing affordability and negatively impact future demand for apartment units? Will Americans travel a lot more, thus stoking demand for hotel rooms, or will they become more stationary due to the gradual aging of the U.S. population? Will teleconferencing affect business travel? Will businesses continue to lease the types of industrial properties they've always found necessary, or will some new form of business practice render many of the current facilities obsolete?

And there are more questions. Will companies continue to absorb space in large office buildings as they have in the past, or will telecommuting stage a revival and make a large dent in the demand for traditional office space? Will businesses seek out locations in major cities or look more favorably on suburban locations—perhaps with lower tax rates? What effect will the continued growth in Internet shopping have on traditional retailers? Will malls lose their allure as a fun destination? For how long will consumer spending remain muted following the Great Recession?

These are questions about basic trends in how we live, how we play, and how we work. No one can answer them with any confidence, but if REIT investors ignore signs of changing trends, their investment returns from some REIT stocks may prove disappointing.

Credibility Issues

Probably the most common type of REIT-specific risk to which investors are exposed is the error in judgment that raises significant management credibility questions.

Here, for example, are a few management miscues that REIT investors have suffered from in prior years:

- Overpaying for acquired properties and later having to sell them at a loss (e.g., American Health Properties).
- Expanding too quickly and taking on too much debt in the process (e.g., Patriot American Hospitality and Factory Stores of America).
- Underestimating the difficulty of assimilating a major acquisition (e.g., New Plan Excel).
- Expanding into entirely new property sectors, especially without adequate research and preparation (e.g., Meditrust).
- Providing investors with unreliable information by, for example, underestimating overhead expenses (e.g., Holly Residential Properties).
- Overestimating future FFO growth prospects (e.g., Crown American Realty).
- Being unable to generate expected returns on newly developed properties (e.g., Horizon Group).
- Setting a dividend rate, upon going public, that exceeds reasonable expectations of FFO levels, thus raising concerns about the adequacy of dividend coverage (e.g., Alexander Haagen).
- Engaging in aggressive hedging techniques such as forward equity transactions (e.g., Patriot American Hospitality).
- Proposing a merger that makes little strategic sense (e.g., Mack-Cali and Prentiss Properties).

- Failure to entertain a reasonable buyout offer (e.g., Burnham Pacific Properties).
- Investing in new technologies or Internet initiatives and having to write them off (too many to mention).

The common denominator in most of these situations is the perception among investors that management has lost control of its business, that it lacks discipline, or that it is otherwise taking undue risks with the shareholders' capital. Have you noticed that, with only one exception, all of these REITs have vanished from the scene? (Mack-Cali remains and is back in shareholders' good graces).

Yet another kind of credibility issue arises when an executive compensation program is implemented that doesn't align the interests of management with those of the REIT's shareholders, for example, a bonus plan that rewards the executives for volumes of acquisitions or development—without regard to their risk-adjusted returns. A related issue is excessive executive compensation, or compensation that is disconnected from the value created for the REIT's shareholders over the applicable time period. Poor corporate governance and weak or incomplete disclosure of financial information are other concerns that are likely to have a negative impact on a REIT's stock price.

The umbrella partnership REIT (UPREIT) format is now widely accepted, but can create conflict-of-interest issues. UPREITs, as you may recall from an earlier chapter, are those REITs whose assets are held by a limited partnership in which the REIT owns a controlling interest and in which REIT insiders may own a substantial interest. Since these insiders may own few shares in the REIT itself, the low tax basis of their partnership interests creates a conflict of interest should the REIT be subject to a takeover offer, or in the event it receives an attractive offer for some of its properties.

Most problems like these can be remedied by a REIT's management team if it is forthright with investors, quickly recognizes any mistakes it has made, and promptly takes action to rectify the situation.

For example, in September 1999, Duke Realty sold $150 million of new common stock to ABP Investments, a large Dutch pension fund, at a price below what most analysts determined to be Duke's per-share NAV. REIT investors never like seeing their REITs sell equity at a price that is dilutive to NAV, and indeed, many investors are willing to pay price premiums for REITs that are able to consistently increase their NAVs at above-average rates over time. Thus, they were not happy that Duke, a well-regarded office and industrial REIT, would sell new shares at a dilutive price, and they trashed the price of Duke's stock by 15 percent shortly after the secondary offering. Some wondered about management's ability to make sound capital market decisions. Management reacted promptly, however, and soon announced a new "self-funding" strategy, whereby its development pipeline would be funded by retained earnings and asset sales, and it stated that it did not contemplate additional equity offerings. Duke's stock price then recovered nicely over the next few months.

The key issue in these situations is management's loss of credibility with investors. When a REIT has disappointed investors as a result of poor judgment, it can be very hard to regain their confidence; in extreme cases, the only alternatives for such a REIT are to sell out or to obtain new management. Such a loss of confidence was a key factor in causing Chateau Communities, a manufactured home community REIT, to sell off its assets and liquidate some years ago.

 TIP

Allocation of capital is very important to capital-intensive companies; furthermore, REITs can retain only a modest portion of their earnings. Accordingly, a loss of management credibility can shut down a REIT's access to capital and thus substantially diminish its market value.

There is obviously no way for REIT investors to avoid such problems altogether; human nature is such that no executive is immune to the occasional lapse in judgment; furthermore, some of these problems become apparent only in hindsight. Conservative investors will thus favor blue-chip REITs that have demonstrated solid property performance, good capital allocation discipline, and excellent balance sheets over many years (and preferably over entire real estate cycles). Of course, investing exclusively in only the most highly regarded REITs may result in missing out on lesser-known

REITs whose shares are selling at cheap prices or those REITs that are due for a turnaround.

Another strategy that may appeal to the risk-averse investor is to avoid REITs that have been public companies for only a short time, as most of these management credibility issues seem to have arisen in "unseasoned" REITs. Again, this approach could mean missing out on some very promising newcomers. The "right" investment strategy depends, in large part, on the individual investor's risk tolerance, as well as his or her total return requirements. To repeat myself, there is rarely a "free lunch" in the investment world.

Balance Sheet Woes

Debt is always a potential problem, as well as an opportunity—for people, for nations, and, no less, for REITs. If management overburdens the REIT's balance sheet with debt, investors will be particularly wary. High debt levels often go hand in hand with impressive FFO growth and high dividend yields, but investors need to discount such apparent benefits when they have been subsidized by excessive debt. Too much debt, particularly short-term debt, can virtually destroy a REIT, a fact to which shareholders of General Growth Properties, before its rebirth, can certainly attest. Earlier, we noted that a blue-chip REIT is conservatively financed. The importance of a strong balance sheet cannot be overemphasized, because those REITs that are overloaded with debt will not only make investors wary, but may, if their property markets deteriorate, or credit markets freeze, have to be sold to a stronger company at a fire-sale price or, worse, be dismembered for the benefit of creditors.

A balance sheet can be judged "weak" from a number of different perspectives, as we discussed in Chapter 8. A weak balance sheet can seriously restrict the REIT's ability to expand through acquisitions or developments, and excessive debt leverage will magnify the effects of any decline in NOI. Further, a weak balance sheet can make equity financing expensive (new investors will have substantial bargaining power); it also creates the danger that lenders will not roll over existing debt at maturity, that covenants in credit agreements will not be complied with, and that, should interest rates rise substantially, the REIT will be exposed to a rapid deterioration in cash flows.

The market has usually factored potential problems like these into the stock price before the REIT actually feels their effects. A REIT, therefore, that is perceived to be overleveraged or to have too much short-term (or even variable-rate) debt will see its shares trade at a low P/FFO ratio in relation to its peers and to other REITs, and may trade at an NAV discount. Accordingly, careful REIT investors will continually monitor their REITs' balance sheets.

Guilt by Association

Another risk should be mentioned here, although it is usually temporary in nature. There have been times when one REIT in a sector has had operating or financial problems and all the other REITs in its sector suffer from guilt by association.

The following is a good illustration: In early 1995, two of the recently public factory outlet center REITs, McArthur/Glen and Factory Stores of America, angered REIT investors—the former by being unable to deliver the new and profitable developments it promised Wall Street, the latter by expanding too aggressively and taking on too much debt. The market, often prone to shooting first and asking questions later, assumed that these problems pervaded the entire sector, and destroyed the stock prices of solid factory outlet REITs Chelsea and Tanger, as well as the two problem-plagued outlet REITs. However, by the end of 1995, Chelsea's stock was back near its all-time high, and Tanger's stock was in the process of recovering as well.

Investors who dumped their Chelsea and Tanger shares at very depressed prices because of their inability to distinguish between a major, sector-wide problem and problems encountered by a couple of individual REITs had to swallow a bitter pill but learned a valuable lesson. And the lesson we current REIT investors need to remember is that some REITs will, at times, be mistakenly judged guilty by association. The *good* news is that these situations can create very attractive buying opportunities.

Modest Market Valuations

REIT investors need to recognize that despite REITs' 50-year history, very few are large companies when compared with many major U.S. corporations. Let's take Hewlett-Packard (symbol: HPQ) as an example. In early 2011, HPQ had 2.19 billion shares outstanding; at its market price of approximately $48 per share, HPQ's total equity market cap exceeded $105 billion. An even larger company, Procter & Gamble, then had shares outstanding worth almost $180 billion. Moving away from the real giants, let's look at Costco, a large discount retailer. In February 2011, it had an equity market cap of $32.7 billion.

Compare these market caps to some major REITs' market caps. Simon Property Group, the largest REIT at the end of 2010, had an equity market cap of approximately $29 billion. The next two largest were Public Storage and Vornado Realty, with equity market caps of $17.3 billion and $15.2 billion, respectively. Only 10 REITs, including those just noted, had equity market caps in excess of $10 billion, and just 20 had equity market caps of over $5 billion.

Table 12.1 shows the average equity market caps of equity REITs within each property sector at the end of 2010, from NAREIT data.

The market cap of the entire REIT industry, as well as the individual REITs within it, will fluctuate with changing market conditions, but has certainly grown over time. As of December 31, 2010, the total equity market cap for all equity REITs was $359 billion, up from

Table 12.1 Average Sector Market Caps

Property Sector	No. of REITs	Equity Market Cap
Office	18	$2.5 billion
Industrial	8	$2.2 billion
Mixed Office/Industrial	6	$1.5 billion
Shopping Centers	17	$1.9 billion
Regional Malls	7	$8.1 billion
Free Standing	4	$1.9 billion
Apartments	15	$3.5 billion
Manufactured Home Communities	3	$0.8 billion
Diversified	14	$2.0 billion
Lodging/Resorts	13	$1.8 billion
Health Care	13	$3.3 billion
Self-Storage	4	$5.2 billion
Timber	4	$5.4 billion

just $11 billion at the end of 1992, $50 billion at the end of 1995, and $147 billion at the end of 2001 (but down from $401 billion at the end of 2006).

Nonetheless, while the "typical" REIT is by no means a tiny company, it is hardly a major U.S. corporation. As of December 2010, the equity market cap of the *entire equity REIT industry*, at $359 billion, was smaller than the equity market cap, at that time, of just one huge corporation, Exxon Mobil ($363 billion), but was ahead of that of Apple ($297 billion).

But this chapter is about risk, so let's consider how small market size can present risks for the REIT investor.

A REIT with a small market cap, perhaps $300 million or less, may not be able to obtain the public awareness and sponsorship necessary to enable it to raise equity capital. Further, although increasing pension and institutional ownership of REITs is likely to be a new trend fostering the growth of the entire REIT industry, a small market cap may discourage such funds from investing in a REIT due to its stock's lack of market liquidity.

Also, higher general and administrative costs as a percentage of assets or cash flows, including costs to comply with Sarbanes-Oxley requirements, will be proportionately greater for smaller REITs; this could result in permanently lower profit margins. Finally, a minor misjudgment on the part of management of a small REIT (see "Credibility Issues" earlier in this section) could have a greater impact on the REIT's future business prospects, FFO growth, and reputation with investors.

It would seem that a small company must do everything right if it wants to attract a greater number of investors and see its stock priced fairly.

Depth of Management and Management Succession Issues

Perhaps a more serious potential issue for many REITs is not size, as such, but rather management depth and succession. Smaller companies, whether REITs or other businesses, because of their limited financial resources, are often unable to develop the type of extensive organization found in a major corporation. We must ask ourselves whether the REIT might be at a competitive disadvantage if, perhaps, it cannot afford to hire a staff of employees of the highest caliber or obtain the very best market information concerning supply and demand for properties in its market area. Other questions might relate to the depth and experience of the REIT's property acquisition team or property management department, or perhaps the sophistication and strength of the REIT's financial reporting, budgeting, and forecasting systems.

There are certain efficiencies that can be enjoyed by companies of substantial size, including greater bargaining power with suppliers and even tenants. These are issues that must be addressed separately for each REIT, but small size can limit any company's ability to attract high-quality executives, particularly at the middle-management level, and lack of management depth can affect a REIT's ability to remain a strong competitor in its markets.

Even if we, as investors, are comfortable with a small REIT's management strength and depth, modest size often means we must rely on the management of a few brilliant people to produce superior long-term results with the least risk. It is certainly true that investors sometimes embrace "superstars" at large public companies, for example, Warren Buffett at Berkshire Hathaway or Steve Jobs at Apple. However, shareholders will be at risk of a sudden departure of one of these outstanding individuals.

A very highly regarded REIT executive is certainly an important positive for REIT investors. Executives such as Kimco's Milton Cooper (who remains at Kimco as executive chairman), Simon Property's David Simon, Taubman Centers' Bobby Taubman, and Vornado's "dynamic duo"—Steve Roth and Mike Fascitelli—have helped their REITs to create much value for shareholders (and for themselves as large shareholders) over many years. However, if the REIT—whatever its size—has not developed an outstanding group of executives, one of which can step easily into the CEO's position at a moment's notice, it will see its "franchise value" decline, perhaps along with its stock price, when the superstar departs. It's never good for any organization to be excessively dependent on a single individual, no matter how talented.

Management succession is a sensitive issue that is, for obvious reasons, difficult for both investors and REIT management teams to discuss, but it is of vital concern to investors. Genius is tough to replace in any organization, but it's particularly tough to replace in small and mid-cap companies like most REITs. The earlier generation of smart, entrepreneurial managers will eventually retire, and REIT investors need to assess the capabilities of those who will be replacing them. However, as important as the succession issue is, it is only a part of the larger issue of how successful a particular REIT has been in building a strong, deep, and motivated management team.

Summary

- REIT investors are subject to such potential industry-wide hazards as an excess supply of available rental space (or weak demand for space), rising interest rates, and declining commercial property values, as well as other risks.
- While a recessionary economy sometimes results in a temporary decline in demand for space, the excess supply that is brought on by overbuilding can be a much larger and longer-lasting problem.
- To the extent that REIT stocks compete with other, higher-yielding investments, higher interest rates can cause REIT stocks to decline so that they will remain competitive on a yield basis.
- Rising interest rates can also soak up purchasing power from consumers as well as businesses, and can cause recession; they also can affect REIT profits and asset values, leading to declines in REIT shares.
- REIT stocks can become unpopular with investors at times, even when the REITs' businesses are performing well.
- Overleveraged (or "broken") balance sheets, poor capital allocation decisions, and management credibility issues can create problems for specific REITs—and their investors.
- Fortunately, financial or business disasters have been very rare among REITs, and share price collapse has been infrequent.
- The small size of some REITs and a lack of management depth can be a competitive disadvantage, and may cause the REIT's stock to be a perpetual underperformer.
- Succession planning is important for all businesses, but is particularly important for smaller companies, such as many REITs, that may be highly dependent on a single individual.

CHAPTER

13

Tea Leaves: Some Thoughts about the Future

"Forecasts usually tell us more of the forecaster than of the forecast."
—Warren Buffett

Investors' relationships with REIT stocks are like some love affairs—they can change very quickly from hot to cold and back again. REITs were greatly admired by investors from 1993 through 1997, and then hated from 1998 until 2000. Investors rediscovered them in 2000, when value and income investing became fashionable, and drove REIT prices to very lofty levels in 2006 and 2007. But real estate became a dirty word for the next few years, and it was debatable whether I'd ever be asked to write another edition of this book. But reports of the death of REITs seem always to be greatly exaggerated, and they emerged, Phoenix-like, from the ashes of the Great Recession and related credit crunch—and have again become popular with investors.

We should expect that, sooner or later, REITs will again be relegated to investors' doghouses—from which they will yet again emerge, perhaps even more popular than ever. Meanwhile, let's remember that despite the frequent sound and fury emanating from the stock market, REIT organizations have been quietly fulfilling their responsibilities to their shareholders. Except during the Great Recession and its aftermath, they have grown their cash flows, dividends, and asset values, and their stocks have been very good investments. Most continue to look for the intelligent acquisition, some seek attractive development opportunities, and all work doggedly to create long-term value for their shareholders.

REITs will never again be stranded in the murky backwaters of the investment world; they are now too well established for that to happen. But because their popularity will ebb and flow, like all asset classes, we cannot predict the near-term direction of REIT stock prices, and I certainly won't attempt to do so. However, in this last chapter I'd like to break out the crystal ball, murky though it is, and review some of the issues that could affect the size, landscape, and characteristics of the REIT industry over the next 5 to 10 years.

Before we start forecasting the future, though, let's quickly try to gain some perspective by reviewing the past and the present. The REIT industry was a late bloomer. There were only 12 publicly traded equity REITs at the end of 1971, fully 11 years after being authorized by Congress. The total equity market cap of equity REITs did not reach $1 billion until 1982, 22 years after the first REIT was organized, and as recently as 1992 it was still just $11 billion. However, equity REITs' market cap reached $274 billion by the end of 2004, and exceeded $300 billion by the end of 2010. So most of the REIT industry's growth occurred in just the past 20 years, driven by the initial public offering (IPO) boom of 1993 and 1994, the huge wave of secondary offerings in 1997 and 1998, and the increasing size of many REITs. The rise in the value of most REIT stocks, particularly from 2000 through 2010, was also a major factor.

Despite this impressive growth, the REIT industry, as we discussed briefly in the last chapter, remains small in comparison with both the broader stock market and the total value of commercial real estate in the United States. Equity REITs owned approximately $500 billion in net real estate investments as of the end of 2010 (per the National Association of Real Estate Investment Trusts' [NAREIT's] estimate), but that's only 10 to 15 percent of the total value of all institutionally owned commercial real estate in the United States.

Thus, the additional growth prospects for the U.S. REIT industry are substantial, and its total market cap could expand dramatically over the next decade. But will this actually happen? In order to hazard a guess, we will need to consider two key questions: (1) will a significant number of private real estate owners want either to become REITs or to sell their properties to REITs; and (2) will individual and institutional investors want to expand their REIT holdings or otherwise decide to own more commercial real estate in securitized form?

Additional Real Estate Owners Will "REITize"

A successful and growing real estate organization could list several reasons why it might choose to go public as a REIT. Some of these have to do with the pricing of real estate on Wall Street compared with its pricing on Main Street, while others are attributable the advantages of the REIT format.

Arbitrage

REIT stocks have traded at prices above their estimated net asset values (NAVs) during most periods over the past 15 years (the primary exceptions being 1999 to 2001 and 2008 to 2009). To the extent this trend continues and NAV premiums expand, many private real estate owners—and particularly real estate organizations—will be tempted, for this reason and several others we'll discuss shortly, to go public as a REIT. Doing so would enable the organization to capture the "spread," or "arbitrage," between the pricing of real estate assets in private markets versus public markets. Of course, there would be less motivation to become a public company at those times when REIT shares are trading at prices that are *below* underlying real estate values. Indeed, if NAV discounts become very large, many REITs will elect to capture that "reverse arbitrage" by either going private or being acquired at a premium to the depressed market price—this occurred from late 1999 to early 2000, and again from the latter part of 2005 to the spring of 2007.

We saw in an earlier chapter that when REIT stocks were priced at significant NAV premiums, for example, from the end of 1992 through mid-1994, a major REIT IPO boom followed. Another sizable wave of real estate companies went public as REITs from

1997 through mid-1998, during which time the average REIT stock traded at a substantial NAV premium. Another, albeit smaller, wave of IPOs crested in 2003 to 2004; this wave ended in 2005, and the pace of new IPOs has been modest since then. Thus, the rate at which the REIT industry expands beyond its present size—or even contracts—may be significantly affected by how REIT shares are priced in public markets. As noted earlier, if the trend of REIT stocks trading at moderate to significant NAV premiums persists, we can expect to see more real estate organizations go public as REITs, the only issue being size and number.

But there are also reasons beyond arbitrage for a strong real estate company to go public as a REIT. These include tax advantages, greater access to capital, the ability to strengthen and motivate the organization, and liquidity and estate planning. Kimco Realty had been very successful as a private real estate company for 25 years and completed its IPO in November 1991 when REIT shares were still relatively unknown. Kimco did not go public to capture any arbitrage, but rather for these other (and more permanent) reasons. And there have been many other companies that have taken advantage of the REIT structure. Let's now consider them.

Tax Advantages

Perhaps one of the most obvious reasons a corporation owning substantial commercial real estate might choose to become a REIT is that, unlike most corporations, REITs generally don't pay corporate income taxes; rather, their shareholders pay taxes on the REIT's earnings as they are distributed in the form of dividends. This enables REITs and their shareholders to avoid double taxation—albeit, in recent years, at dividend tax rates higher than those paid by holders of most common stocks.

Although many property-owning companies can substantially reduce, or even avoid, taxation entirely by taking on a large amount of debt and writing off the interest expense (as well as a real estate depreciation expense), the REIT format allows a private real estate organization to go public and do business with less debt leverage and thus less risk. This is no small advantage in fickle and—at times—challenging credit markets.

Even existing publicly traded real estate–owning corporations might elect to become REITs in order to take advantage of the lack of double taxation. In 2010, for example, Weyerhaeuser, the large timber and forest products company, became a REIT—notwithstanding many years of successful operation as a traditional corporation. Host Hotels, which owns a large number of upscale and luxury hotels, also elected REIThood some years ago. And Catellus Development Corporation, a successful real estate developer for many years, became a REIT in 2004 before being acquired by another REIT, ProLogis. Other timber companies, Plum Creek Timber and Rayonier, also became REITs in recent years.

TIP

That REITs generally pay no corporate income taxes is a factor that will motivate many real estate companies to follow the REITization trend.

Access to Capital

Perhaps an even more important inducement for going public as a REIT is the greater access to capital and financing flexibility that publicly traded REITs enjoy. The commercial real estate business is capital intensive, and successful and growing real estate organizations constantly need additional capital for building and buying real estate, for improving and upgrading individual properties, and to otherwise take advantage of opportunities. But, as Kimco's executive chairman, Milton Cooper, has reminded us, lenders have been manic-depressive over the years when it comes to lending to real estate owners, developers, and operators. During some periods they seem almost to be throwing money at these enterprises, while at other times they are absolute skinflints. We were reminded again of this truth during the credit crunch of 2009. Access to multiple sources of capital, including equity capital, is a huge advantage enjoyed by public REITs and is particularly valuable when others don't have it; the best opportunities seem to arise during such times.

Of course, traditional sources of financing won't be discarded by companies that become REITs. Successful REITs normally obtain short-term financing and mortgage loans from banks, as well as longer-term, private debt financing from various lenders—such as insurance companies—in the same way that they did earlier as private companies. These financing sources are particularly important at times when public markets are reluctant to provide equity or debt capital. REITs also can enter into joint ventures with pension funds and other institutions in order to obtain additional liquidity; they may sell interests in some of their assets to these joint ventures and use the proceeds for higher-profit opportunities, while continuing to manage the fund assets and retain tenant relationships. The point here is that public REITs have much more flexibility and financing opportunities than do private real estate organizations.

 TIP

Access to the public markets provides flexibility and financial resources to REITs and allows management teams to have access to reasonably priced capital to plan for the long term and to provide some insulation from the occasional perversity of private lenders.

The issuance of common stock provides the most permanent type of financing—there is no obligation to repay it. Furthermore, common stock issuance allows the REIT to leverage this additional capital by adding debt to it. Before a borrower becomes eligible for unsecured loans, most lenders will insist on a substantial cushion of shareholders' equity, as well as a certain minimum "coverage" of interest payment obligations. Thus, selling common stock provides permanent capital and allows the REIT, if it so chooses, to add a debt component to the total capital raised, reducing the total cost of the new capital.

The sale of preferred stock is another avenue normally open only to publicly traded companies. Preferred stock is a form of leverage and magnifies changes in a REIT's cash flows, but it is not recorded as debt on the company's balance sheet and is generally not treated as such by lenders or credit rating agencies. Furthermore, nonconvertible preferred stock does not dilute common shareholders' equity interest in the REIT. Public Storage and PS Business Parks use preferred stock extensively, rather than debt, to keep their balance sheets strong and flexible, but many other REITs have also found preferred stock advantageous as a financing tool.

The issuance and public sale of unsecured notes and debentures enables the REIT to diversify away from heavy reliance on banks and other private lenders, while providing them with more flexibility in asset recycling strategies. It's simply easier to sell an asset that isn't burdened by a mortgage. The broad mix of available financing options is of significant value to a real estate company. We have seen that public markets will sometimes be closed to a REIT as a result of depressed market conditions or for some other reason; private financing may then be readily available. Conversely, at other times, private lenders may be exceedingly tightfisted, while the public markets extend an open hand.

Finally, becoming an umbrella partnership REIT (UPREIT) or a DownREIT may give the real estate organization a significant potential competitive advantage in the acquisition of properties from sellers who, by accepting operating partnership units (OPUs), can defer capital gains taxes. This financial tool has, at times, worked well for some REITs.

Expanded access to capital via common stock, preferred stock, and unsecured debt, as well as through the issuance of OPUs, is a key reason why more well-run and growing real estate companies will become REITs in the years ahead.

Building a Stronger Organization

Today, more than ever, owning and operating commercial real estate successfully is a *business*—whether the real estate is apartments, office buildings, retail properties, or any other type. And a strong organization is essential to the success of any business; competition is fierce everywhere, but well-run real estate organizations can often operate at lower costs and frequently enjoy more bargaining power—they are likely to have a significant competitive edge.

Although private companies can certainly build solid organizations and motivate employees and management, share liquidity makes it is easier for a public company to accomplish these objectives. Stock options and stock bonus or purchase plans that are flexible and provide liquidity are effective motivational tools for employees—from the most recently hired all the way to top management.

TIP

Today, stock options, restricted stock, and stock purchase plans (allowing employees to buy company stock at a discount) are strong employee incentives for public companies, including REITs.

Disciplined decision making, adequate financial controls, and incisive forecasts are becoming increasingly important to management teams as they seek to get ahead of the competition. Many public companies find that the corporate governance requirements imposed on them, while often nettlesome and costly, strengthen the organization in the long run. These requirements include having a board that includes several independent outside directors with whom business plans and projects must be discussed and justified; having to answer to the shareholders with respect to allocation of capital, expense control, compensation programs, and other shareholder concerns; and implementing strong financial systems and controls.

Thus, strengthening the organization and its financial discipline allows public REITs to become more efficient owners and managers of real estate. As such, they should be able to increase market share relative to many smaller, less well capitalized, and less disciplined real estate owners.

Liquidity and Estate Planning

Another factor likely to induce well-run real estate companies to go public is the ability of the public markets to provide liquidity for the ownership interests of management and employees. In all businesses—real estate, manufacturing, or services—management changes from time to time, and individuals who have devoted years to a successful operation may want to cash out upon retirement. Even key personnel who stay with the company will need to convert some of their capital to cash from time to time, perhaps to buy a house or to pay their children's college tuition, or simply to diversify their investments. The public market provides the necessary liquidity, as transfers of privately held shares or partnership interests can be costly and time consuming, and sometimes is just not possible.

Estate planning concerns may also induce successful real estate companies to "REITize." Uncle Sam takes a big bite out of substantial estates, and going public won't change that. However, it should keep heirs from having to sell all or part of the business or dumping real estate assets to pay estate taxes. Shares can be sold in the public markets, which will allow the business itself to remain undisturbed.

But Being Public Isn't for Everyone   We should keep in mind, however, that there are some reasons why a company might *not* want to go public. Management will have to operate in a fishbowl, as almost every major decision must be explained to analysts and shareholders, who will be constantly looking over management's shoulders. The Sarbanes-Oxley legislation imposes severe penalties on careless management teams, and its compliance costs are substantial. Independent directors will need to be selected and consulted on all major plans, policies, and strategic decisions. There will be significant pressure to perform, often on a very short-term basis. The costs of running a public company will be large, including premiums for directors' and officers' insurance, expensive audit fees, costs of maintaining an investor relations department, transfer agent fees, and legal and accounting costs for Securities and Exchange Commission (SEC) and federal law compliance. And as mentioned earlier, the prospect that REIT shares may, at times, trade at discounts to estimated NAVs can discourage some private real estate companies from going public as a REIT.

Notwithstanding these concerns, the benefits of a strong and growing commercial real estate enterprise's going public as a REIT, or electing to become one, are substantial. And their value has been proven by the significant growth of the REIT industry over time, in both the number of REITs and total market cap.

It's fair to question, however, whether the REIT industry will experience the kind of dramatic growth through a large number of new IPOs of major private real estate organizations that occurred in 1993 and 1994. The REIT industry has been known and widely respected for a number of years, and large private real estate organizations have had ample opportunity to become REITs if they wanted to do so, for example, the San Francisco–based Shorenstein Company and several large New York City real estate companies.

Many of these firms may have decided that they just don't want to deal with the annoyances inherent in being a public company. If these large private companies continue along their present path, the continuing expansion of the REIT industry will be driven by many smaller IPOs, as well as by property acquisitions and developments—including joint ventures with institutional real estate owners—by existing REITs and a gradual increase in the values of REIT-held properties over time.

Increasing Investor Demand for REITs

Although investor interest in REIT stocks will wax and wane from time to time, what should be important to long-term investors is whether the underlying demand for REIT stocks will build over time—and what long-term forces might drive that increasing demand. Rising demand for REIT investments can help to fuel industry growth and provide more liquidity and choice for REIT investors.

Individual Investors

A perceptive observer once noted that the Baby Boomer generation is like a large rat that has just been swallowed by a python—it greatly changes the form of the snake as the meal wends its way through the snake's long torso. The Baby Boomers created overcrowded classrooms when they started school in the 1950s, and spiraling tuition rates as they pursued higher education in the 1960s; they stoked demand for BMWs and other consumer goods in the 1970s and 1980s as they got jobs and began climbing the corporate ladder. They bought dot-com stocks, fueling the Internet stock bubble in the late 1990s, then poured money into houses several years ago—driving their prices to unsustainable levels. Perhaps instead of "following the money," we should follow the Boomers. They now are rapidly approaching (and even into) retirement; the oldest Boomers turned 65 in 2011.

What will they be doing to fund their living needs in their retirement years? Many of them will seek to supplement their Social

Security checks by investing for income. Most of these new investment dollars will flow into bond and equity mutual funds that focus on current yield. However, REITs' excellent track record and above-average dividend yields should induce many Baby Boomers to place more of their investment dollars into REIT stocks, directly or through mutual funds or exchange-traded funds (ETFs). Many are investing on their own, and others are turning to stockbrokers, financial planners and investment advisers.

How much of the new investment funds that will be deployed by these new yield-oriented investors will REITs be able to capture? The signs point to a significant amount. New investors start with small investments, and mutual funds are one obvious beneficiary; a mutual fund is a cost-effective way for new investors to get into a regular investment program. Mutual fund investors don't need to be financial analysts or even to follow specific stocks.

Popular 401(k) plans also encourage employees to invest through mutual funds. Although company-sponsored 401(k) plans that offer a REIT option are still in the minority, this will change over time—possibly even helped by readers of this book who will ask their employer to create one! Recent developments have been encouraging. NAREIT reports that the Profit Sharing/401(k) Council of America released a survey for the 2009 plan year, which concluded that "the proportion of DC (defined contribution) plans now including a real estate fund as an investment option jumped from 24.8 percent in 2008 to 33.4 percent in 2009." Ten years ago, only about 5 percent of such plans offered a real estate option.

From an Investor's Standpoint

The motivation for investing in REITs is clear: REITs have, over many years, delivered total returns to their investors that equal and, during many time periods, exceed, those of the Standard & Poor's (S&P) 500 index; they have fairly low correlations, which means that the REIT segment of one's portfolio won't move in lockstep with price movements of other asset classes; and they have shown themselves to be, during most market cycles, less volatile. They provide substantial dividend yields—well in excess of most other common stocks—and they respond to a different set of economic and market conditions from other common stocks and asset classes.

Over time, investors' needs will grow and may become more complex. Some investors will want to get more personally involved. For tax reasons, they may want to time their investment transactions. Stockbrokers and professional financial planners and investment advisers will help them to do this. Fortunately, more of these professionals are becoming REIT knowledgeable.

Even more important, investors will want to diversify their investments among different asset classes to minimize the adverse effects of the occasional bear market within a particular asset class. The major debacle in tech stocks that began in 2000 has taught many new investors the value of diversification. As we saw earlier, REIT stocks' correlations with other asset classes are fairly low, while their historical total returns have been impressive. If a large slice of the investment community decides on a 10 to 20 percent allocation to REITs, the impact would be quite substantial. In January 2011, Pimco (Pacific Investment Management Company), the huge and highly regarded investment management firm, released a paper, "Designing Outcome-Oriented Defined Contribution Plans," which recommended a REIT allocation of as much as 15 percent for "target-date glide paths." As investors' assets grow and they become more knowledgeable about the investment world, they will want to make sure that they have a meaningful allocation to REIT investments.

Back in 1997, Bernard Winograd, CEO of Prudential Real Estate Investors, observed that "the kind and quality of the offerings and the players are beginning to improve, and the REIT business is shifting from being a cottage industry to a mainstream investment choice." He added that as more large real estate companies go public, the growing liquidity will draw still more investors to the sector.

Despite occasional setbacks and bear markets, Mr. Winograd's observation has proven valid and perceptive. Financial publications catering to individual investors are again discussing the benefits of REIT investing, and individual investors are listening.

Brokerage firms, too, are expanding their coverage of REIT investments, and today virtually all of the major brokerage firms now have REIT analysts. Additionally, NAREIT has a program to educate financial planners about REIT investing as an excellent form of diversification for their clients' assets, and is helping to expand the number of REIT options in the all-important 401(k) market. More investment advisers than ever before are looking at REITs as a strong supplement to bonds and other higher-income equities. As our Baby Boomers retire in ever-greater numbers, the high, steady, and growing dividend income provided by REITs, as well as their other favorable investment attributes, will become even more attractive to them.

Institutional Investors

Earlier, we noted that institutions and pension funds have been slow to embrace REITs. But, for many reasons, that is changing—perhaps not as quickly as the REIT industry would like, but changing nonetheless. First of all, until fairly recently, REIT stocks focused only on a limited number of property sectors. Now, however, virtually all real estate types can be found among the assets of REIT organizations. Until 1993 to 1994, the REIT industry was dismissed as insignificant, and many desirable types of properties, such as offices, malls, hotels, and self-storage facilities that are key sectors in the REIT industry today, weren't even represented or were available only in very limited choices.

Objections were raised with respect to the small market caps of REITs, which made it difficult for institutional investors to buy and sell REIT shares in large blocks without affecting their market prices. If an institution found a REIT in which it would like to

Institutional Ownership of REITs

Institutional investors historically have elected to own real estate as one asset class within their broadly diversified portfolios. And REITs, which are both liquid real estate and operating real estate businesses, can be an outstanding supplement to direct ownership of real estate:

1. REITs provide much greater liquidity and transparency than ever before.
2. Institutions can now choose from an increasing number of high-quality real estate organizations with management depth and attractive institutional-quality assets.
3. The number of REIT sectors and geographies has expanded significantly.

The bottom line is that investing in REITs is a sound long-term strategy for institutional investors, and can add a new dimension to their commercial real estate investment portfolios.

invest, it couldn't buy a significant position without finding itself owning a controlling position in the REIT. As we'll discuss below, liquidity is a waning issue in the REIT industry; the market caps of many REITs have grown dramatically, while liquidity has increased substantially.

Many pension funds already have substantial investments in REITs. Others have "put their toes in the water" by entering into joint ventures with experienced REIT organizations. Eventually, as their comfort level rises, many of these institutions will increase their commitments via direct purchase of REIT shares. But before we consider whether major pension, endowment, and related funds will increase their allocations to REIT shares in the years ahead, let's try to understand where we are today.

It is difficult to determine the extent of REIT share owner- ship by pension funds and other institutional investors. Geoffrey Dohrmann, founder, president, and CEO of Institutional Real Estate Inc. (IREI), a firm that provides consulting services to, and supplies the information needs of, institutional commercial real estate investors, noted that institutions invest in REITs in many different ways. He told me recently that some "treat REITs as a sep- arate asset class," and many others "invest in REITs through their money managers or through direct investments by their own staffs, as well as those who are invested through index funds."

However they invest, it appears that institutional ownership of REIT stocks is already substantial. SNL Financial tracks such data, which shows that, particularly with respect to some REITs, institutional ownership is already very large. For example, their figures compiled in 2010 show that 649 institutions, including mutual funds, own about 96 percent of the outstanding shares of Simon Property Group, the largest REIT. And yet large institu- tional investors are still placing only a modest portion of their "real estate" allocations in REIT stocks. The 2011 study by IREI and Kingsley Associates, referred to in Chapter 5, noted that only about 7.4 percent of the funds expected to be allocated in 2011 toward commercial real estate by major institutions were intended for REIT shares.

But momentum is building. The 7.4 percent noted above is more than double the 3.5 percent target of the prior year. In October 2010, Callan Associates, a large institutional investment consulting firm with nearly $1 trillion under advisement, issued a white paper, "REITs: A Balanced Perspective." It noted REITs' "strong and measurable diversification benefits," and concluded that "performance relative to private core real estate is compelling. ..." Although the larger institutional investors will never replace all their real estate investments with REIT shares, it is probable that REIT shares will find their way into many more institutional portfolios over time. Let's consider then, in a bit more detail, why this might be so.

REITs' Quality and Management Strength   From the time that the REIT industry was born in 1960 until about 20 years ago, most REITs were managed in a passive way by small real estate staffs or by outside advisers. Those days are gone, and internal management is now the order of the day. To have called these old-style REITs "organizations" would have been generous indeed. As we discussed in Chapter 6, insider stock ownership was, in most cases, insignificant, conflicts of interest were numerous, and most REITs had only limited access to capital. Institutional investors would have found investing in such REITs almost laughable.

Today, however, a large number of the experienced and widely respected real estate firms that had operated successfully for many years as private companies have become REITs and, despite the inevitable hiccups along the way, have earned solid reputations— no less as public REITs than as private companies. Some of these include: in mall REITs, Macerich Company, Simon Property Group, and Taubman Centers; in neighborhood shopping centers, Developers Diversified, Kimco Realty, and Regency Centers; in apartments, AvalonBay Communities and Post Properties; and in the office and industrial sectors, AMB Property, Boston Properties, and Duke Realty. Yes, there were some outstanding organizations operating under the REIT format before 1991, such as Federal, New Plan, United Dominion, Washington REIT, and Weingarten, but they were few in number. Investors' choices among quality REIT organizations are greater than ever today.

A related and even more important factor that has contributed to, and will continue to increase, the amount of institutional funds flowing into REIT investments is that investors are now recognizing the strength of many REITs' management teams and their skill sets.

In the late 1980s and early 1990s, and again in the past few years, institutions learned, to their great sorrow, that management can be as important as location as a determinant of success for a portfolio of properties. REITs' extensive property management skills, tenant contacts, strong financial resources, access to capital, in-house research capabilities, and, in many cases, development and redevelopment expertise, should enable them to create shareholder value in ways not available to passive commercial real estate owners, and can help to provide total investment returns greater than those provided by direct commercial real estate or private equity funds that invest in this asset class. REITs' track record in this respect, as noted earlier in this book, has been impressive.

Increased Market Caps and Share Liquidity   If small market caps were a factor in deterring institutional fund managers from investing in REIT shares in the past, they must have been gratified to see REIT market caps increasing, thus providing increased liquidity. Before the 1993 to 1994 IPO boom, not a single REIT could boast an equity market cap of as much as $1 billion. According to NAREIT, by the end of 1997, a total of 47 REITs had passed that milestone, and there were 83 of them by December 2010. Market caps will shrink at times, due to the occasional bear market (and some REITs will go private), but REITs will continue to issue equity from time to time to acquire and develop properties; and although new equity offerings have the effect of reducing the ownership interests of the existing shareholders, they also increase REITs' equity market cap and the public "float" of available shares. Furthermore, to the extent that REIT shares trade at sufficiently high prices so that they may be used as "currency" to acquire private real estate companies, the REIT industry will see a larger number of REIT organizations with very substantial market caps.

The trading volume of many REIT stocks today matches that of many mid-cap and larger non-REIT companies, and such volumes will increase with their increasing market caps. According to NAREIT, the average daily dollar trading volume of the shares comprising the NAREIT Composite Index rose from approximately $100 million in 1995 to more than $400 million by the end of 2000, to approximately $1.4 billion by March 2005, and to approximately $3.4 billion by December 2010 (see Figure 13.1).

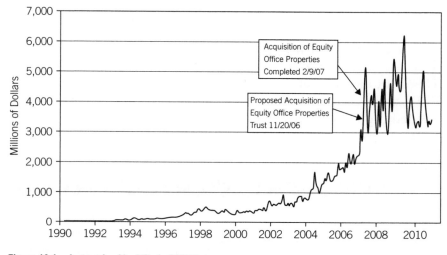

Figure 13.1   Increasing Liquidity in REIT Shares
Source: NAREIT, *REITWatch,* January 2011.

Most institutional investors are now able to establish sizable positions in many REIT stocks without significantly affecting the current market price. Further, as institutions become more comfortable with REITs, they might find it less important to be able to dump hundreds of thousands of shares within 20 minutes.

An experienced REIT observer, William Campbell, has suggested several other advantages for pension funds and other institutions owning REITs rather than specific real estate. Some of these include the use of debt leverage in real estate investing (which is often not legally permitted in direct investments by pension funds); the greater ability of REITs to assemble multiple properties in a single geographic area, which can increase operating efficiency, provide tenants with more location choices, and generate better real estate returns; the ability of most institutional owners to obtain greater real estate diversification with respect to management style, geography, and property sector; and the ease with which the investment can be liquidated should it prove disappointing.

In what form will institutions continue to invest in REITs? There are several. They can, of course, simply buy REIT shares in the open market. They can form a joint venture with a REIT, putting up the funds for the acquisition of properties meeting specific guidelines or for the development of one or more new properties. Or they can swap properties they already own for REIT shares. And they have, at times, negotiated private placements of common stock directly with a REIT, and have participated in new preferred stock offerings. This institutional interest will continue to augment the credibility of REIT stocks as real estate–related investments, provide REITs with needed capital at reduced costs, and motivate many more privately held, successful real estate companies to become REITs.

TIP

It's not important *how* institutions and pension funds choose to invest in REITs; it is important only that they are choosing REITs as a strong supplement to direct ownership of real estate and that they continue to increase their investments in them.

Matt Gilman, formerly senior portfolio manager at ABP Investments, a large Dutch pension plan (and now CEO of Starwood Real Estate Securities), has stated that REIT liquidity is "infinitely better" when compared with buying or selling individual buildings. Also, he notes, REIT investing makes it much easier to obtain the required diversification.

An occasional issue for institutions is the question of whether REITs should be considered "real estate." As we've discussed, REITs are a unique blend of both real estate and equities, and any attempt to assign them a single label will be doomed to failure. A study published in 2003, in the *Journal of Portfolio Management*, authored by Joseph Pagliari, Kevin Scherer, and Richard Monopoli, compared REIT stock price performance, based on the NAREIT index, to the performance of private real estate, as represented by the National Council of Real Estate Investment Fiduciaries (NCREIF) Property Index. After adjusting to make the NAREIT and NCREIF indices more comparable, the authors concluded that "public and private [real estate investment] vehicles ought to be viewed somewhat interchangeably…, offering investors a risk-return continuum of real estate investment opportunities." If this is so, then it isn't unreasonable to conclude that REITs combine the best of both real estate *and* equities. Nonetheless, the modest pace with which institutions have increased their investments in REIT stocks may have been partially due to this "equity versus real estate" conundrum, as well as the REITs' modest, albeit growing, liquidity in prior years.

Eventually, however, many more institutional investors will conclude that while REIT stocks are subject to the fashions and vagaries of the equities markets in the short term, they will deliver real estate–like returns in the long run—and, quite likely, somewhat better than that. Of course, as we saw in Chapter 8, the quality of REITs' management teams—and how they perform over time—will be essential in attracting new institutional, as well as individual, REIT investors.

But don't take my word for it. Geoffrey Dohrmann, the consultant I referred to earlier in this chapter and who has very close ties to the institutional commercial real estate community, told me in late 2010:

> I think it's safe to say that institutions have been allocating a greater share of their real estate allocation to REITs, and that this trend is likely to continue. In addition, as REITs are added to major indices, money managers are encouraged to add the corresponding securities to their portfolios as a means of meeting or beating the indices. Finally, the shift from defined benefit to defined contribution pension fund formats should continue to create opportunities for REIT stock investment management firms to more broadly distribute their fund products as alternative choices for fund participants. So institutional, professionally managed ownership of REIT shares is likely to continue to grow over the next 5 to 10 years.

The bottom line here is that, although the larger pension funds and other similar institutions will never replace all their direct real estate investments with REIT shares, it is probable that REIT shares will find their way into many more institutional portfolios over time. Indeed, the trend has been slowly moving in that direction, particularly in recent years.

Larger REITs: Is Bigger Really Better?

A crucial point concerning the nature of today's REITs is that, until the IPO boom of 1993 to 1994, most REITs were fairly small companies with limited capabilities. They acquired real estate, and most were able to manage their holdings reasonably well. Many were able to upgrade their properties from time to time, and thus increase their enterprise value and FFO at a faster pace than if they had employed a purely passive buy-and-hold strategy, but very few were able to develop properties. In 1993 and 1994, however, all of this changed when a large number of new REITs with well-established development capabilities went public.

There are times in various real estate cycles when it is simply not going to be profitable, at least on a risk-adjusted basis, to develop new properties, such as when existing rental rates are insufficient to justify the costs of land acquisition, property entitlement, and construction, when interest and financing costs are excessive, or when tenant demand for space is weak. At other times, however, new development is clearly warranted and can generate strong investment returns if conceived and executed intelligently. REITs capable of such development clearly have an advantage, since they will be able to avail themselves of opportunities when conditions are appropriate, and thus can increase their FFO and NAV faster than those not so well situated.

Although some investors will choose to invest in the smaller REITs, some of which pay higher dividends and have lesser growth capabilities, it's likely that even more investors, particularly the institutional type, will focus on those real estate organizations that can create the most additional value for their shareholders. These companies will have the acquisition skills to know when to buy properties and where to find them at bargain prices, the research abilities to determine where long-term growth will be strongest, the staff necessary to manage existing properties in the most creative and efficient manner, the size necessary to become the low-cost space provider and to negotiate the best deals with suppliers and tenants in their markets, the capability of developing the kinds of properties most in demand and in the best locations, and the foresight to create highly incentivized management teams and intelligent succession plans. Such REIT organizations, through their ability to attract new capital at appropriate times during most market cycles, will become significantly larger and will attract increasing institutional followings.

And yet, despite the promise and potential of these larger REIT organizations of the future, REIT investors should question whether there are also disadvantages in large size. Some will question the value to shareholders of becoming a "national REIT" with assets in far-flung locations, while others have noted that, at times, REITs have paid excessive prices—in cash or in stock—to attain greater mass. A proposed merger of Prentiss Properties and Mack-Cali Realty in 2000 was given the Bronx cheer by investors, and was subsequently abandoned when investors could detect no value creation from such a business combination. New Plan Realty's merger with Excel Realty in 1998 also offered questionable value. Did the large Rouse acquisition benefit the shareholders of General Growth? Probably not. We'll consider merger-and-acquisition (M&A) activity later.

Many REITs certainly have become national in scope and will continue to seek a presence in promising new markets. But they are also, even at the same time, exiting markets and shedding assets, focusing more intensely on markets in which they are strong and dominant or where they see the best long-term potential growth. Thus, many REITs are realizing that "local sharpshooters"—as SL Green has long been in Manhattan—may create the most value for shareholders.

Although a large REIT can become a local sharpshooter in a number of markets, it has not been easy, historically, for an apartment, office, industrial, or neighborhood shopping center REIT to be a highly effective competitor in more than a dozen of such markets, particularly if their assets are scattered across the United States. A few very large REITs, for example, Equity Residential and Simon Property, have done so, but others have stumbled.

Today, there are many large geographically diversified REIT organizations (e.g., Camden, Equity Residential, Kimco, Simon, and UDR), others with a heavy emphasis on selected markets nationally (e.g., AvalonBay, Boston Properties, ProLogis, and Regency), and still others that remain very focused regionally (e.g., Essex, Federal, Kilroy, SL Green, and Vornado). There are advantages and disadvantages to each business model, and the REIT investor should determine whether a REIT has the financial strength, the infrastructure, and the management expertise that fit the chosen model. What might be a smart strategy for one REIT to pursue may be folly for another. Geographic diversification is not a sufficient reason for a REIT to enter new markets; we REIT investors can diversify on our own by buying a package of REITs.

Let's now consider, in the context of larger REIT sizes, the issue of mergers and acquisitions in the REIT world. Despite the likelihood that more well-run, privately-held real estate companies will become REITs in the years ahead, we have also, at times, seen periods of merger and consolidation. Prior editions of *Investing in REITs* described, probably in excessive detail, many of the "public-to-public" mergers of REIT organizations from 1995 through 2004, and I won't repeat that exercise or update it in this edition. Suffice it to say that a large number of REIT names that we veteran REIT investors had invested in no longer haunt the streets of REITland, and have been absorbed by many of today's larger REITs or sold to private equity firms or other real estate investors.

TIP

What seems to have driven many public-to-public mergers was the perception by some, at least in the REIT industry, that "bigger is better." Is it?

The really important questions for investors are these: Is a larger REIT truly better—or, at least, a stronger competitor that will generate higher-than-average rewards for its shareholders over time? And, if so, do mergers with, or acquisitions of, other REITs make sense? The proponents of large size make the following points:

- The acquirer, due to economies of scale, can easily improve the profitability of acquired assets.
- Mergers deliver "synergies" in the form of overhead and other cost reductions.
- Larger companies have stronger bargaining positions with their suppliers and can obtain substantial price concessions.
- Larger companies also have more bargaining clout with tenants, particularly in the retail sector.
- Larger companies can offer more services to tenants, thus increasing retention rates.
- Larger size reduces the cost of capital—both debt and equity.
- Investors appreciate—and will pay a premium for—the greater liquidity that large public real estate companies provide.

These are certainly valid points. But there are contrary arguments. Those who are skeptical of the value of a REIT buying other REIT organizations (or even large real estate portfolios) argue:

1. Operating cost savings are minimal, particularly when a well-run REIT or property portfolio is acquired.
2. Most REITs are not bloated with overhead, so any corporate general and administrative expense savings will also be minimal.
3. It is always difficult to blend corporate cultures, and many valuable and experienced executives will depart, thus negatively affecting the long-term value of any such mergers.
4. A "synergy gap" is often created when a premium price is paid for a company that substantially exceeds the cost savings, which may take years, if ever, to recover—and it often destroys value for the acquiring company's shareholders.
5. REIT organizations only occasionally enjoy attractive "currency," in the form of expensive stock that can be effectively used in acquisitions.
6. Becoming ever larger makes it much more difficult for that splendid "one-off" acquisition or unique development project to create a meaningful amount of incremental value for shareholders.

It's my view that mergers can sometimes create value for the acquiring company's shareholders—and bigger is sometimes better—but mergers can also destroy shareholder value. Much depends on the property sector, the structure of the deal (and its pricing) and how well it is executed in years two through five. Each deal must be evaluated on its own. Investors are becoming smarter and more discriminating, and they will reward growth and larger size only if value is created as a result. Large REITs will certainly be strong competitors in real estate markets throughout the twenty-first century but many smaller, more focused REITs have shown that large size and huge footprints are not prerequisites for success in the REIT industry.

In 2000 many of the larger, more aggressive REITs enjoyed substantial appreciation in their share prices, while the stocks of the smaller and quieter REITs languished. This situation gave rise to the thought that consolidation in the REIT industry would accelerate following the "year of separation," as the larger REITs with strong share "currencies" (trading at NAV premiums) would be able to acquire many of the smaller REITs at bargain prices. This did not happen, as many of the large-cap REIT stocks that did so well in 2000 gave up much of their performance edge to the smaller, higher-yielding REITs in 2001. As long as smaller REITs can compete effectively, and create value for their shareholders, it will be difficult to argue that REIT M&A activity will be an accelerating trend.

We will, of course, continue to experience mergers and acquisitions in REITville, for example, the merger of AMB Properties and ProLogis, announced in January 2011 and the merger of Nationwide Health and Ventas announced in February 2011; however, a major wave of large deals is probably not likely. Even General Growth Properties, as it prepared to emerge from bankruptcy in 2010, was able—with the help of some large-money investors—to remain independent, rebuffing a buyout offer from Simon Property Group. In any event, speculating on the "next" buyout candidate is unlikely to be very productive for REIT investors. Although the rigors and aggravations of compliance with Sarbanes-Oxley and other costs of being a public company may drive some smaller REITs to seek a merger partner, and even larger REITs may choose to combine forces or to go private, we cannot identify them ahead of time.

REITs, of course, can grow their real estate portfolios in ways other than buying entire companies, such as Macerich's acquisitions of the Westcor portfolio in 2002 and the Wilmorite assets in 2005, or Regency's $2.7 billion 2005 acquisition, along with Macquarie Countrywide (an Australian property trust), of a Calpers–First Washington portfolio of shopping centers. Large property transactions that are well conceived, priced attractively, and offer many of the potential advantages discussed earlier, while minimizing the problems and concerns also noted, will be greeted with enthusiasm and will benefit the shareholders of both the acquiring and the acquired companies. Others, less well conceived or poorly executed, will leave many disgruntled shareholders in their wake. The REIT industry will certainly expand over time, but, with the exception of shopping malls, where the vast majority of the most productive malls in the United States are owned by REIT

REITs in the S&P 500 Index

For several years the REIT industry had been seeking to have one or more of its members included within the Standard & Poor's major U.S. indices, including the S&P 500, the S&P MidCap 400, and the S&P SmallCap 600 (the S&P had a separate index for REIT shares prior to 2001). The principal argument for inclusion was that modern REITs have evolved from being relatively small ($10 to $50 million) passive pools of investment properties with outside advisers and external property management into fully integrated, self-managed companies, many having market capitalizations larger than some companies already included in the S&P 500. Thus, the contention has been that REITs should be as entitled to membership in such an index as any other company if the S&P selection criteria are met.

The S&P decision makers finally became convinced, and announced on October 3, 2001, that it would regard REITs as eligible for inclusion in their broad-based U.S. indices. S&P also then announced that Equity Office Properties, the largest REIT in 2001, was selected to replace Texaco (which merged with Chevron) in the S&P 500; several other REITs were then designated for inclusion in the S&P MidCap 400 Index and in the S&P SmallCap 600 index. S&P stated that it had "conducted a broad review of Real Estate Investment Trusts (REITs), their role in investment portfolios, treatment by accounting and tax authorities, and how they are viewed by investors," and that "Standard & Poor's believes that REITs have become operating companies subject to the same economic and financial factors as other publicly traded U.S. companies listed on major American stock exchanges."

The long-term consequences of S&P's decision are substantial. According to S&P's web site, funds indexed to the S&P 500 in late 2010 amounted to $915 billion, while the index itself represents $3.5 trillion in stocks. The first REIT included in the S&P 500, Equity Office Properties, initially represented approximately 0.1 percent of the S&P 500, or about $1 billion of new investment. Later in 2001, the largest apartment REIT, Equity Residential, was also added to the S&P 500. These REITs were followed by a number of others and, at December 2010, 14 REITs were included in the S&P 500 index. The long-term benefit of REITs' inclusion has been a major boost to REITs' credibility as solid, long-term equity investments. Equity fund managers must now take REITs seriously, and their failure to do so risks underperformance versus their benchmarks.

Some industry leaders have suggested that REIT organizations ought to be viewed as mainstream equity investments and should compete with all other equities for the attention of investors. But "be careful what you wish for."

(Continued)

A substantial part of the appeal of REIT stocks is that many investors regard them as a separate asset class, like bonds or international stocks, and the inclusion of such a separate asset class within a broadly diversified investment portfolio has many advantages, particularly in view of their modest correlations, in most periods, with other asset classes. If REIT shares become viewed simply as equities, like tech stocks or health care stocks, will this advantage be lost?

Perhaps—but not necessarily. It should not matter what label is placed on a group of stocks if owning them as part of a diversified portfolio continues to provide the investor with significant advantages. If their investment characteristics are favorable, including modest risk, low correlations, and strong total returns, should investors really care whether financial advisers call REIT shares a separate "asset class" or merely an "industry group"? In any event, the inclusion of a number of REIT stocks within the S&P 500 and other smaller S&P indices has become a watershed event for the REIT industry.

organizations, it's doubtful that commercial real estate ownership will be dominated by a few huge companies, REITs or otherwise.

Additional New Trends

In Chapter 6, some recent new trends in the REIT industry were noted, such as joint ventures with institutional investors and asset recycling strategies (in which existing assets are sold to upgrade portfolio quality or to fund development projects). Investors have also seen several other recent trends in the REIT world, many of which may affect REIT valuations and growth rates; let's discuss a few of them.

Debt Leverage

We've discussed in other places in this book the wisdom and rationale of REITs' use of debt to increase investment returns. In looking ahead, an obvious issue is how much debt the best-regarded REITs will carry on their balance sheets. Perhaps I am excessively skeptical, but I've not been convinced that the use of debt creates any long-term value for REIT investors, except during extraordinary periods when commercial real estate can be acquired at abnormally cheap prices. Debt leverage can be a mild positive when the economy and space markets are performing well, but can be a time bomb on those occasions when conditions reverse quickly and credit markets freeze.

But debt has *always* been used by real estate investors, and perhaps that mind-set won't ever change. Many REITs had ample opportunity to raise huge amounts of equity capital in 2010 and will into 2011 to reduce debt to very low levels and, while plenty of equity was raised to repair broken balance sheets, by the spring of 2011 no major REIT (except for a very few, such as Public Storage, which has never taken on much debt) had leverage ratios of less than 30 percent of total assets. This may happen, however, in the years ahead. My guess is that any REIT that substantially reduced debt leverage would be cheered by many investors, particularly if signaled and explained ahead of time. And there's hope: Kimco's Milton Cooper, a REIT industry leader, has stated his goal of seeing Kimco reduce its debt leverage to 25 percent over a reasonable period of time; perhaps it will be able to do so, becoming a model for a REIT industry with less debt.

But let's be realistic. Few REITs are likely to reduce debt leverage ratios to below, say, 40 percent, particularly when interest rates are very low (as they were in the past few years and into 2011). And leverage at that level shouldn't be all that worrisome to investors if the REIT has structured its debt maturity schedule very conservatively and its ratio of debt to free cash flow before interest expense isn't burdensome. The problem, of course, is that "black swans" don't advise us ahead of time when and where they intend to land.

Better Disclosure

TIP

Reporting and disclosure by REIT organizations have become much more comprehensive, and it's now easy, by going to a REIT's web site, for the individual investor to obtain access to financial and other information that was previously available only to analysts and institutional investors.

Just one example of many is AvalonBay's web site (www.avalonbay .com), which includes quarterly financial information and numerous attachments and supplements, describing, among other matters, the status of the company's development pipeline, acquisitions and sales, and submarket profiles. Greatly encouraged by SEC disclosure rule Regulation FD, most public companies, including REIT organizations, are broadening their dissemination of important business and financial information, and a large number of quarterly earnings conferences are now available to all investors, either by phone or by Webcast (and replays are readily available).

And disclosure itself is improving. Although REIT investors continue to be troubled by, among other things, the fact that different companies even within a single sector sometimes calculate FFO differently—despite continual efforts by NAREIT to refine and improve the definition—progress is steadily being made toward more uniform disclosure and accounting practices, as well as the disclosure of more detailed property and other data. Investors are demanding ever more precise and meaningful financial information, and REIT organizations are increasingly complying with their wishes.

Perhaps one day, in the not-too-distant future, we'll have "fair value" accounting in the United States, and REITs will be disclosing the fair market values of their properties. That process has already begun.

REITs Investing Overseas

REITs have traditionally avoided investing in real estate abroad—and for good reason. The laws, industry practices, and economics of owning and managing real estate are often very different outside of the United States; real estate everywhere tends to be a very specialized business, demanding a strong local presence and employees who understand governmental regulations, tenant requirements, supply-and-demand trends, and land and building values, among much other information. But recently we have seen exceptions, as a few of the more aggressive REITs have been making real estate investments in foreign countries.

Perhaps the earliest—and, quite likely, the most successful—of such efforts was made by Chelsea Property Group, which was acquired by Simon Property Group in 2004. Chelsea formed joint ventures with two major Japan-based corporations to build and manage outlet centers in Japan, and the results have been outstanding. Other retail REITs have also been active in acquiring interests in properties overseas. Simon, in addition to its Chelsea Premium Outlet properties located in Japan, Mexico, and South Korea, has made investments in Warsaw (Poland), Naples (Italy), and Hangzhou (China)—but later disposed of some of them. In 2007 Developers Diversified invested in a joint venture development project in Russia. Taubman Centers is working on development projects in Macao, Puerto Rico, and South Korea, and Kimco Realty began investing in Canada and Mexico several years ago, and has more recently been investing in Latin America.

Two industrial property REITs have also been active beyond U.S. borders. ProLogis expanded into 18 countries, including Canada, China, Europe, Japan, and Mexico (although it sold many of these assets to reduce debt leverage in the wake of the Great Recession), and AMB Properties has established a presence in Canada, Mexico, Europe, Japan, China, and Singapore. Shurgard Self-Storage, since acquired by Public Storage, developed a number of storage properties in Europe, and Host Hotels now owns lodging properties in six European countries. However, office, residential, and health care REITs have not been particularly interested in investing capital outside the United States.

Investing in foreign real estate certainly introduces new risks (e.g., foreign currency losses, issues involving relationships with foreign partners, unique regulatory and tax issues, etc.). However, a judicious amount of such investment can also be very profitable to the REIT and its shareholders if planned and executed with care and foresight, particularly if these business plans can take advantage of a combination of the expertise—and perhaps tenant relationships—of both the REIT and the foreign partner. But a merely passive investment by a REIT in a foreign country would seem to offer little advantage to the REIT's shareholders. As Kenneth Campbell and Steve Burton explained in Chapter 11, U.S. investors can participate in foreign real estate investments through ownership of foreign REIT stocks, widely available mutual funds and even ETFs. The devil is, indeed, in the details, and some REITs will create value for their shareholders from these endeavors while others will not.

New Spin-Off REITs?

A 2001 event, one that may eventually be significant for the REIT industry, was the issuance of IRS Revenue Ruling 2001-29. This ruling, concluding that REIT organizations are engaged in "an active trade or business," makes it possible, if other criteria are satisfied, for corporations to spin off to their shareholders stock in a new organization that could elect to become a REIT and would own the real estate previously owned by the larger corporation. Upon the issuance of this revenue ruling, investors immediately focused upon fast-food giant McDonald's Corp., wondering whether it might put all its real estate into a new REIT (McREIT?) that would lease these assets back to McDonald's. Any major corporation that owns substantial real estate assets could be motivated to pursue a spin-off of its properties into a new REIT, hoping to increase its profitability and return on equity, while possibly reducing corporate taxes.

But there are major obstacles. Such a spin-off would diminish the corporation's control over the locations where it does business. And, as a practical matter, investors would be unlikely to embrace a REIT of this type, which would, at least initially, lease substantially all of its assets to one large tenant. Investors prefer their REITs to be diversified by tenant mix, and to have an arm's-length relationship with each tenant. A new "captive" REIT could promise to buy additional properties over time and lease them to others, but would be investors be sufficiently patient?

The first spin-off transaction completed as a result of the 2001 revenue ruling was the merger of Plum Creek Timber with a new REIT formed by a spin-off of Georgia Pacific's timber assets. Indeed, this transaction was the reason the revenue ruling was requested; Plum Creek became a REIT in 1999. Rayonier, a large timber, fiber and wood products company, converted to a REIT in 2004, and Weyerhaeuser, another major timber and forest products company, elected to become a REIT in 2010.

Until very recently, only timber and forest products companies have so far taken advantage of this revenue ruling. But in January 2011, Dillard's, a large retailer, announced plans to form a new REIT subsidiary that would receive real property interests from Dillard's and its related companies. The intent is for these properties to be leased to Dillard's under triple-net leases. A number of large retailers own many or most of their own stores and, given the very competitive retail environment, one may speculate whether additional retailers may also form REITs. We should keep in mind, however, that the Dillard's spin-off, if it occurs, could amount to merely a financing device, and may not create a new business model of interest to REIT investors.

Real Estate–Related Businesses

The discussion of the REIT Modernization Act of 1999 in Chapter 3 noted that, under such law, a REIT can organize a taxable REIT subsidiary (TRS) to engage in business activities for which it was not previously authorized. Many REITs have been forming new business ventures outside of the traditional REIT business of acquiring, developing and operating commercial real estate, quite often through a TRS. A number of retail, office, and industrial REITs have developed new properties for clients or captive joint venture funds and, with the assistance of a TRS, have the flexibility of selling them quickly upon completion—often reaping a substantial development profit (even after taxes) and deploying it into other traditional or nontraditional investments.

Before it was sold to a Tishman Speyer-Lehman Brothers partnership in a 2007 $22 billion deal, Archstone-Smith, through its Ameriton TRS, managed properties for others, even developing and trading properties. During the frothy housing market a few years ago, Equity Residential and Post Properties developed condominiums to take advantage of then-strong demand for such properties (rather than, or in addition to, selling some of their own properties to condo converters). Kimco Realty has for many years provided venture capital financing to retailers. A number of REITs have made investments in real estate technology, such as broadband, cable, and Internet access. Others have even organized their own start-up technology, e-commerce, or telecommunications ventures, although these have not fared as well. Ventas, a health care REIT, has used its TRS to increase its ability to profit directly from increases in net operating income at its seniors communities by eliminating third-party lessees (but this strategy, of course, also increases the REIT's exposure to deteriorating business conditions).

The report card on these ventures has been mixed. Most of them outside of the technology sector have performed reasonably well, at least until they were adversely affected by the Great Recession, but they seemed to have flunked "Technology 101"— most technology-related investments were written off by REIT organizations in 2001. REIT management teams should be given credit if new and profitable revenue streams can be created in this manner, but REIT executives are experts in owning, acquiring, managing, and sometimes developing commercial real estate and should be wary of allocating substantial capital to new ventures in which they have had little experience. Most of these new investments will probably deliver the best rewards, certainly on a risk-adjusted basis, when they enable the REIT to leverage its existing development and property management expertise or to become more competitive in its basic real estate business by increasing tenant satisfaction, in other words, acting as a "gatekeeper" for other service providers, and offering cost-saving opportunities to their tenants. And, of course, some REITs will earn better returns with their TRS strategies than others. As always, risk needs to be balanced with prospective rewards.

So Much More to Come

In the autumn 1996 issue of *REIT Report*, Peter Aldrich, founder and co-chair of the real estate advisory firm Aldrich Eastman Waltch, prophesied that "the industry's right on track now for a 25 percent compounded annual growth of market cap. Nothing should slow it now unless there's bad public policy." Seven years later renowned real estate investor Sam Zell noted that the securitization of real estate, through REITs, is a long-term trend that will continue. Doug Crocker, former president and CEO of Equity Residential, said more recently, "I think the industry will grow in size. The size of the individual REITs will continue to expand, and the investor base will continue to expand exponentially from where it is today."

REIT organizations and their investors naturally remain very optimistic about the future of the REIT industry, for good reason, even though the volume of rhetoric has been turned down a notch or two as the industry has become wiser and more sophisticated.

We may no longer be in the early innings, and industry growth, going forward, will be far less than 25 percent per year. As noted throughout this book, disheartening bear markets and occasional poor capital allocation decisions have, at times, clawed at the REIT industry; and, at times, some very good REITs have been taken private, for example, Archstone-Smith and Equity Office. However, bear markets are invariably followed by bull markets, and the industry continues to grow—both in size and sophistication. REIT investors and REIT management teams have, for the most part, refrained from engaging in "irrationally exuberant" strategies, and have remained focused on old-fashioned blocking and tackling, as well as capital preservation, during some very difficult real estate markets, including recently. The REIT industry has certainly matured.

The ebbs and flows of investor sentiment will always influence price movements of individual stocks and entire equity sectors in the short term, but, over longer time periods, investors will base their buying and selling decisions on business prospects, investment merits and expected risk-adjusted total returns. REIT organizations, led by some of the most experienced and innovative management teams that have ever been assembled in the world of real estate, are truly capable of continuing to deliver outstanding returns for their investors, particularly when adjusted for their lower risk. This fact—more than any other— will insure a home for REITs in virtually all investors' portfolios. The best, I firmly believe, is yet to come!

Summary

- The rapid growth of the REIT industry has created abundant opportunities for investors—both individual and institutional—as they now have many more investment choices.
- The REIT vehicle also provides experienced and successful real estate organizations with increased access to needed capital and wide flexibility in financing, enabling them to more easily grow their businesses and attract and motivate quality management teams.
- The trend toward larger and more capable REITs enables individual investors and large institutions alike to diversify

their investment portfolios, while offering the prospects of very competitive total returns.

- REITs still own only a modest percentage of institutional-quality commercial real estate in the United States, and thus have ample opportunities to expand their assets and operate them with even greater efficiency.

- The rationale for investing in REITs is simple and compelling: REITs provide substantial and, during most periods, growing, cash dividends, along with significant opportunities for capital appreciation, with only a modest amount of risk and relatively low correlations with other asset classes.

- As REITs become larger in size, through property acquisitions, new developments and even, at times, acquisitions of other REITs, investors should ask themselves whether increased size for any particular REIT is a net advantage or disadvantage.

- New trends in the REIT industry include capital recycling, joint venture strategies, increasing transparency, ever-improving corporate governance, more share liquidity, and the development of real estate-related businesses.

- The REIT industry has certainly matured in recent years, but numerous avenues still exist for REIT organizations to become stronger, to attract new investment capital, and to grow their businesses by seizing the ample opportunities that will unfold over time.

Death and Taxes

When REIT stocks are held in taxable accounts, i.e., outside of individual retirement accounts (IRAs) or other tax-advantaged accounts such as 401(k) plans, they have two significant disadvantages with respect to their non-REIT cousins. Assuming an 8 percent total return expectation and a dividend yield of 2 percent for the typical non-REIT stock, about 75 percent of such total return will consist of capital appreciation, which—if held for more than 12 months—is taxed at long-term capital gain rates. Congress recently extended for two years the maximum capital gain tax rates in effect at the end of 2010, which were 15 percent (5 percent for low-bracket taxpayers). Thus, most of the expected returns from non-REIT stocks will be taxed at favorable rates. Furthermore, non-REIT ("qualified") dividends are presently taxed at a rate not to exceed 15 percent.

With REITs, however, approximately 50 percent of investors' expected total return will come from dividend income, which is taxed at regular, rather than qualified, rates.

Nevertheless, ownership of REIT shares does frequently provide the shareholder with some tax advantages. Very often, a significant portion of the dividends received from a REIT is not fully taxable as ordinary income; some of the dividend may be treated as a long-term capital gain, and another portion may be treated as a "return of capital," which is not currently taxable to the shareholder. This return of capital portion of the dividend reduces the shareholder's cost basis in the shares, and defers the tax until the shares are ultimately sold (assuming the sale is made at a price that exceeds the cost basis). If held for at least

12 months, the gain is taxed at long-term capital gain rates and the shareholder has, in effect, converted dividend income into a deferred, long-term capital gain. NAREIT data indicate that in 2009, for example, approximately 13 percent of REIT dividends were comprised of capital gain distributions and 10 percent was a return of capital.

How does this happen? As we saw earlier, REITs base their dividend payments on funds from operations (FFO) or adjusted funds from operations (AFFO); net income is a lesser consideration. FFO, simply stated, is a REIT's net income but with real estate depreciation added back, while AFFO adjusts for straight-lining of rents and recurring expenditures that are capitalized and not immediately expensed. As a result, many REITs pay dividends to their shareholders in excess of net income as defined in the Internal Revenue Code (IRC), and a significant part of such excess is often treated as a "return of capital" to the shareholder and not taxable as ordinary income. The return of capital component of a REIT's dividend has, since 1995, ranged from 9 percent (2007) to 28 percent (2005), and has been between 12 percent and 17 percent in a typical year.

If a REIT realizes long-term capital gain from a sale of some of its real estate, it may designate a portion of the dividend paid during the year of the sale as a "long-term capital gain distribution," on which the shareholder will pay taxes, but normally at lower capital gain rates. Thus, dividend distributions paid to REIT shareholders will consist primarily of ordinary income, return of capital, and long-term capital gain.

Table A.1 shows how the dividends that Duke Realty paid in 2009 were allocated among ordinary dividends, qualified dividends, capital gain distributions, and return of capital. Each REIT, of course, will have a different allocation, and the allocations for a REIT will vary–sometimes widely–from year to year.

Table A.1 Treatment of Dividends: Duke Realty

Duke Realty 2009	Dividend per Share	Percent of Total
Total Distributions per Share	$0.760000	100%
Ordinary Dividends	$0.524687	69%
Qualified Dividends	$-0-	0%
Total Capital Gain Distributions	$0.035125	4.6%
Return of Capital	$0.200188	26.3%

Example

Let's assume an investor purchased 1,000 shares of Duke Realty (DRE) at the end of 2008 at $11 per share, for a total cost of $11,000 (for simplicity, we'll ignore commissions). We will also assume a dividend rate of $0.76 per share. By the end of 2009, he or she will have received $760 in dividends. Based on the components of DRE's 2009 dividends set forth above, of the total of $760 in dividends, $524 will be taxed at ordinary income rates, $35 will be taxed at the more favorable capital gains tax rates, and $200 will be tax deferred as a return of capital. The investor must reduce his or her cost basis by the amount of the return of capital (in this case, $200, or $0.20 per share), so that the new cost basis of the 1,000 shares of DRE would then be $10,800. Finally, let's also assume that the shares are sold in early 2010 for $13 per share, or a total of $13,000 (again ignoring commissions). The investor would then report a total long-term capital gain of $2,200 (the difference between $13,000 and $10,800) on Schedule D.

Shareholders cannot predict the amount of the dividend that will be tax deferred merely by looking at reported net income in the REIT's annual or quarterly reports, as the tax-deferred portion is based on distributions in excess of the REIT's taxable income pursuant to the IRC. The differences between net income available to common shareholders for financial reporting purposes and "taxable income" for income tax purposes relate primarily to:

- Differences between IRC depreciation (usually accelerated) and "book" (usually straight-line) depreciation.
- Accruals for preferred stock dividends.
- Deferral for tax purposes of certain capital gains on property sales (e.g., tax-deferred exchanges).

There is generally no publicly available information allowing us to determine, ahead of time, the portion of the dividend distribution from a REIT that will be taxed as ordinary income. This is because, as noted earlier, for tax purposes, certain income and expense items are calculated differently from what appears in the current year's financial statements. This number must be determined by the REIT at the end of its tax year, and the shareholder will have to wait until early the following year to obtain the final figures.

Of course, none of the foregoing discussion is relevant if REIT shares are held in an IRA, 401(k) plan, or other tax-advantaged account. The dividends won't be taxable while held in such an account, but the distributions (when eventually withdrawn from the account) will normally be taxable as ordinary income.

What happens upon death of the shareholder? Under current tax law, the heirs get a "step-up in basis," and no income tax will be payable with respect to that portion of the dividends classified as a return of capital (although estate taxes may have to be paid). In this scenario, it's therefore possible, merely by dying, to escape income tax entirely on a significant portion of a REIT's dividends—but this is not a recommended tax-planning technique!

State tax laws, of course, may differ from federal law. Investors should check the status of their dividends under federal *and* state tax laws with their tax accountant or financial adviser.

None of the foregoing tax advantages will induce a REIT skeptic to own REIT shares; furthermore, the lower tax rates on qualified dividends still give other common stocks an edge over REITs if tax savings are one's only investment consideration. Nevertheless, the ability to defer a portion of the tax on REITs' dividends, and to treat another portion as capital gain taxed at lower rates, can have significant advantages over time and should not be overlooked.

Case Study: FFO, AFFO, FAD, and CAD

The following example in Table B.1 is an income statement derivation of adjusted funds from operations (AFFO) and funds (or cash) available for distribution (FAD or CAD), contained in a quarterly earnings report by Post Properties, an apartment REIT. Although the calculation below was published by the REIT a number of years ago, it is nevertheless still typical of how AFFO, FAD, or CAD can be derived for most REITs.

Table B.1 Post Properties (PPS): Third Quarter, 1996

(In thousands of dollars, except for per share.)

Revenue

Rental—Owned Property	$40,583
Property Management	722
Landscape Services	1,199
Interest	50
Other	1,661
Total Revenue	$44,215
Property Expenses	
Property Operating & Maintenance	$15,115
Depreciation—Real Estate Assets	5,877
Total Property Expenses	$20,992
Corporate and Other Expenses	
Property Management—Third Party	$558

Table B.1 Continued

Revenue	
Landscape Management	1,013
Interest	5,970
Amortization of Financing Costs	293
Depreciation—Non–Real Estate Assets	197
General and Administration	1,769
Minority Interest	0
Total Corporate & Other Expenses	$9,800
Total Expenses	$30,792
Income before Minority Interests and Extraordinary Items	$13,423
Gain on Sale of Assets	$693
Minority Interest in Operating Partnership	(2,535)
Net Income	$11,581
Plus	
Depreciation and Amortization—Real Estate Assets	$5,877
Minority Interest	2,696
Less	
Net Gain on Sale	$(854)
Amortization of financing costs	(55)
Funds from Operations (FFO)	$19,245
FFO per Share	$0.71
Less	
Recurring Capital Expenditures	$(692)
Adjusted Funds from Operations	$18,553
AFFO per Share	$0.69
Less	
Nonrecurring Capital Expenditures	(687)
Funds or Cash Available for Distribution	$17,866
FAD or CAD per Share	$0.66
Weighted Average Number of Shares/ Operating Units	26,929

Discussion

Note that Post Properties reduced its AFFO of $18,553,000 by $687,000 to account for "nonrecurring capital expenditures." This provides a fairly accurate picture of cash available for distribution for Post's 1996 third quarter; however, because of the nonrecurring nature of those expenditures, it may not provide an accurate "run rate" of free cash flow going forward (which may be higher by $687,000).

Depreciation of real estate assets such as apartment buildings and other structures under accounting conventions can be deceptive. Real estate (most notably the underlying land) tends, over time, to appreciate in value, particularly if well maintained; however, for accounting purposes, depreciation must be deducted in order to derive net income. Funds from operations (FFO) is calculated by adding back real estate depreciation and amortization to net income. However, property owners incur recurring capital expenditures that are certainly real and that need to be taken into account to provide a true picture of the owner's recurring cash flow from the property.

Examples include the necessary replacement from time to time of carpets, drapes, external lighting fixtures and roofs. In some cases, property owners may make tenant improvements (and/or provide tenant allowances) that are necessary to retain the property's competitive position with existing and potential tenants, and may pay leasing commissions to outside brokers. Since many of these expenditures are capitalized rather than expensed as incurred, they must be deducted from FFO in order to determine adjusted funds from operations, or AFFO, which is a more accurate picture of economic cash flow.

Some REITs and investors who use funds (or cash) available for distribution (FAD or CAD) often distinguish it from AFFO in the manner that Post has done. Unlike AFFO, which deducts the amortization of real estate-related capital expenditures from FFO, FAD or CAD is often derived by deducting *nonrecurring* (as well as normal and recurring) capital expenditures. And some REITs or their investors who calculate FAD or CAD may also deduct repayments of principal on mortgage loans. Unfortunately, there is no widely accepted standard for making these adjustments when calculating CAD or FAD.

The following additional points may be helpful to keep in mind when analyzing REITs' existing and prospective revenues and free cash flows.

When reviewing a REIT's revenues, it is a good idea to analyze lease expirations and existing lease rates and compare them to market rental rates within the REIT's property markets. This approach may help in determining whether rental revenues may increase or decrease when leases are renewed at current market rates. This is often referred to as *embedded rent growth* or *loss to lease* (for lease rates that are below market rents) or *rental roll-down* (for lease rates that are above market rents).

Always distinguish revenues from services (whether from property management, a fee-development business, joint venture fees, or consulting services) from revenues from rents. *Rental* revenue tends to be more stable and predictable, as fee-only clients are able, at some point, to terminate the relationship (and the resulting service or fee revenue streams). Revenues from some joint ventures, however, tend to have reasonably long lives.

Always analyze the REIT's type of debt and its debt maturities. REIT investors will normally prefer long-term debt to short term, and fixed-rate debt to variable rate. Some REITs have more exposure to rising interest rates than others.

Watch for recurring capitalized property expenditures that are maintenance-oriented and do not improve the REIT's properties or prolong their useful lives, as well as unusual financing devices (e.g., "buy downs" of loan interest coupons, forward equity transactions, etc.). These items will affect the quality of reported FFOs and help to calculate AFFOs.

Cost of Equity Capital

Important as the concept is, there seems to be no general consensus on how to calculate a REIT's "cost of equity capital." There are, however, several ways to approach this issue. One quick way to determine a REIT's *nominal* equity capital cost is to estimate the REIT's expected per-share FFO for the next 12 months. When issuing new equity, this per-share FFO should be adjusted for the new shares being issued and the expected incremental FFO to be earned from the investment of the proceeds from such new share issuance (or interest costs saved from the pay-down of debt). Finally, we would then divide such "pro forma" FFO per share by the price the REIT receives for each new share sold.[1]

Let's assume, for example, that Apartment REIT USA has 10 million shares outstanding, trading at $15 per share, and is expected to earn $10 million in FFO over the next twelve months. It intends to issue an additional 1,000,000 shares and receive net proceeds of $15 per share (we'll ignore underwriting commissions), which will be used to buy an apartment building providing an initial yield of 6 percent; this investment of $15 million will thus provide $900,000 of additional FFO (6 percent of $15 million).

---

1. Some investors have simply looked at a REIT's dividend yield, which is quite misleading; FFO and AFFO, as well as other valuation metrics, such as whether new shares are sold at an NAV premium or discount, are far more important than dividend yields in the context of determining REIT valuations, and thus the dilution from issuing additional shares.

Therefore, on a pro forma basis, this REIT will have $10.9 million in FFO which, when divided by 11 million shares outstanding, will produce FFO of $0.99 per share. Dividing this by the $15 offering price results in a nominal cost of equity capital of 6.6 percent. Note that this is higher than the entry yield (6 percent) available on the new apartment investments, as a result of which this stock offering would be mildly dilutive to current FFO per share.

However, if we were to hypothesize that Apartment REIT USA were able to sell its new shares at a net price of $17, its nominal cost of equity capital would be 5.8 percent. Thus, the higher the price at which a REIT can sell new shares, the cheaper its nominal cost of capital will be; this would make it more likely that the offering and the investment of the offering proceeds would be "accretive" to FFO.

But the above approach measures only a REIT's *nominal* cost of equity capital; its true cost of equity capital is much more important, and should be measured in a very different way. In the first approach, we divided pro forma expected FFO per share by the net sale proceeds per share, using expected FFO only for the next 12 months. But what about the FFO that will be generated by the REIT for many years into the future? This FFO will be forever diluted by the new shares being issued, and, for this reason, a short-term look is very incomplete. How can longer time periods be taken into account?

One way that a REIT's true cost of equity capital may be measured is to use the total return expected by investors on their investment in the REIT. For example, if a REIT's shares are being priced in the market to provide for an expected internal rate of return of 10 percent (including both dividend income and capital appreciation, and on the basis of projected FFO or AFFO and dividend growth rates, debt leverage and other factors), shouldn't the REIT's true cost of equity capital also be the same 10 percent? A few REITs may be so conservative (perhaps because of little or no debt on the balance sheet and a very cautious business strategy) and well-regarded, and their FFO and dividend growth so predictable, that a more modest 7 percent annual return might satisfy most investors; in such a case, the REIT's true cost of equity capital might be 7 percent.

A major difficulty with this approach, however, is determining the total return that is demanded by investors; this isn't as easy as it might appear, as shareholders rarely broadcast to the world what they expect. And, of course, some investors will expect higher returns than others. All of this discussion moves us into capital asset pricing models, "modern portfolio theory," and the like, which try to determine the return investors should demand in excess of a "risk-free" return such as 6-month T-bills or 10-year T-notes, based on various measurements of risk such as standard deviations and betas. But these topics are beyond the scope of this discussion, and disagreements prevail there also.

Nevertheless, REIT investors who want to delve into this issue might want to try to determine the total returns expected, or that *should* be expected, by investors in particular REIT stocks and use those figures to determine the REIT's true cost of equity capital. (There are discussions and papers available on the Internet that cover this topic, e.g., "The True Cost of Capital," Institutional Real Estate Securities, January 1998.) One might argue that, in view of REITs' historical total returns of 11 to 12 percent, REITs should expect that their true cost of equity capital would be in that neighborhood. However, during periods of unusually low interest rates, low real estate cap rates, or when returns from other investments are expected to be uncharacteristically modest, REIT investors' return expectations should be reduced, and REITs' cost of equity capital should be lower than their long-term historical averages.

It's important to emphasize that much of the cost of equity capital calculation depends on the extent to which the REIT uses debt leverage; the more debt, the higher the cost of equity capital. The cost of *debt* capital (which is more straightforward) can be blended with the cost of equity capital to determine a weighted average cost of capital (WACC) to help determine the wisdom of any new investment made by the REIT, that is, the internal rate of return (IRR) on any new investment should equal or exceed its WACC.

REITs' legal requirement to pay out 90 percent of net income to their shareholders each year in the form of dividends makes it difficult for a REIT to generate substantial external growth in FFO or AFFO (e.g., through acquisitions or new development) without either an aggressive capital recycling strategy or frequently coming back to the markets for more equity capital. Keeping low debt levels certainly helps to reduce the overall cost of equity capital, as does periodically selling off properties with very modest long-term IRR potential.

That said, those REITs that continue to find attractive opportunities will normally need to raise additional equity capital from time to time. It is therefore important for REIT investors to understand how to analyze a REIT's cost of equity capital, particularly its true longer-term cost of equity capital—even though such calculations will be imprecise. The investment returns expected from external growth initiatives should be carefully compared with REITs' capital costs to make sure that shareholders' interests aren't permanently diluted—or value destroyed—when new equity is sold.

APPENDIX

REIT Portfolio Management

Following is a discussion of how one might go about managing his or her REIT stock portfolio. It is excerpted (and updated) from one of the author's newsletters, "The Essential REIT."

Those who own only two or three REIT stocks and intend to buy no more of them should ignore this entire Appendix D. It's intended primarily for REIT enthusiasts who have a significant allocation to REITs, perhaps owning 10, 20, or even 30 of them, and who are curious about the many potholes and forks in the road leading to effective REIT portfolio management.

First, a caveat. This is not a topic that one sees discussed regularly in *Money* magazine or the financial press; portfolio management tends to be the province of academic types, quant jocks, and professional portfolio managers, and most articles on the subject are apt to be filled with arcane and incomprehensible formulae of the type that we might find on the blackboard at an MIT postgraduate seminar on string theory. If you don't believe me, check out any issue of the *Journal of Portfolio Management*. However, as I went to law school, not business school, the following discussion will be notably devoid of higher mathematics (or even lower mathematics, for that matter). That's the good news; the bad news is that it offers no five-step programs for immediate capital gain.

All right, let's get to it. We know that all REIT organizations are not created equal, nor *are* they equal. They each own different assets in different locations, pursue different business strategies, and structure their balance sheets differently. The quality and depth of their management teams differ substantially. Perhaps all classical music sounds the same to the uninitiated, but its enthusiasts certainly know the difference between Schubert and Schoenberg. Likewise, all REITs are similar in many ways—they all own, or lend on the security of, commercial real estate—but can be quite different from one another.

These different characteristics, as well as the relative valuation levels of various REIT stocks, make the long- and short-term return prospects and risk profile of one REIT stock quite different from that of another. So, to think of REITs as one might think of many investment grade bonds—"who cares which one you own?"—can a big mistake. Property markets, management teams, balance sheets and business strategies affect both risk and growth profiles, and *do* count in REIT investing. Over time, they will certainly affect performance and volatility. Think of it this way: If you want to invest in the "energy" sector, how do you build your portfolio? Do you buy the integrated majors, for example, Chevron, Exxon, and Royal Dutch? Small "exploration and production" companies? Drillers? Natural gas pipelines? Master limited partnerships? Do you prefer oil or gas? Do you focus on big reserves in "exciting" places such as the western Canadian tar sands or off the coast of Brazil, or are you more comfortable in proven locations such as the San Juan Basin? Your answers will clearly affect your portfolio performance and risk profile.

It's the same with REITs. REIT portfolio management, I believe, should be driven by one's investment objectives. Is it getting the best possible performance, risk be damned? To beat the benchmark by 100 basis points annually? To be a closet indexer? How important is risk—not just volatility, but the prospects of a near-permanent decline in portfolio values due to excessive debt leverage or a very aggressive development strategy? Is volatility important? High dividend yields? Maximizing after-tax returns? We learned long ago that there is no free lunch in the perverse world of investing, and one's strategy should be tailored to one's return requirements and degree of risk aversion. So let's take a closer look at some possible investment objectives.

1. **Beating Benchmarks—and Risk Management.** We all want to beat the benchmarks, right? For those who get paid to manage portfolios, it's their raison d'être—and justifies their fees. For those managing portfolios on their own, superior performance gratifies the ego and justifies the extra work; otherwise, index funds would be the way to go. But we often don't focus enough on what's required to beat the benchmark—especially if we want to shatter it. Let's be honest: while the REIT industry has expanded by more than 20-fold since the end of 1992 (and had an equity market cap of over $300 billion at the end of 2010), it's still a somewhat small industry and our investment choices aren't unlimited, particularly if liquidity is an issue. And there are lots of new investors grazing in REITland, some of whom are quite intelligent. Companies now regularly issue guidance, and most FFO/AFFO estimates out on "The Street" are very similar; a REIT beating, or failing to meet, consensus numbers by more than a few pennies—when nonrecurring items are filtered out—only happens a bit more often than seeing pigs fly.

So it's very competitive out there—if not a jungle. A select few may be able to beat the benchmark somewhat regularly by simply being very astute stock-pickers—but they won't beat the index by more than, say, 2 percent a year over a 5-year time horizon. However, clobbering the benchmark by 5 percent annually, and on a regular basis, requires one to embrace risk as one would embrace a cold lager after a 10-mile hike. So let's assume that a portfolio manager wants to significantly beat the benchmark; how should he or she manage an all-REIT portfolio?

There are several ways, including:

(a) Very active trading, seeking to scrape or claw an extra one or two percent here and there, albeit at the cost of high portfolio turnover.
(b) Heavily overweighting or underweighting specific real estate sectors—REIT industry performance can vary widely by

sector from year to year (and even quarter to quarter), and finding oneself greatly overweighted in a strongly performing sector can do wonders for performance.

(c) Ditto for specific companies, particularly if they are not heavily represented in the benchmark, for example, taking 6 percent positions in, say, Chesapeake Lodging, Monmouth Real Estate, Retail Opportunity Investments, or Terreno Realty can put us well ahead of—or way behind—the benchmark.

(d) Straying outside of REITland and owning non-REIT real estate stocks such as Brookfield, the St. Joe Company, or even homebuilders such as PulteGroup.

Risk comes in many shapes and sizes, and can also be increased or decreased in ways other than overweighting or underweighting sectors or stocks, or indulging in heavy trading. Some sectors are inherently more risky than others; the cash flows of hotel REITs, for example, are less predictable. And, of course, risk differs substantially by company. While nobody can say whether there is more exposure to a short-term stock price decline in MPG Office Trust or in Boston Properties, there is little doubt that the former is simply a riskier company to own—and not just because of its greater stock price volatility.

There are also differences in company-specific risk; this can be due to a number of factors, including management strategies (how risky is the strategy, and how much capital is being devoted to it?), stability and predictability of cash flow streams from real estate (and real estate–related businesses), and the extent of development risk and overseas investment risk. How reliable has management—and its forecasts—been in prior quarters? Is there risk that it will misallocate capital? And, of course, some balance sheets are simply riskier than others—due to high amounts of debt leverage, substantial variable-rate debt and/or near-term debt maturities. Liquidity in REIT shares can also be an issue, particularly if the company disappoints.

The bottom line here is that one might generate better near-term performance from a portfolio chock full of MPG Office, Felcor Lodging, and First Industrial, but it will be a riskier portfolio than one heavily weighted with the likes of Equity Residential, Public Storage, and Simon Property Group. So let's not kid ourselves: superior performance is wonderful, but it usually comes at a price—and that price is spelled R-I-S-K.

2. **Reducing Volatility.** If low volatility is our objective, there are some things we can do. One obvious approach is to focus heavily on those REIT shares that have had a history of not moving around much from day to day, that is, the REIT industry's version of Johnson & Johnson or Kimberly-Clark. But keep in mind that yesterday's sleeping dog can, for various reasons, become tomorrow's kangaroo on steroids, and vice versa. Several additional tools can also be effective in reducing portfolio volatility. Let's look at a few of them:

One obvious tactic is increasing cash levels. Nobody's going to call you a wimp for maintaining a cash position of 5 to 8 percent, and doing so will certainly reduce volatility (though it will, of course, punish you in a bull market). Another is to make sure that positions aren't concentrated, in other words, don't put more than, say, 3 percent of your total investment assets into any single position. Again, this may entail a cost in performance if we are right about our stock picks, but volatility will be reduced. Volatility can also be reduced by spreading one's investments out over many sectors of real estate, as this will tend to even out daily and weekly performance.

Risk may or may not be defined exclusively in terms of volatility but, as was true of highly levered REITs in 2008 through 2009, stocks that are more likely to self-destruct due to any number of future events are likely to be more volatile. If this is so, focus on the safer companies in REITdom—from the perspectives of management quality, business strategies, development risk, cash flow predictability and stability, balance sheet strength, share liquidity, dividend coverage, and other issues that can affect a REIT's stock price level 12 months later. Shares of companies like AvalonBay, Boston Properties, Federal Realty, Public Storage, and Simon Property are likely to be less volatile due to their investment characteristics, including size and modest debt leverage. So, if low volatility is your game, load up on the stalwarts.

3. **Maximizing After-Tax Returns.** Many smart financial planners continue to remind us that what we *keep*, after tithing to Uncle Sam and our state government coffers, is what really counts. We may make $10,000 on a successful short-term

trade, but if we live in California or another high income tax state, we'd be lucky to keep $6,000 of that, and we'd need to earn a very high return on any new substitute investment just to recover those tax payments. Of course, many investors own REITs in individual retirement accounts (IRAs) and 401(k) plans, and "don't need no stinkin' tax planning." Fine. But others do need to think about their taxes, perhaps even more in REIT investing than elsewhere.

Why? Think about it this way. Even long-term capital gains may be taxed at rates up to 25 percent (not 15 percent), when state taxes and alternative minimum tax (AMT) phase-outs are tossed into the equation. Can another REIT stock bought with the proceeds of a REIT we sell generate enough capital appreciation to make us whole within a year or two? Not likely—not if we reasonably expect only 4 to 5 percent in capital appreciation annually for the typical REIT stock. So those of us who invest in REIT stocks with personal funds need to think seriously about taxes and tax bills resulting from taking profits.

Fortunately, REIT shares are at much lower risk of vaporizing than, say, a biotech or Internet stock. It's highly unusual for a REIT to miss consensus estimates badly, and REIT assets seldom melt away like obsolete semiconductor inventory. Most REITs' cash flows are protected by long-term leases. So, it's not going to kill us to hold onto a REIT investment with a large embedded capital gain that we would otherwise like to sell to take advantage of some other apparent bargain in REITville. For those who want to keep capital gain taxes to a minimum, the best strategy, therefore, is to resist the temptation to sell or pare back every time a stock looks expensive or the risk profile increases modestly. Thus, tax-sensitive investors should be particularly focused on those REIT stocks they'd be happy to own for many years. And watch those REIT mutual funds carefully; they are tasked to outperform their peers or a REIT benchmark, and so most of the portfolio managers care as much about taxes as my golden retriever, Sammy, cares about who's on the cover of next week's *People* magazine.

4. **Investing for Yield.** Many believe that yield is the name of the game in REIT investing. And who can blame them? In recent

years, about half of the total returns from REIT investing have come from the dividend yield alone. I know a number of REITsters who profess, "Hey, capital appreciation is nice, but I'll be perfectly content if my REITs provide me with a steady dividend, with occasional increases as circumstances warrant."

Should a REIT investor focus only on yield? Of course not. But should he or she pay attention to yield? Yes indeed. Yield is certainly one of the distinguishing factors setting REIT stocks apart from their cousins in the broader world of equities, and a Chevron or a McDonald's, clad in a 3 percent or 4 percent dividend yield taxed at lower rates, will be a formidable competitor to REITs with similar or lower yields.

But let's assume that Mr. Yield Hogg is highly motivated by dividend yields. How should he structure his portfolio? "Here there be dragons." As many investors have learned to their eternal sorrow, a yield that looks too good to be true usually isn't. But just as it's a truism that even though you may be paranoid doesn't mean that others aren't out to get you, those who have a thing for yield can still invest in REITs successfully. Some of my best friends in REITdom prefer REIT stocks with higher than average dividend yields, and I cheerfully own some of them (the stocks, not the friends).

Of course, the "no free lunch" principle means that we must make certain sacrifices when we focus heavily on yield. Growth rates of higher-yielding REITs are apt to be lower; this is so for several reasons. First, a higher dividend yield resulting from a REIT's paying out close to, or more than, 100 percent of its free cash flow means that less retained earnings can be invested for future cash flow growth (and companies that pay more in dividends than provided by free cash flows are liquidating themselves unless they can continually sell assets at high prices and replace them with new developments at positive spreads). Second, a higher yield is often an indication that Mr. Market is less than impressed with prospective future growth prospects and so demands that the current yield be high enough to offset this perceived sluggish growth rate. And, third, a high dividend yield is frequently a sign that the REIT owns higher cap-rate properties, which may suggest lower-quality or higher-risk assets.

Another trade-off is greater risk. If a particular REIT is perceived as an animal having sharp teeth and unpredictable behavior, investors often will price its shares at a higher current dividend yield so that they will be compensated for the heightened risk. Mortgage REITs tend to have high yields for this reason, among others. Historically, some of the highest yields in REITdom have been attached to shares that you shouldn't take home to mother.

Thus, there are usually good reasons why one REIT will yield 3.5 percent and another will yield 7 percent. But those who work hard, study management teams and balance sheets, and have a firm handle on the risks inherent in some higher-yielding REIT stocks can build a pretty good portfolio with them. And, of course, these investors will probably want to add a component consisting of fairly safe, higher-yielding REIT preferreds—although with these one normally gives up all opportunity for capital appreciation.

5. **Personal REIT Investment Strategy.** What's my personal REIT investment strategy? For broad diversification, I try to blend several of the foregoing styles. However, my primary emphasis at this stage of my life is risk avoidance; most investors, including your humble author, buy REIT stocks not for the purpose of hitting home-runs and bragging to their neighbor about their most recent coup but, rather, to preserve their capital (including earning a good and predictable return on it) and to avoid disasters—and as many potholes as possible. As a result, I tend to focus on those companies in which I have a high level of comfort that they aren't going to do something really stupid. They have superb, proven management teams, own good-quality properties in good locations, enjoy strong balance sheets, and—well, if you've read the book, you know the rest.

But here's a final thought. There is no one "right way" to invest in REIT stocks; various strategies can work well if intelligently executed. An old saw claims that "bulls make money, bears make money, but pigs get slaughtered." Similarly, only those investors who flip-flop from one investment style to another, perhaps chasing "the hot REIT of the week"—and who try to trade in and out of them—will get hurt owning REIT stocks.

The key, of course, is knowing one's financial objectives, performance criteria, risk and volatility tolerances, yield requirements, and willingness to pay capital gains taxes. But every active investment strategy requires knowing something about the REIT that's being bought or sold, including its management team, business strategy, assets and geographic locations, balance sheet, and related considerations, as well as having a pretty good conception of relative valuations and risks. Those who don't want to play that game can always buy a REIT mutual fund or exchange-traded fund (ETF), perhaps often with little or no loss of performance (but, in the case of some mutual funds, with the risk of dealing with substantial tax bills at the end of each year).

APPENDIX **E**

Largest Global Real Estate Companies as of December 2010

		As of:		12/31/2010					
				Percent of Total					
Security	Ticker	REIT/	S&P Dev	EPRA	Div [1]	Crnt	Equity Mkt [2]	Equity Mkt	Free
Name	Symbol	REOC	Weight	Weight	Yield	Price (Local)	Value (USD) Bil.	Float (USD) Bil.	Float %
Americas									
Argentina (ARS)									
IRSA-Inversiones y Rep. S.A. (B)	IRSA AR	REOC	0.0%	0.0%	0.9%	6.32	$0.92	$0.35	37.5%
Total Country	1		**0.0%**	**0.0%**	**0.9%**		**$0.92**	**$0.35**	**38.0%**
Total Majors	1		**0.0%**	**0.0%**	**0.9%**		**$0.92**	**$0.35**	**37.5%**
Brazil (BRL)									
PDG Realty S/A Empreendimentos e Participacoes	PDGR3 BZ	REOC	0.0%	0.0%	2.2%	10.16	$6.77	$6.75	99.7%
Cyrela Brazil Realty S/A Empreendimentose e Participacoes	CYRE3 BZ	REOC	0.0%	0.0%	1.0%	21.85	$5.57	$3.77	67.7%
MRV Engenharia e Participacoes S/A	MRVE3 BZ	REOC	0.0%	0.0%	1.0%	15.61	$4.54	$2.99	66.0%
BR Malls Participacoes S/A	BRML3 BZ	REOC	0.0%	0.0%	2.0%	17.10	$4.19	$3.50	83.6%
Multiplan Empreendimentos Imobiliarios S/A	MULT3 BZ	REOC	0.0%	0.0%	0.9%	36.90	$3.72	$2.38	64.0%
Gafisa S/A	GFSA3 BZ	REOC	0.0%	0.0%	1.0%	12.04	$3.13	$3.02	96.5%

Total Country	**24**		**0.0%**	**0.0%**	**1.4%**		**$48.03**	**$33.36**	**69.5%**
Total Majors	**6**		**0.0%**	**0.0%**	**1.4%**		**$27.91**	**$22.41**	**80.3%**
Canada (CAD)									
Brookfield Properties Corp.(B)	BPO CN	**REOC**	0.5%	0.8%	3.1%	17.56	$8.88	$8.88	100.0%
RioCan Real Estate Investment Trust	REI-U CN	**REIT**	0.3%	0.7%	6.3%	22.00	$5.72	$5.70	99.7%
H&R Real Estate Investment Trust	HR-U CN	**REIT**	0.2%	0.4%	3.7%	19.43	$2.85	$2.79	97.7%
Calloway Real Estate Investment Trust	CWT-U CN	**REIT**	0.1%	0.3%	6.6%	23.37	$2.30	$2.01	87.2%
Canadian Real Estate Investment Trust	REF-U CN	**REIT**	0.1%	0.3%	4.5%	31.05	$2.08	$2.07	99.3%
Brookfield Properties Corp. (B)	BPO	**REOC**	0.0%	0.0%	3.2%	17.42	$8.81	$8.80	99.9%
MI Developments Inc. (Cl A)	MIM/A CN	**REOC**	0.0%	0.0%	1.5%	27.13	$1.26	$1.26	100.0%
Total Country	**29**		**2.3%**	**4.3%**	**3.8%**		**$70.34**	**$65.87**	**93.6%**
Total Majors	**7**		**1.3%**	**2.4%**	**4.1%**		**$31.91**	**$31.50**	**98.7%**
Chile (CLP)									
Parque Arauco S.A.	PARAUCO CC	**REOC**	0.0%	0.0%	2.5%	1140.00	$1.48	$0.36	24.1%
Total Country	**1**		**0.0%**	**0.0%**	**2.5%**		**$1.48**	**$0.36**	**24.3%**
Total Majors	**1**		**0.0%**	**0.0%**	**2.5%**				
Mexico (MXN)									
Urbi Desarrollos Urbanos S.A. de C.V.	URBI* MM	**REOC**	0.0%	0.0%	0.0%	28.99	$2.30	$1.16	50.3%

(Continued)

Security Name	Ticker Symbol	REIT/ REOC	Percent of Total — S&P Dev Weight	Percent of Total — EPRA Weight	Div [1] Yield	Crnt Price (Local)	Equity Mkt [2] Value (USD) Bil.	Equity Mkt Float (USD) Bil.	Free Float %
As of:					12/31/2010				
Corporacion Geo S.A.B. de C.V.	GEOB MM	REOC	0.0%	0.0%	0.0%	45.28	$2.02	$2.02	100.0%
Total Country	**4**		**0.0%**	**0.0%**	**0.3%**		**$5.32**	**$3.76**	**70.7%**
Total Majors	**2**		**0.0%**	**0.0%**	**0.0%**		**$4.31**	**$3.17**	**73.6%**
United States (USD)									
Simon Property Group Inc.	SPG	REIT	3.5%	3.7%	3.2%	99.49	$29.15	$28.47	97.7%
Public Storage	PSA	REIT	1.7%	1.6%	3.2%	101.42	$17.27	$14.35	83.0%
Vornado Realty Trust	VNO	REIT	1.6%	1.9%	3.1%	83.33	$15.22	$13.69	90.0%
Marriott International Inc.	MAR	REOC	0.0%	0.0%	0.4%	41.54	$15.13	$11.86	78.4%
Equity Residential	EQR	REIT	1.8%	1.8%	3.5%	51.95	$14.78	$14.27	96.6%
General Growth Properties Inc.	GGP	REIT	1.3%	0.9%	2.6%	15.48	$14.50	$13.74	94.8%
HCP Inc.	HCP	REIT	1.6%	1.5%	5.1%	36.79	$13.42	$13.33	99.3%
Boston Properties Inc.	BXP	REIT	1.5%	1.5%	2.3%	86.10	$12.06	$11.86	98.3%
Host Hotels & Resorts Inc.	HST	REIT	1.4%	1.5%	0.2%	17.87	$11.90	$11.50	96.6%
Starwood Hotels & Resorts Worldwide Inc.	HOT	REOC	0.0%	0.0%	0.5%	60.78	$11.59	$10.96	94.6%
Weyerhaeuser Co.	WY	REIT	0.0%	0.0%	1.1%	18.93	$10.15	$9.88	97.4%

AvalonBay Communities, Inc.	AVB	REIT	1.2%	1.2%	3.2%	112.55	$9.60	$9.38	97.7%
Ventas, Inc. (A)	VTR	REIT	1.0%	1.0%	4.1%	52.48	$8.24	$8.17	99.1%
ProLogis (A)	PLD	REIT	1.0%	1.0%	3.1%	14.44	$8.22	$8.19	99.7%
Kimco Realty Corp.	KIM	REIT	0.9%	0.3%	4.0%	18.04	$7.32	$7.05	96.3%
CB Richard Ellis Group Inc. (Cl A)	CBG	REOC	0.0%	0.0%	0.0%	20.48	$6.61	$6.51	98.4%
Plum Creek Timber Company Inc.	PCL	REIT	0.0%	0.0%	4.5%	37.45	$6.05	$6.03	99.6%
AMB Property Corp. (A)	AMB	REIT	0.6%	0.7%	3.5%	31.71	$5.34	$5.21	97.6%
Nationwide Health Properties (A)	NHP	REIT	0.6%	0.6%	5.2%	36.38	$4.59	$4.55	99.0%
Rayonier Inc. REIT	RYN	REIT	0.0%	0.0%	4.1%	52.52	$4.23	$4.18	98.7%
Forest City Enterprises Inc. (Cl A)	FCE/A	REOC	0.3%	0.3%	0.0%	16.69	$2.27	$2.03	89.6%
Forest City Enterprises Inc. (Cl B)	FCE/B	REOC	0.0%	0.0%	0.0%	16.62	$0.35	$0.04	12.5%
Total Country	**145**		**39.6%**	**40.7%**	**3.5%**		**$418.72**	**$394.47**	**94.2%**
Total Majors	**14**		**20.0%**	**19.6%**	**2.6%**		**$228.01**	**$215.24**	**94.4%**
Asia									
Australia (AUD)									
Westfield Group Australia	WDC AU	REIT	2.5%	2.9%	6.7%	9.58	$22.67	$20.91	92.2%
Stockland Australia	SGP AU	REIT	1.1%	1.1%	6.1%	3.60	$8.79	$8.76	99.7%
Westfield Retail Trust	WRT AU	REIT	0.9%	0.8%	0.0%	2.57	$8.05	$8.05	100.0%
GPT Group	GPT AU	REIT	0.6%	0.7%	5.4%	2.94	$5.59	$5.11	91.4%
Lend Lease Group	LLC AU	REOC	0.5%	0.0%	3.7%	8.63	$5.00	$4.70	93.9%
Total Country	**35**		**9.2%**	**8.6%**	**5.6%**		**$86.02**	**$77.96**	**90.6%**
Total Majors	**5**		**5.6%**	**5.4%**	**4.4%**		**$50.11**	**$47.53**	**94.8%**

(Continued)

				As of:	12/31/2010				
Security	Ticker	REIT/	Percent of Total		Div[1]	Crnt	Equity Mkt[2]	Equity Mkt	Free
Name	Symbol	REOC	S&P Dev Weight	EPRA Weight	Yield	Price (Local)	Value (USD) Bil.	Float (USD) Bil.	Float %
China (HKD)									
Renhe Commercial Holdings Co. Ltd.	1387 HK	REOC	0.0%	0.0%	7.7%	1.36	$3.85	$1.58	41.1%
Franshion Properties (China) Ltd.	817 HK	REOC	0.0%	0.0%	1.1%	2.34	$2.76	$1.02	37.1%
United Energy Group Ltd.	467 HK	REOC	0.0%	0.0%	0.0%	1.55	$2.55	$0.75	29.3%
Yuexiu Property Co. Ltd.	123 HK	REOC	0.0%	0.0%	0.0%	2.08	$2.48	$1.28	51.7%
Home Inns & Hotels Management Inc. ADS	HMIN US	REOC	0.0%	0.0%	0.0%	318.41	$1.63	$1.63	100.0%
China Vanke Co Ltd B HKD	200002 CH	REOC	0.0%	0.0%	0.8%	9.60	$1.62	$1.62	100.0%
Total Country	**16**		**0.0%**	**0.0%**	**1.6%**		**$19.26**	**$11.34**	**58.9%**
Total Majors	**6**		**0.0%**	**0.0%**	**1.6%**		**$14.89**	**$7.88**	**53.0%**
Hong Kong (HKD)									
Sun Hung Kai Properties Ltd.	16 HK	REOC	3.0%	4.0%	2.1%	129.10	$42.68	$24.79	58.1%
Cheung Kong (Holdings) Ltd.	1 HK	REOC	2.5%	0.0%	2.3%	119.90	$35.72	$20.51	57.4%
Wharf (Holdings) Ltd.	4 HK	REOC	0.0%	1.3%	1.8%	59.80	$21.18	$10.59	50.0%
Hang Lung Properties Ltd.	101 HK	REOC	1.2%	1.3%	2.0%	36.35	$20.89	$10.50	50.2%
Hongkong Land Holdings Ltd.	HKL SP	REOC	1.0%	1.5%	2.5%	56.13	$16.24	$8.09	49.8%

China Overseas Land & Investment Ltd.	688 HK	REOC	0.0%	0.9%	1.6%	14.38	$15.12	$7.05	46.6%
Swire Pacific Ltd.	19 HK	REOC	0.0%	0.0%	2.5%	127.80	$14.89	$11.61	78.0%
Henderson Land Development Co. Ltd.	12 HK	REOC	0.8%	0.9%	1.5%	53.00	$14.84	$6.67	45.0%
Wynn Macau Ltd.	1128 HK	REOC	0.0%	0.0%	0.0%	17.40	$11.61	$3.22	27.7%
Shangri-La Asia Ltd.	69 HK	REOC	0.0%	0.0%	0.8%	21.10	$7.84	$3.50	44.6%
Evergrande Real Estate Group Ltd.	3333 HK	REOC	0.0%	0.0%	0.2%	3.78	$7.29	$2.36	32.4%
Longfor Properties Co. Ltd.	960 HK	REOC	0.0%	0.0%	0.9%	10.82	$7.18	$1.66	23.1%
Link Real Estate Investment Trust	823 HK	REIT	0.8%	0.9%	4.0%	24.15	$6.89	$6.89	100.0%
Total Country	**96**		**13.5%**	**15.4%**	**2.3%**		**$376.98**	**$170.09**	**45.1%**
Total Majors	**13**		**9.3%**	**10.9%**	**1.7%**		**$222.37**	**$117.43**	**52.8%**
India (INR)									
DLF Ltd.	DLFU IN	REOC	0.0%	0.0%	0.4%	291.95	$11.08	$2.39	21.5%
Unitech Ltd.	UT IN	REOC	0.0%	0.0%	0.1%	66.20	$3.72	$1.73	46.4%
Housing Development & Infrastructure Ltd.	HDIL IN	REOC	0.0%	0.0%	0.0%	194.25	$1.80	$1.00	55.6%
Indian Hotels Co. Ltd.	IH IN	REOC	0.0%	0.0%	1.0%	96.60	$1.56	$1.09	69.9%
Indiabulls Real Estate Ltd.	IBREL IN	REOC	0.0%	0.0%	0.0%	139.55	$1.25	$0.93	74.4%
Total Country	**20**		**0.0%**	**0.0%**	**0.7%**		**$28.55**	**$9.48**	**33.2%**
Total Majors	**5**		**0.0%**	**0.0%**	**0.3%**		**$19.43**	**$7.14**	**36.8%**

(Continued)

	As of:			12/31/2010						
				Percent of Total		Div[1]	Crnt	Equity Mkt[2]	Equity Mkt	Free
Security	Ticker	REIT/	S&P Dev	EPRA				Value (USD)	Float (USD)	
Name	Symbol	REOC	Weight	Weight	Yield	Price (Local)	Bil.	Bil.	Float %
Indonesia (IDR)										
Bumi Serpong Damai	BSDE IJ	REOC	0.0%	0.0%	0.7%	900.00	$1.75	$0.63	35.9%
Lippo Karawaci	LPKR IJ	REOC	0.0%	0.0%	0.0%	680.00	$1.63	$1.40	85.7%
Total Country	**13**		**0.0%**	**0.0%**	**0.3%**		**$9.33**	**$4.73**	**50.7%**
Total Majors	**2**		**0.0%**	**0.0%**	**0.3%**		**$3.38**	**$2.03**	**59.9%**
Japan (JPY)										
Mitsubishi Estate Co. Ltd.	8802 JP	REOC	2.8%	2.4%	0.8%	1506.00	$25.82	$19.88	77.0%
Mitsui Fudosan Co. Ltd.	8801 JP	REOC	2.0%	2.2%	1.4%	1619.00	$17.59	$15.21	86.5%
Sumitomo Realty & Development Co. Ltd.	8830 JP	REOC	1.2%	1.4%	1.0%	1939.00	$11.38	$8.24	72.4%
Daiwa House Industry Co. Ltd.	1925 JP	REOC	0.8%	0.0%	1.7%	998.00	$7.38	$5.81	78.8%
Daito Trust Construction Co. Ltd.	1878 JP	REOC	0.6%	0.0%	3.5%	5560.00	$8.06	$5.09	63.2%
Nippon Building Fund Inc.	8951 JP	REIT	0.6%	0.7%	3.9%	833000.00	$5.57	$4.97	89.3%
Japan Real Estate Investment Corp.	8952 JP	REIT	0.6%	0.6%	3.8%	842000.00	$5.08	$4.75	93.4%
Japan Retail Fund Investment Corp.	8953 JP	REIT	0.4%	0.4%	4.6%	155700.00	$2.97	$2.75	92.7%

Advance Residence Investment Corp.	3269 JP	REIT	0.3%	0.0%	4.5%	181800.00	$2.20	$2.05	93.2%
Aeon Mall Co. Ltd.	8905 JP	REOC	0.2%	0.3%	0.9%	2180.00	$4.87	$2.04	41.8%
Total Country	**64**		**13.5%**	**10.4%**	**3.3%**		**$144.78**	**$106.96**	**73.9%**
Total Majors	**10**		**9.5%**	**8.1%**	**2.6%**		**$90.91**	**$70.78**	**77.9%**
Korea (KRW)									
Lotte Shopping Co. Ltd.	023530 KS	REOC	0.0%	0.0%	0.3%	473000.00	$12.10	$3.65	30.1%
Hyundai Development Co.	012630 KS	REOC	0.0%	0.0%	1.2%	34000.00	$2.26	$1.70	75.2%
Total Country	**3**		**0.0%**	**0.0%**	**0.5%**		**$14.53**	**$5.37**	**37.0%**
Total Majors			**0.0%**	**0.0%**	**0.7%**		**$14.36**	**$5.34**	**37.2%**
Malaysia (MYR)									
UEM Land Holdings Bhd	ULHB MK	REOC	0.0%	0.0%	0.0%	2.44	$2.88	$2.85	98.8%
SP Setia Bhd	SPSB MK	REOC	0.0%	0.0%	2.0%	5.95	$1.96	$1.53	77.8%
Boustead Holdings Bhd	BOUS MK	REOC	0.0%	0.0%	6.9%	5.38	$1.64	$1.51	92.1%
Total Country	**26**		**0.0%**	**0.0%**	**2.9%**		**$17.22**	**$10.50**	**61.0%**
Total Majors	**3**		**0.0%**	**0.0%**	**3.0%**		**$6.48**	**$5.88**	**90.7%**
New Zealand (NZD)									
Kiwi Income Property Trust	KIP NZ	REIT	0.1%	0.1%	7.0%	1.00	$0.76	$0.72	94.7%
Goodman Property Trust	GMT NZ	REIT	0.1%	0.0%	8.1%	0.95	$0.68	$0.56	82.9%
AMP NZ Office Ltd.	ANO NZ	REOC	0.1%	0.0%	7.8%	0.78	$0.61	$0.61	100.0%

(Continued)

Security Name	Ticker Symbol	REIT/ REOC	Percent of Total S&P Dev Weight	EPRA Weight	Div [1] Yield	Crnt Price (Local)	Equity Mkt [2] Value (USD) Bil.	Equity Mkt Float (USD) Bil.	Free Float %
Argosy Property Trust	ARG NZ	REIT	0.0%	0.0%	7.9%	0.73	$0.31	$0.30	95.5%
Property for Industry Ltd.	PFI NZ	REIT	0.0%	0.0%	5.4%	1.14	$0.19	$0.18	94.6%
Total Country	**5**		**0.3%**	**0.1%**	**7.2%**		**$2.55**	**$2.37**	**92.9%**
Total Majors	**5**		**0.3%**	**0.1%**	**7.2%**		**$2.55**	**$2.37**	**92.9%**
Philippines (PHP)									
SM Investments Corp.	SM PM	REOC	0.0%	0.0%	1.5%	543.00	$7.59	$2.09	27.6%
Ayala Land Inc.	ALI PM	REOC	0.0%	0.0%	1.5%	16.46	$4.89	$2.25	45.9%
SM Prime Holdings Inc.	SMPH PM	REOC	0.0%	0.0%	3.1%	11.38	$3.61	$1.49	41.3%
Metro Pacific Investments Corp.	MPI PM	REOC	0.0%	0.0%	0.0%	3.89	$1.79	$0.79	44.3%
SM Development Corp.	SMDC PM	REOC	0.0%	0.0%	0.6%	9.00	$1.51	$0.57	37.5%
Total Country	**12**		**0.0%**	**0.0%**	**1.3%**		**$24.78**	**$8.77**	**35.4%**
Total Majors	**5**		**0.0%**	**0.0%**	**1.3%**		**$19.38**	**$7.19**	**37.1%**
Singapore (SGD)									
CapitaLand Ltd.	CAPL SP	REOC	1.2%	1.2%	2.8%	3.71	$12.35	$12.29	99.5%
City Developments Ltd.	CIT SP	REOC	0.7%	0.8%	0.6%	12.56	$8.92	$4.74	53.2%

As of: 12/31/2010

Global Logistic Properties Ltd.	GLP SP	REOC	0.4%	0.4%	0.0%	2.16	$7.60	$4.00	52.6%
CapitaMall Trust	CT SP	REIT	0.4%	0.5%	4.8%	1.95	$4.85	$2.76	56.9%
Keppel Land Ltd.	KPLD SP	REOC	0.3%	0.3%	1.7%	4.80	$5.43	$2.55	47.0%
Total Country	**50**		**5.8%**	**5.1%**	**3.5%**		**$94.12**	**$53.52**	**56.9%**
Total Majors	**5**		**3.1%**	**3.2%**	**2.0%**		**$39.15**	**$26.33**	**67.3%**
Taiwan (TWD)									
Farglory Land Development Co. Ltd.	5522 TT	REOC	0.0%	0.0%	7.7%	78.50	$1.90	$0.69	36.4%
Highwealth Construction Corp.	2542 TT	REOC	0.0%	0.0%	7.7%	65.40	$1.59	$1.39	87.4%
Ruentex Development Co. Ltd.	9945 TT	REOC	0.0%	0.0%	1.9%	51.30	$1.34	$0.95	71.4%
Huang Hsiang Construction Corp.	2545 TT	REOC	0.0%	0.0%	2.6%	97.40	$1.21	$0.69	56.7%
Cathay Real Estate Development Co. Ltd.	2501 TT	REOC	0.0%	0.0%	2.7%	18.40	$1.05	$0.58	55.0%
Total Country	**24**		**0.0%**	**0.0%**	**3.3%**		**$16.40**	**$11.44**	**69.8%**
Total Majors	**5**		**0.0%**	**0.0%**	**4.5%**		**$7.08**	**$4.30**	**60.6%**
Thailand (THB)									
Land & Houses PCL	LH TB	REOC	0.0%	0.0%	5.1%	6.45	$2.15	$1.45	67.6%
Central Pattana PCL	CPN TB	REOC	0.0%	0.0%	1.0%	26.75	$1.93	$0.92	47.6%
Cent Pattana Pub Thb1(Alien)	CPN/F TB	REOC	0.0%	0.0%	2.8%	21.00	$1.52	$1.52	100.0%
Pruksa Real Estate PCL	PS TB	REOC	0.0%	0.0%	3.0%	18.50	$1.35	$0.32	23.5%
MBK PCL	MBK TB	REOC	0.0%	0.0%	4.6%	104.00	$0.65	$0.38	57.7%

(Continued)

Security Name	Ticker Symbol	REIT/ REOC	S&P Dev Weight	EPRA Weight	Div [1] Yield	Crnt Price (Local)	Equity Mkt [2] Value (USD) Bil.	Equity Mkt Float (USD) Bil.	Free Float %
			Percent of Total						
CPN Retail Growth Leasehold Property Fund	CPNRF TB	REOC	0.0%	0.0%	7.6%	11.90	$0.65	$0.43	66.5%
Total Country	**17**		**0.0%**	**0.0%**	**4.5%**		**$13.11**	**$8.31**	**63.4%**
Total Majors	**6**		**0.0%**	**0.0%**	**4.0%**		**$8.25**	**$5.01**	**60.8%**
Vietnam (VND)									
Vincom JSC	VIC VN	REOC	0.0%	0.0%	0.0%	97500.00	$1.84	$0.76	41.0%
Tan Tao Investment-Industry Corp.	ITA VN	REOC	0.0%	0.0%	0.0%	16600.00	$0.29	$0.27	93.0%
Total Countries	**2**		**0.0%**	**0.0%**	**0.0%**		**$2.13**	**$1.03**	**48.4%**
Total Majors	**2**		**0.0%**	**0.0%**	**0.0%**		**$2.13**	**$1.03**	**48.1%**
Europe									
Austria (EUR)									
Immofinanz AG	IIA AV	REOC	0.5%	0.0%	0.0%	3.19	$4.47	$3.89	87.1%
CA Immobilien Anlagen AG	CAI AV	REOC	0.2%	0.2%	0.0%	11.91	$1.40	$1.26	90.1%
Atrium European Real Estate Ltd.	ATRS AV	REOC	0.1%	0.0%	2.7%	4.37	$2.18	$1.57	71.8%
conwert Immobilien Invest AG	CWI AV	REOC	0.1%	0.1%	2.3%	10.76	$1.23	$0.93	75.4%

Atrium European Real Estate Ltd.	ATRS NA	REOC	0.0%	0.0%	0.0%	2.8%	4.30	$2.15	$2.15	100.0%
CA Immo International AG	CAII AV	REOC	0.0%	0.0%	0.0%	0.0%	5.60	$0.33	$0.33	100.0%
Total Country	**10**		**1.0%**	**0.3%**		**1.4%**		**$12.99**	**$10.82**	**83.3%**
Total Majors	**6**		**0.9%**	**0.3%**		**1.3%**		**$11.76**	**$10.13**	**86.1%**
Belgium (EUR)										
Cofinimmo S.A.	COFB BB	REIT	0.2%	0.2%		6.7%	97.41	$1.79	$1.68	93.9%
Befimmo S.C.A.	BEFB BB	REIT	0.1%	0.2%		6.4%	61.30	$1.38	$1.08	78.4%
Warehouses de Pauw S.C.A.	WDP BB	REIT	0.1%	0.1%		8.0%	36.65	$0.62	$0.43	69.0%
Intervest Offices S.A.	INTO BB	REIT	0.0%	0.0%		7.7%	23.49	$0.44	$0.20	45.3%
Wereldhave Belgium C.V.A. S.C.A.	WEHB BB	REIT	0.0%	0.0%		4.8%	68.50	$0.49	$0.15	30.7%
Total Country	**17**		**0.4%**	**0.5%**		**5.4%**		**$7.81**	**$5.35**	**68.5%**
Total Majors	**5**		**0.4%**	**0.5%**		**6.7%**		**$4.71**	**$3.53**	**75.0%**
Denmark (DKK)										
TK Development A/S	TKDV DC	REOC	0.0%	0.0%		0.0%	23.90	$0.18	$0.15	85.2%
Jeudan A/S	JDAN DC	REOC	0.0%	0.0%		2.7%	408.00	$0.78	$0.26	33.2%
Total Country	**3**		**0.0%**	**0.0%**		**0.9%**		**$1.11**	**$0.48**	**43.2%**
Total Majors	**2**		**0.0%**	**0.0%**		**1.3%**		**$0.96**	**$0.41**	**43.0%**
Finland (EUR)										
Sponda Oyj	SDA1V FH	REOC	0.1%	0.2%		3.3%	3.88	$1.44	$1.21	83.9%

(Continued)

Security Name	Ticker Symbol	REIT/ REOC	S&P Dev Weight	EPRA Weight	Div [1] Yield	Crnt Price (Local)	Equity Mkt [2] Value (USD) Bil.	Equity Mkt Float (USD) Bil.	Free Float %
			Percent of Total						
Citycon Oyj	CTY1S FH	REOC	0.1%	0.1%	4.5%	3.08	$1.01	$0.57	56.0%
Total Country	**3**		**0.2%**	**0.3%**	**3.9%**		**$2.80**	**$2.07**	**73.9%**
Total Majors	**2**		**0.2%**	**0.3%**	**3.9%**		**$2.46**	**$1.78**	**72.4%**
France (EUR)									
Unibail-Rodamco S.A.	UL FP	REIT	2.2%	2.3%	5.4%	148.00	$18.21	$17.80	97.8%
Klepierre S.A.	LI FP	REIT	0.4%	0.4%	4.6%	27.00	$6.87	$3.44	50.0%
Fonciere des Regions S.A.	FDR FP	REIT	0.4%	0.3%	6.6%	72.40	$5.21	$3.40	65.3%
Gecina	GFC FP	REIT	0.3%	0.3%	5.3%	82.31	$6.91	$2.70	39.0%
ICADE S.A.	ICAD FP	REIT	0.3%	0.3%	9.5%	76.35	$5.30	$5.25	99.1%
Nexity S.A.	NXI FP	REOC	0.0%	0.0%	4.6%	34.16	$2.37	$1.08	45.7%
Total Country	**31**		**4.0%**	**4.0%**	**5.5%**		**$75.95**	**$48.41**	**63.7%**
Total Majors	**6**		**3.6%**	**3.5%**	**6.0%**		**$44.86**	**$33.67**	**75.0%**
Germany (EUR)									
Deutsche Euroshop AG	DEQ GR	REOC	0.2%	0.3%	3.8%	28.98	$2.01	$1.59	79.2%
Deutsche Wohnen AG BR	DWNI GR	REOC	0.1%	0.1%	1.9%	10.50	$1.15	$1.15	100.0%

As of: 12/31/2010

Gagfah S.A.	GFJ GR	REOC	0.1%	0.1%	7.4%	6.71	$2.04	$0.81	40.0%
IVG Immobilien AG	IVG GR	REOC	0.1%	0.0%	0.0%	6.45	$1.09	$0.65	59.8%
alstria office REIT-AG	AOX GR	REIT	0.0%	0.1%	4.9%	10.50	$0.87	$0.34	38.9%
GBW AG	GWB GR	REOC	0.0%	0.0%	0.5%	13.80	$1.01	$0.08	8.0%
Total Country	**15**		**0.7%**	**0.7%**	**2.1%**		**$10.78**	**$6.03**	**55.9%**
Total Majors	**4**		**0.5%**	**0.6%**	**3.1%**		**$8.16**	**$4.62**	**56.6%**
Greece (EUR)									
Eurobank Properties Real Estate Investment Co.	EUPRO GA	REIT	0.0%	0.0%	8.0%	5.95	$0.49	$0.11	23.5%
Total Country	**3**		**0.0%**	**0.0%**	**65.2%**		**$0.79**	**$0.24**	**30.4%**
Total Majors	**1**		**0.0%**	**0.0%**	**8.0%**		**$0.49**	**$0.11**	**23.5%**
Italy (EUR)									
Beni Stabili S.p.A.	BNS IM	REIT	0.1%	0.1%	3.2%	0.63	$1.63	$0.76	46.9%
Prelios S.p.A.	PRS IM	REOC	0.0%	0.0%	490.1%	0.45	$0.50	$0.37	74.4%
Total Country	**5**		**0.2%**	**0.1%**	**99.3%**		**$3.00**	**$1.48**	**49.3%**
Total Majors	**2**		**0.1%**	**0.1%**	**####**		**$2.13**	**$1.14**	**53.4%**
Netherlands (EUR)									
Corio N.V. REIT	CORA NA	REIT	0.7%	0.7%	5.5%	48.02	$5.86	$5.80	98.9%
Wereldhave N.V.	WHA NA	REIT	0.3%	0.3%	6.4%	73.06	$2.10	$2.10	100.0%

(Continued)

405

				12/31/2010					
	As of:								
Security	Ticker	REIT/	Percent of Total		Div [1]	Crnt	Equity Mkt [2]	Equity Mkt	Free
Name	Symbol	REOC	S&P Dev Weight	EPRA Weight	Yield	Price (Local)	Value (USD) Bil.	Float (USD) Bil.	Float %
Eurocommercial N.V.	ECMPA NA	REIT	0.2%	0.2%	5.3%	34.45	$1.89	$1.84	97.4%
Vastned Retail N.V.	VASTN NA	REIT	0.2%	0.2%	7.1%	51.98	$1.29	$1.29	100.0%
ProLogis European Properties	PEPR NA	REOC	0.1%	0.1%	0.0%	4.81	$1.23	$1.23	100.0%
Total Country	**11**		**1.6%**	**1.7%**	**5.0%**		**$15.90**	**$15.22**	**95.7%**
Total Majors	**5**		**1.4%**	**1.5%**	**4.9%**		**$12.37**	**$12.26**	**99.1%**
Norway (NOK)									
Norwegian Property ASA	NPRO NO	REOC	0.1%	0.1%	0.0%	10.35	$0.89	$0.70	78.6%
Total Country	**3**		**0.1%**	**0.1%**	**0.3%**		**$2.86**	**$1.23**	**43.0%**
Total Majors	**1**		**0.1%**	**0.1%**	**0.0%**		**$0.89**	**$0.70**	**78.6%**
Poland (PLN)									
Globe Trade Centre S.A.	GTC PW	REOC	0.0%	0.0%	0.0%	24.50	$1.82	$1.04	56.9%
Total Country	**6**		**0.0%**	**0.0%**	**0.3%**		**$3.49**	**$1.87**	**53.6%**
Total Majors	**1**		**0.0%**	**0.0%**	**0.0%**		**$1.82**	**$1.04**	**56.9%**

Russia (RUD)

LSR Group	LSRG LI	REOC	0.0%	0.0%	0.0%	0.00	$4.74	$4.74	100.0%
LSR Group	LSRG RU	REOC	0.0%	0.0%	0.0%	0.00	$3.40	$3.40	100.0%
Gruppa Kompany PIK OAO GDR (Reg S Sh)	PIK LI	REOC	0.0%	0.0%	0.0%	0.00	$2.00	$2.00	100.0%
Gruppa Kompany PIK OAO Reg S Sh	PIKK RU	REOC	0.0%	0.0%	0.0%	0.00	$1.87	$1.87	100.0%
Total Country	**7**		**0.0%**	**0.0%**	**0.0%**		**$13.46**	**$13.42**	**99.7%**
Total Majors	**4**		**0.0%**	**0.0%**	**0.0%**		**$12.02**	**$12.02**	**100.0%**

Spain (EUR)

Inmobiliaria Colonial S.A.	COL SM	REOC	0.1%	0.0%	0.0%	0.06	$1.67	$0.15	8.8%
Realia Business S.A.	RLIA SM	REOC	0.0%	0.0%	0.0%	1.56	$0.58	$0.14	24.4%
Actividades de Construccion y Servicios S.A.	ACS SM	REOC	0.0%	0.0%	4.7%	35.08	$14.81	$6.07	41.0%
Ferrovial S.A.	FER SM	REOC	0.0%	0.0%	4.5%	7.44	$7.32	$3.65	49.9%
Acciona S.A.	ANA SM	REOC	0.0%	0.0%	4.6%	53.00	$4.52	$1.61	35.6%
Sacyr-Vallehermoso S.A.	SYV SM	REOC	0.0%	0.0%	0.0%	4.75	$2.51	$0.72	28.7%
Total Country	**11**		**0.1%**	**0.0%**	**5.9%**		**$34.42**	**$12.77**	**37.1%**
Total Majors	**6**		**0.1%**	**0.0%**	**2.3%**		**$31.40**	**$12.34**	**39.3%**

Sweden (SEK)

Castellum AB	CAST SS	REOC	0.3%	0.3%	4.2%	91.55	$2.34	$2.07	88.5%
Fabege AB	FABG SS	REOC	0.2%	0.2%	4.0%	78.55	$1.93	$1.61	83.5%

(Continued)

Security Name	Ticker Symbol	REIT/ REOC	Percent of Total S&P Dev Weight	EPRA Weight	Div [1] Yield	Crnt Price (Local)	Equity Mkt [2] Value (USD) Bil.	Equity Mkt Float (USD) Bil.	Free Float %
Hufvudstaden AB	HUFVA SS	REOC	0.2%	0.2%	2.7%	78.55	$2.37	$1.27	53.5%
Kungsleden AB	KLED SS	REOC	0.2%	0.2%	4.1%	61.50	$1.25	$1.22	97.7%
Wallenstam AB	WALLB SS	REOC	0.1%	0.0%	1.8%	177.00	$1.40	$0.76	54.3%
JM AB	JM SS	REOC	0.0%	0.0%	1.6%	157.50	$1.95	$1.94	99.1%
Total Country	**15**		**1.2%**	**1.1%**	**2.7%**		**$17.25**	**$11.61**	**67.3%**
Total Majors	**6**		**0.9%**	**0.9%**	**3.1%**		**$11.25**	**$8.87**	**78.9%**
Switzerland (CHF)									
Swiss Prime Site AG	SPSN SW	REOC	0.4%	0.4%	5.0%	69.75	$4.07	$3.43	84.3%
PSP Swiss Property AG	PSPN SW	REOC	0.3%	0.5%	3.6%	75.00	$3.69	$2.78	75.3%
Mobimo Holding AG	MOBN SW	REOC	0.1%	0.0%	4.5%	199.70	$1.10	$1.01	92.5%
Allreal Holding AG	ALLN SW	REOC	0.1%	0.1%	3.7%	136.20	$2.00	$1.27	63.4%
Total Country	**7**		**1.1%**	**1.0%**	**3.8%**		**$12.06**	**$9.07**	**75.2%**
Total Majors	**4**		**1.0%**	**1.0%**	**4.2%**		**$10.85**	**$8.49**	**78.2%**

As of: 12/31/2010

United Kingdom (GBP)

Land Securities Group PLC	LAND LN	REIT	1.0%	1.0%	4.2%	6.74	$8.09	$7.66	94.7%
British Land Co. PLC	BLND LN	REIT	0.9%	0.9%	5.0%	5.25	$7.27	$7.08	97.5%
Hammerson PLC	HMSO LN	REIT	0.6%	0.6%	3.9%	4.17	$4.62	$4.46	96.6%
Capital Shopping Centres Group PLC	CSCG LN	REIT	0.4%	0.6%	3.9%	4.18	$4.52	$2.61	57.8%
Segro PLC	SGRO LN	REIT	0.4%	0.4%	5.2%	2.86	$3.33	$3.29	98.9%
Derwent London PLC	DLN LN	REIT	0.2%	0.3%	1.9%	15.61	$2.47	$2.03	82.1%
F&C Commercial Property Trust Ltd.	FCPT LN	REOC	0.0%	0.1%	5.6%	1.06	$1.13	$0.74	65.8%
UK Commercial Property Trust Ltd.	UKCM LN	REIT	0.0%	0.1%	4.7%	0.82	$1.54	$1.54	100.0%
Songbird Estates PLC	SBD LN	REOC	0.0%	0.0%	0.0%	1.41	$1.69	$1.33	78.4%
Total Country	**51**		**4.9%**	**5.5%**	**2.9%**		**$53.69**	**$46.28**	**86.2%**
Total Majors	**9**		**3.5%**	**4.0%**	**3.8%**		**$34.65**	**$30.74**	**88.7%**

Middle East/Africa

Israel (ILS)

Azrieli Group Ltd.	AZRG IT	REOC	0.1%	0.1%	0.0%	100.00	$3.42	$0.86	25.0%
Gazit-Globe Ltd.	GLOB IT	REOC	0.1%	0.0%	4.0%	45.40	$1.98	$0.81	41.0%
Total Country	**14**		**0.5%**	**0.1%**	**2.4%**		**$11.83**	**$4.27**	**36.1%**
Total Majors	**2**		**0.2%**	**0.1%**	**2.0%**		**$5.40**	**$1.67**	**30.9%**

Other

South Africa (ZAR)

Growthpoint Properties Ltd.	GRT SJ	REOC	0.0%	0.0%	6.6%	18.33	$4.35	$4.07	93.5%

(Continued)

	As of:			12/31/2010					
			Percent of Total						
Security	Ticker	REIT/	S&P Dev	EPRA	Div[1]	Crnt	Equity Mkt[2]	Equity Mkt	Free
Name	Symbol	REOC	Weight	Weight	Yield	Price (Local)	Value (USD) Bil.	Float (USD) Bil.	Float %
Redefine Properties Ltd.	RDF SJ	REOC	0.0%	0.0%	8.5%	7.99	$3.25	$2.03	62.3%
Hyprop Investments Ltd.	HYP SJ	REOC	0.0%	0.0%	6.0%	57.00	$1.43	$1.35	94.7%
Total Country	**14**		**0.0%**	**0.0%**	**7.4%**		**$18.49**	**$14.25**	**77.1%**
Total Majors	**3**		**0.0%**	**0.0%**	**7.0%**		**$9.03**	**$7.45**	**82.5%**
Turkey (TRY)									
Akmerkez Gayrimenkul Yatirim Ortakligi A.S.	AKMGY TI	REIT	0.0%	0.0%	2.7%	82.50	$0.73	$0.56	76.1%
Total Countries	**3**		**0.0%**	**0.0%**	**1.8%**		**$1.92**	**$1.19**	**62.0%**
Total Majors	**1**		**0.0%**	**0.0%**	**2.7%**		**$0.73**	**$0.56**	**76.1%**
United Arab Emirates (AED)									
Al Dar Properties Co.	ALDAR UH	REOC	0.0%	0.0%	2.2%	2.28	$1.60	$1.20	75.0%
Sorouh Real Estate PJSC	SOROUH UH	REOC	0.0%	0.0%	0.0%	1.63	$1.16	$0.94	81.0%
Total Country	**3**		**0.0%**	**0.0%**	**0.7%**		**$3.10**	**$2.30**	**74.2%**

Total Majors	2	0.0%	0.0%	1.1%	$2.77	$2.14	77.5%
Total All Countries	830	100.1%	100.0%	2.72%	$1,732.71	$1,188.34	68.6%
Total All Majors	175	62.1%	62.7%	3.53%	$958.47	$708.15	73.9%

NOTES:
A - Mergers in process: Ventas to acquire Nationwide Health; AMB Property and ProLogis to combine.
B - Dually listed on New York Stock Exchange.
[1] Divided yields are calculated using CBRE Clarion analyst updated dividends when available; or Factset's reported dividend when unavailable.
[2] Security market cap is sourced from Factset and represents a full market cap in USD.

Glossary

The following is a glossary containing some terms used frequently in the worlds of commercial real estate and REITs. Many of these terms are not always used in the same way by all investors; therefore, you will undoubtedly encounter definitions elsewhere that are somewhat different. Another good source of REIT and commercial real estate terminology can be found at NAREIT's web site, specifically, www.reit.com/IndividualInvestors/GlossaryofREITTerms.aspx.

Adjusted funds from operations (AFFO). FFO (see **FFO**), less normalized recurring expenditures that are capitalized by the REIT and amortized, and which are necessary to properly maintain and lease the property (e.g., new carpeting and draperies in apartment units, leasing expenses, and tenant improvement allowances); adjustments are also made to eliminate the straight-lining of rents, which is an accounting convention.

Base year. In a commercial lease, the year used as a reference against which revenues or expenses in subsequent years are measured to determine additional rent charges or the tenant's share of increased operating expenses of the property.

Basis point. One one-hundredth of 1 percent (0.01 percent). Thus, a 30-basis-point increase in the yield of a 10-year bond would result in a yield increase from, say, 3.35 percent to 3.65 percent.

Beta. The extent to which a stock's price moves with an index of stocks, such as the S&P 500.

Bond proxies. A slang term used to refer to the shares of a REIT that provide an above-average dividend yield to its shareholders but where FFO/AFFO and dividend growth rates are expected to be quite low, for example, 1 to 3 percent annually.

Book value (per share).   The dollar amount of a company's assets less its liabilities, as reflected on its balance sheet pursuant to GAAP (see **GAAP**), divided by the common shares outstanding. Book value will reflect all prior depreciation and amortization, which are expensed for accounting purposes and may have little relationship to a company's net asset value when valued at current market prices or prevailing cap rates. See also **Net asset value.**

Cap rate.   The initial return expected by the buyer of a property, expressed as a percentage of an all-cash purchase price. It is normally determined by dividing the property's expected net operating income (before depreciation expense, interest expense, and income taxes), or NOI, during the next 12 months by the purchase price. Cap rates for specific properties will vary widely at any time and from time to time but, generally speaking, high cap rates indicate greater perceived risk or, perhaps, lower-than-average NOI growth prospects. When calculating the expected NOI from a property, most buyers and investors exclude normal but often capitalized expenses such as new carpeting or draperies (e.g., in apartment units), tenant improvement expenditures, or leasing commissions; the cap rate so calculated is often referred to as a "nominal" cap rate. An "effective" or "economic" cap rate includes the effects of normalized capital expenditures.

Cash flow.   With reference to a property (or group of properties), the owner's rental revenues from the property minus all property operating expenses, including property management expenses, utility costs and property taxes. The term ignores depreciation and amortization expenses and income taxes, as well as interest on loans obtained to finance the property. Sometimes used interchangeably with net operating income or EBITDA.

Commercial mortgage-backed securities (CMBS).   An acronym for commercial mortgage-backed securities, these are bonds that are backed by a number of mortgages on commercial real estate properties. They are usually structured as real estate mortgage investment conduits (REMICs) so that the interest payments are not taxed at the entity (or trust) level and are passed through to the investors. CMBS securities are often sliced and diced into various "tranches" of different levels of seniority and risk.

Correlation. The extent to which the price of one type of investment, e.g., REIT stocks, moves with those of other investments. A perfect correlation of 1.0 suggests that the price movement can be exactly predicted by the price movement of the investment to which it is compared. A correlation of zero suggests that there is no correlation at all, while a correlation of −1.0 indicates that the investment will move in price exactly the opposite of its compared investment.

Cost of capital. The cost to a company, such as a REIT, of raising capital in the form of equity (common or preferred stock) or debt. The cost of *equity* capital should take into account the dilution of the interests of the existing equity holders in the company. The cost of *debt* capital is merely the interest expense on the debt incurred.

Debt capital. The amount of debt (as opposed to equity) that a REIT carries on its balance sheet. This would include the combination of fixed-rate or variable-rate debt, secured or unsecured debt or debentures issued to public or private investors, borrowings under a bank credit line, and any other type of indebtedness. It does not include equity capital, such as common or preferred stock.

Discounting. When used in financial markets, the process by which expected future developments and events that will affect an investment are anticipated and taken into account by the price at which the investment currently trades in the market.

DownREIT. A DownREIT is structured much like an UPREIT (see **UPREIT**), but is usually formed *after* the REIT has become a public company and generally does not include the REIT's directors and/ or executive officers among the partners in the REIT-controlled partnership.

Earnings before interest, taxes, depreciation, and amortization (EBITDA). Earnings before interest, taxes, depreciation and amortization. See **Cash flow.**

Equity capital. Permanent capital that has been raised through the sale and issuance of stock that has no right to repayment or redemption by the issuing company. This normally takes the form of common stock. Preferred stock is also generally regarded as equity capital, although occasionally a few preferred stocks are issued with a company obligation to redeem such shares at certain times or under certain conditions. Most REIT preferreds may, but are not required to be, redeemed by the issuing company after a period of time, normally five years from issuance.

Equity market cap.   The total value of all issued shares of a public company, such as a REIT, which is determined by multiplying the company's total common shares outstanding by the market price of the shares as of a particular date (see also **Market cap**). Sometimes "equity market cap" includes operating partnership units issued by an UPREIT or DownREIT that are convertible by the holder into common shares, and some investors include the stated (or par) value of outstanding preferred stock.

Equity REIT.   A REIT that owns, or has an equity interest in, real estate (rather than one making loans secured by real estate collateral).

Funds from operations (FFO).   Net income (determined in accordance with GAAP), excluding gains or losses from debt restructuring and sales of property, plus depreciation of real property, and after adjustments for unconsolidated entities, such as partnerships and joint ventures, in which the REIT holds an interest.

Generally accepted accounting principles (GAAP). Principles to which financial statements of public companies must conform.

Gross leasable area (GLA).   A measurement of the total amount of leasable space in a commercial building.

Hurdle rate.   In the investment world, the minimum acceptable return (often expressed as an internal rate of return [see Internal rate of return]) required before making an investment.

Interest coverage ratio.   In REIT world, the ratio of a REIT's operating income (before amortization, depreciation, income taxes and interest expense) to total interest expense for any particular period. This ratio measures the extent to which interest expense on outstanding debt is covered by existing cash flow.

Internal rate of return (IRR).   This concept allows the real estate investor to calculate his or her projected and actual investment returns, including both returns *on* investment and returns *of* investment. It takes into account all cash receipts from the investment (forecasted or actual), balanced against all cash contributions, so that when each receipt and each contribution is discounted to net present value, the sum is equal to zero. For real estate investors, it is usually calculated without regard to debt leverage. The sale of the investment at the end of the holding period, at a price above or below the purchase price, will affect the actual IRR.

Many investors believe that IRR is the best way to measure their return on an investment. It is a longer-term, and more comprehensive, measurement of one's investment return than merely the current income. Green Street Advisors has estimated that commercial real estate near the end of 2010 was priced, in very general terms, to provide the buyer with an estimated IRR of approximately 7.7 percent.

Leverage.   The process by which the owner of a property may expand both the economic benefits and the risks of property ownership by adding borrowed funds to his or her own funds that have been committed to the acquired asset or to the venture.

Market cap.   The total market value of a REIT's (or other company's) outstanding securities and indebtedness. For example, if 20 million shares of a REIT are trading at $20 each, 1 million shares of the REIT's preferred stock are trading at $25 each, and the REIT has $100 million of debt, its market cap would be $525 million ($400 million in common stock, $25 million in preferred stock, and $100 million in indebtedness). See also **Equity market cap.**

Mortgage REIT.   A REIT that owns mortgages secured by real estate collateral. This term also sometimes refers to REITs that lend money in real estate–related transactions though not always secured by real estate mortgages, for example, "mezzanine" loans.

National Association of Real Estate Investment Trusts (NAREIT). The REIT industry's trade association, NAREIT provides substantial data and information about REITs to investors, sponsors conferences and educational forums, and works with Congress on legislation that may affect the REIT industry.

Net asset value (NAV).   The estimated net *current market value* of all of a REIT's assets, including but not limited to its properties, after subtracting all its liabilities and obligations. Some analysts also make other adjustments, for example, marking debt up or down to reflect current interest rates. Such net asset value, which is usually expressed on a per-share basis, must be estimated by analysts and investors, as US REITs don't normally obtain periodic property appraisals, nor are they required to do so by generally accepted accounting principles.

Net income. An accounting term used to measure the profits earned by a business enterprise after all expenses are deducted from revenues. Under GAAP (see **GAAP**), depreciation of real estate owned is treated as an expense of the business.

Net operating income (NOI). Recurring rental and other income from a property, or portfolio of properties, less all operating expenses attributable to that property or portfolio of properties. Operating expenses will include, for example, property management (including repairs and maintenance), insurance, utility and snow removal costs, and real estate taxes. They do *not* include items such as corporate overhead, interest expense, property improvements, capital expenditures, property depreciation expense, or income taxes.

Overage rents. A provision in a retail or other lease that requires the payment of rent in addition to the base rental prescribed in the lease if the tenant's store sales or revenues exceed certain specified levels during the measurement period.

Overbuilding (or "overdevelopment"). A situation in which so much new real estate has been recently completed and offered to tenants in one or more markets that the supply of available space significantly exceeds the demand by renters and users, leading to falling occupancy rates, pressure on rental rates, and/or increasing tenant concessions.

Payout ratio. The ratio of a REIT's annual dividend rate to its FFO or AFFO, on a per share basis. For example, if FFO is $1 per share and the current dividend rate is $0.80 per share, the FFO payout ratio would be 80 percent.

Sometimes investors will use "coverage ratio" rather than payout ratio; the former measures the extent to which the current dividend is being covered by FFO or AFFO. In this calculation, investors divide FFO or AFFO by the dividend rate; that is, if the dividend is $0.80 per share and FFO is $1 per share, the FFO coverage ratio is $1 divided by $.80, or 1.25×.

Positive spread investing.   The ability to raise funds (both equity and debt) at a nominal cost that is less than the initial returns that can be obtained from real estate acquisitions. This term measures only current returns, and does not take the true, or long-term, cost of capital into account.

Price-to-earnings (P/E) ratio.   The relationship between a company's stock price and its per-share earnings. It is calculated by dividing the stock price by the company's earnings per share, on either a trailing twelve-month basis or a forward-looking basis. A similar measure used in the REIT world is a "price-to-FFO" ratio (P/FFO) or a "price-to-AFFO" ratio (P/AFFO).

Real estate investment trust (REIT).   Either a corporation or, less often in recent times, a business trust, that has certain tax attributes prescribed by federal legislation, the most important of which is that the entity obtains a federal tax credit equal to dividends paid to its shareholders if certain requirements are satisfied (such as the requirement to pay out at least 90 percent of pretax net annual income to shareholders).

Real Estate Investment Trust Act of 1960.   Legislation passed by Congress and signed into law in 1960 authorizing the formation of REIT organizations, for the purpose of allowing individuals (and institutions) to make investments in real estate and receive benefits similar to those they would receive from direct ownership.

Real estate operating company (REOC).   Refers generally to a public company that owns, manages, and/or develops real estate but has not elected to qualify for REIT status under federal law. These companies are thus not required to make any dividend payments whatsoever to their shareholders, nor are they subject to other requirements applicable to REIT organizations; this gives them more flexibility with respect to their use of capital. They pay income taxes at normal corporate tax rates, however. Due to their normally very low dividend yields, their shares can be more volatile than REIT shares. Examples include Brookfield Properties, Forest City Enterprises, the St. Joe Company, most homebuilders, and many hotel companies.

Same-store sales. This term has historically been used in the analysis of retail companies (e.g., JC Penney), and refers to sales from stores open for at least one year; it excludes sales from stores that have been closed and from new stores, which often have unusually high sales growth. The "same-store" concept is applied to REITs' rental revenues, operating expenses, and net operating income from those of its properties that have been owned and operated in the same fiscal period of the prior year.

Securitization or equitization. The process by which the economic benefits of ownership of a tangible asset, such as real estate, are divided among numerous investors and often represented in the form of publicly traded securities. Some mortgage loans, however, are packaged together as bonds and sold off in tranches of different risk levels to investors, as in the CMBS market; these are normally not publicly traded. See **CMBS.**

Specialty REIT. A REIT that owns, or lends on the security of, a type of real estate other than the standard property types such as offices, industrial properties, apartments, or retail stores. Thus, a timber REIT or a movie theater REIT would be a "specialty REIT."

Total return. A stock's dividend income plus capital appreciation, before taxes and commissions. For example, if a stock rises 4 percent in price and provides a 4 percent dividend yield during the measurement period, the investor's total return would be 8 percent.

Triple-net lease. A type of lease that requires the tenant to pay its pro rata share of all recurring operating costs of the property, such as utilities, maintenance, property taxes, and insurance.

UPREIT. A REIT that does not own its properties directly, but owns a controlling interest in a limited partnership that owns the REIT's real estate. Other partners (besides the REIT itself) might include management and other private investors. See also **DownREIT.**

Value creation. Although this is not a precisely defined term in the REIT industry, it is extremely important for investors. It generally refers to the ability of a REIT's management team to take certain actions, above and beyond managing and leasing its properties appropriately, that make the REIT's shares more valuable to investors over time. These actions, which may not be reflected in current earnings accretion, cover a wide range of activities, including attractive property (or even enterprise) acquisitions, profitable property developments and joint venture strategies, forming and operating nonrental real estate businesses, and managing the balance sheet effectively (including selling equity at opportune times and refinancing debt when interest costs are low).

Volatility.   The extent to which the market price of a stock tends to fluctuate from day to day, or even hour to hour. The volatility of a REIT stock, or all REIT stocks, will vary over time. It is likely that the shares of REITs with modest debt leverage and more secure cash flows will be less volatile than others during most market periods.

About the Author

Ralph L. Block has been a participant in the REIT industry in various professional investment and advisory capacities since 1993, and has been investing in REIT stocks since the early 1970s. Until his semiretirement in 2005, he was a principal and senior REIT portfolio manager for Phocas Financial Corporation, a registered investment advisory firm, and is presently the owner and proprietor of Essential REIT Publishing Company, an independent advisor to, and publisher of information for, the REIT industry and its investors. From 1993 through August 2003, he was chief REIT portfolio manager with Bay Isle Financial LLC, a San Francisco, California, investment advisory firm. From 1998 through 2003, Ralph was co–portfolio manager, with William Schaff, for Undiscovered Managers REIT Fund, which earned a five-star rating from Morningstar.

Ralph is also the author of *The Essential REIT*, a newsletter dedicated to REITs and REIT investing, has written regular columns for *REIT* magazine, and writes weekly blog posts on REITs for SNL Financial, under "Block Party." He has been quoted in numerous media articles, has spoken at various investment forums, and, in recognition of his books, articles, and newsletters, received the NAREIT Industry Achievement Award in 2004.

Prior to becoming a REIT professional, Ralph practiced corporate and securities law in Los Angeles, California, for 27 years, and served as a director of various private and public companies. He is a graduate of UCLA and the UCLA School of Law, where he was on the board of editors of the *UCLA Law Review*. He lives in Westlake Village, California, with his wife Paula, and their irrationally exuberant golden retriever, Sammy.

About the Contributors

Steven D. Burton has 27 years of investment experience in real estate. He currently serves as a member of the CBRE Clarion global portfolio management team responsible for overseeing CBRE Clarion's European securities research team. He is active in both EPRA and NAREIT. He joined the CBRE Clarion team in 1995 after service as an asset manager with GE Investment Corporation in Stamford, CT. Prior to that, he was a credit analyst with PNC Financial Corporation in Philadelphia.

Steve is a 1982 graduate of Middlebury (VT) College (*cum laude*) and received his MBA from the Kellogg School at Northwestern University. He is a chartered financial analyst (CFA) and member of the CFA Institute and the CFA Society of Philadelphia.

Kenneth D. Campbell has been active in the REIT industry since 1969. He currently serves as managing director of CBRE Clarion, based in Radnor, Pennsylvania. He is a member of CBRE Clarion's Global Investment Policy Committee and previously served as portfolio manager and chief Investment Officer. CBRE Clarion is an investment adviser managing approximately $23 billion in global portfolios for a group of diversified global clients including pension funds, sovereign wealth funds, mutual funds, closed-end investment funds, and other institutional investors. CBRE Clarion affiliated in the second half of 2011 with the Investment Group of CB Richard Ellis, a global real estate services company listed on the New York Stock Exchange. CBRE Clarion previously was affiliated with ING Group, an international banking and insurance company headquartered in The Hague, Netherlands.

Ken founded Audit investments, Inc., of New York City in 1969 as an investment advisory firm devoted to serving investor needs in the real estate industry. He founded and edited its advisory service

Realty Trust Review (later *Realty Stock Review*), which became the leading investment service for REITs and real estate securities until its sale in 1990. Audit began managing institutional accounts in 1984 and contributed this business to CBRE Clarion's predecessor in 1992.

Ken edited and was principal author of *The Real Estate Trusts: America's Newest Billionaires* (1971) and was editor and principal author of several of Audit's investment studies, including *Mortgage Trusts: Lenders with a Plus; Profits and the Factory Built House; REITs: Their Banks and Bondholders;* and *New Opportunities in Realty Trusts.* He is a graduate of Capital University and the New York University Graduate School of Business Administration (*with distinction*).

Index